COMPANY MEN

STUDIES IN INDUSTRY AND SOCIETY

Philip B. Scranton, *Series Editor*

Published with the assistance of the Hagley Museum and Library

Related Titles in the Series

JoAnne Yates
Control through Communication:
The Rise of System in American Management

Charles W. Cheape
Strictly Business:
Walter Carpenter at DuPont and General Motors

Pamela Walker Laird
Advertising Progress:
American Business and the Rise of Consumer Marketing

COMPANY MEN

White-Collar Life and Corporate Cultures in Los Angeles, 1892–1941

Clark Davis

The Johns Hopkins University Press
Baltimore & London

Printed in the United States of America on acid-free paper

Johns Hopkins Paperbacks edition, 2001
2 4 6 8 9 7 5 3 1

An earlier version of Chapter 2 appeared in *Business History Review*.

The Johns Hopkins University Press
2715 North Charles Street
Baltimore, Maryland 21218-4363
www.press.jhu.edu

Library of Congress Cataloging-in-Publication Data will be found at the end of this book.
A catalog record for this book is available from the British Library.

ISBN 0-8018-6275-2 (pbk.)

To my parents

M. Jerry Davis
Sylvia Clark Davis

CONTENTS

PREFACE

American corporate executives confronted a daunting challenge during the 1990s. The rapidly growing ranks of American stockholders heightened already intense pressure to show regular and large quarterly profits, even as fierce international competition, dramatic revolutions in business technologies, and ever-turbulent market and political imperatives threatened company balance sheets. The dilemma led many companies to simultaneously trim ranks while demanding even greater employee loyalty and production. Few corporations faced a more treacherous business climate than Southern California Edison, which, amidst mounting investor pressures, confronted a government-forced restructuring of the utility industry that broke up the virtual monopoly the company had enjoyed since the passage of a 1913 state regulatory compact. SCE prepared for the new competitive pressures by sharply reducing its workforce through both forced layoffs and voluntary retirement programs. Yet, even as they cut ranks and reduced employee benefits, SCE officials knew that success in the increasingly competitive utility market would depend on employees' dedication, loyalty, and superlative performance. Corporate officers had taken to heart a fundamental adage of business management: in the consumer's eyes, employees are the company. A series of radio and television advertisements in the late 1990s, featuring SCE personnel engaged in community service, underscored the company's dedication to this principle. One spot showed a worker before a group of school children, saying, "Hi kids, my name is Mike and I work for Southern California Edison. Today I am going to read you a story from the *Jungle Book* called 'Rikki-Tikki-Tavi.'" In another, a little boy tells his father that he wants to work for the company when he grows up so he can read books to children. SCE showcased its employees—the vital link between the company's product and its customers—as efficient, compassionate, skilled, and, most importantly, involved in their communities.

The dueling imperatives to keep labor expenses low and to cultivate dedicated workers has dominated corporate administration across various economic sectors from the early days of big business. Managerial efforts to deal with these inherent conflicts proved especially explosive as the twentieth century drew to a close. Cost-cutting schemes in the wake of longstanding commitments to career employees attracted considerable national attention. "Corporate downsizing" became a topic of heated national debate, emerging as an issue in the 1992 and 1996 presidential elections when both political parties sought to capitalize on the popular issue of the economic insecurity created by this trend. A particularly poignant moment occurred on April 7, 1996, when CBS's *60 Minutes* reporter Lesley Stahl cornered AT&T chief Robert Allen and demanded to know why the suddenly nervous and shaken-looking boss had raised his salary while eliminating the jobs of thousands of subordinates.

The downsizing furor surfaced everywhere. One *Newsweek* cover described the nation's leading executives as "Corporate Killers." Menacing photographs of four major American business leaders and the number of employees each had laid off, figures totaling 131,000, accompanied the bold red headline. Inside, the article announced that "firing has gotten to be trendy in corporate America in the same way that building new plants and being considered a good corporate citizen gave you bragging rights twenty-five years ago." According to the *Newsweek* writer, "Now you fire workers—especially white-collar workers—to make your corporate bones."[1]

Mass firings were hardly new to American business in the 1990s, yet at the time the *Newsweek* article appeared, the nation's official unemployment rate hovered below 6 percent. Why then the fuss? At the root of the downsizing controversy lay a fundamental shift in the nature of corporate management. Leaders' efforts to streamline operations increasingly focused on white-collar ranks. Those middle managers once thought to be the safest in corporate hierarchies started to eye their mailboxes nervously when news spread of coming pink slips. Furthermore, many employees perceived a distinct lack of regret on business leaders' part for the assault on loyal staff. Executives often introduced layoffs as measures in efficiency and even growth, rather than unfortunate and painful actions. It did not comfort workers when these strategies generated bonuses for those wielding the axes. One *Los Angeles Times* headline conveyed this bottom-line attitude when it opened a story on AT&T layoffs with the headline: "AT&T Lays Out Bold Plan for the Future."[2]

For many in the nation's workforce, cries of injustice over this situation likely fell on deaf ears. Cyclical employment and the ever-present possibility of financial decline already shadowed many other American workers, be they laborers, small business owners, or independent professionals. For the nation's white-collar salaried employees, however, those Americans working in comfortable offices in large corporations, it seemed that a contract had been broken. White-collar jobs in large companies (like those many in the news media held, not coincidentally) had been thought to be safe, steady, and secure. "Give your life to IBM and it will take care of you," the feeling had been. "Cradle-to-grave security" had been an unwritten clause in the job description of white-collar life.

The frustrations felt by thousands of big business employees around the nation who faced declining salaries and shrinking benefit packages, as well as the possibility of layoffs, (even as their firms expected higher performance) reflected neither a naive understanding of business fortunes nor an arrogant overvaluing of their importance to their firm. Rather, they represented an outrage motivated by an implicit contractual agreement widely promoted in American corporations throughout the twentieth century. The belief that employment in large firms, particularly in white-collar salaried positions, ensured career security and a host of specific perquisites had emerged as part of early twentieth-century negotiations between business leaders and white American men. That agreement became central to corporate cultures by the 1920s and emerged as a hallmark of the nation's modern middle-class culture.

This book explores how the first generation of career employees in corporate America, who were largely educated, young white men, negotiated an occupational culture that defined core tenets of white-collar employment and middle-class culture that persist to the present day. These men not only constructed new managerial bureaucracies, but they also reconfigured a host of middle-class values and mores. Their efforts to build meaningful careers entailed more than issues of task and income. These men's expectations and dreams were shaped by prevailing gender norms, racial constructions, ever-shifting economic conditions, factors of geography, unique familial pressures, and innumerable other social and cultural pressures. American business and culture thus evolved in tandem. The prominent place that white-collar themes and issues have held throughout the history of twentieth-century popular culture speaks to the ongoing relationship. In prominent cultural texts, from Arthur Miller's *Death of a Salesman* to the cartoon strip "Dilbert" and from *The Man in the Gray Flannel Suit* to the steady stream of late 1990s films rooted in bureaucratic angst, such as *In the Company of Men*, *Clockwatchers*, and *Office Space*, Americans have continually wrestled with the social tensions inherent in the corporate order.

The term *company men* best captures the occupational cohort of male white-collar employees who negotiated the corporate cultures that have defined the twentieth-century middle class. White-collar work encompassed a broad variety of salaried nonmanual jobs ranging from clerks to executives. Attachment to the firm united these men from different strata; whether one was a clerk, manager, professional, or executive, his occupational identity lay not in his tasks or skills but with his employer. Corporate dictates and cultures dominated even those on the payroll with highly specialized training and restricted professional associations, such as lawyers, accountants, and engineers. Despite position, duty, or tenure, these individuals were, in the end, employees.

In the minds of boards of directors and top executives, this cohort stood distinctly apart from blue-collar ranks and female office workers, for officials believed that white-collar men represented both their company's "brain" and its public face. Company men either managed others or were, theoretically, en route to administrative posts. They also often held those positions most visible to the public and were, therefore, most likely to symbolize the company within the community. While descriptions of production and clerical jobs often focused on skills and abilities, those of white-collar positions more often emphasized less tangible interpersonal traits. One scholar has aptly noted that these encompassed such nebulous qualities as rationality, ambition, thoroughness, "enthusiasm," "personality," leadership skills, and executive ability.[3] These subtle identifying characteristics, encoded with gendered and racialized assumptions, indeed became the keys that white American men used to assume the corporate jobs that emerged as planks in the platform of middle-class America.

What it means to be middle class in the United States has perplexed scholars throughout this century, and I will not presume to settle the debate here, but I do argue that one key component of middle-class identity during the Progressive Era was the assumption of economic survival and the luxury to wrestle with "quality of life" issues when it came to occupational decisions. By virtue of being white and even marginally educated, millions of American men gained access to a privileged category of jobs that offered decent pay, working conditions, and prestige. The young men who entered downtown business offices across the nation, however, did not pause to marvel at their good fortune. Instead, they fought to carve out the best possible futures based on their interests, needs, and dreams. Jobs other Americans yearned for they considered too stifling or unworthy of consideration for a plethora of personal reasons. The executives who recruited employees from this privileged labor pool interacted daily with these ambitious young men who had high expectations and distinct desires. White-collar men rarely obtained all they wanted from employers, and business leaders never fully accomplished their personnel goals, but both sides did gradually develop a set of parameters that came to define middle-class career expectations and the characteristics of a good job.

Believing place to be a critical element in the history of corporate cultures, I tell this story from the vantage point of Los Angeles. I use, however, a broad definition of "Los Angeles." Business and market operations rarely correspond to city limits, and the process of cultural formation is not city-specific. "Los Angeles" will thus at times refer specifically to the city and county but more often will indicate the heart of a business and labor network connected to points throughout southern California, the American West, and even the nation and world. Certainly no region, whether it be town, city, or state stands in isolation. Los Angeles developed within a national and global community, and its history is a part of these larger histories.

ACKNOWLEDGMENTS

Writing this book has been an exceptionally rewarding and exciting journey, for it has connected me to smart and wonderful people who have provoked and stimulated my understanding of the world and who have become cherished colleagues and friends in the process of intellectual discovery. I can trace this study's origins to a seminar paper on labor relations at Union Oil that I wrote for University of Southern California professor Steven J. Ross. I remember keenly his enthusiastic reaction when I first shared my ideas, and from that time to the present day his encouragement, rigorous critiques, constant reminders to focus on "the big picture," and the sterling example of his own scholarship have been of inestimable value. USC provided me a wonderful environment in which to become an historian and I will always be proud to have studied with Elinor Accampo, Lois Banner, Philip Ethington, Ron Gottesman, Paul Knoll, Mauricio Mazon, Frank Mitchell, and Terry Seip. I owe my mentor and friend, Ed Perkins, a special debt of thanks for his unflinching support of my work and career.

Over the course of researching and writing this book I have benefited from the comments, critiques, and encouragement of many who have read chapters, responded to conference papers, and, through conversations, letters, and by example, sharpened my thinking and writing. For these contributions I would like to thank Eric Avila, Hal Barron, Mansel Blackford, Ann Carlos, Greg Dickinson, Sarah Elkind, Michael Engh, Janet Fireman, James Gilbert, John Gilkeson, Kevin Gilmartin, James Gregory, Melanie Gustafson, Sanford Jacoby, Robert Johnston, John Landry, Kate McGinn, Natalia Molina, Elizabeth Munson, Laurie Pintar, Anthony Rotundo, Tom Sitton, Robert Slayton, Andrea Tone, Mary Yeager, and the members of the Huntington Library Los Angeles History Research Group and the L.A. Cultural History Seminar.

While the burden of any weaknesses in this study lies wholly with me, for its strengths I must acknowledge a number of scholars who went far beyond the call in devoting time and energy toward supporting my research, strengthening my analysis, and shoring up my resolve. Bill Deverell offered valuable criticisms and suggestions on an early and then the final draft of this manuscript and provided generous advice, encouragement, and friendship at innumerable points in between. David Igler and Rennie Schoepflin each read and commented on more of my work than they likely care to remember, and offered critical feedback and comradeship at crucial moments. Angel Kwolek-Folland and Olivier Zunz strengthened this book significantly not only by offering valuable reads but through the example of their own excellent scholarship, which helped to spark my interest in this topic. Robyn Muncy's piercing insight, combined with her unflinching generosity, often aided and inspired me. Greg Hise, Philip Goff, and Becky Nicolaides proved empathic sounding boards, confidants, and advisors as I completed this project. Daryl Maeda's wit, wisdom, and friendship energized my scholarship at many points.

My greatest debts are to the incomparable Doug Flamming, who has been my toughest critic and most staunch ally throughout this process. Nobody expressed such enthusiasm for my findings, engaged my work so deeply, or proffered such valuable personal and professional support. Nothing I write would adequately express my respect for his intellect or appreciation for his friendship.

The resources and personnel of several institutions made this study possible. The Huntington Library is an intellectual's paradise and I am grateful to Alan Jutzi, Kate McGinn, Martin Ridge, Roy Ritchie, Jennifer Watts, and the entire Huntington staff for their gracious support of scholars. I join all southern California historians in my gratitude to Dace Taube at USC's Regional History Center and also wish to thank Cynthia Graham at Pacific Mutual Life archives, Marilyn Ghausi at Bank of America archives, and the fine historian of Southern California Edison, William Myers. The Huntington Library, the John Haynes Foundation, the Fletcher Ford Foundation, and the Historical Society of Southern California provided grants and support at key junctures. La Sierra University consistently nurtured this study, not only with a sabbatical and several research grants, but also with many layers of personal support, and I want to thank specifically Lawrence T. Geraty, Adeny Schmidt, Gary Bradley, and Rennie Schoepflin. A special thanks to the many brilliant La Sierra students from whom I have learned much, in particular to my superb research assistants: David Brooks, Greg Cushman, Brian Guth, Jessica Kim, and Adrian McIntyre.

My association with the editor of this series, Phil Scranton, has been one of the great joys of this project. His ability to help historians magnify their strengths and surmount their weaknesses has improved our profession immeasurably and has made this a much better book. Johns Hopkins University Press's history editor, Robert Brugger, provided generous and professional support at every step, and the thoroughness and insight of JHUP manuscript editor Anne Whitmore made this project's final stretch a pleasure.

There are several people who have bolstered my life and this project in ways that are difficult to describe adequately. I wrote much of this work in the La Cañada home of Drew and Betsy Hamlin and the Paris studio of Andrée Desormière, and I will always be grateful to them for accepting me into their families. Perhaps no debt is more difficult to quantify than the one I owe Keith Black, John Childs, Brian Morrison, Carol Mangione, Pam Miner, and Joseph Perloff, all of whom saved my life following a mycotic aneurysm in 1994. And Mark and Jan Davis are probably unaware of the many ways they have contributed to this work by prodding me to rethink assumptions and perceptions about historical experience. I am proud to be their brother.

Cheryl Koos has journeyed with me every day of this project as my intellectual comrade, always willing to offer insightful reads of new drafts, propose alternative explanations, suggest additional sources, and keep me abreast of new historiographical and methodological trends. More importantly, she has been my best friend, partner, and soulmate. Both this book and my life are better for her presence.

I dedicate this book to my parents, whose utter virtue and unwavering devotion to my interests has laid the groundwork for every good fortune I enjoy. It is a pleasure to have them as parents and friends.

COMPANY MEN

INTRODUCTION

> Men of California, the world is ours! . . . The twentieth century and the centuries which are to come, belong to the Pacific, and the imperial gateway to the Pacific is our own matchless empire of California.
>
> —George Hart, Los Angeles Chamber of Commerce Banquet, 1905

In October 1876, James and Mary Crank "bade good-bye to the East" and embarked on a week-long journey to a new life in California, a land they described as "a far country." James Crank, born in rural New York in 1842, had spent most of his young career in Chicago, where he had enjoyed considerable success in the insurance business and other financial enterprises. Mary was in poor health, however, and this sent them west in search of a more arid climate. They first settled in San Francisco, but the city's "raw and moist winds" exacerbated the respiratory trouble she had hoped to escape. In January 1877, they moved south to Los Angeles where they found the dry weather that indeed bolstered Mary's health. For several months James and Mary resided at the Pico House, an elite hotel in what was then a rustic, 8,000-resident community. They soon took a liking to the local San Gabriel Valley and, later that year, purchased the 200-acre Fair Oaks Ranch fifteen miles northeast of Los Angeles, next to the "Indiana Colony," which would become Pasadena. One could drive to and from the town of Los Angeles "without passing a soul," Mary recalled, and neighbors were few and miles away. Daily pleasures included carriage rides, hunting, and visiting friends.

During the next quarter-century, a steady stream of immigrants to southern California transformed the region. The swelling population marred Mary's cherished countryside but stoked James's ambitions. Mary complained that he spent fewer and fewer hours at the ranch, devoting himself instead to numerous business initiatives. In subsequent years James organized the First National Bank of Los Angeles, built the first cable street railway in the West, and helped found the Los Angeles suburb of Monrovia. By the 1920s he enjoyed a reputation as an important local entrepreneur who had assisted in laying the region's twentieth-century urban infrastructure.[1]

When George and Helen Ward moved to California in 1905 and bought a home in bustling South Pasadena, barely a mile from where the old Crank ranch had been, they, unlike the Cranks just a generation before, settled amid a booming urban center. Born in White Plains, New York, in 1863, George had graduated from Andover Academy in 1882 with special training in engineering and mathematics. For sixteen years he worked as an engineer and then manager for several local railroads and bridge-building firms. George's future took a major turn in 1898 when eastern railroad magnate Collis P. Huntington hired him to engineer a New York railway line. Collis Huntington died the following year, but before he did, he told his heir, Henry E. Huntington, "Stick to Ward, you can trust him." Henry took Collis's advice, and it led to a long, profitable partnership. He initially hired George to manage rail lines in Ohio and New York but relocated him to southern California in 1905 to help coordinate a growing network of local business interests. George initially served as assistant general manager of the Huntington Land and Improvement Company, the Pacific Electric Land Company, and the Los Angeles Railway Land Company, but he soon moved into the vice presidency and general management of these operations. In 1911, George became vice president of Huntington's Pacific Light and Power Corporation and in 1914 assumed the presidency of two Huntington electric and railway subsidiaries. George left Huntington's employment in 1917 to become vice president of operations and marketing for Southern California Edison Company (SCE), the nation's fifth largest electric utility. He spent the 1920s climbing SCE's corporate ladder and became the company's president in 1932.[2]

James Crank and George Ward grew up in New York state only twenty years apart, but more than a generation separated their lives in California. While Crank had worked to build new businesses in a sparsely populated region, George Ward arrived a "company man" and spent his career managing major metropolitan corporations. From their first days in Los Angeles, neither social isolation nor entrepreneurial ventures characterized the Wards' lives. They instead became immersed in an emerging urban corporate culture.

In the half-century or so between the Cranks' arrival in southern California in 1876 and George Ward's ascendancy to the presidency of Southern California Edison in 1932, Los Angeles grew rapidly from a rural and remote western town of less than 10,000 inhabitants to the American West's leading financial, entertainment, and industrial center, with 2,000,000 residents. Fueled by enormous population growth and massive capital investment, the region's agricultural, small business, and fledgling industrial economy evolved to an entrenched corporate capitalism. Nowhere in the country did this process occur with greater scope, speed, or cultural impact. From the turn of the century through the onset of the Great Depression, Los Angeles served as the nation's "corporate frontier," a setting where the country's twentieth-century service and commercial economy would not have to displace a well-established industrial economy but would emerge alongside the modern city itself.

Southern California's corporate revolution spawned a prominent new personality in America's urban landscape—the company man. By the time SCE named George Ward president, Los Angeles had become home to a new white-collar middle class that included men, and increasingly women, working in office jobs, professional posts, and other nonmanual positions for companies they did not own. While local boosters continually touted men like James Crank as emblematic of regional opportunities, far more southern Californians worked as clerks, agents, salesmen, and managers than would ever found or run local companies. For every film star or business tycoon, hundreds of men and women worked for modest pay in diverse and scattered offices. In fact, by 1930, nearly one in four working male Angelenos held a white-collar job. The most fortunate, like Ward, climbed to the upper rungs of white-collar bureaucracies, where they found considerable wealth, status, and power; but for the majority, such goals proved illusory. Steadily growing numbers of local residents lived within the modest boundaries of a new white-collar middle-class culture characterized by bureaucratic employment and organizational life.

By 1930, more than fourteen million Americans, greater than 30 percent of the civilian labor force, were employed in office, sales, or professional jobs.[3] Throughout the twentieth century, scholars and critics have sought to understand this social group. As early as 1929, Robert and Helen Lynd recognized the significance of this "business class" in reshaping American culture. During the Cold War era, corporate personalities became the subjects of provocative caricatures and critical theoretical constructs, including C. Wright Mills's "power elite," David Riesman's "lonely crowd," William Whyte's "organization man," and Sloan Wilson's "man in the gray flannel suit."[4] Unfortunately, in the 1960s and 1970s these company men sank into obscurity within popular historical narratives, in which they were generally portrayed as simply average, unexceptional, and even boring. When they are remembered at all now, it is as passive drones in our national experience.

The history of southern California during the early twentieth century belies such images. From 1892, when Edward Doheny discovered oil in Los An-

The cover of a 1930 Los Angeles Chamber of Commerce brochure, illustrating the city's evolution from a Spanish village to a modern corporate industrial center. Courtesy of Department of Special Collections, University Libraries, University of Southern California.

geles, leading numerous entrepreneurs to form companies that could capitalize on the region's "black gold," until 1941, when a tidal wave of federal defense monies launched a second era of corporate growth, the region's business community struggled to transform a remote desert into a corporate metropolis. White-collar workers became pivotal if unheralded actors in this drama. The challenge of building and running large-scale businesses proved as daunting as the historically famous task of finding adequate water supplies for the city, and it remained a challenge long after massive aqueducts had sated the city's thirst. The look of emerging firms, how they would work, and what exactly employment would entail took shape over the course of a long, haphazard, and heterogeneous process in individual companies, industries, and cities.

This book tells the story of white-collar company men in early twentieth-century southern California and of the new urban corporate cultures they helped to create. As large firms began to dominate the region's economy, securing the talents and loyalties of hundreds and thousands of employees preoccupied Los Angeles's business elite. In their efforts to build a white-collar

labor force, executives like George Ward met with a host of questions. Of the hundreds of thousands of immigrants pouring into southern California from thousands of farms, towns, and cities across the globe, who would answer white-collar job advertisements? Whom would firms hire? Which employees would prove loyal, which would not, and who would most successfully climb company ladders? As executives and employees answered these questions, they negotiated nothing less than the nature, demands, and rewards of white-collar life, the meaning of corporate employment, and, ultimately, the tenets of a new middle-class culture.[5]

From the outset, white men dominated this story. Few people of color occupied staff positions in business offices. In a random sample of clerical employees in Los Angeles taken from the 1920 U.S. census, 99 percent were classified as white.[6] The absence of a single African American bank teller in San Francisco before 1930 sheds light on the racial boundaries of white-collar life. Sensing that white-collar corporate work was largely out of their reach, upwardly mobile blacks, Asian Americans, and Latinos pursued professions with fewer barriers, such as teaching, social work, and preaching, or channeled their energies into small businesses. By the mid 1920s, however, African Americans in Los Angeles had opened at least one large corporation of their own—the Golden State Life Insurance Company—which grew rapidly into the largest black-owned business west of Chicago. Golden State provided the one significant corporate door for black men, as well as secretarial positions for black women.[7]

Outside of Golden State Life, however, most corporate offices in Los Angeles were not simply "white," they were explicitly Anglo-Saxon. A cult of Anglo-Saxonness prevailed and business elites staffed their firms with men of British descent. In 1933, for instance, when the Security-First National Bank appointed Adolph Nordling to the position of assistant trust officer, bank publications devoted considerable attention to the fact that the firm now had a "Scandinavian in its official ranks" (though this "Scandinavian" happened to have been born in Iowa), a rarity among its otherwise Anglo-Saxon leadership. Photos from Los Angeles business offices portray a workforce of young, square-jawed, Nordic-appearing men with typically British surnames, all seemingly cut from a common mold.[8]

In narrowing their "career employees" largely to young men of British descent, Los Angeles's business elites assumed a difficult challenge. That these privileged Americans filled the managerial ranks of southern California firms does not mean that most men of such heritage merrily gravitated to white-collar work. Rather, young Angelenos typically held considerable reservations about big business employment. The growing numbers of office jobs in large businesses compelled such gentlemen, along with millions of other Americans, to question the meaning of work and to reconsider their jobs in the context of independence, mobility, security, and community. The formation of big business challenged prevailing conceptions of what it meant to be a man, to be a woman, and to be successful in America.

The first generation of American men to be raised in a significantly white-collar economy—the group that laid the foundation of corporate Los Angeles—struggled to align personal ambitions and cultural ideals with the rapidly shifting occupational realities wrought by corporate concentration. White-collar jobs in growing companies challenged key tenets of a still-pervasive nineteenth-century middle-class worldview that stressed the distinction between physical labor and office work. By the late nineteenth century, office jobs in small firms had become established embarkation points for middle-class futures. White-collar employment around the turn of the century appeared to open up the same avenues to sizable numbers of Americans. The types of jobs that became widespread by the early twentieth century, however, undermined earlier middle-class notions of economic independence. Entry-level male office jobs in large firms paid poorly, often required troubling degrees of workplace subservience and conformity, and offered no realistic opportunity to direct the enterprise. Furthermore, women's increasing presence in the corporate workplace posed disturbing challenges to manly identities.

Confusion over what the work entailed, where it would lead, and what status and lifestyle it would afford provoked much discussion—and no little consternation—in families seeking appropriate futures for their children. The changing nature of "middle-class work" led Americans to ponder the shifting meanings of and relationships between middle-class identities and white-collar work.

The life of Clarence Bowerman, who directly confronted the rising new corporate culture, demonstrates these tensions. In 1929, Bowerman became manager of Security-First National Bank's Van Nuys Branch. This lucrative position assured his family a comfortable middle-class life. At first, there seems little of note in an educated Anglo-American male rising to a position of power in an urban bank, but upon closer examination Bowerman's tale proves complicated. Bowerman grew up in Monrovia (the suburb founded by James Crank) in the 1880s. His family had moved there hoping the salubrious climate would cure their invalid mother who, in fact, "recovered" as soon as she was west of the Rocky Mountains. After finishing high school, Bowerman took coursework at the University of Southern California and the Throop Polytechnic Institute in Pasadena (now Caltech). Business courses at Throop helped him secure his first job, in 1900, as a stenographer and balancer of passbooks with the First National Bank of Monrovia. By 1906, he had become an assistant cashier, but his desire to work outdoors led him to join the ranks of a local contracting company. After seven years, he left that job to start up a general merchandising business in the San Fernando Valley. His business put him in contact with the president of a small, local institution, the Bank of Lankershim, who offered him the position of vice president and manager in 1919.

Bowerman entered the 1920s an icon of middle-class success, but he ended the decade a less noteworthy white-collar manager. In 1928, the massive Security-First National Bank of Los Angeles acquired the Bank of Lankershim. Suddenly, Bowerman found himself in effect demoted, one of more than 150 branch managers in a 3,500-employee institution. Ironically, Security-First assigned this former entrepreneur and business leader, now reduced to midlevel manager, the task of solving its worker turnover problem. Bank executives aimed to develop a dedicated staff of educated Anglo-American men, but they found these men difficult to retain. The annual turnover rate among this group exceeded 35 percent in the late 1920s. Many aspired to the kind of career Bowerman had previously had, and they would not long remain white-collar employees in a large and often stifling bureaucracy.[9]

Although Security-First's public relations machine promoted Bowerman as the epitome of corporate success, his own pursuit of more individualistic and entrepreneurial opportunities for much of his career, as well as his assignment to dissuade others of such goals, alludes to tensions that not only plagued local bank operations but festered throughout the nation's white-collar workforce. Security-First executives, like all those who worked to build and manage vast hierarchies of salaried employees, endeavored to turn talented and ambitious young hires into loyal company men. But these men often proved reluctant partners in the corporate enterprise. Their backgrounds and aspirations frequently clashed with the constraints and demands of bureaucratic employment, and therein lay the central drama in the rise of big business.

Both market imperatives and new technologies spurred the growth of large Los Angeles firms. Successfully building and operating big companies, though, required more than technical and organizational designs; it mandated the cultivation of human capital. As young Angelenos searched for work, interviewed at local firms, and joined the ranks of growing businesses, their interests and needs shaped corporate dictates, practices, and strategies. The creation of white-collar bureaucracies thus both reflected and forged middle-class values and mores.

Few things better illuminate the social and cultural dimensions of business management than the relationship between gender and white-collar work. The men who clutched corporate reins rarely considered women full potential players in the business enterprise and often expressed hostility at their mere presence. In 1908, for instance, the new president of the Alfred Dodge Felt Company proudly told directors that he was "employing ambitious young men who have shown ability, push and energy, instead of a lot of women as practiced by the former office manager." To be sure, most leaders expressed less exclusionary sentiments, and the growth of large firms provided women with a new spectrum of job opportunities. By 1925, one third of all white-collar workers nationwide were women, and their presence profoundly shaped business cultures. Still, distinctly masculine forms dominated white-collar work during this period. From 1910 to 1930, for instance, the number of Americans working as proprietors, managers, and officials, and as agents in real estate and insurance, more than doubled; women, however, never composed more than 6 percent of this group. Conversely, the percentage of stenographers who were female grew from 5 percent in 1870 to 96 percent in 1930. With only rare exceptions (notably in the insurance industry), employers relegated women to the lower-rung clerical positions. This was especially true in Los Angeles. In 1926, women held 98 percent of the city's stenographer positions, a higher proportion than in most cities, but infrequently occupied higher clerical posts. Women held 26 percent of high clerical positions in Kansas City, 47 percent in New York City, and 56 percent in Chicago, but only 22 percent of such slots in Los Angeles.[10]

In Los Angeles and across the nation, white-collar work came to mean very different things for men and women. For women, who were excluded from many other sectors of employment, clerical work provided interesting new opportunities, higher pay, and more status than most other available jobs. Yet, because company offices beckoned largely to young, middle-class, unmarried women who would, presumably, quit upon marriage, female employees tended to be young and single. Samples taken in 1910 and 1920 of female Los Angeles clerical workers shows an average age of twenty-seven, while the percentage of married workers dropped during the intervening decade from an already low 18 percent to 6 percent. Nationally at that time, the majority of female office employees were under twenty-five, and 90 percent were unmarried. By comparison, the average age of male clerical workers stood at thirty-four, seven years higher than the women's average age. Moreover, while the percentage of married male clerical workers dropped during the 1910s, as it did for women, it remained considerably higher, declining only from 55 to 40 percent.[11]

The demographics of female clerical workers actually reveal as much about the gendering of managerial strategies as they do about societal norms regarding working women. Most firms claimed that female employees quit upon marriage, and statistical data superficially supports their assertions. One Los Angeles bank, for instance, did not count women quitting to marry in its turnover statistics, for officials considered this an expected occurrence, not a personnel problem to be solved. Evidence suggests, however, that companies themselves often imposed this "marriage bar" in forcing out married women. Employers additionally sought to discredit female clerical workers' grievances by claiming that they had left for marital reasons, rather than out of frustration over poor pay, tedious work, and no opportunities for advancement. One scholar notes that by invoking the marriage bar, "employers helped to ensure that women would continue to 'fail' to live up to the ideal male model of a 'career,' and thus make the convention a reality."[12]

In direct contrast, the concept of a corporate ladder came to define male white-collar employment and to clearly distinguish "company men" from female clerical workers—whom many dubbed "office wives." One historian has captured this distinction in the inverse relationship between corporate employment, class status, and men's and women's career histories. White-collar work for young women, which essentially meant clerical employment, provided a respectable, middle-class livelihood, but if they remained in such positions throughout their lives they would slide into working-class status. Conversely, entry-level white-collar jobs for men, also clerical posts, offered what seemed working-class wages and tedium, but over the course of their lives men could advance into high status and high-paying positions.[13]

While some scholars have sought to divide white-collar employees based on clerical, managerial, and executive ranks, such categorizations obscure the profound emphasis on male career paths and a corporate life cycle that dominated big business in the early twentieth century. The corporate ladder rationalized an enormous gulf in status, authority, and remuneration. Despite the reality of severe material distinctions, all male jobs, from clerk to president, were, in the abstract, linked. Executives argued that these positions presented a pathway of opportunity, and many men believed them. While few entry-level male clerks honestly thought they would become company presidents, most aspired to climb much higher over the course of their careers. By providing their male employees more opportunities for promotion, higher salaries, and greater authority than they did female employees—men, for instance, earned as much as 50 percent more than women in entry-level posts—companies promoted solidarity among white-collar men and discouraged resentment among male clerical workers.[14]

Managerial efforts to ennoble white-collar work by defining it as an Anglo sphere within a multicultural society and as a masculine bastion atop a marginalized female clerical staff assured a white male workplace, but it did not guarantee those men's enthusiasm for corporate life. Business executives encountered considerable resistance in their efforts to link in workers' minds their success with the firm's. High rates of turnover, widespread evidence of employee apathy, and an awareness of their personnel's capacity to help or hinder corporate operations in innumerable ways plagued leaders' designs. Their solution lay in the crafting of a new, white-collar middle-class culture, and at the heart of this story lay the creation of distinct corporate cultures in individual firms. One general definition of corporate culture is "the formal and informal rules and understandings that make corporations distinct institutions." These rules include not only organizational charts but "the sort of informal knowledge about how to 'get things done' that are part of any large, bureaucratic system."[15] This definition works on the level of individual firms but needs to be pushed beyond the office. Such internal company cultures could succeed only if they resonated with broader American values. Corporate cultures, both formal and informal, functioned only when congruent with prevailing middle-class practices and mores, or when designed to subtly reshape rather than contradict these norms. The emergence of large firms thus required businesses to build working environments that were both acceptable to middle-class Americans and able to shape middle-class ideals and customs to mirror corporate interests.

The formation of corporate cultures originated in simple interactions. Security-First National Bank leaders, for example, wanted the services of Clarence Bowerman. He, in turn, needed a job. But Bowerman had certain expectations regarding income, duties, workplace conditions, and future opportunities. His superiors, similarly, dealt with Bowerman alongside many competing pressures. In Los Angeles and throughout the nation, executives and employees worked on a daily basis to mold corporate cultures that would accommodate their mutual interests. In this process, big businesses slowly became the shopfloor of the nation's new middle class.

The explicit construction of white-collar cultures proceeded most dramatically in firms employing hundreds and even thousands of workers, where executives felt threatened and vulnerable in the face of their inability to control daily operations. The need to recruit, motivate, and retain large numbers of personnel prompted such companies to experiment with new occupational cultures and structures considered critical to company success. Among the largest and most important Los Angeles firms were the Union Oil Company of California, Security-First National Bank, the Pacific Mutual Life Insurance Company, Southern California Edison, and the Pacific Electric Railway Company (PE). Each of these enterprises experienced massive corporate growth during the 1910s and 1920s and emerged with thousands of employees scattered over numerous counties and offices, or, in the case of Union Oil and Pacific Mutual, other states and countries as well. Each company ranked among the nation's largest in its respective industry; each struggled to staff expansive white-collar ranks; and each wrestled with the challenges of developing and administering vast bureaucracies.[16] Yet while all confronted similar issues of corporate growth and management, each operated in very different economic, political, and cultural contexts. PE encountered declining revenues and business, while Union Oil expanded continuously at a staggering pace. Pacific Mutual maneuvered relatively autonomous of state intervention, while SCE lost a significant portion of its territory to municipal ownership. And while PE hired a fairly small number of female employees, Pacific Mutual not only had an unusually high proportion of female office workers in the 1920s, but by decade's end it also aggressively recruited women as underwriters and as managers to supervise them.

A handful of companies occupied center stage in Los Angeles's business community, but smaller peripheral firms also played roles in the evolution of local corporate cultures. Older, embattled firms such as the Pacific Mail Steamship Company, as well as new and innovative businesses such as the

Western Air Express Company also turned to salaried personnel and similar strategies to weather their differing challenges. Neither firm could enact the broad personnel programs of larger, more prosperous companies, but each had to respond somehow to the same personnel dilemmas.

The anonymous white-collar legions who reshaped southern California's economy and society during the process of corporate growth unknowingly helped to build what would became a cradle of American economic and cultural life. Early business activity in the region occurred far from the locus of American political and economic power, but the era of corporate formation witnessed Los Angeles's rise to national and international prominence. The site of Native American populations as far back as 900 B.C., the town of Los Angeles, founded by Spanish settlers in 1781, had given no hint of its future as an American urban center through much of the nineteenth century. In the 1850s, for instance, Los Angeles housed only 1,600 residents. The town had no hospital, public school, college, library, bank, or English language newspaper.[17] As late as the 1870s, the city remained a distant western outpost. *Los Angeles Times* editors countered eastern perceptions of Los Angeles as a "half Mexican pueblo and half wild west cow town," declaring that "Los Angeles people do not carry arms, Indians are a curiosity, [and] the gee string is not a common article of apparel here."[18] Los Angeles's population explosion began in the mid 1880s when the Atchison, Topeka and Santa Fe Railroad constructed a line there from the east; but during the depression of the 1890s, Chamber of Commerce officials fretted about the city's growing population and the inability of newcomers to find work. At the annual banquet in 1895, the Chamber's president cautioned against encouraging new migrants, noting, "Since the knowledge of our sunny skies and equable climate has extended to the ends of the earth, multitudes come hither in the hope of . . . securing lucrative employment. The outcome is, the supply so far exceeds the demand that many and sore disappointments result."[19] These concerns would prove short-lived. By 1900, business leaders and city officials enthusiastically beckoned newcomers to an economy that boomed with few interruptions until the Great Depression.

By 1930, Los Angeles was the fifth most populous city in the country and housed more people than thirty states individually and more than the seven least populated states combined. Southern California firms ranked among the nation's elite in diverse industries, including transportation, utilities, financial services, entertainment, petroleum, and construction. The Second World War sparked an even more rapid ascent in population growth and corporate concentration, which lasted through the Cold War era. By the 1990s, when more than fourteen million people inhabited the region, southern Cal-

This exhibit, sponsored by the Los Angeles Chamber of Commerce, was one of many sent to cities around the nation during the 1920s to lure new residents and businesses. Courtesy of Department of Special Collections, University Libraries, University of Southern California.

ifornia stood as the cultural and economic heart of a state that ranked fifth among national economies.

Los Angeles's twentieth-century rise also entailed its development into a defining center of middle-class life. One acute observer has noted that "southern California became America's first western 'culture hearth' during the 1920s and, along with the rest of the state, gained even greater influence on American civilization during the mid-twentieth century."[20] One could actually describe this as understatement, for Los Angeles became one of the world's few truly global creators of popular culture. The region's cultural power has operated on many levels. Hollywood, which became the dominant site for the creation and production of American cinema in the 1910s and 1920s, emerged concomitantly with and also inside of corporate Los Angeles.

While Hollywood depictions of white-collar life were, more often than not, set in New York City, southern Californians created and produced them in Los Angeles. As Hollywood's images played in theaters throughout the country, local civic associations engaged in well-organized and expensive campaigns to promote the region and its occupational and residential opportunities. While Los Angeles was not unique in its boosterism, few places so successfully attracted not only new migrants but national and international interest. Perhaps best epitomized in the ranks of those who watched the Rose Parade each year, not just for the floats, but to marvel at the sunny climate and vacationlike atmosphere, southern California came to occupy a unique status as a sometimes bizarre yet tantalizing region.[21]

Despite southern California's economic and cultural significance, probing its corporate life raises difficult questions about the issue of regionalism in the American experience. Historians of western cities and towns have long had an ambivalent relationship with their subject. On one hand, many question why investigations that focus on New York, Philadelphia, or other eastern cities are often considered national while those about the West are thought of as regional. Conversely, the field of western history has enjoyed remarkable success in modern historiography, as some of the profession's most invigorating recent scholarship has focused on examining the distinctiveness of experience in the American West.[22]

This book dissolves the synthetic dichotomy of regional versus national studies and draws on both sides of the divide. It argues that southern California's social, political, and economic landscape distinguished the locale in three important ways from other urban centers. First, Los Angeles businesses did not have to displace an existing industrial structure and were, therefore, poised to influence the local culture more profoundly. Second, Los Angeles's economy had a comparatively large service sector and, thus, a larger proportion of nonmanual employees than eastern industrial centers. While the number of industrial workers in the city grew by 127 percent during the 1920s, the percentage of workers engaged in manufacturing actually dropped, because white-collar, small business, and professional positions grew even more. By 1930, more than 40 percent of employed male southern Californians worked in nonmanual positions, a figure significantly higher than the national average.[23] Third, the region's population comprised an unusually diverse mix of racial and ethnic minorities. By 1930, Los Angeles ranked second only to Baltimore among large cities in the proportion of people of color, including Mexican Americans, Asian Americans, and African Americans. The city's Anglo-American elite made this racial and ethnic fragmentation, compounded by communities of southern and eastern Europeans, a central issue in labor strategies. They ultimately racialized the region's workforce and carved out a near Anglo-Saxon monopoly on white-collar jobs.[24]

Despite these differences in the nature and process of southern California's economic development, the evidence suggests that, while emerging western corporations had greater opportunities than eastern firms to innovate policies and procedures and shape the local milieu and greater opportunities to negotiate corporate cultures, business experience there differed by degree, not kind. Distinctive features of western life affected the way southern California companies operated and dealt with employees, but *process* took precedence over *place* in molding corporate cultures. Large businesses, whether in Los Angeles, Chicago, or Atlanta, ultimately faced similar organizational dilemmas when it came to recruiting, securing, and motivating talented young men. More often than not, they adopted common strategies. While southern California's distinctive environment shaped the interaction between companies and employees, a national corporate culture, however varied, had developed by the 1920s. Frank Lloyd Wright once said, "If you tilt the whole country sideways, Los Angeles is the place where everything loose will fall."[25] Despite such popular images of southern California as distinctive, or bizarre, local corporations innovated, enacted, and turned to largely shared *national* strategies in securing the loyal service of Americans, loose pegs or otherwise.

This book explores this history, not as a smooth transition from a precorporate to a bureaucratic society, but more as the participants themselves viewed it—as a confusing period of dramatic social and economic shifts in which corporate leaders and white-collar workers sought to adapt to, resist, and shape change. Only through a process of negotiating corporate cultures in individual firms did the transition to a corporate America occur. The white, male, salaried employees who drove this new order ultimately demanded much in return for their services. In this process, they constructed new definitions and understandings of middle-class experience that would shape American culture for generations to come.

ONE

THE RISE OF CORPORATE LOS ANGELES

> The amazing industrial progress of Los Angeles compares more than favorably with that of any part of the nation. Within the lifetime of a boy you have doubled the number of your manufacturing establishments, trebled your wage earners, multiplied their payroll by more than 400 percent, and quadrupled the value of your products.
>
> —*Southern California Business*, June 1925

As they surveyed the region's economy in the spring of 1926, southern California's business leaders had every reason to feel enormous pride. Most either remembered or knew that only a generation before Los Angeles had been a small city with limited economic activity. Yet, while few executives hesitated to gloat about the area's rise to global prominence, most had little time for self-congratulation, as new pressures and challenges loomed constantly. That winter, for instance, heavy rains had suppressed department store traffic and slashed profits. In April, several major refinery fires and accidents limited oil production and stirred labor unrest. Throughout the spring, area furniture companies reported difficulty with collections, automobile sales stagnated, and bakeries complained of grocery stores stealing their business. Every day in 1926, just as they had every day of their company's histories, officials grappled with the task of building and running business enterprises in sometimes threatening, often tenuous, and continually shifting environments.[1]

The rise of corporate Los Angeles occurred not as a simple story of business expansion but as a complex web of strategic plotting by individual firms to boost sales and profits. Knowing that large corporations became the dominant institutions in American business and industry during the early twentieth century makes it all too easy to understate the human drama and agency in the process. Companies evolved in different ways and for different reasons as a variety of needs and forces shaped their growth.

The year 1926, for instance, proved a particularly challenging period for local aviation executives. In May, only a month after the Los Angeles–based Western Air Express Company initiated the city's first private air mail and freight operations, its leaders asked themselves, "Why not increase revenue by carrying people as well as mail and cargo?" In answering their question, they learned that carrying passengers entailed more than simply adding pounds to the gross weight each flight carried. Passenger service created numerous additional difficulties; humans proved more temperamental than freight. In subsequent months, Western Air sought to train employees to meet these new demands by circulating innumerable memoranda outlining instructions for passenger care. Safety dominated their concerns. Western Air management feared that passengers would find the idea of wearing parachutes alarming and urged employees to persuade customers that "the parachute is the life preserver of the air." The company also worried that passengers would resist wearing the required helmet, goggles, and flying suit and so instructed personnel to make sure these items fit comfortably: "when we say fitted, we mean fitted. Nothing can be more uncomfortable than to be in the air with a poorly fitted helmet or goggles." Proper signing of release forms provided yet another concern. Leaders instructed employees to make certain that passengers, prior to take-off, signed forms absolving the company from any liability for their injury or death. Finally, there existed the problem of airplane boarding procedures. Management instructed employees to firmly grasp people's arms and personally lead them to the plane's door, always remaining between the passenger and the wing: "This is to avoid the danger of possibility of the passenger walking into the propeller. This is our most serious problem and must not be forgotten for one moment."[2]

Air travel has become so routine today that the safety instructions now given prior to take-off bore both flight attendants and passengers. As the excerpts from this memo reveal, in the early days of commercial aviation such familiarity or apathy did not exist. In their efforts to build a profitable company, Western Air executives not only had to lure a curious but nervous public onto their planes, they also had to find employees comfortable and proficient in this new business environment. Western Air and other aviation firms created the structure and rules of commercial air travel only after a process of much experimentation with company policies and industry procedures.

Far from unique, the Western Air experience typifies the nimble, experimental, and adaptive mindset that was needed to develop new businesses in the region's emerging corporate economy. Throughout Los Angeles's history, executives struggled to make sense of new and evolving business climates and to create organizational structures and cultivate workforces that would assure success. This story played out in southern California as a number of large corporations emerged out of hundreds of small businesses. This did not occur as part of a natural, inevitable process, but rather because the leaders of these large corporations, with both luck and foresight, molded a workforce and operational apparatus tailored to their unique situations. When young Los Angelenos searched for work, they applied for positions in businesses and industries that were more often than not new and unsteady. Even when growing and apparently successful, individual businesses struggled to adapt to new circumstances, conditions, and challenges; they developed the rules of operations as they stumbled forward.

Big businesses became the site around which a new white-collar corporate culture developed, and Los Angeles provided a cradle for the subsequent new middle class of salaried employees. The city came of age in the 1920s with the nation's most rapidly developing economic infrastructure and a popular culture industry that blared news of its growth around the country. The emergence of Los Angeles as one of the nation's most important economic centers was in itself a Hollywood tale. Its rise seemed as unlikely at the start of its modern growth as many of the movie scripts for which the city became famous. In an 1876 publication boosting Los Angeles County, Ohio immigrant Robert Widney declared that the region's abundant fertile acreage would assure future prosperity as "all wealth comes from the earth." To explain his point, he described how regional products provided economic bases for New York City, Chicago, and San Francisco, but added a disclaimer that Los Angeles "will never rival these. They are only mentioned to illustrate the principles." By the turn of the century, events had proved Widney wrong. Los Angeles did grow to rival those other cities both in population and economic development. Widney did not anticipate the extent to which the city would grow, in part because he could not envision the scale and diversity of firms that would come to form the basis of modern urban economies. The city's wealth ultimately came not just from the sale or development of regional commodities but from a sprawling service sector, including insurance, entertainment, banking, utilities, and transportation. The place that twenty-two-year-old Kansas City immigrant William Spalding called a "dull town" in 1874 and thirty-three-year-old Iowa-born Jackson Graves referred to as a "sleepy, ambitionless adobe village" in the 1880s would become one of the nation's leading corporate metropolises by the 1920s, with nearly half its vast workforce engaged in distributive and service industries.[3]

Just as the nation's white-collar men have often escaped critical scrutiny, so too has Los Angeles enjoyed a mythologized past. The dramatic story of its rise, from the opening of the first transcontinental railway line into the city in 1876 through the onset of the Depression in 1929, has seduced many a commentator to join in the region's booster tradition. Throughout its long legacy of aggressive self-promotion, boosters, commentators, and historians alike have recounted the city's growth with awe, have endowed Los Angeles with human qualities, and have described its rise with a sense of inevitability. In this vein, one historian recently declared that "Los Angeles envisioned itself, then materialized that vision through sheer force of will."[4]

To be sure, the city's vast growth, as well as that of the region's economy, is a remarkable story. Because its emergence as a major urban center occurred alongside the appearance of modern corporate bureaucracies, a sketch of corporate growth in Los Angeles offers a particularly dramatic tale. The city's "downtown" in the 1870s, prior to the first major population boom, encompassed a village plaza dominated by a Roman Catholic church and several small businesses, closely surrounded by fields where farming and cattle-raising flourished. In following years, the heart of the city edged several blocks southward to a bustling new central business district. By the 1920s, "downtown" referred to a sprawling district of office buildings that housed regional, national, and even international corporations. Six new bank offices opened in 1921 alone. In 1924, twenty-two major new downtown buildings welcomed tenants. Subsequent years witnessed the opening of several new business complexes with millions of dollars of construction under way. By 1930, office buildings occupied 30 percent of the land in downtown Los Angeles, compared to less than 5 percent in 1890.[5]

According to the common narrative of the region's business and economic history, Los Angeles grew into a modern city as much from self-conscious planning and promotion as from the dictates of location and resources. Following the opening of rail lines into the city, local residents and investors faced the challenge of developing a sparsely populated region that lacked water, a port (the nearest significant natural harbor was 120 miles away in San Diego), a local transportation system, and important natural resources. Regional entrepreneurs responded by combining capital investment in the local infrastructure with well-funded promotional campaigns to attract settlers. With the climate as bait, they attracted emigrants by building new communities. Each arrival provided additional labor as well as new consumers for their enterprises. In the words of one historian, "Los Angeles, it should be understood, is not a mere city. On the contrary, it is, and has been since 1888, a COMMODITY."[6]

Citrus crops became the region's first major commercial export. Venture capitalists planted southern California's initial commercial orchard in 1841, and by the 1880s local growers were winning prizes at international expositions. The arrival of Santa Fe's transcontinental railroad in 1886 and the development of the refrigerated railroad car in the 1890s provided the opportunity for exporting fruits on a large scale. By the 1890s, southern California's citrus industry, which boasted more than five million trees, ranked as the most important local industry.[7]

Oil emerged as the second major industry, and ultimately the more lucrative one. Speculators drilled scattered wells around the city beginning in 1865, and after Edward L. Doheny discovered oil within the Los Angeles city limits in 1892, an oil boom attracted numerous drillers and massive capital investment. By the end of the century, several companies were operating a total of more than six hundred local wells. One-fourth of the nation's oil supply came from Los Angeles by 1930.[8]

During the 1910s and 1920s, the nation's fledgling film industry coalesced in southern California. The cinema business generated many jobs and much revenue. By 1920, led by Los Angeles's climate, geography, and open-shop tradition, every major national motion picture company had opened production centers there; in 1921 the city hosted fifty-three motion picture companies. The industry's product value rose from $79 million to $129 million between 1921 and 1929, and it spawned related booms in tourism and merchandising.[9]

Throughout this period, Los Angeles grew steadily as an important trading center. In hopes of remedying the city's lack of a natural harbor, its civic, Chamber of Commerce, and business leaders in the 1890s had lobbied the federal government for funds to create a deep-water port. Construction of the new harbor began in 1899, following a bitter battle between two railway factions over its location, in which San Pedro emerged victorious over Santa Monica. By 1929, federal and local government harbor expenditures had surpassed $40 million. The Panama Canal's opening in 1914 affirmed the foresightedness of such investments. The new route allowed regional industries more direct access to eastern and European ports, and by 1925, 70 percent of the canal's traffic passed through Los Angeles. The city became the largest port on the West Coast in 1923. By 1930, it handled more than one billion dollars in products and ranked first among American ports in intercoastal business, second in exports, and third in total commerce.[10]

During the 1910s, Los Angeles's municipally operated port helped to lure significant local and eastern capital into a bustling industrial sector. The Panama Canal spurred rapid industrialization, as regional products could now reach northeastern ports in barely two weeks. From 1910 to 1920, more than 2,700 factories opened in the metropolitan area. By the 1920s, the city ranked tenth among the nation's industrial centers, boasting major glass, garment, furniture, metal, and tire factories. In constant 1914 dollars, industrial output rose from $355 million in 1920 to $895 million by 1926.[11]

Booming population growth and massive industrial development fueled continuous growth in southern California's service sector. Banks, insurance companies, transportation firms, utility companies, and other service industries expanded to meet growing demands. From 1905 to 1920, for example, bank deposits in Los Angeles jumped from $71 million to $444 million.[12]

This 1930s aerial view shows Los Angeles's early-twentieth-century business district. In the 1950s, the district picked up and moved from downtown to a new location to the south and west. Courtesy of Department of Special Collections, University Libraries, University of Southern California.

This quick survey offers a factual description of Los Angeles's economic growth, but such a narrative obscures much of the story. Simply recounting the rapidity and scope of the city's transformation from a small agricultural community to the West's leading financial, entertainment, and industrial center feeds into the argument that the city was predestined for great heights and masks the diversity and tenuousness of the course of urban development that took it there. Such an approach deletes human actors from the story. To concentrate on such condensed and aggregate dimensions of economic growth contributes to a sense that corporate emergence proceeded as a linear, homogeneous, and faceless process. To the contrary, developing corporate economies represented the efforts of thousands of individuals trying to build businesses in complicated, uncertain, and challenging environments. These firms needed to procure the services and loyalties of many thousands of employees in order to succeed. Companies in every industry faced unique hurdles; within single industries, the strategies and designs of firms varied widely and depended on leaders, the local workforce, geography, and regional culture and politics. For all of the Chamber of Commerce tracts marveling at the region's booming economy, many Los Angeles investors, managers, and employees lay awake at night worrying about their future livelihoods.

Tremendous diversity characterized the city's business life. The companies that formed the core of corporate Los Angeles in the 1920s ranged from longstanding firms dating well back into the nineteenth century, struggling to stay alive in new economic environments, to new firms created by technologies and consumer demands that arose suddenly in the 1920s. The Pacific Mail Steamship Company exemplifies the former. Chartered in 1848, the San Francisco–born company initially operated steamers between Panama and several West Coast ports. The California Gold Rush provided an early boom to Pacific Mail's fortunes, which lasted to the turn of the century. By 1865 the company owned twenty ships and by 1875 had expanded its operations to China, Japan, New Zealand, and Australia. In 1900, the powerful Southern Pacific Railroad acquired Pacific Mail.[13]

With the development of the Los Angeles harbor in the first two decades of the new century, Los Angeles became a critical center for Pacific Mail operations. An office staff of several dozen struggled to control hundreds of employees who handled cargo and passenger operations between the city and numerous Pacific Rim ports. The persistent need to hire new agents, stewards, and office personnel amidst high turnover rates preoccupied the local office. The demands of monitoring the quality and activities of these scattered and often distant employees provided an additional challenge. Letters and reports detailing worker quality and activities arrived continually, noting how employees were either helping or hurting the firm. To further complicate matters, the company's efforts to direct its unruly staff and operations occurred amidst stiff competition from rival lines.

After over half a century of steady growth, Pacific Mail fell on hard times after 1915. Passage of the La Follette Seaman's Act, requiring partial replacement of Chinese crews with white crews, increased company expenses. Concurrently, the Panama Canal Act of 1915 included regulations preventing ties between shipping and railroad companies. For these reasons, Southern Pacific sold its interests in Pacific Mail in 1915. The maritime demands of World War I, however, provided a boom and the company flourished anew. That success lasted until 1925, when the United States Shipping Board put five of the company's primary vessels up for sale, and Pacific Mail's failure to retain the ships in the subsequent bidding led to its quick dissolution.[14]

While Pacific Mail's executives struggled to make a nineteenth-century industry prosper under twentieth-century conditions, leaders of the Western Air Express Company sought to create an entirely new business enterprise. Founded in July 1925, Western Air Express capitalized on the recent passage of the Kelly Act, which opened up previously government-monopolized air mail service to private companies. In April 1926, Western Air began air mail service between Los Angeles and Salt Lake City, with a stop in Las Vegas. From the outset Western Air officials hoped to add passenger service. In an incident that would garner the company much publicity, humorist Will Rogers, wanting to fly from Los Angeles to Las Vegas, purchased enough air mail stamps to convey 180 pounds and then sent himself. Within a month of its initial run, Western Air began carrying passengers.[15]

Western Air tapped into a booming new market for aviation services and initially struggled to keep up with the demand. On several occasions, the company rejected proposals that would have expanded its operations in favor of assuring tight local control. In 1928, for instance, the Pennsylvania Railroad proposed the formation of a plane-train service from the East Coast to the West; passengers would ride planes by day and trains by night. Western Air rejected that proposal in hopes of gradually establishing its own national network. By 1929 it appeared that these expectations might soon be fulfilled. With the aid of hundreds of employees, the firm directed a transportation network extending as far east as Kansas City. In 1930, however, declining demand and lower government mail rates created financial problems that curtailed Western Air's dreams of its own national network. That year, the company joined with eastern carriers to create a national system.[16]

Western Air's rapid growth came despite considerable turmoil in its early efforts with passenger service. On its initial passenger flight, the company simply set up folding chairs on the cargo plane's floor. This and many other awkward arrangements forced managers to rethink operations. Passengers complained about the difficulty of boarding the planes without ladders or footstools. Many women complained that screws and nails sticking out of seats and joints in the cabin tore their clothing. Passengers also expressed displeasure when flight stewards sat on their armrests or fell asleep during the flight, when the pilot left his seat during the flight, flew too low, or struggled to clean the windshield after it was struck by birds, and when the flight crew became ill because of turbulence. One by one the company addressed these issues, though others continually arose. Complaints about lost luggage, bad food, and the frightening nature of air travel pervaded early Western Air operations.[17]

The experiences of Pacific Mail and Western Air are significant on two levels. First, both companies, like their peers throughout the region's business community, tried to prosper amidst numerous unique internal and external challenges. Both faced stiff competition from other firms, greeted a demanding and often difficult public, and weathered specific industry problems as well as economic forces beyond their control. Second, leaders of both companies had to turn to their broad ranks of employees, who interacted daily with the public, to navigate these challenges. In this too, these executives were not alone. By 1930, over half a million individuals were responsible for the daily operations of individual firms in Los Angeles's economy.[18]

Both the many dimensions of business success and the human face of company growth become clear in the histories of five of the largest Los Angeles–based corporations. The stories of Union Oil, Southern California Edison, Pacific Mutual Life Insurance, Security-First National Bank, and Pacific Electric Railway illustrate the complex and varied natures of modern corporations and how such firms, with their need to corral the talents and loyalties of thousands of employees, became the birthplace of the nation's modern middle class.

Union Oil Company of California

Tourist brochures and Chamber of Commerce materials produced about Los Angeles during the 1920s featured palm trees, beaches, and movie stars, but Los Angelenos themselves might have suggested a very different icon—the oil derrick. Thick, black, sticky oil gushed from wells situated throughout the region during the early twentieth century. Oil provided investors either fortunes or failure, and thousands of working- and middle-class jobs for others. Movies, tourism, and citrus may have been southern California's most celebrated industries, but oil bolstered the region's economy and permeated its consciousness. Oil derricks dominated local landscapes. The rush to tap into elusive subterranean pockets quickly overcame any concerns about the eyesores of derricks and refineries scattered throughout the city. Culturally, oil speculation provided something like a local civic sport. Many Angelenos engaged in oil schemes that received extensive coverage in newspaper stories and advertisements. Many more watched the frenzy with varying degrees of intrigue and disgust. More practically, many residents found employment in the oil companies. The downtown business sector housed the headquarters of several significant petroleum corporations where thousands of office workers congregated each morning to direct their firms' sprawling operations.[19]

It would be difficult to overstate the importance of oil to Los Angeles's pre-Depression economy. City boosters in the 1920s bragged about presiding over one of the nation's ten leading industrial centers, but they ignored important details. While Los Angeles did rank ninth among American cities in the value of its industrial output, petroleum refining alone accounted for over one-third of it. Only during the manufacturing boom of World War II would the region have a diversified industrial section of national significance.[20]

Union Oil, known today as Unocal, emerged early as one of the region's dominant firms. Its thousands of employees handled nearly $300 million in capital stock and directed the production, distribution, and sale of eleven million barrels of oil annually by the late 1920s. As a locally owned corporation, its emergence and success proved a source of considerable interest and pride among boosters in the local business community.[21]

Union Oil's formidable presence in the early twentieth century belied a tenuous past and insecure present. Its story began on October 17, 1890, when Pennsylvania immigrants Lyman Stewart and Wallace Hardison merged their seven-year-old Hardison and Stewart Oil Company with two smaller oil-drilling operations (the name *Union* referred to the uniting of these companies). Based in Santa Paula, a community northwest of Los Angeles, the new company initially sold fuel oil, kerosene, greases, and lubricating oil. With an initial capital stock of $5 million, the company produced eleven thousand barrels of oil its first year.[22]

An office of just fifteen people originally controlled Union Oil's operations, and company directors wielded a heavy hand in daily affairs. For instance, they were deeply involved in employment decisions. During a slowdown in the summer of 1895, the company president personally released two office staff members and placed his son in charge until business picked up again. Simultaneously, he tinkered with a number of job descriptions and chains of commands throughout the small firm.[23]

From its founding, Union Oil leaders argued over issues of strategy and structure. Two central figures clashed repeatedly over the company's nature and direction. Thomas Bard, Union Oil's first president, viewed the enterprise as a tool to make profits that he could direct toward other ventures. Bard wanted the company to produce and sell crude petroleum and to stay out of the more complicated areas of refining and manufacturing. However, Lyman Stewart, the firm's vice president, had been a part of the industry since its beginnings in Pennsylvania and envisioned developing Union Oil into a fully integrated company that would become an industry leader. The two battled for ten years and continually destabilized operations. Finally, in a fierce power struggle involving the board and investors in 1900, Stewart and his son ousted Bard. From that point on Union Oil pursued a strategy of aggressive expansion.

Stewart and his ever-increasing cadre of subordinates recognized that opportunities for expansion included both new geographic markets and new products and services. Adding to its initial offices in San Francisco, Los Angeles, and Santa Paula, Union Oil opened its first sales and marketing facility in San Pedro in 1899. The headquarters moved to Los Angeles in 1900, where the company could interact better with supporting industries. Union Oil continually opened additional offices until, in 1926, it had sales departments in seven western states plus Canada, Mexico, the United Kingdom, and Asia.[24]

The company's growth also reflected technological achievements that provided new uses for its products. In particular, the development of the automobile gave the firm a vast new market for gasoline and motor oil, and the company became an industry leader in marketing automobile products. Union Oil opened its first Los Angeles service station in 1913, and by 1930 it owned 722 stations. In the 1910s and 1920s, the company also entered the booming aviation fuel markets and became a national innovator in transport operations.[25]

Union Oil grew steadily but not without encountering a stream of threats and challenges. Overproduction loomed as an ever-present industrywide crisis. With wildcat speculators exploring for reserves throughout the West in hopes of quick profits, new supply sources threatened to collapse the cash base of large oil companies. Union Oil joined its competitors in advocating a variety of complicated private and state-managed production regulations. Its relations with rival firms were otherwise not so harmonious, however. Competition intensified for oil and gasoline sales and Union Oil's market share remained precarious. Even the company's own workers at times seemed to threaten its existence, at least from leaders' perspective. Labor union activity at its refineries and production sites continuously challenged management's efforts to cut costs.

An unrelenting managerial problem underlay each of these issues. With each stage of expansion, company officials strove to enlarge administrative hierarchies in effective ways. Maintaining control of sprawling operations grew more difficult and complicated as the number of employees soared and the organizational apparatus expanded. Company propaganda spoke paternalistically of the Stewart family's leadership, but in fact, thousands of nameless employees became the real agents in its operations.

Union Oil's managerial bureaucracy expanded on three levels throughout its history, and with each new employee hired, the control of daily operations became increasingly diffused throughout its ranks. The company's first dimension of organizational growth occurred as leaders endeavored to manage the diversification of its operations. Not only did each phase of the company's operations—exploration, production, refining, distribution, and marketing—become more complicated, but each new product also required its own managerial apparatus. Over time Union's administration grew into a complex hierarchy with operations subdivided into specific departments. In 1908, Union had four departments: accounting, secretarial, field operations, and sales. By 1921, directors had reorganized and enlarged the company's administration to include a comptroller's division, treasurer's office, and secretarial office, along with eight additional departments: geological and land, field, manufacturing, stations, fuel oil, transportation, purchasing, and engineering. The personnel needs of each division and department varied, but all employed a staff of clerical and managerial personnel.

Union Oil's second dimension of bureaucratic expansion occurred spatially. As its operations became more diffuse geographically, the firm chose to replicate the structure of its single initial office in different cities, states, and countries. As it expanded into the Pacific Northwest in 1905, for instance, Union opened a Portland, Oregon, office with two employees. By 1922, more than 200 people worked in the office's many departments.[26] Every time Union Oil entered a new market, new managing offices opened. Ultimately, the company's Los Angeles headquarters oversaw division offices, which oversaw district offices, which in turn oversaw city offices.

On a third level, the managerial apparatus deepened. Not only did more divisions of management scatter over larger geographic areas, but every office encompassed an increasingly elaborate chain of command. Sales offices came to include clerks, salesmen, agents, an assistant sales manager, and a sales manager. In nearly every department in every office, a similar hierarchy with many and often minute distinctions in rank and authority appeared.

During the 1920s, Union Oil mushroomed into a major corporate bureaucracy. Its original office staff of fifteen grew to three thousand people in

1916, and to ten thousand by 1929. Although records showing the exact numbers and breakdown of Union Oil personnel over time do not exist, in 1926, nearly half of its nine thousand employees filled white-collar positions, with the rest in drilling and field operations.[27]

Pacific Mutual Life Insurance Company

During the early twentieth century, Los Angeles boosters took enormous pride in constructing downtown business complexes. The city's youth and its geographical remoteness created in many local promoters tinges of insecurity that led to enthusiastic celebrations of every indicator of economic growth and achievement. The opening of the Pacific Mutual Life Insurance Company's new headquarters building in 1926 garnered just such fanfare. The opulent structure adjoined the company's earlier Central Park (later Pershing Square) building and placed it not only at the focal point of downtown development but also on the western, cutting edge of the city's shifting business district.

By the 1920s, Pacific Mutual stood as one of the nation's ten largest insurance companies. For the city's business community, however, the firm represented much more than its balance sheet would suggest. Like Union Oil, its local management earned it special status and support. Additionally, Pacific Mutual symbolized Los Angeles's growing position as the capital of western business development, for it was an "immigrant company," having relocated from San Francisco, which vied with Los Angeles for regional economic supremacy.

Pacific Mutual's founders would have been shocked to see their company based in Los Angeles. When entrepreneurs opened the firm in Sacramento in 1868, Los Angeles was a barely accessible and little-known village. Even in 1881, when Pacific Mutual moved to San Francisco with $1.7 million of insurance in force, Los Angeles remained a remote town. Between 1881 and 1906, Pacific Mutual and San Francisco grew together, and each overshadowed its respective neighbors to the south. In the early part of the new century, however, the firm began to encounter financial difficulties. Then, on the morning of April 16, 1906, a powerful earthquake and ensuing fires destroyed San Francisco's business district. Pacific Mutual's eight-story headquarters lay among the casualties.[28]

Although a much smaller city at the time of the San Francisco disaster, Los Angeles was in the midst of dramatic population gains. A local insurance company's meteoric rise testified to the region's development: Conservative Life Insurance Company opened in 1900 with $200,000 capital stock.[29] The firm sold nearly $1.4 million of insurance during its first year. By 1903, with $21 million of insurance in force, Conservative Life claimed to be the nation's fastest growing insurance company. In 1905, it surpassed Pacific Mutual within the state of California; and, in a move that foreshadowed the shifting locus of regional power, Conservative Life acquired the floundering Pacific Mutual in a hostile takeover four months prior to the earthquake. While the merged entity retained the name Pacific Mutual because of its greater recognition, Conservative Life commanded the new enterprise.

For Pacific Mutual's new owners, the San Francisco disaster provided a fitting opportunity for consolidating the corporation in Los Angeles. As if Pacific Mutual's acquisition by a smaller and younger company had not been unsettling enough, the relocation stunned its older leadership and provided another blow to San Francisco's devastated business community. When the embers from earthquake-related fires cooled, Pacific Mutual's San Francisco leadership met amidst the rubble and vowed they would carry on, stronger than before. Their public relations efforts included a photograph of executives standing amidst the ruins in front of the building's seven-story vault, which had survived the quake and fire. Future company publications touted the vault as a symbol of the firm's ability to endure. The scene, however, symbolized poignantly not the company's former strength but rather its destruction in San Francisco and subsequent rebirth in Los Angeles. The move proved fortuitous, for while Los Angeles's population did not exceed that of San Francisco until 1920, that of metropolitan southern California had already surpassed the Bay Area's by 1910. Even Pacific Mutual's older leaders would in later years hail the move. They recognized that the company otherwise might have missed opportunities in the West's primary urban market.[30]

The two firms' consolidation created a vast and booming enterprise. The disorganized leadership that allowed Pacific Mutual to succumb to Conservative Life's January 1906 takeover did not reflect its powerful standing. At that time, Pacific Mutual operated in forty states with $64.7 million of insurance in force. The new firm grew at an extraordinary rate and by 1909 ranked among the nation's top fifteen insurers. In a form of corporate expansion similar to that of Union Oil's, Pacific Mutual developed by increasing both its product lines and its market penetration. The company mirrored industry trends in offering new and broader forms of insurance coverage. Pacific Mutual initially specialized in death benefits, but between 1904 and 1915 the firm began to introduce policies that provided benefits in the event of accidents, sickness, and disabilities, as well as retirement income for the elderly.[31]

Pacific Mutual also expanded by increasing its market coverage. Following its reorganization in 1906, the company had agents working in forty of the

The Los Angeles headquarters of Pacific Mutual Life Insurance Company, 1915. Reproduced by permission of the Huntington Library, San Marino, California.

country's forty-eight states. It added only two states and the District of Columbia to its roster by 1928 but operated many more agencies overall; their number rose from 70 in 1906 to 141 in 1927. As the number of agents and agencies around the country increased, Pacific Mutual found that it could not rely on its home office alone to coordinate all of its business, and subsequently opened up branch offices in key states to direct regional activities.[32]

At the core of this business expansion lay the development of a carefully coordinated staff of white-collar employees. Because Pacific Mutual did not produce a physical product and thus did not have to deal with production or distribution issues, officials could create a highly streamlined managerial structure. Initially, the company rested on a pyramid-shaped hierarchy with a central home office coordinating scattered sales agents. Pacific Mutual began in 1868 with only three officers. From that point until the merger with Conservative Life, most employees served as agents, and the home office staff remained comparatively small. Conservative Life's initial workforce had included three employees to run the home office and six insurance agents. By 1905, the company employed a home office force of approximately 100, who coordinated the activities of roughly 350 agents.[33]

The 1906 consolidation of the two companies coincided with a period in which many new forms of insurance found large markets. The company's management subsequently began a period of two-tiered expansion. First, as the number of agencies grew, the home office in Los Angeles gradually lost direct responsibility for individual agents and deferred control of daily operations to its 150 branch offices. This helped Pacific Mutual address two major threats to its stability, a lack of agent loyalty and a lack of community support. The fidelity of agents proved troublesome throughout its history. Insurance companies competed fiercely to employ well-known and successful salesmen and -women in local communities, and agents often pulled rival firms into bidding wars for their services. Also, because insurers considered trust so critical to business success, they needed agents who were sensitive to the concerns, personalities, and needs of individual communities. Localizing control to as great an extent as possible became key to Pacific Mutual's managerial structure.

A second form of bureaucratic growth occurred at both Pacific Mutual's headquarters and many branch offices as the firm reorganized its managerial structure into specific departments under umbrella divisions. The company organized three general divisions based on types of insurance and, within each division, numerous departments to handle specific functions. This bureaucratization entailed burgeoning office staffs to manage an exponentially expanding roster of agents. In all, the number of executive officers grew from eight in 1906 to twenty-five by 1927. The total number of employees at the home office rose from 234 in 1906 to 763 in 1927, with several hundred additional employees staffing branch offices. By the 1920s, the firm's agents numbered in the thousands.[34]

Southern California Edison Company

For entrepreneurial-minded southern Californians, the region's dramatic population gains provided tantalizing opportunities for amassing wealth. The rush to provide goods and services to the swelling populace motivated innumerable ventures in every economic sector. Among these, few seemed more promising than electric utilities. Even given the general rapidity of corporate growth during this era, few industries matched the speed with which power companies developed, or experienced as vividly the rise of new markets for their product.

Nationally, efforts to produce and sell electricity began in the 1880s and initially centered on generating power for industry and public transportation. Yet if these provided the early catalysts for electric power growth, the electrification of urban areas and later the countryside made this growth explosive. The process of electrification, entailing first indoor lighting, then commercial lighting, and finally the development of electric appliances, swept through American cities and towns between 1885 and 1915. As Americans clamored for electric power, the utility industry raised its capacity twelve fold, utility sales increased sixteen times, and capital investment grew from $500 million to $4.5 billion.[35]

Early utility growth usually occurred as businesses brought electricity to existing regions. Southern California's exploding population added particular allure for investors and entrepreneurs, making the region a magnet for new power companies. On December 31, 1882, the Los Angeles Electric Company, with an employee roster of three, became the first utility to bring electric light to the city of Los Angeles. Over the next forty years, nearly 200 other firms attempted to enter southern California's power market. Few of these companies survived for long; other more aggressive firms acquired most of them. From these mergers, the Southern California Edison Company (SCE) gradually became the region's primary supplier.[36]

Southern California Edison considered its earliest ancestors to be electric companies in the communities of Visalia, Santa Barbara, and Riverside, each founded in 1886. The most significant firm in its lineage, the West Side Lighting Company (1896), developed from the need to supply power to a rapidly growing Los Angeles. Company officials quickly discovered, however, that a San Francisco group had organized the Los Angeles Edison Electric Company in 1894, not to provide service, but to obtain copyrights on "Edison three-wire" circuit technology for purposes of speculation. West Side company officials subsequently merged with the San Francisco–based group to form the Edison Electric Company of Los Angeles in 1897. The following year, they acquired the Southern California Power Company and began the process of purchasing small electric operations throughout the region. John B. Miller became the company's president in 1901 and gained a reputation as "the great amalgamator" for the number of firms he acquired. By 1909, the $30-million company, which served over 600,000 people in five southern California counties, incorporated as Southern California Edison.[37]

SCE's growth occurred amidst the regulatory impulses that dominated Progressive Era politics, and its executives constantly grappled with legislative threats and opportunities. Passage of the state's Public Utilities Act in 1911 formalized SCE's growing monopoly and accelerated its development. Many Los Angeles politicians, however, opposed the measure and sought instead to develop a publicly owned municipal electric utility. SCE officials believed they would eventually lose the Los Angeles market and thus worked to expand interests in surrounding areas. In 1910, Los Angeles provided two-thirds of SCE's revenues. By 1922, when the city indeed established its own electric service, Los Angeles furnished only 10 percent of SCE's revenues.[38] By the 1920s, SCE, now a suburban company, provided service for everything between San Diego and central California except the city of Los Angeles.

Given the loss of the Los Angeles market in the middle of this period, SCE's dramatic growth from its incorporation in 1906 through the 1920s speaks well of its leaders' effective management and foresight. They steadily forayed into new markets, largely through the acquisition of other companies. From 1917, when city voters forced Edison to sell its Los Angeles operations, until 1923, when Los Angeles's utility independence became final, the company doubled its assets and capital stock and acquired most of the region's other utility firms.[39] Heightened industrial demand and increased per capita consumption of electricity also bolstered SCE operations. In 1910, Edison customers each consumed an annual average of 2,504 kilowatt hours of electricity; the number had jumped to 4,072 by 1917. By 1928, SCE stood as the nation's fifth largest electric utility.[40]

The actual running of SCE's daily operations lay on the shoulders of thousands of employees in an unusually elaborate managerial bureaucracy. In the 1920s it would become common for the firm to give its employees organizational charts. Its operations were so diverse, vast, and complex, that leaders devoted considerable effort to ensuring that individual employees understood the broader enterprise in which they worked. At the apex of SCE's hierarchy stood a central administrative office. The company divided its central administration into three departments: operating, engineering, and accounting. Each department, in turn, organized its activities into multiple divisions.

Despite the creation of a large, central administrative structure, SCE's greater bureaucratic growth occurred at the level of its local operations. Fearing that individual communities would move to assume control of utility operations if unsatisfied with its service, the company in the 1920s adopted a decentralized organizational structure designed to assure that local employees would promptly and effectively meet community needs. By 1924 the company divided its activities into thirty-one districts. Each served as a comprehensive operational unit with a manager and staff who directed all aspects of local operations. In effect, SCE became a collection of local utility companies.[41]

This expanding bureaucracy at both the local and main offices drew increasing numbers of employees. In 1915, the company employed approximately 1,800 persons. By 1923, SCE had 5,000 persons on its regular payrolls plus an additional 5,000 temporary workers on construction projects. By 1929, its "permanent workforce" had risen to 9,000. Most of the later growth came in white-collar positions, as the number of sales agents, local office staff, and customer representatives grew disproportionately to workers.[42]

Security-First National Bank of Los Angeles

In 1929, Los Angeles's financial community celebrated a merger between the banking empires of its two leading financiers, Henry M. Robinson and Joseph Sartori. The merger combined the Security Bank with the Los Angeles First National Trust and Savings Bank to create the Security-First National Bank of Los Angeles, the nation's eighth largest bank, with total assets of over $600 million. Local boosters hailed the merger as symbolic of the city's continued rise as a leading national economic center. In fact, the merger did not result from a mindset of aggressive growth and expansion. Rather, it reflected a defensive posture designed to preserve two locally owned banks in the face of overwhelming competition from a San Francisco rival. Los Angeles may have won the insurance battle during this period, but San Francisco retained the supremacy in western banking that it had held since Gold Rush days and continued to plague the aspirations of Los Angeles's business elites.[43]

That Los Angeles banks would ever compete with those of any other major city would have surprised its earliest nineteenth-century bankers. In 1868, a former California governor, John G. Downey, organized the first bank in Los Angeles. Downey had argued for the establishment of a bank since his first visit to the city, in 1850. Active in the practice of subdividing old ranchos from the era of Spanish rule, he wanted to lend money, in large part to make possible his acquisition of the debt-ridden properties. Yet Downey's contemporaries found the idea of establishing a bank in this farming outpost ludicrous. Downey remembered that, in the 1850s, his calls for a bank had fallen on deaf ears: "I tried to induce some Los Angeles friends to join me, not having sufficient funds myself. They all laughed at me." A close friend of Downey's commented, "I hope, Downey, that you and I will never see a bank established in Los Angeles." Even in 1868 when Downey realized his goal, conditions in Los Angeles were less than ideal for a local bank. The capital for the institution had to be raised from San Francisco financiers.[44]

In late 1868, Hellman, Temple, and Company became the city's second bank. Isaias Hellman, a local storekeeper, became involved in banking because he had been one of the few residents who owned a safe, and the miners searching for gold in local hills would bring their gold dust to him for safekeeping. Recognizing the potential complications from this casual practice, and the corresponding opportunity for profit, Hellman founded a bank.[45]

By 1890, following its first modern boom, Los Angeles had four savings banks and eleven chartered commercial banks with $13.9 million in total assets. By 1908, the number of financial institutions had increased to forty-six and the combined assets to $100 million. In the following years, mergers and consolidations reduced the number of banks, but the scope of the city's banking network continued to expand. Throughout the 1910s and 1920s, a rapidly growing populace, the capital needs of a burgeoning new business community, and banking innovations (such as broader checking and savings services, which increased the role of banking in consumer households) fueled a dramatic expansion in local banking. Between 1910 and 1930, local bank deposits grew from $118 million to $1.4 billion.[46]

The consolidation of individual banks and the development of banking networks began in earnest after 1908, when new state legislation required larger amounts of capital to charter banks and the Los Angeles clearing house adopted a policy of working only with banks having capital greater than $200,000. Larger banks thus began to acquire smaller banks, which could not survive in the more demanding environment. Pressure on local banks increased in 1913 when A. P. Giannini, owner of the San Francisco–based Bank of Italy, sought to extend his empire into southern California. After he opened his first branch office, southern California bankers conspired to prevent his further expansion. Under intense pressure, the state agreed to restrictions on branch banking that effectively prevented links between northern and southern California banking markets until 1927.[47]

Los Angeles area banks gradually consolidated into several major branch networks. By 1920, six major local banks had amassed twenty-eight branches, and by 1927, eight of the largest local banks had over two hundred branches. That year, however, witnessed a change in state regulations that allowed Giannini's bank to absorb several local banks and become the city's largest. It was in response to this consolidation that local banking leaders Sartori and Robinson formed the Security-First National Bank of Los Angeles in 1929, creating the largest locally owned bank.

As consolidations and mergers engulfed area banks, and as branch offices proliferated, the nature of bank management and employment changed considerably. The ideal of a small local bank in which the bank's officers dealt directly with customers and in which customers knew bank employees personally dominated marketing campaigns through the 1920s. Such situations were, however, increasingly rare. By the 1920s, the major Los Angeles banks encompassed large white-collar bureaucracies. At its creation in 1929, for instance, Security-First operated 157 branch offices. Most branches employed dozens of people divided into departments based on the type of banking service. A main headquarters office with a much larger roster of white-collar employees, again divided into specific departments, oversaw the branch offices. Security-First's total workforce surpassed 3,500 people. Although executives pared this number during the Depression, the institution (which came to be known as Security Pacific) flourished throughout most of the twentieth century, until 1989, when San Francisco's Bank of America finally acquired it in a hostile take-over.[48]

Pacific Electric Railway Company

In the City of Angels, as everywhere during the 1910s and 1920s, some industries declined, many companies struggled, and businesses often failed. In their quest to lure investors and residents, boosters often spoke of southern California's unique features, but firms in the region were no more free from the threats posed by aggressive competitors, fickle and changing markets, and potentially hostile government regulation than were companies elsewhere. The Pacific Electric Railway Company, for instance, emerged in the 1910s as the nation's largest interurban rail system. During the 1910s and 1920s, however, the company, like the railway industry nationally, suffered declining demand and revenues. According to railway historians, "No industry of its size has had a worse financial record." The once successful Pacific Electric (PE) could not escape this history, or the reputed subversive challenges from local oil firms, and is a fitting reminder of the tenuous nature of corporate operations.[49]

Few companies in southern California boasted a prouder early history than Pacific Electric. By the 1910s, it stood as the nation's largest and most successful electric interurban. The surprise of many today who learn that Los Angeles once had a comprehensive public railway system testifies to the completeness of its dissolution. At its height the system criss-crossed southern California with over 1,200 miles of track, operated by more than 6,500 employees, but the company faced severe financial constraints as early as 1913 and faded badly after 1923.[50]

Los Angeles's first public transportation service, upon which PE would ultimately build, appeared in 1873 when D. V. Waldrom opened a horse-drawn "carry-all" line to provide access to his bar and public garden on the city's "outskirts" at Spring and West Sixth Streets. In the following decade, interurban railway lines replaced this and subsequent scattered horse-drawn operations. In the 1890s, local entrepreneurs began to consolidate these lines into regional networks, hoping not only to serve local transit needs but also to provide access to development projects. Railway operations were one route to immense prosperity, because of the increased value they brought to the outlying areas they made accessible. For this reason, southern California venture capitalist Henry Huntington became involved in Los Angeles's transit system. His presence helped to provide the capital necessary for a period of tremendous railway expansion. In 1898, Huntington purchased the Los Angeles Railway Company, along with a number of other local systems, in the hope of creating a single urban railway network. Huntington merged these into the Pacific Electric Railway Company, incorporated in 1901. By 1910, PE operated six hundred railway cars and carried 225,000 passengers each day.[51]

Huntington sold his interest in PE in 1910 to the Southern Pacific Railroad, which reorganized the company the following year in a merger with eight other local electric railway systems. Now a massive railway network, PE expanded further in late 1912 when it extended service northward into the San Fernando Valley and in 1914 with an additional line running sixty-five miles east to San Bernardino. By 1924, the company had become the nation's largest interurban transit system, running six thousand trains each day and carrying 110 million revenue passengers annually on 144 routes over a 1,200 mile network.[52]

During its early years of rapid growth and expansion, PE built a large bureaucracy. In 1903, the company employed two thousand persons, of which approximately 150 worked in managerial or office positions; the rest served as conductors, engineers, trackmen, mechanics, or on various construction and maintenance teams. By the 1910s, Pacific Electric's organizational structure included six thousand employees, with more than one thousand filling white-collar or managerial positions in several administrative departments. More than eighty persons served in its General Passenger Department alone; the department included a main office managed by a general passenger agent supported by general agents in promotion and advancement, publicity and relations, solicitation and service, and passenger and freight solicitations. It also ran two separate ticket offices and an information service.[53]

Despite the company's steady expansion through 1923, Pacific Electric never prospered, as did most other major local firms. In fact, after 1913, pas-

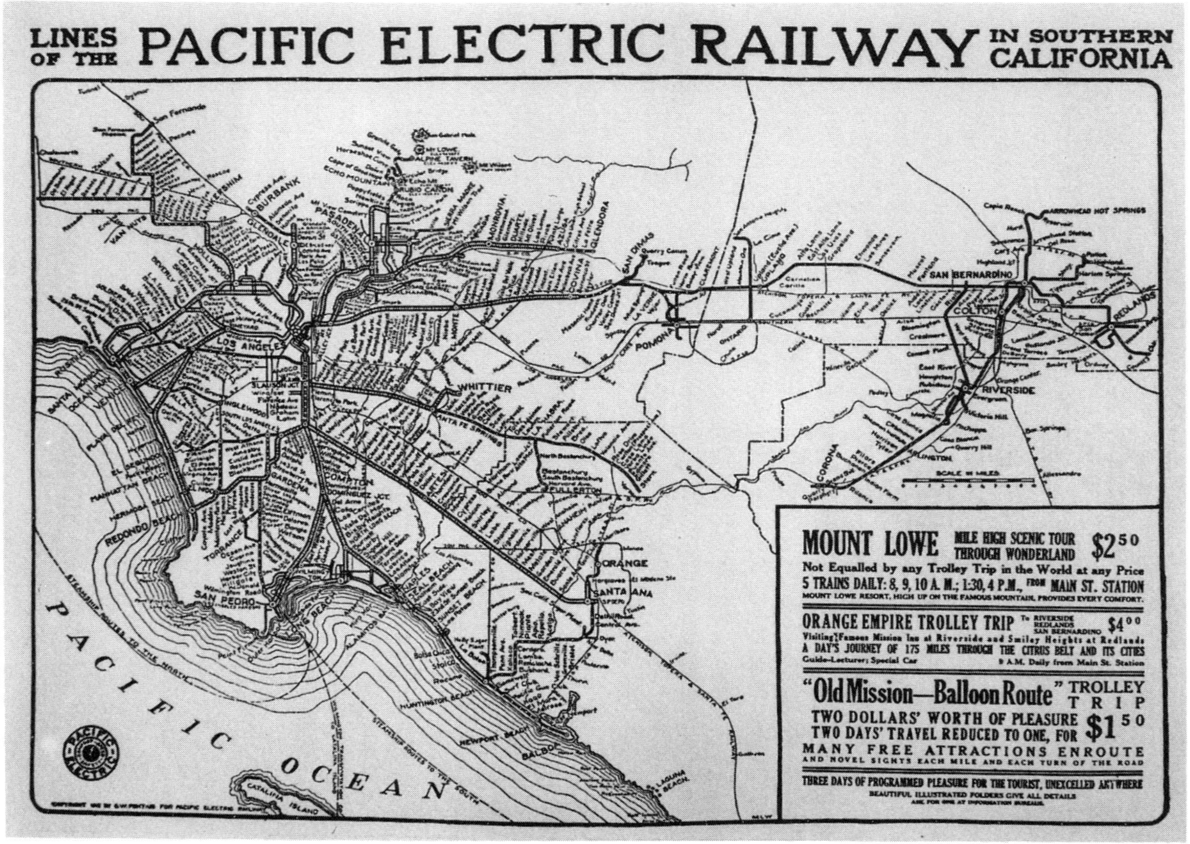

Map of the lines operated by the Pacific Electric Railway in 1912. Courtesy of Andrew Rolle, private collection.

senger operations showed a profit only during World War I. In 1923, the company began to reduce operations. Southern Californians' love for the automobile proved the death knell for PE, despite its leaders' claim that the automobile market had reached "saturation" in the 1920s. In vain, the company tried to educate its employees and the public about the drawbacks to car travel, reproducing with glee, for instance, news of a five-fold increase in auto-related deaths between 1913 and 1923. Unfortunately for PE, not only did southern Californians seem to prefer automobiles to electric railways, but increased automobile traffic on Los Angeles streets slowed PE's operation and made the service even less desirable to commuters. Local residents preferred to invest their money in private transportation than to support development of the significant new underground subway system that PE was proposing to alleviate the congestion. The number of revenue passengers carried annually by PE trains had increased from sixty million in 1912 to one hundred million in 1923. A prolonged drought reduced the production of hydroelectric power in 1924 and forced the company to curtail some electric lines in favor of buses. Many of these routes never reopened. Passenger volume dropped to eighty-one million by the decade's end, with declining revenues imperiling many employees' security.[54] The company's structure reached its apex in the 1910s, but thereafter revenues were not sufficient to further enlarge it. Rather, the company began to trim its workforce. Pacific Electric did not eliminate whole departments during the 1920s but gradually reduced its operations.

The Human Face of Corporate Growth

The growth of southern California's economy during the early twentieth century, like that of other urban centers around the nation, clearly reflected the corporate revolution. Economic change during this period entailed more than simply an increase in the volume of business, caused by growth in the population. A fundamental change in the nature and organization of business activity occurred as large firms grew and dominated their respective sectors. Instead of a few local companies multiplying to hundreds of midsize enterprises, a handful of giants acquired most of the available trade. Instead of the number of oil companies multiplying from several to dozens, for example, a few giant firms emerged. This oligopolistic development occurred throughout southern California's economy, as it did across the nation.

PE, SCE, Security-First, Pacific Mutual, and Union Oil were among those major firms that rose to dominate economic activity in the city of Los Angeles and its environs. By the 1920s, downtown Los Angeles had become a major corporate hub where the activities of regional, national, and international corporations originated. Yet when one looks inside the corporate headquarters, the idea of a monolithic corporate America crumbles. Each firm faced particular challenges and opportunities and would work to create a unique organization and corporate culture.

Yet, while the differences between these companies were many, there existed a common theme. As each grew, leaders gradually lost control of daily operations and had to rely on the activities of hundreds of subordinates, most of whom they did not know personally and probably never would. For most companies, however large, success eventually rested on cultivating positive relations with individual customers and local communities. In the realm of daily operations stockholders and executives turned over the reins to hundreds and thousands of company employees. Behind raw statistics of corporate growth and earnings lay the activities of individual employees. Their backgrounds, enthusiasm, loyalty, and interests would ultimately dictate a company's level of success. Cultivating dedicated employees subsequently became one of the most critical tasks of corporate leadership.

TWO

DEFINING CORPORATE EMPLOYMENT

There are occasions when the sacrifice of a few minutes of your own time may save the company as much as your regular time is worth for several years. You are not loyal if you do not make that sacrifice.

—*Edison Current Topics* 1912

As small Los Angeles businesses grew into large regional, national, and even international corporations, they became civic celebrities. In the booster-oriented local media, stirring biographies of corporate executives and features on the construction of impressive downtown office complexes dominated coverage of the city's business life. The society magazine *Saturday Night*, for instance, regularly reported on the opening of new corporate headquarters and presented glowing accounts of executives in ways that seemed to identify both building and leaders as the company itself. Portraits of corporate presidents frequently adorned the magazine's cover, with banner headlines such as: "Further Evidence of Commercial Growth of Southern California's Metropolis," and "Southern California's Substantiality Reflected in Costly Business Buildings." Executives themselves were complicit in these strategies. Local banks, in particular, used imposing edifices and the names of prominent executives to convey auras of success, strength, and confidence. Typifying these strategies, Farmers and Merchants National Bank advertisements from the 1910s showcased the institution's ornate downtown headquarters along with a solemn quotation: "Upon the Character of the Men Who Direct its Affairs, Depends the Security of a Bank." Promotional materials for nearly every other major Los Angeles bank similarly included a photograph of its headquarters and a listing of its directors and executives.[1]

Efforts to identify a corporation by a building or its prominent leaders harkened back to the days of small town and small business economies, when local residents often knew and dealt directly with proprietors. In these instances, business leaders were, in fact, the company. In Los Angeles's booming corporate economy, however, such constructs belied the reality that customers rarely interacted with executives and in many cases dealt with the firm at a branch office or venue other than its main headquarters. Most Los Angelenos came to know a business by the individual employees they encountered in local shops and offices. While advertisements for Farmers and Merchants National Bank proclaimed that the quality of its directors assured successful operations, its leaders knew all too well that the loyalty of their customer base rested on the competence and worth of individual tellers, clerks, cashiers, and other employees who met bank clients every day, often far from executive offices.

While Los Angeles's business elite celebrated their roles in building powerful corporations, they confronted daily a new business risk—the fact that their firms' success depended largely upon hundreds and even thousands of subordinates, few of whom they would likely ever even meet. No single executive could ensure his firm's success. They instead had to rely on the daily efforts of employees who rarely held any ownership in the firm or had any direct stake in its level of success. To leaders' chagrin, these nameless workers were in positions to help or hinder the firm in many ways every day. A Union Oil executive summarized the situation: "A corporation may spread itself over the whole world, and it may employ a hundred thousand men, but the average person will usually form his judgment of it through his contact with one individual."[2]

The subjects of employee loyalty and dedication reverberated incessantly throughout corporate cultures. Business leaders fiercely resisted the notion that their employees should feel less commitment to the company than they themselves did. Companies feared workplace apathy, for they knew that their salaried ranks played a decisive role in their enterprise's success and quality. The size and structure of corporate operations meant that those at the top had to rely on hundreds or even thousands of subordinates to conduct most day-to-day operations. However skilled a company's leadership, excellent its products, or efficient its structure, a single employee had the power to either cost the firm business or bolster its prosperity. Circumstances often reminded executives of the crucial role individual employees played in a company's success. Most leaders had personal knowledge of situations in which poor service had driven away customers; they frequently discussed the topic in their business associations. In a 1921 speech before the Los Angeles Associated Advertising Club, for instance, the organization's president noted that high quality advertising and "clerical efficiency" must go hand in hand: "Advertising doesn't sell goods, it only brings customers into the store. If the clerks fail to make sales, the cost of advertising is a sheer waste." The president then asserted that while 50 percent of the results of the advertising depended upon the retailer, "in that 50 percent, 49 percent is attributable to the manner in which store patrons are treated."[3]

In addition to their control of internal business operations, salaried employees affected a company's ability to withstand external public pressures. The rise of big business spurred protests against large firms on numerous fronts. Antitrust legislation, federal regulatory agencies, public ownership campaigns, and third political parties all channeled public reaction against big business initiatives. Individual firms encountered this popular disfavor in different forms. For instance, state and local governments threatened utilities with public ownership. Large regional banks faced restraints on growth when prominent local banks exerted political pressure. Whatever the nature of the external challenges, most firms became keenly sensitive to their image and knew that employees provided the critical point of contact between a company and the public.[4]

Airline stewards do not exactly typify white-collar workers, but aviation industry labor relations during the 1920s exemplify the central tensions inherent in corporate management. Los Angeles's Western Air Express Company leaders confronted early the fact that employees represented the company to customers, and securing their hard work and commitment thus dominated managerial agendas. Company executives had initially focused their attention on acquiring airplanes, pilots, and skilled mechanics. Impressed with the new technology, they felt that the ability to move people quickly from one place to another would itself fuel their business. On early Western Air flights, ground personnel simply led passengers to their airplane where, once aboard, pilots would nod and say "nice day," and passengers would then be expected to sit quietly until the plane landed. The need for flight attendants soon became apparent, however, as pilots had to make premature stops after passengers became ill or too terrified to continue. Western Air responded by hiring "stewards" to attend to passengers. Their presence halved the number of emergency landings and proved valuable in numerous additional ways. In fact, executives learned that passengers worried more about their treatment by stewards than all of the expensive technology behind the flight. A Western Air leader noted, "The attention rendered by a steward in a transcontinental air trip is what determines the future patronage of our guests." A slow, rude, or ill-informed steward could drive away a customer permanently, while exemplary employees cultivated repeat business and invaluable word-of-mouth advertising.[5]

Amidst their costly airplanes and skilled personnel, comparatively inexpensive stewards increasingly struck Western Air executives as the key to successful passenger operations. Most southern California corporations similarly confronted the fact that the individual employees who interacted directly with customers were often the most pivotal component in company success. This situation posed a troubling challenge for local business leaders. How could they ensure total commitment from salaried employees who did not own the company and benefited only indirectly from its success? How could they get them to act like limited partners, or stakeholders? How could they persuade them to view the firm's success as their very own?

The Los Angeles business community responded to these organizational dilemmas by vigorously demanding nothing less than total commitment. In a period in which officials scripted the workings of corporations on the fly, executives unabashedly rebuffed the idea that employees would not assume the posture of ownership. They defined corporate employment in the broadest terms and insisted on ardent twenty-four-hour-a-day loyalty to the firm's interests.

While Western Air executives initially resisted the idea of spending money on stewards, they came to recognize that these employees could help assure the company's success and began to demand they do so. Western Air expected stewards to go beyond the call of duty in exhibiting a zealous passion for passenger comfort. For a salary of $100 per month, from which the firm expected them to furnish their own uniforms (except the white dinner jacket), pay lodging costs on overnight flights, and purchase their own in-flight meals, leaders asked each steward to act as "porter, waiter, nurse, baggage and mail clerk, courier, tour escort, etc." The "etcetera" in the job description signified that the company expected stewards to serve in nearly any capacity passengers demanded. Rather than list tasks, officials found it more useful to provide examples of superlative employee actions, such as the steward who fed children and changed babies' diapers during flights, one who arranged bridge parties and other amusements for passengers during layovers, and the one who ventured to bring in as much as $600 in new business during a single month.[6]

When Western Air officials made these demands on its employees, flight attending was a new profession and its roles were unclear. Despite scattered anecdotes about exemplary stewards, most men the company hired did not meet its idealized expectations. Few, for instance, gleefully offered to change soiled diapers. Western Air and most airlines would eventually turn to female attendants, believing them better suited for such "care and nurturing tasks"; but in the profession's early years, executives struggled to mold young men. Throughout the terrain of corporate Los Angeles, businesses in all industries similarly struggled to define the shifting meaning of corporate employment on their terms. While historians of emerging corporate management often emphasize the increasingly precise division of tasks within these new bureaucracies, early leaders would have been aghast at the notion that they were limiting employees' responsibility. Whether naive about how different the corporate workplace looked to those farther down the ladder, or in recognition of that difference and fearful of its consequences, company leaders, like those at Western Air, expected much from employees as they expanded their firms. However proud of their own leadership and achievement, executives knew well the power of dedicated employees, as well as the threat of disloyal ones. A Southern California Edison executive put it succinctly in a 1921 letter to employees: "You are the company."[7]

The bumper stickers reading "How am I driving?" seen on company vehicles today offer a contemporary example of the idea that employees represent the company. Leaders know that drivers do more than transport products or services, they come into contact with the public and thus have the power to hurt or help the firm. Early Union Oil executives similarly asked that its drivers exhibit extreme caution and politeness. A 1928 company editorial noted that drivers could destroy any positive impression created by its thousands of billboards and should instead take care to give a friendly wave to passers-by and say: "Go ahead sir, I could have dashed across in front of you, but may you live long and buy lots of Union Gasoline."[8] Quite obviously, corporate public relations efforts extended both horizontally and vertically throughout large firms, but they were particularly intense for white-collar ranks. Many in these categories had direct customer contact, but even those who did not played public roles. Customers, at least potential customers, were everywhere, and executives wanted to make sure that everyone on their staff knew it and acted accordingly. Local businesses expected each employee to be a salesperson, an ambassador to the community, and a political activist on the firm's behalf, whatever the specific tasks of their job.

The Changing Meaning of Work

As Los Angeles business leaders worked to cultivate dedicated employees, growing white-collar bureaucracies with large salaried staffs shifted the meaning of work for many Americans. During the nineteenth century, middle-class occupational cultures in the United States recognized little distinction between "work" and "private life." The nation's small businessmen, farm owners, and professionals found the roles thoroughly intertwined. Work consumed these men's time, energy, and identity, for not only were most responsible for their enterprises, be they a farm, company, or office, but they also had to tend its interests in their private dealings as well. Their prosperity often rested on active involvement in the local community's organizations, society, and politics.

In contrast, early-twentieth-century corporate employees had limited responsibility for the enterprise and experienced a clearer separation between work and private life. To be sure, salaried employees in large firms worked at vastly different steps on large bureaucratic ladders and had widely varying duties, degrees of authority, levels of status, and incomes. Yet they all shared an occupational culture keenly distinct from middle-class friends and neighbors engaged in professions, small businesses, and even skilled labor. Most corporate employees performed precise and limited tasks under another's direction and played but a small part in decision making. They worked a specific number of hours on narrowly defined projects for a fixed salary and then went home to a life and identity at least partly removed from the firm.[9]

The changing nature of California banking well exemplifies how corporate concentration and the increasing role of salaried employees in business operations entailed a distinctive new occupational milieu. When the first meeting of the California Bankers Association (CBA) convened in 1891, most attendees were part owners or played leadership roles in small, single-branch banks. The published proceedings suggest that banking consumed their lives. Not only were most immersed in the details of their bank's operations, but they also knew their reputation affected its success. One speaker noted that a typical day started well before banking hours, when he arrived to open the vault, clean the office, read the mail, and prepare for a wide variety of customers. Many customers would call on personal and community matters as well as banking, and these interactions could either solidify business relationships or impair them. Only a generation later, CBA meetings differed dramatically. By the 1910s, most attendees were salaried managers and employees of large city banks. Lacking ownership in the bank, they did not subsume their personal interests to those of their employer. The meetings became a time for learning specific information about one's duties and for informal networking, a process that could perhaps lead to better opportunities at another firm.[10]

While this shift in the nature of work may appear today a natural component of new economic structures, leaders and employees at the time found the change perplexing and struggled to understand bureaucratic employment. Few Americans found corporations natural or logical institutions. While in retrospect the distinction between owner and employee and between small businessmen and salaried managers seems clear, leaders and employees in emerging firms thought in terms of nineteenth-century small business occupational cultures, and they tried to make sense of twentieth-century corporate employment in those terms. Industrial workers could look back upon a long tradition of artisanal production in their efforts to define large-scale industrial work, but the first national generation of white-collar employees wrestled over the meaning of a position within a large enterprise or even the exact nature of their connection to the firm.[11]

As young male Los Angelenos assumed white-collar posts in large companies, they inevitably asked tough questions about their jobs. If they worked for a fixed salary, what could they gain from working harder? If they did not own the firm, would they benefit from increased profits? If they saw their job merely as a stepping stone to more personally rewarding opportunities elsewhere, why should they care about the firm's larger needs? Corporate managers were all over the map in finding ways to respond to employees. Some chose emotional manipulation. A department store employee in the late 1920s, for instance, noted one such example: "Mr. Smith is a man who is very emotional. Lots of these people who work here are ignorant, and Mr. Smith plays on their emotions. In our store assemblies on Saturday mornings he will make a speech, and just about cry. He will tell how he needs everyone's help, and how he isn't making any money. If he made one penny last year he made a million."[12]

On other occasions, leaders tried more authoritarian strategies. Because the size and structure of many businesses demanded that employees play exact and carefully delineated roles, executives often became rather harsh in their efforts to maintain strict workplace standards. The Pacific Mail Company, for instance, frequently distributed memos to employees complaining of nonadherence to office hours: "We expect everyone to be ready to get down to business when the clock registers 8:30." The memo then warned: "If employees fail to get down to business promptly, we will have to make some changes."[13]

Many firms turned to rational persuasion in their efforts to corral employees, emphasizing the need for effective, enthusiastic performance of routine tasks. The Security-First National Bank instructed employees: "A task seemingly obscure and routine takes on a majesty and sublimity when looked upon as a necessary contribution to the well-being of the entire business."[14] Yet even as they struggled to improve their employees' daily performance of office tasks, most executives insisted that workers help the firm in broader ways, beyond their specified duties. As an SCE executive wrote: "Loyalty to your employer means a step out of your way, whenever that step is necessary to conserve his interest."[15]

Unfortunately for leaders, company sermons often proved ineffective and management expressed frequent frustration about their employees' apparent lack of commitment to the enterprise's larger success. From the earliest days of American big business, executives bemoaned the lack of employees who met their expectations, who, in the words of one historian, "failed to accept the overweening importance of a job as the defining center of the self." Throughout the era of corporate emergence, businessmen complained that young hires did not evidence bureaucratic values, and then they proceeded to re-echo their standards and demands.[16] In a vocational guidance text representative of those used widely in southern California schools and colleges during the 1920s, a chapter entitled "The Kind of Worker Employers Want" hammered away at the dangers of viewing white-collar work in too limited a fashion. One employer summarized these sentiments in saying, "The fault I find with most young people is that they do not take any interest in the firm. They regard it only as the source of a meal ticket. They seem to think it exists solely for their own benefit." Another employer commented that an employee could prove his worth by "trying to enlighten himself about the firm's problems and studying phases of the business other than the one in which he is immediately engaged." Continuing, he described an excellent employee as one "who tackles his job not merely as an isolated job but also sees it in relation to the rest of the work of the firm."[17]

In 1913, Pacific Electric executive Paul Shoup read an article in *World's Work* magazine entitled "The Soul of the Corporation" that seemed to capture his and other leaders' feelings on job performance. The author, an eastern railroad president, complained, "No corporation is soulless. The trouble is that they too frequently have the wrong kinds of souls . . . For many years, the utterly unnecessary and senseless incivility of corporation employes [*sic*] has been a striking fact." Impressed with these sentiments, Shoup mailed a copy of the article to every Pacific Electric employee. The bulk of the lengthy text encouraged employees to go beyond the call of duty in customer service and customer stewardship: "We are all working together for the good of each other, as well as for the good of the company and of the community." The author noted that in his own firm, "We have devoted much effort, therefore, to the creation of a body of picked men who will feel a genuine interest in establishing this policy. When a man applies for a position . . . he may be rejected on the sole ground of deficient personality."[18]

PE employees could hardly miss the message. The company expected them to do more for the firm than simply their assigned tasks. Employees were to express keen dedication to PE's larger interests. This theme appeared often in the corporate communications of PE and every other major Los Angeles firm. A typical PE announcement read: "Who could be more directly interested in the success of a railroad . . . than the employee who serves it? His daily bread depends for the time being at least upon its ability to meet its weekly or monthly payrolls. Why then, should he not be in duty bound to render whatever business as will tend to make it more successful?"[19]

Alarmed by the severity of internal business needs and the external public pressures their companies faced daily, and cognizant that the dedication of salaried employees offered the only effective solution, Los Angeles executives aggressively confronted the issue of employee commitment and loyalty. They hoped to instill in their workforce a sense of ownership. Such efforts were hardly new in American business life, but with the widespread growth of large bureaucracies, these managerial imperatives took on heightened importance and had to be woven thoroughly into corporate cultures. With widescale corporate employment a relatively new and rapidly evolving prospect, leaders tried to capitalize on this instability by defining white-collar work on their terms. On a broad level, top managers repeatedly urged employees to consider themselves "partners" in the enterprise. The Pacific Mutual Life Insurance Company told employees in 1925: "Happy is he who speaks, not of the boss's business, but of our business, who considers himself an integral part of the concern, who thinks not of personal gain or satisfaction but of the welfare and greater success of the organization."[20] Executives repeatedly argued that it was "natural" for employees to support enthusiastically the firm's interests.

Platitudes about employee dedication reverberated throughout corporate cultures in the early twentieth century. But too much rested on their efforts for leaders merely to issue admonitions. They took much greater pains to make their expectations and demands very clear.

The Employee as Salesperson

Although corporate enterprises rested on the sale of products or services, the precise division of tasks in most firms meant that few employees directly encountered customers. Most personnel performed limited functions, whether in production, distribution, accounting, legal services, or other areas. In the 1890s, for example, the owner of a fledgling Los Angeles oil company on a given day might have purchased land for explorations, made decisions about new drilling, delivered oil to a client, and placed an advertisement in a local newspaper. By contrast, most employees in the vast oil oligopolies of the 1910s and 1920s spent their days performing a single narrow task, whether writing copy for advertisements, auditing service station accounts, or tracking employee hours and payroll records.

In the development of these product- and function-specific bureaucracies, sales and marketing became specialized activities. Many historians have noted the rise of modern advertising and the development of mass consumerism during this period. The aggressive efforts of big business to market products and services were critical to the development of both of these aspects of modern business. Most large corporations began to cultivate professionalized sales staffs and marketing divisions. Advertising become a "science" critical to business success. At Union Oil, for instance, marketing rivaled geology in importance.[21]

Yet even as companies carefully professionalized sales and advertising, leaders resisted limiting marketing duties to particular employees. Instead, they expected all personnel to bring the firm new business. Though few companies made sales an explicit part of job descriptions, they urged their white-collar ranks to promote products or services to friends and acquaintances. Leaders believed that in contrast to paid advertising, which required company outlays to boost sales, employees could bring in new business without costing the firm money. If every worker became a salesperson, their every friend or acquaintance became a potential customer.

Corporate designs for employee sales efforts varied widely depending on the nature of the business and its products or services. Most banks, for example, concentrated on increasing customer accounts; consistent growth rested primarily upon the continual acquisition of new depositors. Los Angeles banks found considerable potential for customer growth in the region's expanding population and skyrocketing need for banking services. Local banks engaged in fierce competition to secure new business, and all demanded their employees' help.

Bank leaders wrote extensively about employees' critical role in recruiting depositors. While most firms assigned specific agents to find new customers, executives knew an important source of clients would be local residents who knew and respected bank employees. People wanted their money handled by those they trusted. A Pacific Southwest Savings Bank development manager explained: "There is no doubt that making friends is considered one of the best means of securing new business that is known . . . we have found in checking the location of our customers that many of them are living in localities that are entirely outside of the area served. They are coming for a manager or teller who is particularly friendly or whom they have known or done business with."[22]

Many banks asked employees to seek new customers through formal campaigns. Successful employees often received special prizes, or at least their boss's high praise and good favor. Beginning in 1921, the Pacific Southwest Savings Bank held annual "tribute campaigns," two-week contests during which personnel competed to bring in the most new depositors and loan applications. Each day during the campaign, the company issued a mimeographed newspaper called *The Tribute* to update employees on how their activities compared with those of their colleagues. Most campaigns were major successes. The sixth anniversary campaign in 1927, for instance, brought in nearly 5,000 new accounts, as well as other transactions totaling more than $3 million.[23]

Public utilities, operating in a different business context, made other demands upon their employees. By the 1920s, most utility companies functioned as state-regulated regional monopolies. They did not have to worry about attracting more customers, since those in their districts were automatically "loyal" patrons. Utility companies benefited from other business enhancements, such as increased capital support. They aggressively promoted the sale of their stock and often asked employees to help in their efforts. Southern California Edison urged employees to persuade friends and relatives to become stockholders. According to company claims, employees did in fact solicit new investors. In a 1922 report discussing an increase in stockholders, management commented that the remarkable showing stemmed from the "intense loyalty" of SCE employees who "in their spare time and whenever opportunity presented itself, sold our securities to the people they came into contact with in their everyday life."[24]

Utility companies also benefited from increased use of their product and asked employees to encourage electricity consumption, primarily by urging them to tout electric appliance usage. Throughout the 1920s, SCE held an annual "Electrical Christmas Campaign," in which each department sold these products for Christmas presents. In 1928, SCE executives commended the company's steam generation department for selling 1,000 appliances. To promote employee familiarity with the benefits of electric services, the firm offered awards for projects encouraging electric usage. In 1930 it sponsored a contest for the best essay with the title: "Better Home Lighting and What I Can Do About It." SCE awarded eighty-nine prizes; the overall winner received $100. SCE also urged employees to set good examples in power and appliance usage and helped them purchase appliances at reduced rates. Leaders noted that it was "inconsistent for the employee of a light and power company to advocate the use of electrical appliances which he does not have in his own home." A 1926 company report bragged, "Two of the SCE districts now have 100% of married employees using electric ranges."[25]

Edison's efforts to encourage electric usage exemplified prevailing marketing strategies. In an era of significant technological change, many firms not only had to win converts to their brand name, but they also had to promote the use of their product itself. Oil companies, and to a certain extent even banks, joined utilities in pushing use of their product or services, and they insisted that employees join these endeavors. Oil executives pressed employees to support new industries and technologies that would create a heightened demand for petroleum. Union Oil specifically urged employees to advocate motoring. Elaborate company magazine articles prodded employees to purchase automobiles and take automotive vacations, and to nudge their friends to do the same. Union Oil also touted the aviation industry and asked its workforce to patronize air mail in their own correspondence: "One letter a week from each of us would substantially increase the air mail business." The firm similarly requested that employees advocate other petroleum-related industries, including asphalt, bus service, and pesticides. Union Oil distributed detailed information about these new industries through its corporate communications, in the hope that employees would pass the news on to others.[26]

In addition to promoting petroleum products generally, oil firms of course wanted to sell their own brand. Ironically, even as Union Oil demanded employee loyalty, it recognized a need to earn it, and provided employees with detailed explanations of the superiority of the company's products and servcies. The company placed full-page advertisements in nearly every issue of its in-house magazine and treated its employees as consumers whose loyalty needed to be earned. Executives combined subtle strategies with more direct orders to purchase and sell Union products. In one such example from 1923, Union told employees that "the greatest sales insurance" a business could have was "an army of recommenders" and that employees should believe in the company's products "to the point of enthusiasm."[27] Several months later, Union Oil launched the "Put It Across" campaign, asking all employees and stockholders to fill out a pledge that they would persuade one person to switch to Union Oil products each week. The company reported enthusiastic support for the program and "Put It Across" campaigns became regular themes of company life thereafter.[28]

Whatever the real degree of success in sales campaigns, the continuous and fervent efforts of Los Angeles corporations to motivate employee participation suggest the difficulty of stimulating and maintaining such loyalty. Companies facing particularly tenuous and challenging economic circumstances had to pursue the goal of across-the-board employee salesmanship even more aggressively. The struggling and embattled Pacific Electric Rail-

Grows Like a Snowball

"PUT IT ACROSS"
THIS WEEK

THE percentage of loyal "Put it acrossers" who returned the cards of acknowledgment was amazing. Nothing could be more encouraging to all of us than the knowledge that our stockholders and employees are actively behind us.

We can feel the influence you are exerting. There are definite signs that many of you are really talking Union *Non-Detonating Gasoline* and Aristo Motor Oil.

But the more the better.

Every new convert to our products means a steady buyer whose purchases will run to many dollars during the balance of the year.

And a convert a week per "Put it acrosser" means 10,000 new buyers every seven days.

Tell one motorist today about the advantages of Union *Non-Detonating* Gasoline and Aristo Motor Oil. The story is interesting and convincing.

Let's "Put it across" this week and every week. It's worth real money to every member.

In its employee magazine, the Union Oil Company urged employees to secure new business. Reproduced from the *Union Oil Bulletin* 3 (June 1923): 25, by permission of the Huntington Library, San Marino, California.

way Company urged its employees to be "Pacific-Electric minded," meaning they were to promote the company "24 hours a day." Through the 1910s and 1920s, Pacific Electric leaders relentlessly prodded employees to drum up new business. With titles such as "Wanted!—5,000 Business Getters" and "Are You Helping to Increase PE Revenues?," company magazine articles asked for help increasing ridership and bringing in new freight accounts. Executives proposed numerous ways for employees to secure new business: take excursions around the region, then recommend such trips to friends and neighbors; look out for tourists, strike up a conversation, and herald PE service and its various tours; and listen for news about local firms or organizations planning outings, then propose traveling on PE. Pacific Electric also asked employees to note agricultural harvests, new residential developments, new industries, or any other business or economic change on which the company could capitalize. Employees were to notify management of such potential markets so that company representatives could inquire about opportunities for new routes or customers.[29]

Pacific Electric relied more on praise than monetary rewards to motivate its staff. Employees who brought in or directed the company to new business became subjects of glowing features in the company press. Beginning in the mid 1920s, Pacific Electric's magazine printed the names of all personnel who provided tips. In the summer of 1926, for example, the firm's general passenger agent wrote an editorial, complete with photographs, praising four employees who had secured the business of several large vacation groups.[30] Pacific Electric publicized such news more fervently than other firms. As revenues fell, it needed support from employees more than ever.

Even in sales-oriented firms with predominantly commissioned employees, such as insurance companies, leaders pushed for more aggressive efforts. The earnings of most Pacific Mutual Life Insurance Company employees directly reflected their success. Leaders wondered, however, whether employees would stop selling at a certain level, or on evenings and weekends. To prevent such "disloyalty," Pacific Mutual urged employees to remain sales agents in their personal dealings.[31] The company held that the desire to acquire new customers should infuse all aspects of an agent's life. A story that appeared in the company magazine in 1911 typified the firm's attitude: "I chanced to be in a barber shop in a small suburban town last Saturday, and as I believe it to be my duty as an insurance man to preach the gospel of life insurance whenever occasion offers, I said to the proprietor, 'Where do you carry your insurance?'" This desire for employees to spend their leisure time with friends and acquaintances selling insurance became a prominent theme of Pacific Mutual communications. Executives told agents, "No one in any line of work

MAY have so many leisure hours as the life insurance agent, as he is the master of his own time, but no one SHOULD have so few such hours."[32]

In a small business economy, few owner-managers needed to be convinced of their stake in their enterprise. Corporate executives, however, labored to instill some sense of employee ownership. Most employees played only small roles in the company's organization, but leaders insisted that this in no way freed them from also serving the company's bottom line — selling its products and services. Leaders believed personnel should identify so strongly with the company that promoting its products and services would be a logical part of every job description.

The Employee as Activist

Of all the challenges to corporate stability and growth, few seemed more threatening to Los Angeles executives than regulatory politics. None of the region's major firms grew and prospered apart from some interaction with governmental bodies.[33] The prospect of state regulation as a potentially helpful or threatening force prodded many companies to politicize their employees. Just as most believed it "logical" that all personnel would promote company products and services, so too did they assume employees would share its political agenda.

When it came to matters of labor politics, business leaders could usually count on white-collar support. As we will see, local corporate cultures prodded white-collar men to identify with the firm, not with a class of workers. If company men were indeed on a ladder leading to management, then distinguishing themselves from superiors in workplace negotiations made little sense. While not all of southern California's white-collar men bought into this creed, few engaged in collective bargaining efforts or appear to have openly supported their blue-collar colleagues who did. Despite concerted campaigns, particularly during the 1930s, attempts to unionize America's office and professional ranks proved largely unsuccessful prior to the post–World War II era. In 1935, only 5 percent of the nation's white-collar workers belonged to unions. At Pacific Electric, there is even evidence that white-collar men directly aided in combating union activity. During a PE platform-worker strike in 1918, some office staff filled in for striking workers.[34]

The effort to keep Los Angeles an open-shop city was but one of many political issues facing regional business leaders, and it was not one that led them to seek openly the help of white-collar employees. In responding to the wide array of other political pressures, however, many executives came to see their company men as an army of lobbyists who could influence elections and arouse political support or opposition. Firms asked employees to become advocates for a vast range of specific issues and to canvass their friends, neighbors, and relatives for support—to become political activists on the company's behalf.

The utility industry offered a clear example of the intricate relationship between business and the state and of how utilities expected employees to support their company's political interests. Because the growth of local communities required reliable utilities, public sentiment generally favored proposals to stabilize utility operations and to reduce costs. The capital investment required to build a powerplant made it wasteful of both investors' and the local community's resources to have several competing firms. Companies such as Southern California Edison acquired competing interests in their region by arguing that area monopolies would produce increased efficiency and ultimately lower rates to customers. Utility executives sought public acceptance of monopolies, a move most voters viewed with suspicion, but they resisted what some proposed as the next logical move in the industry's stabilization—public ownership. Firms such as SCE found themselves in a delicate position, desiring government sanction of their operating monopolies but resisting public ownership. State legislators enacted a compromise with the passage of the California Public Utilities Act of 1911, allowing regional monopolies in the electric utility industry in exchange for state regulation of rates and policies. The statute enabled SCE to monopolize southern California's utility market.[35]

Passage of the California Public Utilities Act did not free SCE from further political turmoil. The company's status remained a matter of public debate throughout the 1910s and 1920s, as differing groups urged repeal of the act in favor of municipal and state ownership. In 1917, the city of Los Angeles voted to seize control of its own utility services and forced SCE to sell its operations within city limits. SCE then faced not only public oversight of its rates and operations but the continual threat of state acquisition of its remaining suburban markets.

The clear connection between SCE interests and local politics led its executives to spend tremendous energy politicizing employees. The first third of the company's 100-page employee handbook in the 1920s talked not of the workplace, nor even of the company itself, but dealt instead with political issues relating to public utility corporations. Whole chapters in these handbooks, with titles such as "Financing a Corporation," "Political Ownership and Taxation," and "Ownership of Public Utilities," offered information about and analyses of the horrors of governmental regulations and municipal utility ownership. In showcasing these matters in its handbook, SCE let employees know that the firm's well-being depended on a cooperative relationship with the government. Workers needed both to understand the significance of that fact and to help implement the creation of government policies beneficial to the firm.[36]

In addition to the extensive political features in employee handbooks, SCE devoted considerable space in routine corporate communications to educating employees about public utility issues. Editorials with titles like "Public Interests and Private Interests Synonymous" described the threats municipal ownership posed. In the months prior to the city's seizure of utility operations, the firm published numerous attacks on the idea of public-owned services. One writer declared, "The right of ownership is based upon possession through honest and legitimate acquisition . . . there can be no justice, therefore, in laws that confiscate, in whole or in part, directly or indirectly, the capital of those who have saved for the benefit of those who have not."[37]

Whenever a public utility measure came before voters, SCE invested considerable resources into instructing its employees to vote appropriately. In 1913, for instance, Los Angeles residents voted on a bond measure allowing the city to construct its own power plants. For several weeks prior to the election, SCE urged its employees to campaign among friends and neighbors against the measure. On election eve the company held a political rally under the guise of an "employee's banquet." Seven hundred attended the fête, at which speaker after speaker decried the measure. Following the bond's defeat, SCE executives thanked and praised employees for their efforts.[38] Such political campaigns became a common element in the firm's organizational culture. One of the largest company-backed efforts occurred in 1922 when the California State Water and Power Act, which would have put all public utilities under state control, came before voters. The company mobilized employees to oppose the measure and took significant credit for its electoral defeat. Edison leaders noted proudly that statewide the ratio of no to yes votes was 2.45:1, while the ratio in SCE territory was 4.07:1.[39]

As another partially regulated public utility, the Pacific Electric Railway Company faced similar political challenges and also responded by mobilizing its employees. The issue of what constituted fair taxation preoccupied PE leadership. They argued that PE should not be required to pay state taxes, since California used those monies in part to build highways for the firm's competition — trucks and automobiles. In effect, executives charged, the state forced PE to subsidize rival industries. Throughout the 1910s and 1920s, company editorials lambasted the "inequities" of corporate taxation and sought to cultivate employee anger. With articles such as, "Taxes One of Greatest Burdens of the Nation and the State," and "Increased Taxation versus Economy," PE protested its tax burden and enlisted employees in its political efforts.[40]

Like SCE, PE sought to mobilize employees during crucial elections. In the spring of 1921, the company geared up to fight a proposed increase in public utility taxes. The firm's vice president wrote a letter to all personnel, in which he threatened that if voters passed the "King Tax Bill," the company might have to reduce wages. In 1923, when the city of Los Angeles voted on a new bus company franchise, PE leaders again wrote to employees and urged them to vote no and to persuade their friends to do so as well. Whether writing in support for Calvin Coolidge's candidacy in 1924, or in opposition to the development of new steam rail lines in Southern California in 1926, or opposing rail construction parallel to that of its parent company, Southern Pacific, in 1929, PE's editorial writers repeatedly advised employees to take political stances that would benefit company operations.[41]

While not all businesses faced such direct political challenges, most experienced at least some interaction with local, state, or federal governments, and most made political demands on their personnel. Banks, for example, operated under detailed state regulations. Many of them, therefore, participated in political lobbies and campaigns and asked employees to become part of those efforts. California banks sought to form a united front on political issues through the California Bankers Association, founded in 1891.[42] The Security-First National Bank in Los Angeles gave the CBA's political concerns major coverage in its company newspaper. In 1929 the vice president of the bank's head office served as chairman of the CBA's committee on legislation and taxation and regularly chronicled his activities and reported on the potential consequences of proposed legislation in company magazine editorials. Bank leaders urged staff members to write their legislators on matters affecting banking policies and to vote appropriately when ballot measures appeared.[43]

Oil companies also participated in state and national politics. Overproduction, regulation of pipelines, and water damage were three major issues affecting the industry in California. In each case, most firms became active in political and community organizations in an effort to bolster their interests. Overproduction deeply concerned Union Oil, one of the largest companies. Throughout the 1920s, its leaders condemned overzealous drilling by upstart firms. Surplus production lowered the price of oil and cut into Union's profits. Company management bluntly told employees about the problem but provided them less self-serving arguments to limit production: that new businesses wasted millions of dollars (ultimately paid by consumers) in duplicating unnecessary facilities, that over-drilling wasted valuable natural resources and damaged petroleum pools, limiting the firm's ability to recover oil in the future when it might be most needed. Union Oil hoped to convince employees to turn public sentiment in favor of legislation restricting drilling licenses and setting production limits.[44]

Union Oil asked its employees to become activists on other political issues affecting the company. Primarily, leaders lobbied the government to undertake programs such as highway construction that would promote automobile usage and to reject legislation such as increased registration fees for automobiles that could hurt the industry. Prior to 1923, for instance, California residents who owned automobiles paid only a "horse-power tax," which usually amounted to between eight and ten dollars per year. In 1923, however, a new law held that all car owners instead would pay a three dollar registration fee and two cents a gallon gasoline tax. Union Oil feared a decline in automobile usage and actively opposed any increases in auto fees. In 1925, when the state legislature considered a bill to raise the registration fee to five dollars a year and the gasoline tax to three cents a gallon, the company gave the matter extensive coverage in its *Bulletin*, carefully explaining how this would hurt the auto industry and Union Oil business. The firm urged employees to write their representatives and convince friends to oppose the measure.[45]

The *Union Oil Bulletin* also promoted state and federal measures to build new roads and highways. Union officials recognized the boost this would give to automobile usage and thus company products, and, in turn, the company became a proponent of increased funding for such projects. On numerous occasions, executives sought to educate employees about and asked for their support of political measures to further those projects. In 1925, for example, employees came across an article entitled, "Getting the Most for the Highway Dollar," which emphasized the need for new roads and highways in the western United States and how state and federal funds could be used for such purposes.[46]

Amidst the widespread rhetoric of laissez-faire capitalism in Los Angeles, local corporations knew that government entities could affect their operations in both friendly and damaging ways. Most firms became deeply involved in efforts to manipulate state and federal legislation, to assure that new laws would serve their interests. As well, they expected employees to advance the company's political agenda.

The Employee as Ambassador

In sales efforts and in politics, large firms made specific demands on employees above and beyond their daily tasks. Less specifically, local corporations expected employees to act as their gregarious and public-minded ambassadors. Fearing competition from other firms, community disfavor, and state regulation, leaders of large companies added positive and gracious interaction with customers and the general public to employees' informal job descriptions. Companies urged employees to treat every customer they encountered with extreme courtesy. Even employees in positions with little direct customer contact were to be vigilant about the feelings of customers. Most firms also asked employees to advance their interests within the community. Whether through professional societies, neighborhood associations, or community organizations, officials expected all personnel to represent the firm as a vital local institution.

The notion of employees as ambassadors to the public appeared frequently in corporate communications. Because workers served as the vital link between a company and its public, management cared deeply about staff members' personalities and the quality of their community involvement. In August 1924, for example, Pacific Mail Steamship Company director T. A. Graham sent one of his executives, C. C. Mallory, to tour the company's Asian offices and bring back a report on the quality of their operations. Mallory devoted considerable attention to analyzing not only the local office's efficiency and profitability, but also to their workers' personalities and private lives. According to Mallory, an employee's character and reputation were important determinants of company success and were of interest to the firm. He noted in one report, "This man should be selected, first, of course, as to ability, second and none less, as to personality." In another discussion of company policies toward its bureau managers, Mallory suggested that employees be expected to mix with locals in social settings: "it seems to me that we should require these men to appear at the golf club every so often because there seems to be no better way of keeping in touch with the public and also establishing friendships." Commenting on a specific employee, Mallory discussed his personality traits and community involvement: "He is well liked by all with whom I have talked and I am satisfied that he will make his place in the community."[47]

Most firms wanted public-minded employees, but corporate needs and expectations varied widely. Public utilities and other companies subject to government regulation were keenly concerned with public opinion. The Pacific Electric Railway Company found public sentiment a major factor not only in its profitability but in its very existence. As a state-regulated industry, PE required public approval for rate increases. Electoral support joined consumer demand as crucial to company success. Local opinion further affected PE's operations because of routine review by regulatory agencies. For example, the automobile's increasing popularity created much pressure in Los Angeles to limit PE operations on major streets.

With so much public and governmental scrutiny, PE maneuvered in what it considered a hostile environment. The declining market for interurban services only exacerbated this attitude. In response, PE acted with a hypersensitive concern for customer satisfaction. Equating consumer favor not only with increased ridership but also with greater public support in debates over regulation, the company conducted extensive campaigns urging employees to be sensitive to customer needs. Though it had a virtual monopoly on public interurban transportation, the firm exhorted employees to be courteous and publicly praised those who seemed particularly alert to these concerns. In the late 1920s, for instance, PE began publishing positive comments received about employees, noting, for example, that A. W. Young evidenced "exceptionally courteous conduct," and H. J. White had a "pleasant attitude at all times."[48]

PE also asked its employees to nurture public goodwill by actively participating, in the company's name, in community and national service projects. Leaders hoped their employees' involvement would show the firm's value as a local institution. During World War I, for example, PE asked its employees to contribute to a Liberty Loan Drive and to purchase war savings stamps. Executives enthusiastically reported that 99.1 percent of employees, or 3,720 persons, had contributed to the loan drive by war's end. In-house publications touted the number of personnel in local offices who had purchased war stamps. PE also asked its employees to contribute to community charities. The company set an annual quota for participation in the Los Angeles Community Chest Organization, begun in 1924. PE used local and national projects such as war bond and charity drives as a means to nurture public appreciation for the company, and it expected its staff to participate enthusiastically in such endeavors.[49]

Southern California Edison was even more vulnerable than Pacific Electric to public regulatory bodies and surpassed PE's efforts to promote employee ambassadorship. Top officials fervently emphasized the importance of customer satisfaction; the topic reverberated throughout its corporate culture. In 1916, for instance, an SCE executive addressed employees about why the issue mattered to them. He warned that the company's success, and therefore each employee's paycheck, rested on customer support, for complaints reported to the public utilities commission could result in the seizure of SCE operations or tighter regulations of company activities.[50]

Throughout the 1910s and 1920s, SCE leaders preached a gospel of courteous service and careful attention to customer needs. They asked employees to be the "eyes and ears" of the company in monitoring public opinion and to report pertinent information to district leaders. Some local offices passed out "little red books" in which employees were to record comments they overheard about the firm. According to management, the book made "each and every one of us an agent in all departments of this company's business." SCE also published a stream of pamphlets instructing employees on consumer interaction, including "A Pleasing Personality," "The Sense of Responsibility," "Business Manners," and "As Others See Us."[51]

SCE's efforts to mold employees into company ambassadors paralleled those of Pacific Electric's concern for community and national charities and campaigns. During World War I, SCE conducted war bond drives among its employees, as well as numerous other fundraisers, such as "work bees" for the Red Cross. Like PE, the company used participation in these efforts to gain public support. Corporate leaders sought publicity for employees' charitable activities and used them to publicize the firm.[52]

In addition to sensitizing employees to the importance of customer satisfaction and urging their support of community projects on the company's behalf, SCE leaders asked them to exhibit individual initiative in enhancing the company's good name. They expected employees to participate actively and visibly in private clubs and community organizations, and to do so as SCE representatives. Throughout the 1920s, executives prodded department heads, district managers, and important agents to join local associations. In his 1921 book, *Winning the Public*, the company's vice president for public relations and business development wrote of the district manager: "It is his duty to be a big man in the community, just as the company is a big and necessary factor in its business life. For this reason, the district manager should be actively interested in all of the business and community organizations." The company specifically requested that leading employees become active in chambers of commerce and boards of trade, as well as the Lions, Rotary, and Kiwanis Clubs, and similar institutions. SCE paid at least partial if not full dues for department heads and managers to join these organizations.[53]

Operating in a political context of widespread support for municipally owned utilities, and one in which many citizens saw private firms as greedy betrayers of the public's trust, SCE hoped that management's participation in community organizations would show the firm in a more positive light. The company apparently believed that if members of the local community respected and liked SCE officials, they would be more inclined to side with the company in debates over public utility matters. Through its emphasis on customer satisfaction, participation in community charities, and involvement in local associations, SCE sought to make its employees sympathetic public figures. This process culminated in company efforts to circulate employee news items that would give the firm "a human face." At the urging of its vice president for public relations, SCE forwarded human-interest stories about employees, including notices of marriages and births, to local newspapers.[54]

Insurance officials expressed similar interest in employees' ambassadorship, though for different reasons. Because agents were a company's sole presence in most outlying communities, they alone established the firm's image and determined its success. Pacific Mutual brass told agents, "The company's reputation in your field is what you make it; hence your responsibility." Personality and character took on added importance for life insurance agents because of the nature of their work. Selling insurance required agents to speak with virtual strangers on a frightening topic — death. Cultivating well-liked agents thus became extremely important to executives. One company editorial noted, "The general agent who is popular in his community by reason of services given to his church, his lodge or charitable drives, is usually better equipped to secure new men than the general agent who sits back."[55]

Customer satisfaction and community support concerned few industries more than banking, for banks offered not products as much as service, and more than other businesses they needed customers' trust. Acquiring new customers required banks to exude strength and confidence. Their employees' trustworthiness and reputation were central to their ability to garner this goodwill. Bank executives aggressively cultivated the image of dependability and a deep commitment to their community. So important were these issues that officers and directors removed colleagues who seemed to lack public confidence. In July 1918, Farmers and Merchants National Bank asked two board members to resign following news that each had damaged the bank's standing in the local community. One had refused to donate money to the Red Cross, thus angering many of the bank's customers. Vice President Jackson A. Graves wrote to president Isaias Hellman: "we all regret that it was necessary to ask Mr. Vosburgh to resign, but the war fever is at great height in this community and anything that looks like a lack of patriotism will not be tolerated." The firm asked another to resign because of widespread publicity about his personal financial problems.[56]

As banks grew into large corporations, this concern with image grew to encompass all employees. Customers of large urban banks judged the institution not only on the basis of its leadership and tradition but also on their own level of comfort with and confidence in bank employees. These issues became particularly critical in branch banking networks. The quality of local offices became a high priority for astute leaders eager to ward off legislation against branch banking. Whether a cashier, teller, loan agent, or courier, bank employees learned that confidence, character, and congeniality were central to their job descriptions. A Long Beach bank executive told CBA meeting attendees in 1912 that "There probably is no other line of business where personal friendship counts for so much as in banking." The official noted that while merchants can cut prices and draw trade, banks deal with money: "What has he to offer them? His personal attention." The speaker continued, "He must have the knack of associating with him an office force that is courteous, congenial, accurate, neat, fair-minded, patient, and punctual, from the chief teller to the latest acquired runner . . . your bank will be judged by the business man as he faces this runner."[57]

Many banks assigned specific tellers, agents, or officers to important customers as a means of establishing personal relationships. Beginning in 1905, the Los Angeles First National Bank enacted a system of alphabetical grouping, enabling tellers to become better acquainted with customers.[58] Most urban banks, however, soon became too large for such systems and attention switched to the more general issue of customer satisfaction. Firms preached the "gospel of service." Articles such as "Personality Is an Asset in Trust Relations," along with others that spoke of the importance of being kind and courteous to customers, became staples of bank communications. In a 1929 editorial, Security-First National Bank reminded employees: "Our real employer is not the bank but the bank customer. Without him there can be no bank and no job. Keeping him pleased causes him to bring others to deal with the bank, enlarging its clientele, its volume, its profits, and its salaries."[59]

To further bolster their public image, many banks asked employees to address local organizations on banking and financial matters. They aimed to portray the bank and its employees as the voice of economic wisdom and as the financial custodians of the local economy. Security-First National Bank established a speakers' division with a full-time department head. Every two weeks, Security-First published a list of community presentations given by employees. Nearly a dozen speeches were delivered on behalf of the bank in any two-week period, to churches, clubs, schools, and other groups.[60] Security-First also asked its branch managers and other leaders to write columns for local newspapers as a way of getting the bank's name before the public.[61]

Firms in some industries might be expected to have given less attention to employee ambassadorship than regulated utilities, insurance companies, or banks; but while the success of corporations based on economies of scale, such as oil, did rely more heavily on price and distribution, customer satisfaction still mattered. Union Oil communications frequently noted the importance of employee service, for in the intensely competitive gasoline and service station business, executives desperately cultivated brand loyalty. A pleasant and efficient staff at all levels could ensure repeat customers.[62] Union Oil also asked its employees to advocate its highway safety and courtesy campaigns. Through their employees, company officers hoped to promote auto travel in an era when many Americans were fearful of driving. Leaders also wanted employees to convey the firm's concern with the rising number of auto accidents.[63]

Of Whom Much Is Expected

Throughout the early twentieth century, Los Angeles journalists, civic leaders, and business executives celebrated loudly the region's emerging corporate economy. Yet while company executives cheerfully posed for newspaper and magazine articles that celebrated their firms' accomplishments, they knew well that their successes rested heavily on the shoulders of thousands of men and women whose loyalty and dedication they often doubted. For this reason, executives, while smiling for the cameras, engaged in vigorous behind the scenes efforts to secure dedicated personnel. At the heart of this process were their efforts to define corporate employment broadly. They expected employees not only to meticulously perform their specific duties over a lifelong career but also to assume a sense of ownership in the company.

To the pleasure of business leaders, many employees found meaning in their work and assumed the firm's identity. Indeed, in recounting their life stories to oral historians, many southern California company men construct narratives idealizing corporate responsibilities and rewards. Carl Eichenlaub is among them. Hired by a southern California railroad in 1914, he began a career traveling the region to promote the railroad's interests. Eichenlaub started as a messenger boy, but his eagerness to go the extra mile made him advancement material. He noted that he performed virtually every job in the office and thus became too valuable to lose: "When the big layoff came a year and a half later, they didn't lay me off, because I did every job in the office—did the payroll, cleaned up the office, put all the maps away, did every job that nobody else wanted to do, so when they came to laying me off they thought, well, gee, that kid does everything around here. We can't let him go." The firm ultimately promoted Eichenlaub to superintendent, capping a forty-seven-year career.[64]

Lindsay Buford Little similarly remembers his career as espousing the employment ethos touted by large firms. In 1906 he accepted a position with Standard Oil of California, which in 1927 made him production manager in the firm's Los Angeles headquarters. He served in this capacity until 1941. In a

1963 interview, Little recalled his Standard Oil days with pride and stated that he considered himself responsible for the production of 489 million barrels of oil while at Standard. Little spoke of feeling "a keen sense of proprietorship" that had "not been dampened in the slightest" since his retirement from the firm.[65]

Although we cannot know the extent to which Eichenlaub's or Little's memories realistically capture the attitudes of company men during the early twentieth century, they do speak to the fact that many felt devotion to their employers and worked hard for their company's interests. In all likelihood, however, many others felt no such sense of commitment. And even if one accepts their stories as illustrative of early corporate cultures, Eichenlaub's and Little's memories provide an incomplete picture of white-collar life. Missing from these accounts are discussions of what the companies did to ensure such loyalty.

There is considerable evidence, as we will see, that many employees, in fact, fell short of employers' expectations. As a result, firms undertook more vigorous efforts to make those expectations clear and created other inducements to secure loyal service. In a reversal of the biblical adage, corporate leaders found that much must be given to him of whom much is expected. This was especially true because Los Angeles companies made such demands on an ambitious segment of the labor force that included young, white, native-born men who were determined to chart successful futures for themselves.

THREE

COMPANY MEN

I was just a little cog in a big wheel up there and I thought, "this is no good, I am never going to get where I want to be this way."

—Charles K. Fletcher, employee, Pacific Southwest Savings Bank

In June 1923, a sudden resignation in the Pacific Mail Steamship Company's Los Angeles office provided twenty-four-year-old Leo James Devlin a great opportunity. Since entering San Francisco's labor force in 1915, Devlin had held numerous jobs in an effort to find the one that would open doors to a promising future. For five years he had worked for the Peabody Company where he advanced from order clerk to assistant bookkeeper. Devlin left the company in 1920 for a "better position" as cashier for another local firm, but to his chagrin, the job proved to be a temporary staff post. He soon quit for a more promising opportunity with the Northwestern Electric Company, but that position also proved disappointing. In the spring of 1921, he signed up with the accounting firm of H. Liebes and Company, but here, too, Devlin grew disgruntled; he left the firm several months later when it switched to a different accounting system. It was at this point, in January 1922, that Devlin accepted a place as clerk with Pacific Mail. Though an entry-level position, it provided the decent salary of $110 a month, and the company promised him a great future. Pacific Mail hired Devlin to fill a vacant clerkship; within several months, a superior's resignation allowed for his first promotion. Six months later, another resignation brought another promotion, and after less than two years with the company, the departure of the Los Angeles office's vice accountant opened up a major rung on the company ladder.

Devlin seized the opportunity and moved to Los Angeles. Once there, he rented a room in a neighborhood just west of downtown where large homes had been converted into rooming houses. Earning a salary of $150 a month at a major international corporation, Devlin appeared destined for a successful future. In less than a year, Pacific Mail named him its chief accountant in Los Angeles at a lucrative salary of $175 a month. Months later, Devlin moved into a quaint one-story bungalow just north of downtown in the fashionable Edendale district bordering Echo Park.

Devlin's rapid climb ended abruptly after one year, when changes in the ownership of Pacific Ocean shipping routes forced Pacific Mail's dissolution. At twenty-six years of age, he again entered the job market. Devlin's search led him to the suburb of Inglewood, where he took a position with the Maier Brewing Company. He worked there as a bookkeeper for two years before being promoted to accountant. He stayed with Maier Brewing for four years, but he left in 1930 after being reclassified as a bookkeeper. Devlin soon accepted an accounting position in a prominent downtown firm. He and his new wife, Marie, returned to Los Angeles where they moved into a home on West Seventy-first Street in an affordable middle-class residential community.[1] Over the course of fifteen years, Devlin had held a total of twelve jobs in seven different enterprises.

Leo Devlin's story typified white-collar male experience on many levels. Young, white, and a migrant to the city, he exemplified most company men. As his career matured, he moved farther from downtown, from a boarding house to a single-family home. Most significantly, he continually sought the best position with the best opportunities. Devlin showed little hesitation to quit one job and take another if it looked more promising. That he gained most of his positions by the resignations of others implies that many of his fellow white-collar employees shared this attitude.

Leo Devlin's career history suggests that whatever his employers desired, he was not "the company." Even as growing Los Angeles firms insisted their employees spend every moment working for the company's interest, many young men dreamt of grander futures and kept their eyes open for the job that would best lead them there. Leo Devlin certainly sought the best future for himself, and employers gained his loyalty only when he was happy with the work and confident about his prospects.

Devlin's story reveals a fundamental tension within urban corporate cultures: a direct clash between leaders' and employees' expectations. As we have seen, Los Angeles executives needed a steadily growing workforce to staff their corporations, and they placed enormously high expectations upon these employees. To their good fortune, the city's soaring population translated into a thriving, expansive labor pool. Yet while there were always plenty of applicants for their rapidly expanding white-collar ranks, leaders were selective about whom they considered for such positions. Neither the cost of labor nor education and skills alone shaped hiring and promotion decisions. Rather, leaders added to these criteria a desire for what one of them called the "pearl and white Anglo Saxon" male, a term that spoke volumes about the world-view of Los Angeles business leaders.[2] By fishing for employees only in this "white," male pool, businesses faced a smaller and more challenging labor market. They placed themselves in the position of making heavy demands on comparatively privileged people who often had various occupational options and frequently severe reservations about long-term corporate employment. Devlin, while fitting the gender and racial criteria, did not match the company mold. He and thousands of his peers viewed white-collar careers with critical eyes and moved without hesitation from job to job in search of better opportunities. The friction between leaders' beliefs about who could be "company men" and the career expectations of those very men would ultimately result in the construction of new white-collar corporate cultures throughout the region's economy.

Hiring the Whitest of Collars

Throughout the early twentieth century, Los Angeles's business leaders marveled at the region's complementary population and economic growth. The rush of people moving to southern California in the late nineteenth and early twentieth centuries transformed Los Angeles with a suddenness and scale unique among American cities. No single region experienced urbanization during this period more rapidly than southern California. From 1880 to 1930, Los Angeles's population took a breathtaking 812-percent leap. This growth spurt approached twice that of Seattle (444%) and exceeded by even greater margins those in Denver (316%), Chicago (251%), New York (148%), and San Francisco (112%).[3] The movement of Americans into the region became one of the largest internal migrations in the history of the American people. While demographers note specific population booms in 1906 and 1923, journalist Carey McWilliams aptly suggested that "the growth of southern California since 1870 should be regarded as one continuous boom punctuated at intervals by major explosions."[4] Los Angeles passed San Francisco as the state's largest city in 1920, at which time it ranked tenth among cities nationwide. From 1920 to 1924, the city grew by more than 100,000 each year and would reach one million in 1930. Los Angeles County's population soared from 936,455 in 1920 to nearly 2,250,000 in 1930; an additional million lived in the surrounding four counties.[5]

This booming population provided a vast and steadily growing labor pool for the Los Angeles business community. The number of gainfully employed

Table 3.1 Population growth in greater metropolitan Los Angeles, 1870–1930

Year	*City*	*County*
1870	5,728	6,200
1880	11,093	20,002
1890	50,395	101,454
1900	102,479	172,298
1910	319,198	504,131
1920	577,000	936,000
1930	1,238,000	2,208,000

Source: Robert Fogelson, *The Fragmented Metropolis: Los Angeles, 1850–1930* (Cambridge: Harvard University Press, 1967).

men living in the city in 1910 exceeded the county's entire total population just ten years earlier. The number of working adult men rose from approximately 30,000 in 1900, to 140,000 in 1910, to 250,000 in 1920, and to over 500,000 in 1930.[6]

While the boom in the region's labor market encouraged Los Angeles executives, their selectivity about who could fill white-collar salaried positions often turned their optimism into concern. Rather than seeing a massive population from which to recruit employees, they looked down from their offices onto a community that they divided into explicit categories of desirables and undesirables. Leaders had clear views about what kind of people would best suit corporate interests, and more often than not, these reflected prevailing conceptions of gender, race, and ethnicity. When the Security-First Bank promoted J. A. H. Kerr in 1930, for instance, officials noted in a laudatory article that "Kerr Looks Like a Banker." They meant this explicitly. The square-jawed, silver-haired, handsomely dressed Anglo-American personified their vision of the ideal employee.[7]

The results of a 1919 survey of corporate employee application forms conducted by the National Association of Corporation Schools are telling in this regard. Over half of the businesses surveyed asked about their applicants' weight. More than a third inquired about applicants' "lines of descent," and roughly one in five required a description of hair texture and complexion. In commenting on the importance of such considerations, one managerial theorist noted that personnel directors must add to such knowledge their personal impressions: "Careful observation of the eyes and face of the applicant should give the interviewer a fairly reliable indication of the moral rating of the applicant."[8] Such questions and advice confirm that experience, training, and skills were usually not the only considerations in personnel decisions.

In Los Angeles, where corporate executives were a largely monolithic group intent on replicating themselves among new hires, an infatuation with appearance and lineage dominated personnel practices. Themselves avidly self-proclaimed Anglo-Saxon Protestant males, the city's business elite assumed that only men would fill significant positions. While women would gradually come to dominate many clerical jobs and by the 1920s would be performing a small but varied number of other white-collar tasks, they were virtually absent from managerial ranks and rarely found in positions thought to be en route to such posts. Only in the insurance industry would women

Pacific Electric's administrative office employees, such as those in this 1923 photo, were recruited from the company's young, white, male labor force, and, more often than not, were of specifically British descent. Reproduced by permission of the Huntington Library, San Marino, California.

hold any significant executive posts, but even these were usually limited to directorships of women's divisions.

While corporate management excluded women with generally little discussion or explanation, race and ethnicity factored explicitly into hiring decisions. Business leaders spoke often and fervently about the need to create and maintain racial and ethnic divisions in the region's social and economic structure. Such issues dominated annual Chamber of Commerce banquets, for instance, where, in an atmosphere of self-congratulation, southern California's corporate elites talked openly of their desire to create a populace of primarily native-born whites, with people of Mexican descent available as a surplus labor force.

Chamber members unabashedly promoted this cultivation of a white, native-born, middle-class metropolis. In 1895, the retiring Chamber president happily reported that most newcomers were from "a desirable class who build the comfortable homes and make responsible citizens." Attracting white citizens of means became a point of some obsession for Los Angeles's business elite. In 1904 the Chamber applauded the setting of "colonist's rates" by railroads, special fares for those intending to buy homes. The Chamber's immigration committee chair suggested that "railways be urged to continue to encourage immigration to this section of a desirable class of people." In 1921, following the postwar labor turmoil that engulfed many American cities, officials published a brochure comparing the "socialistic, even Bolshevistic" element of immigrants in eastern cities to the native-born character of Los Angeles's immigrants: "The influx of foreign born into the eastern U.S. has developed a labor situation full of difficulties." In response, according to Chamber propaganda: "the red-blooded energetic American has turned his face westward and in ever-increasing numbers is moving to the land of his dreams—southern California."[9]

Alongside discussions of populating Los Angeles with "real Americans," Chamber members frankly spoke about the role of Mexican and Mexican-American laborers in the local economy. Even as they celebrated the high proportion of native-born residents, leaders often noted to potential business transplants the presence and potential benefits of the region's large Mexican labor force: "We have a Mexican population in this section in excess of 50,000 people, and these people make excellent workers, the men as common laborers in different crafts and the women make splendid workers in textile plants." This 1924 Chamber brochure further noted that Mexican women "come from a race of people who have been workers in textiles, laces and embroideries for centuries and are naturally adept in the use of their hands."[10]

Whether in Caltech laboratories, the offices of city officials, health department boardrooms, or executive office suites, race informed policies and practices in diverse areas of regional life. This was the era when an interest in eugenics flourished in the scientific, political, and medical communities. In their analyses of southern California's population, business leaders moved beyond issues of native-born heritage versus Mexican descent; amidst continuous discussion of the metropolis as the most "American of cities" and home to true "red-blooded Americans," Chamber members and city officials defined "real Americans" in precise terms. Los Angeles, they argued, represented the last American bastion of Anglo-Saxon descendants. They did not treat this issue with vagueness, subtlety, or inference, but laced their annual banquet speeches and toasts with comments about Anglo-Saxon superiority. At the 1895 banquet, J. S. Slauson fondly described southern California as a place of "the soft-voiced Spaniard, the shrugging, pantomiming Frenchman, the guttural German, the musical Italian, the progressive Japanese, the industrious Chinaman, and the sharp, decisive American."[11] The quotation speaks volumes about how Slauson and his colleagues, who responded with frequent applause, defined "Americans." Not only were "Americans" not people of Asian, southern European, or Mexican descent, but Los Angeles's Anglophile elite also at times even placed German or French Americans on the margins of American society.

Racial references became staples of Chamber banquet oratory. In an impromptu speech given after banquet attendees cheered him to the podium, Senator Stephen White declared at the 1900 gathering, "Taking the Anglo-Saxon race and their progress through the ages, we may say perhaps that the American public more typified their progress than any other." Just two years later, Burt Estes Howard spent much of his banquet speech noting the writings of the Reverend Josiah Strong, a favorite among the city's business elite for his harsh opinions about the inferiority of Mexican peoples. Against a backdrop of vigorous cheers, Howard told the enthusiastic crowd that the United States represented the third great republic, following Greece and Rome, and that its greatness marked the culmination of the Anglo-Saxon race.[12]

Los Angeles businessmen were hardly alone in idealizing Anglo-Saxon peoples and culture. The Immigration Act of 1924 codified such attitudes in national policy, resulting in a virtual ban on immigration from Asia and Africa and severe limits to immigration from southern and eastern Europe. Few groups in the country, however, expressed more support of the act's principles than Los Angeles's corporate leadership, who argued that the city had already become the Anglo-Saxon mecca idealized by the new policy. In November 1924, the Chamber of Commerce magazine *Southern California Business* printed a story entitled "The Los Angeles of Tomorrow," which stated, "For centuries, the Anglo-Saxon race has been marching westward. It is now on the shores of the Pacific. It can go no farther. The apex of this movement is Los Angeles County." The history concluded by asserting that "Anglo-Saxon civilization" would climax in Los Angeles.[13]

The activities of southern California businessmen reveal that this cult of Anglo-Saxonness had consequences beyond changes in immigration policy. It would directly affect the ability of the region's young men to find work. Alongside business leaders' efforts to market and celebrate Los Angeles as an Anglo-Saxon community, they presided over corporations that privileged native-born men of British descent in hirings and promotions. As much as possible, local companies hired men of Nordic appearance who were neatly groomed and presented themselves in terms they would have described as "all American." In practice, this meant a normative Anglo physiognomy, "middle-class" attire and mannerisms, and a lack of distinctive regional accents or characteristics. A southern accent or a southwestern twang, for instance, could evoke regional or class biases and dash one's chances during a white-collar interview. This phenomenon, which blossomed in the racial discussions surrounding the Spanish-American War, lasted at least through the Great Depression.[14]

In the rare cases where persons of color had any access to corporate Los Angeles's inner circles, they found themselves marginalized, at times made invisible, and in other cases subject to ridicule. African American William H. Shores, for example, served as banking executive Joseph Sartori's "right-hand man" for more than thirty years. Shores ran errands and performed a variety of tasks for Sartori, apparently acting as a sort of personal assistant. Yet not only did Shores receive no mention in any official bank communications, but he also retained the title of "janitor" his entire career. We do not know for certain how Sartori's employees reacted to Shores's presence, but affirmations of "whiteness" and ridicule of racial and ethnic minorities occurred as staples of corporate cultures. Company magazines, for instance, often identified employees in news features by noting their ethnic backgrounds, and affixed glowing adjectives to English, Scottish, or Welsh ancestry. Alongside these mentions, racist jokes and caricatures appeared as natural and unquestioned themes in business communications. Pacific Electric Railway Company never officially spoke of employment barriers for African Americans, for instance, but occurrences throughout its corporate culture—such as its workers' appearance in blackface at company-sponsored minstrel shows—continually evidenced the racialized traditions and sentiments that pervaded business life.[15]

The ethnic make-up of southern California's population allowed for narrow, race-based hiring practices. The massive immigration into Los Angeles served to maintain its demographic characteristics, notable among American urban centers, of having a comparatively large percentage of American-born residents. In 1890, roughly three out of every four Los Angelenos were native-born whites, a significantly higher percentage than in many other major American cities. Most of Los Angeles's population growth came from native-born persons from the midwestern and eastern United States. The states of Wisconsin, Michigan, Ohio, Indiana, Illinois, Nebraska, and Iowa became the most important sources of southern California's population gains. Between 1910 and 1930, migrants from these states consistently composed approximately 40 percent of the region's native born population. Writer Louis Adamic seemed to have had this in mind when he wrote in 1932 that Los Angeles captured "the imagination of millions of people who for various reasons have become dissatisfied with what life offers them in Gopher Prairies."[16]

Out of this populace, businessmen staffed their firms with the very "whitest" of collars. To begin with, a general racial and ethnic divide emerged between typically working- and middle-class jobs. A sample of men from the 1910 and 1920 censuses suggests that foreign-born persons and people of southern European, Asian, or Mexican descent were largely confined to agricultural work, domestic service, and manual labor. All the other major occupational groups, including clerical and sales workers; craftsmen and foremen; managers, officials, and proprietors; operatives and kindred workers; and professional and technical workers comprised overwhelming majorities of native-born, northern European men. Yet, if white, native-born men dominated most sectors of southern California's nonmanual labor force, a closer look at clerical and sales workers shows that white-collar "company" men were distinctive among most occupational groups on several points. First, they were even more rarely foreign born. In both 1910 and 1920, native-born men composed a higher proportion of white-collar employees than of any other occupational category. Eighty-six percent of the 1910 sample and 80 percent of the 1920 sample were native born. Second, the vast majority of most white-collar men's parents were also native born. In both census years, more than two-thirds of white-collar men were second generation Americans, a figure matched only by professional and technical workers. Third, of those white-collar men whose parents were foreign born, between 35 and 40 percent claimed English as their parents' native tongue, a figure again matched only by professional and technical workers.[17]

Because occupational categorizations made in U.S. censuses can be problematic, and because these samples are small, we must interpret them with care. Other sources, however, confirm their implications. A simple reading of company magazines, for instance, finds Anglo-American faces and names dominating their pages. More convincing are numbers from a random sample of 4,223 white male draft registrants (ages 18–29) from the city in 1917. Of the roughly 1,200 men in this sample who worked for large companies, 96 percent of corporate professionals, 94 percent of men in managerial positions, and 92 percent of the remaining general white-collar employees were native born, figures significantly higher than for any other occupational group. Furthermore, of the 8 percent of general white-collar employees who were foreign born, nearly half were from Canada or the United Kingdom. The remainder hailed largely from Germany, Scandinavia, or Russia. This contrasts sharply with other occupational groupings. Slightly more than one-fourth of all blue-collar workers were foreign born, as were approximately half of all independent proprietors. Individuals in both groups were more likely to hail from Mexico or southern and eastern Europe.[18]

This sample of draft registrants further suggests that ethnic identities may have taken precedence over class background in corporate hiring. Charting the residences of white-collar employees reveals that they lived in virtually every district in the city. Many came from the prosperous Hancock Park and Highland Park areas, but significant numbers lived in working-class and more racially heterogeneous southern and eastern Los Angeles. In addition, some lived on the eastern edge of downtown in one of the city's poorest districts. While the wide diffusion of white-collar men in Los Angeles alludes to the broad range of such jobs, it also points to the critical place of physical appearance and demeanor in corporate personnel decisions. It seemed to matter little if one came from the "good" side of town, or the "wrong side of the tracks," or whether one came from a family of means or a working-class home. Even educational requirements were minimal or at least flexible for many positions. Ultimately, one could realistically aspire to a white-collar job if one could present the desired white-collar appearance. Indeed, company men wore the very whitest of collars.

The White-Collar City

That salaried, long-term white-collar jobs became the domain of native-born Anglo-Saxon men testifies more to the significance of the "collar line" and to office work's growing dominance in the city's economy than to these men's affinity for such positions. By the early twentieth century, the divide between "office jobs" and manual labor had become key to American conceptions of status and success. This distinction began to emerge in the mid-nineteenth century alongside the nation's fledgling service and commercial economy. Jobs in bookkeeping, clerical work, sales, and the professions became associated with improved social status, including an annual salary rather than daily wages, higher overall pay, the ability to specialize in certain trades or professional activities, greater likelihood of continuous, year-around employment, and physical separation from the more grueling and dangerous environments of factory work, farming, or labor in extractive industries. Based on these and other experiences, nonmanual laborers began to assume higher status than manual workers; and by the late nineteenth century, nonmanual work had emerged as a badge of middle-class respectability.[19]

On these terms, Los Angeles appeared to young men as a distinctly middle-class city. Its stunning economic growth rested on a swelling workforce in every economic sector, but professional service, public service, and clerical occupations led the way. This white-collarization of Los Angeles's economy becomes clear when using federal government models for evaluating occupational demographics. The Bureau of the Census divided American workers into three major categories: farmworkers, manual and service workers, and white-collar workers. Under this model, the term *white-collar workers* encompassed virtually every occupation not engaged in manual labor or domestic service or directly connected to farming. Using this formula, the proportion of nonmanual workers in Los Angeles surpassed the national average by a significant margin. By 1930, close to half of all gainfully employed adult men in Los Angeles served in nonmanual positions.

If the divide between physical labor and some form of nonmanual labor or office work had indeed become the crucial distinction between working and middle-class status by the end of the nineteenth century, then Los Angeles had a significantly middle-class economy. Such a generalization, however, belies the increasing complexity of nonmanual work. The federal census def-

Table 3.2 Percentage of male labor force in white-collar, professional, and entrepreneurial jobs

Year	*Los Angeles*	*United States*	*Chicago*	*New York*	*St. Louis*	*San Francisco*
1910	35.7	20.0	33.7	38.2	33.4	27.8
1920	36.3	21.0	30.6	36.3	32.0	27.7
1930	42.4	25.0	35.1	40.0	35.5	37.8

Source: Bureau of the Census, U.S. Department of Commerce, *Historical Statistics of the United States, Colonial Times to 1970, Part 1* (Washington, D.C.: U.S. Government Printing Office, 1975), pp. 139–40. For metropolitan figures, see *Thirteenth Census, Volume 4*, 132–49, 166–79, 186–203, 205–21, 222–38; *Fourteenth Census, Volume 4*, 153–207; *Fifteenth Census, Volume 4*, 173–83, 208–9, 447–49, 884–90, 1130–32.

Table 3.3 Percentage of male labor force in white-collar jobs

Year	*Los Angeles*	*Chicago*	*New York*	*St. Louis*	*San Francisco*
1910	18.0	20.6	21.7	21.3	13.8
1920	18.6	18.9	18.9	19.0	14.5
1930	22.0	21.8	23.0	22.6	23.5

Source: Bureau of the Census, U.S. Department of Commerce, *Historical Statistics of the United States* (Washington, D.C.: U.S. Government Printing Office, 1975), *Thirteenth Census, Volume 4,* 132–49, 166–79, 186–203, 205–21, 222–38; *Fourteenth Census, Volume 4,* 153–207; *Fifteenth Census, Volume 4,* 173–83, 208–9, 447–49, 884–90, 1130–32.

inition of white-collar work conflated the "old middle class," composed largely of proprietors, professionals, and scattered office employees, with the "new middle class," of the twentieth century, which included significant numbers of office employees and managers in medium to large firms. This governmental classification ignored what most young men knew well or learned quickly: doctors, lawyers, and small businessmen lived very different lives from clerical employees. While young Angelenos gazed upon a world where a large variety of middle-class opportunities seemed to beckon, they encountered clear limits on their ability to pursue the job of their choice. When they actually set out to find work, the diversity of opportunities seemed to shrink. While small businessmen, professionals, and managers dominated the city's landscape, young men rarely constituted their ranks. The entry-level jobs where they instead found work offered a much less appealing range of choices, and it was unclear where these positions would lead.

Draft records from 1917 offer some perspective on how the labor market looked to these men. Approximately 40 percent of the men in this sample held some kind of nonmanual job. Yet, while citywide half of all men in this sector worked as independent professionals or small businessmen, such opportunities were more rare for young men. Many highly desirable professions, such as medicine and law, were becoming more difficult to enter because of stricter educational and licensing requirements, whereas others, such as teaching, grew problematic because of women's increasing presence. Despite the appeal of owning one's own business, most young men recognized this route's limitations and precarious nature. Would-be entrepreneurs needed start-up capital; even if one had the resources, competition was fierce and rates of business failure high.[20] Perhaps because of such dilemmas, only 10 percent of men in the entire draft sample worked as professionals or owned their own business. These two groups accounted for just over 15 percent of all nonmanual male employees.

If a young white man hoped to acquire middle-class occupational status via nonmanual work, finding an office job in a local business seemed the best option. One-quarter of all the men in this sample and well over half of those in the nonmanual world worked in white-collar jobs. These positions, however, were not a natural career pathway for young men. Despite the rapidly increasing prominence of office work, white-collar careers loomed as a new and confusing proposition. Such posts in small businesses had long represented an obvious starting point for young men's careers, but as companies grew larger and their management bureaucratized, these positions seemed less and less appealing.[21] Young men who, accurately or not, felt that they understood professional or small business life must have stared at the office buildings in downtown Los Angeles and pondered: Whom do these companies hire? What kind of opportunities are available? What would a corporate career mean? Although many young Los Angelenos pursued white-collar jobs as their best pathway to a middle-class life, they did so with ambivalence.

Ambitious Young Men

Twenty-nine-year-old Scott Hazel numbered among the many native-born young white men that Los Angeles companies wanted and found. An émigré from Minnesota and the son of native-born midwesterners, he arrived in the 1910s and took a job as bookkeeper in a furniture company. The apparent success of local firms in recruiting men such as Scott Hazel proved deceptive, however, for neither he nor thousands of his peers in the city believed they were signing on for dutiful, lifelong service in a single firm. To the contrary, the white-collar labor market proved exceptionally fluid. Hazel, for instance, proved a disappointment to his employer, remaining in Los Angeles only a short time before leaving to pursue opportunities elsewhere.

Privileged by their race and sex and emboldened by their age, many young white men like Scott Hazel took seriously American culture's ideal of "rags to respectability and riches." Their upbringing occurred in a society that had for generations held social mobility leading to economic independence as the cultural ideal for white males, even the very essence of what it meant to "be a man." Those raised in working-class homes anticipated rising to middle-class status; those from middle-class families envisioned futures framed by security, independence, and prosperity. They each had unique hopes and expectations, but in one way or another, they were all men on the make. They expected to rise in standing and comforts over the course of their lives.

Southern California's social and cultural milieu fanned these young men's ambitions. It was not just white-collar jobs that lured native-born Americans from the Midwest and the East to cross the great western deserts and continue on to the Pacific Coast. If they sought only the opportunity to secure such work, most would have found it sooner along the way and settled there, as many indeed did. Rarely pushed to migrate by social, political, or economic despair, those who migrated to Los Angeles prior to the 1930s were largely a self-selected class of people willing to relocate far away in hopes of finding the many rewards southern California seemed to offer. The region's celebrated, incessant, and precision-drill booster campaigns only fueled their hopes. Because promoters promised not only great weather and a booming economy but also the lifestyle afforded by a "Mediterranean oasis," Los Angeles attracted settlers for whom "better quality of life" meant many different things.[22] Emma Johnson Bennie recalled her father's moving their family to southern California from Iowa in 1908 because "the winters were so very cold and he wanted his family to have a better life." Seventeen-year-old Elmer Wilson spent six weeks hitch-hiking from Pennsylvania to Pasadena in 1916 to see the New Year's Day football game. He enjoyed his stay so much he returned the following year for good.[23]

Once in California, young white men in search of better things found their status heightened by the lower status of the region's significant numbers of Mexicans, Japanese, and African Americans. The proportion of people of color in Los Angeles's population ranked high among American urban centers throughout this period, as migrations of Mexicans, African Americans, and Japanese matched proportionately the immigration of native-born whites. In 1930, when the Census Bureau reclassified Mexicans from "white" to "nonwhite," (a fitting act given the racial discrimination they confronted throughout the history of Anglo Los Angeles), the city ranked among the nation's highest in the percentage of nonwhite residents.[24] The city's sizable number of people of color, who were particularly vulnerable to economic exploitation, strengthened the social and economic position of white immigrants, who already had comparatively privileged backgrounds.[25]

Young Anglo men in southern California were thus an ambitious group on many levels, but while their demographic characteristics may have rendered them part of a local elite, the white-collar world they confronted challenged their ideals. When twenty-year-old Frank Graves moved to Los Angeles with his Vermont-born parents in the 1910s and accepted a position as a clerk in a downtown bank, he followed the footsteps of many before him who had taken such entry-level white-collar jobs as stepping stones to promising futures. By the 1910s, however, the size, systematization, and dominance of the big banks and other corporations that gripped Los Angeles's economy foreshadowed a more ominous career trajectory. Could Frank, from his position as a bank clerk, fulfill his highest career aspirations? Although business historians today write of the modern business enterprise as a "logical" development in the evolution of economic structures, aspiring young men did not always see the logic in the lack of autonomy, authority, or control typical of bureaucratic employment. Many white-collar employees seemed entangled in complex operational hierarchies and subordinated to a rigid chain of command, and they lacked any realistic opportunity to direct the enterprise.

Company life was not always like this. In the very early years of big business formation, employees in fledgling companies could find exciting opportunities to exercise considerable control and initiative. As Los Angeles firms bureaucratized in the early twentieth century, however, individual workers felt bound by strict hierarchies. Corporate guidelines subjected them to paternalistic, if not authoritarian, working environments. In 1913, for instance, the vice president of the Pacific Mutual Life Insurance Company declared to employees that "when a certain agent once told me that he was going to take a week off, I wondered how or why. He had not really been on the job and therefore could not, logically, get off. His week would be a dismal one because he had not earned it." By the mid 1920s, Pacific Mutual required its employees to keep elaborate productivity reports charting the number of clients interviewed per hour, the number of policies sold per hour, and thereby the value of their time per hour. Employees also faced constant scrutiny. The Pacific Mail Steamship Company frequently sent inspectors to evaluate it employees. They often examined not only job performance but also conduct and demeanor. One such inspection report read: "Rutherford I am convinced has the brains to handle his work satisfactorily, [but] he has certain characteristics which are not altogether the best, at least he impressed me as one of the more hard-boiled types."[26]

While vulnerable to larger market forces as well, white-collar workers had little control over the firm's ability to survive adversity inflicted by such forces. Many employees found their jobs abruptly terminated when their employers suffered financial setbacks. When changes in the ownership of shipping routes forced the dissolution of the Pacific Mail Steamship Company in 1925 and 1926, employees received sudden dismissal notices. Men such as Eugene C. Walsh, who had served the company as clerk for seven years and had been promoted twice, opened a letter that said "as stated today we very much regret the necessity of severing your connection with the company." Walsh's boss noted this his services had been "most satisfactory" and expressed his "utmost regret" at the termination. More-junior employees read less-compassionate notices stating, "Owing to the discontinuance of shipping board operations it is necessary to reduce forces and therefore advise you that effective immediately you will be released."[27]

Although, as prevailing cultural norms suggested, white-collar work conferred middle-class status while blue-collar work did not, money was less of a factor in this distinction. Lower-level white-collar employees often received working-class wages. A pay schedule from the Pacific Electric Railway shows that male clerks and other office personnel in 1912 made anywhere from $35 to $90 a month. The lower-paid of these employees took home amounts similar to what the company's blue-collar workers made each month from their hourly earnings. In 1929, nearly two decades later, Security-First National Bank, one of the city's elite financial institutions, still paid its entry-level male employees just over $70 a month, only marginally more than what local factory operatives made. Nationally, white-collar male incomes spanned a large range. A survey of clerical salaries in 1926 showed that entry-level male clerks averaged $60-$80 a month, amounts less than many skilled workers and often comparable to packers, drivers, and porters, though within this spectrum, employees in the largest firms tended to do better.[28]

Status and semantic distinctions formed much of the difference in employment policies and compensation for blue- and white-collar jobs. Even though the amounts of payment were often similar, American companies paid "wages" to manual "workers," while white-collar "employees" received "salaries." Nor was white-collar work necessarily more stable. Most companies paid white-collar employees on a weekly or biweekly basis with no long-term contract.[29]

For all of these reasons, young white men in Los Angeles viewed white-collar employment with considerable uncertainty. Evidence of middle-class reservations concerning white-collar employment appear in many sources. Local businessmen, remembering with distaste their days on the ladder's lower rungs, often spoke with pride about their positions relative to "mere employees." In a local business magazine story from 1909, the owner of a downtown department store with four hundred employees saw a man (for whom he had worked many years before in Michigan) enter his establishment. The man, appearing startled at finding his former employee in the opulent establishment blared, "Why, what are YOU doing here?" With barely concealed glee, he told his former boss (who, readers learn, paid him very little) that he managed the store.[30]

One does not have to dig far into the lives of southern Californians to find young white-collar men expressing resentment at their employment status. Ray Hindman's early career biography includes a laundry list of grievances. He arrived in San Francisco in 1924 and became a clerk at Woolworth's, a retail chain. The company soon transferred Hindman to a southern California store and promoted him to assistant manager. To his disappointment, however, he found that everyone was eventually given that title, "even janitors." Hindman subsequently sought work in a local lumber company, but it turned out that they wanted him primarily as a laborer, so he again quit and went to work for another retailer, the Kress Company. He became a receiving clerk at Kress with a better salary and more interesting tasks, but he soon found a harsh side to his employment contract: no store employee except managers could own an automobile, because the company had strict expectations for how their salaries should be spent. Hindman recalled that employees were expected to "dress properly—suit, white shirt, and tie—and live in a proper kind of an apartment house," in order to "make the Kress Store look good." Hindman was told that the company did not believe an employee could buy an automobile and still "live the way they thought you should live." Hindman quit yet again and, in 1927, went to work for the National Cash Register Company as a salesman. He stayed with NCR less than two years, however, tired of being continually relocated. "What they were doing with me was making a yo-yo out of me," Hindman remembered. He complained, "whenever a salesman would be pulled out of a territory or quit his job, I could be sent into the territory." He noted that once the firm sent him to Tacoma, Washington, for a short stint to replace a man whose wife "didn't like the rain."

Transferred to distant offices, asked to perform tedious tasks, and finding his private life subject to company policies, Hindman joined the chorus of those who longed to own their own business, or at least to have more control over their working environment. Hindman never did own his own firm, but in 1928 he went to work for a small typewriter shop, essentially becoming a junior partner in the enterprise where he then spent thirty-three years.[31] Unwilling to accept corporate dictates, Hindman joined those in southern California who opted for careers in which they could enjoy more autonomy and exert more control.

Southern California business interests found clever ways to capitalize on young men's resistance to white-collar employment in large firms. Local business colleges, which typically trained young men and women in the clerical skills corporations were seeking, frequently advertised themselves as gateways to entrepreneurship. The Isaacs-Woodbury Business College taught white-collar skills but emphasized that "such an education, coupled with self-confidence, legitimate self-assertion and a pleasing and forceful personality—all of which qualities can be developed" would make their graduates "absolutely independent." Some realtors also preyed upon notions of self-sufficiency. A 1914 advertisement for a ranch that appeared in a local business journal featured the headline "Better than Salary" and touted the ten-acre property as an opportunity to be "your own boss" and "not depend on the payroll." Despite the frequent use of promotional literature promising control over one's destiny, business schools did acknowledge the likelihood of white-collar work in most young men's lives. Here too, however, they nurtured the desire for upward mobility. A 1910 advertisement from the International Correspondence School, for instance, showed a young white-collar employee stuck in a bottle, accompanied by the illustration: "Are You Bottled Up?" With its "practical system of special training," the school promised readers they could easily climb out of a "distasteful surrounding to a congenial position with a higher salary." Isaacs-Woodbury similarly vowed to help young men secure better positions. One advertisement stated, "Many who are now occupying subordinate positions have the NATURAL APTITUDE FOR HIGHER WORK, but cannot go up higher for lack of education and technical knowledge." The school then pledged to remedy this situation.[32]

Corporate leaders must have viewed these advertisements with concern. On one hand, they could appreciate the emphasis on careers spent climbing company ladders, yet they deplored the idea of hopping from firm to firm to do so. They hoped employees would instead choose to remain with their business over the long haul. Executives could not help but note that the same magazine that featured these college ads also enthusiastically reported stories of men who left their jobs for better positions elsewhere. In February 1910, for instance, the *American Globe* printed a notice that Fred Herr, who had served with the Los Angeles Railway for twenty years, had accepted a position as local agent for the Western Pacific and the Denver and Rio Grande Railways. The author praised and congratulated Herr, for whom this was an important opportunity. For Los Angeles Railway leaders, however, the news announced the unfortunate departure of a long-term employee who, if the article is to be believed, was well known locally for his skills in Los Angeles railway matters.[33] The departure of good employees created a continual challenge for local business leaders, as young, ambitious men simply viewed their positions as stepping stones to better opportunities elsewhere.

The Residential Geography of Company Men

Surveying white-collar neighborhoods provides a glimpse into the transient nature of Los Angeles's young corporate male workforce. From the 1910s to the 1940s, these men's residences were dispersed throughout the city,

This correspondence school advertisement from 1910 played on young men's fears about a shortage of opportunities to advance into better jobs. Reproduced from *American Globe* 7 (January 1910): 2, by permission of the Huntington Library, San Marino, California.

though a gradual shift north and west occurred, particularly to the Wilshire Boulevard corridor. Yet, in the midst of this period, near the dawn of the 1920s, the young white men who formed the heart of the white-collar labor force were concentrated in one area. Nearly 40 percent of white-collar men who registered for the 1917 draft lived in an approximately forty-block area just west of downtown, stretching north to south from approximately First to Tenth Streets, and east to west from Spring Street to Figueroa Avenue.[34]

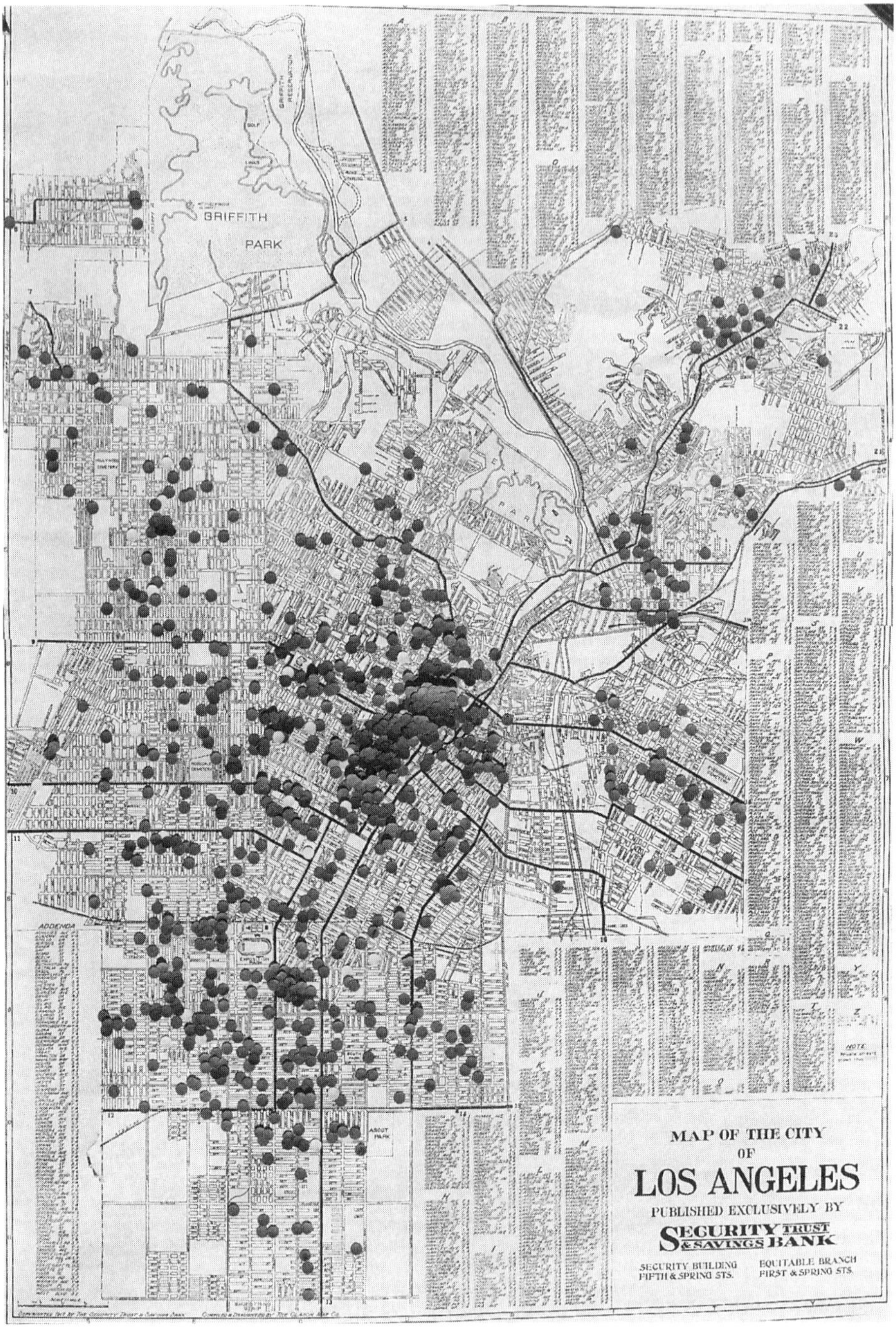

Dots on this map indicate the residences of white-collar male employees. The greatest concentration of white-collar men lay in the district of apartment buildings and boarding houses just west of downtown. Original map provided by the Huntington Library, San Marino, California; adapted and reproduced by permission. Data taken from 1917 draft registration records.

A walk through these neighborhoods reveals much about white-collar experience. In 1920, the intersection of South Grand Avenue and Second Street formed the heart of this district. On Grand Avenue lay a succession of large homes with a few apartments scattered here and there. The first building was a complex called the Minnewska. Most of the fifty-eight units in the building housed married couples spanning a wide age range. Every renter was white and more than 75 percent were native born. The few remaining foreign-born residents came mainly from Canada, the United Kingdom, or Scandinavia. Most Minnewska residents were blue-collar workers or proprietors, with a smattering of white-collar types. Carl Taylor was one of the white-collar residents. A thirty-five-year-old Nebraskan with a wife and two children, he worked as a ticket clerk for a local railway firm.[35]

Adjacent to the Minnewska sat a large house shared by seven young single women, working as either stenographers or nurses. Next to them lay an eight-unit apartment house where eight couples lived, half of whom had children. The residents included both blue- and white-collar workers. Among them was Scott Hazel, whom we have met, and his wife, Ida Pamplin, a twenty-eight-year-old manicurist. Large homes converted into boarding houses occupied the remainder of the block, with one to four families or lodgers residing in each. All of the residents were "white," although people of Mexican descent appeared occasionally on the block. The ages of Grand Avenue occupants varied from the twenties through the sixties, and their occupations were relatively evenly divided among proprietors, blue-collar workers, and white-collar employees.

Farther south on Grand Avenue, the neighborhood slowly changed from one of boarding homes and apartment buildings into a neighborhood with large apartment complexes housing a younger population and fewer families. The 400 block of South Grand Avenue, for instance, included the forty-six-unit Zelda and the eighty-five-unit Granada. These buildings housed an entirely white population that included significant numbers of company men. One Zelda resident, for instance, was John Seiner, a thirty-two-year-old married bill clerk for a local supply company. In the Granada lived twenty-one-year-old Samuel King of Missouri, a single man who worked as a railroad freight clerk. White-collar men shared these buildings with a roughly equal number of blue-collar workers. In the Granada, twenty-two-year-old Ray Roberts, a salesman for a local drug company, lived next to twenty-one-year-old laborer George Roitsch.

By the 700 block of South Grand Avenue, lodging houses filled largely by single white men predominated. The residents continued to be white and mostly native born (immigrants were primarily British or Canadian) and were divided among white-collar employees, proprietors, professionals, and blue-collar workers. In one sixty-eight unit complex, twenty-year-old bank clerk Frank Graves, from New York, lived across from William Read, a twenty-three-year-old laborer from England.[36]

Los Angeles's young white-collar men lived in a remarkably fluid neighborhood. Local residents varied greatly in age, social class, and family status. The only measures of demographic homogeneity, in fact, lay in the fact that residents were renters and mostly white. Even in this latter category, however, some diversity existed. A small number of Jews, Mexicans, and southern Europeans also lived in this corridor, and in its midst sat an apartment building housing fifty-five Japanese American lodgers and families.

In the minds of young white-collar men, all of these factors made their careers seem distinctly in transition. When they left their apartments to go to work each morning, they passed the doors of few neighbors whose lives they hoped to emulate. A small number of their neighbors were recent immigrants from southern or eastern Europe, probably not the "type of people" among whom they expected to live. Many whom they greeted in the halls or on the stairwells were blue-collar men whose presence served to remind them that the rungs on the occupational ladder were slippery.

Perhaps even more troubling, these men lived in immediate proximity to many white-collar women and many older white men working in low-level white-collar positions. Such figures must have kindled considerable anxiety about the status and long-term implications of white-collar work. The increasing presence of women who held jobs with comparable titles, even if such women received less pay, had less authority, and worked in different physical locations within the corporate workplace, forced white-collar men to question their own social status. In the older white-collar men in low-level positions they must have seen the possibility that opportunities for advancement would not materialize for them. Thirty-four-year-old Fred Laughlin, for instance, hoped his position as clerk would provide a future away from his crowded lodging house shared by fourteen people, including a mechanic, marble tiler, and a plasterer. However, knowing one of his neighbors, a forty-seven-year-old clerk named George Mitchell, must have given him some pause about a low-level white-collar man's chances for social mobility. Many young white men shared Fred Laughlin's vantage point. Conditioned by their society to expect grand futures, they found themselves living in mixed lodging houses and working in lower-level white-collar jobs whose status and futures were uncertain.

A residential district of single-family homes in southwestern Los Angeles formed the city's second major hub of young white-collar men. Though historians often label the district lower middle or middle class, quite distinct from the working-class neighborhoods that lay to the east, a walk through the area in 1920 would have shattered stereotypical suburban middle-class images. The physical facades of detached single-family homes camouflaged a very different social reality behind their doors. Known as Vermont Square, the community lay several blocks south of the prestigious though fading West Adams district, home to mansions housing the city's first- and second-generation Anglo elite. Several blocks to the east lay Main Street, a north-south street generally thought to divide the city's working and middle-class districts. Vermont Square itself encompassed primarily modest, single-family homes built just prior to the war, but few properties were occupied by single families. Owners had divided many residences into apartments, duplexes, and triplexes that they rented out to multiple families and lodgers. Only about half of the homes were owner occupied, and in many that were, homeowners rented out rooms to boarders.[37]

Most white-collar men in this neighborhood were sons living with their parents. For them, securing a middle-class future would require a step beyond the standard of their upbringing. Twenty-two-year-old Coloradan Leland Curtis moved with his family to Los Angeles, where they rented part of a home on West Fortieth Street. Leland, whose father worked as a building supplies dealer, found a job as a bank clerk. The position gave Leland a toe-hold in a more secure middle-class world, but the occupations of his neighbors constantly reminded him not only of the ever-present prospect of working-class life but also of the dubious status and future of lower white-collar work. A fifty-year-old unemployed woman shared the property, along with a German immigrant family that included a sixty-eight-year-old mother and her daughter, both supported by the son, a forty-year-old laborer, and his wife, a forty-two-year-old office worker.

Gene Dalton, too, worked as a clerk in a corporate world more middle-class and Anglicized than the one in which he spent his nights. He and his father, a cigar maker, rented one of three units in a home one block from the Curtis family. Next door lived a fifty-year-old Mexican man who owned a house shared by his daughter and two younger sons. When Gene and Leland walked down Fortieth Street each morning to catch the Pacific Electric car into downtown, they passed a wide diversity of people. On one block, for instance, a Mexican rancher and his family rented a house. Next door lived an elderly German couple, who owned the home, and their young son, a jeweler, who supported them. They next passed a rental house inhabited by a middle-aged manufacturer, his wife, daughter, and two grandsons. Next to them resided a forty-one-year-old female Irish immigrant, who owned the home, and her four children. Other properties housed a large Swedish immigrant family, an elderly retired couple, and a mother and two single daughters working as stenographers.

Scattered throughout the neighborhood were married white-collar men and their families. Thirty-two-year-old Frank Miller, for instance, worked as a bookkeeper at Union Oil. He and his wife, a teacher, rented half of a duplex, which they shared with an elderly German cigar maker and his wife. Jacob Streitz, an agent, owned a home along with his wife and three-year-old daughter. A middle-aged Canadian merchant and his wife owned and lived in the house next door.

Like their colleagues in the downtown lodging district, few white-collar men residing in Vermont Square thought they had "made it." While the allure of home ownership reverberated strongly in Los Angeles, many of these men still lived with their parents, and many of those married still rented rooms in crowded homes within this supposedly "middle-class" area. All of them slept in distinctly "mixed" neighborhoods. As a community with many boarders, working-class men and women, German and Scandinavian immigrants, and families of Mexican descent, Vermont Square differed sharply from the homogeneous and elitist Anglo world of corporate Los Angeles. It also differed from the vision many of these men had of their futures. The neighborhood, like their entry-level white-collar jobs, provided but a way station to what they viewed as a solid middle-class future within Los Angeles's WASPish circles.

The Corporate Dilemma

Few white-collar men—young, ambitious, and mobile—cheerfully dedicated their lives to their employers. Executives learned quickly that employee loyalty could not be taken for granted. Lacking the occupational cohesion often seen among skilled laborers and rarely participating in collective bargaining or unions, white-collar men rarely exerted power in ways easily visible to historians.[38] Yet these employees did "bargain" with leaders. They negotiated in subtle ways by simply not offering their best efforts. The size and collective nature of corporate operations made enthusiastic support among all employees—blue- and white-collar alike—crucial to company success. The essential business tasks performed by white-collar employees made their dedication particularly important. Executives never forgot that, on any given day, individual workers could seriously help or hurt the firm. From clerks to senior managers, their frequent contact with consumers and their coordination of daily activities made them important players in company operations.

White-collar employees also bargained with their feet. A 1919 book on office management, published for business executives, noted that "during the last few years much attention has been directed to the loss involved in the frequent leaving of employees." Citing recent research, the author noted that "a high rate of turnover is not confined to factory employees." Indeed, corporate leaders' desire to staff their firms with native-born white men, primarily of Anglo-Saxon descent, doomed them to continual struggles with turnover. With little hesitation, these "men on the make," such as Leo Devlin, whose story began this chapter, willfully changed companies if better opportunities arose. The feminization of lower clerical posts in large part reflected frustration over young men's refusal to stay in such positions for long. Many companies found that turnover rates for male clerks were simply too high, and they considered women more stable.[39]

Job-hopping characterized the career histories of the young men who continually sought opportunities for better pay, status, or more independence. The mobility themes articulated in business college advertisements found fertile ground among young men who accepted less than glamorous white-collar posts but aspired to better things. J. E. Brick Elliott, for instance, came to California with his family from Bozeman, Montana, in 1897. After graduating from Monterey High School in 1906, he worked for a year with a Western Pacific Railway survey party, but then enrolled at Stanford University, where he graduated in 1912. The Southern Pacific offered him a job, but he declined the post for a better position with the Associated Oil Company, which paid him $135 a month and expenses, nearly double Southern Pacific's salary. The following year he left Associated Oil to work as a geologist for the Shell Oil Company. He quit that position in 1920 to teach at Stanford University but resigned the following year to start his own drilling business.[40]

Fred Pearson also transferred from company to company. He became a senior statistician at the Atlantic and San Francisco Railroad Company in 1908. Pearson stayed with the firm until 1918, and received at least two promotions, but left for a better job in the Bethlehem Shipbuilding Corporation. Bethlehem terminated Pearson in 1921 and he signed on with the Pacific Mail Steamship Company. Although he received a promotion six months later, he resigned in 1922 to take a "more remunerative position" elsewhere. Pearson sought upward mobility through white-collar work but in no way limited his opportunities to those found in a single company.[41]

Employee turnover plagued company operations in most southern California firms. While the problem's severity varied from business to business, few escaped the frustrating managerial scourge. When a good employee left, management expended time and money finding a replacement. Leaders would then have to train and educate new employees in company procedures, a process that could take considerable time, depending on the job. The departure of employees additionally drained the pool of candidates available to fill upper-level vacancies. When particularly good personnel departed, a company lost valuable "advancement material."

Turnover could also pose a threat if employees with sensitive information joined rival firms. Union Oil executives found this out as early as 1894 when three former employees divulged "company secrets" about drilling operations to a rival San Francisco firm. In following years, Union Oil and countless other companies fretted over such disloyal acts. This threat especially troubled firms with large sales staffs, for they feared customers would follow employees to new companies. For this reason, insurance companies engaged in ferocious efforts to lure agents from other firms and to retain their own.[42]

Few corporations left for historians detailed records of employee turnover. Those that do exist, however, suggest high rates. From 1904 to 1909, for example, the Pacific Mail Steamship Company hired 252 salaried male clerks. Seventy-seven of them quit shortly after being hired, never having received a raise or promotion, thirty-two were fired shortly after joining the firm, and another eight quit despite having received a raise or promotion within a few months. Barely half of the company's new hires during this period lasted more than several weeks.[43]

Security-First National Bank also encountered marked turnover. Retention difficulties alarmed bank leaders during the 1920s. When "loyalty" improved during the Great Depression, company leaders continually lauded their own "handling" of the problem, oddly neglecting the role played by the national economic crisis in ameliorating it. In 1931, bank executives expressed relief that the turnover rate for 1930 had been "only" 20 percent. The previous year, the bank had experienced an all-time record rate of 35 percent, which, the words of company leaders suggest, was higher than previous years but not an anomaly.[44]

Mobility studies in other parts of the country confirm that most large firms encountered significant turnover, particularly in lower-level positions. In Philadelphia, 42 percent of workers between 1870 and 1936, both blue- and white-collar, left their first job for a better position elsewhere. The percentage leaving for more advantageous posts steadily decreased with each job, but it remained as high as 18 percent for their fifth job. A 1919 office management text devoted significant space to the problem of turnover in white-collar ranks, confirming its prevalence. In 1927, a conference on business education at Northwestern University addressed at length the difficulty of replacing departing managers as a common problem.[45]

Two Ideal Employees

Lester Bradley graduated from a San Diego high school in 1900. For the next seven years he traveled back and forth between southern California and Chicago, never working for much more than a year at any one job. His employers during these years ranged from construction firms to the Chicago Board of Trade. Finally, in 1907, he walked into the Southern Trust and Savings Bank and asked for a job. According to Bradley, "[the manager] told me he didn't have any jobs open and I asked him if it was all right if I worked there for nothing until a job opened up—and he said I could." Four months later the bank offered him a paying position. He stayed there twenty-five years, ultimately becoming vice president and manager. Bradley's willingness to work for free, his loyalty to the bank, and the skills and talents he apparently exhibited suggest that he epitomized the ideal company man.[46] His recollections are most important, however, for their atypicality. Most southern California banks and other firms struggled to cultivate such dedicated career employees—not to mention those who would work for free.

When the Security Trust and Savings Bank hired Lewis Ives Pierce in 1918, the bank assumed a long-term challenge to win his loyalty. Pierce had recently immigrated to the city from Chelsea, Massachusetts. His family had been in the United States for more than seven generations and over that time had come to secure a comfortable existence, of which summers at Cape Cod were but one family tradition. Pierce moved to Pasadena because of fond impressions from a lengthy family holiday there years before. Shortly after his arrival, Pierce accepted a job as statement clerk with the bank's Pasadena branch. Bank officials viewed Pierce—a young, educated Anglo-American male—as exactly the sort of public ambassador they wanted to have interacting with customers; he did not disappoint. Pierce became known for his effective service, late evenings, and active involvement in the bank's speakers bureau, where he spread the message of its merits to the community. Pleased as they were with his performance, however, Pierce proved a problem. He not only met the high expectations of Security Trust but also matched the employee profile of many other local companies, a fact that did not go unnoticed by his superiors. Although he remained with the company for many years, the alliance proved tenuous. Only two months after his hiring, Pierce complained of boredom. Shortly thereafter, the bank transferred him to its head office downtown. This initial promotion began a pattern of continually improving pay, positions, and perquisites in an effort by Security Trust to retain Pierce and other valued employees.[47]

As executives discovered, they could not compel commitment. They operated in a labor market where the talents and loyalties of "quality" employees were hard earned. This predicament led large firms to explore and experiment with ways to mold these men into the dedicated employees they so desperately desired.

FOUR

CREATING AN ESPRIT DE CORPS

> Getting employees to give their best can only be effected thru [*sic*] the adoption of a definite clear-cut policy which recognizes the fact that the welfare and happiness of the employees are inseparable from the success of the organization.
>
> —Joseph French Johnson, *Office Management*, 1919

On a Wednesday evening in 1910, nearly half of the Los Angeles Railway Company's 1,200 employees gathered to present president Henry Huntington a silver trophy cup. They gave the $300 gift as an expression of gratitude for recent salary increases. In making the presentation, employee George Prichard announced that the workforce owed Huntington a debt of thanks for his kind treatment. He promised that in addition to expressing appreciation through the cup, "we will show it in our work." Huntington responded by thanking them for their excellent efforts, noting, "everywhere I go, I am complimented for the effective service given by this company. My answer always is, 'it is because my employees are gentlemen.' I feel that you are and want to tell you I am proud of you."[1]

While little is known about the details or circumstances behind this familial, even patriarchal encounter, both the event and the positive press it generated must have pleased company officials. With each expansion in business operations, Huntington and other executives grew more reliant on their employees to assure corporate prosperity. They welcomed any signs of rigorous dedication and loyalty and this was an example at the positive extreme.

Los Angeles Railway employees would not regularly express such gratitude, however. Through most of the 1910s and 1920s, executives from Pacific Electric, the parent company of the LARC, felt little confidence in their employees' commitment. Postwar strikes were the most visible manifestation of employee "disloyalty," but another challenge proved similarly enduring and threatening, one leaders referred to as "the human challenge of business management." The imperatives of managerial bureaucracies required executives to recruit, motivate, and retain talented young men to serve the company's interest as their own. Yet while leaders went out of their way to make expectations clear, their employees often disappointed them. High rates of turnover and fear of worker apathy dominated managerial concern. Employee error and misbehavior sapped many managers' time and many firms' profits.

Despite the careful selection of employees, the occasional really troubled person slipped into the ranks. Perhaps the most horrific example Los Angeles executives ever faced occurred in December of 1927 when a First National Trust and Savings Bank employee kidnapped the twelve-year-old daughter of a bank official. William Hickman, a "nice-looking, well-dressed," nineteen-year-old from Kansas City kept Marion Parker captive for four days before collecting $1,500 in ransom. He then dumped her mutilated torso on a quiet street corner in the middle of Los Angeles. Oregon police captured Hickman seven days later. Prior to his execution by hanging at San Quentin, he confessed to the crime, reporting that he had kidnapped Marion "to defray his college expenses."[2]

Fortunately, most employees proved less troublesome, but cases of employee error occurred commonly. The Pacific Mail Steamship Company faced one such incident in June 1922 when a passenger, Mr. Wombly, wrote to complain that a Pacific Mail employee, Mr. Holzheiser, had overcharged him sixteen dollars for a Panama Canal cruise. The company immediately acknowledged receipt of the letter and promised to investigate the matter. In an interview on July 7, Holzheiser denied any wrongdoing, though his interviewer noted that he seemed "very evasive." Without a confession, however, Pacific Mail officials hesitated to accept Wombly's claim and instead began their own investigation of both Wombly and Holzheiser. They reviewed Holzheiser's account books and wrote letters to a contact in Wombly's hometown of Norfolk, Virginia. Officials again questioned Holzheiser on August 23 and noted that during this meeting he became "very angry and defensive at the insinuation, given his 'many years of service.'" But when Holzheiser failed to show up for a meeting the next day to discuss the problem further, the company suspended him until the matter could be resolved. Meanwhile, Pacific Mail received letters on August 30 and October 2 describing Wombly as a wealthy and respected member of the Norfolk business community who should be believed. At about the time this correspondence arrived, Pacific Mail discovered that Holzheiser had indeed made an error. On October 13, leaders apologized to Wombly and agreed to repay the disputed money. The following day, Pacific Mail began the process to cash in on a $3,000 bond they had taken out on the departed employee.[3]

The Holzheiser incident illustrates the trouble even small mistakes or transgressions could cause management. From their San Francisco offices, Pacific Mail leaders had to trust subordinates whom they had never met to conduct the company's business in offices far away. When Wombly's claim appeared, they were hesitant to blame their employee and investigated at length before accepting the charge against him. Like most corporations, they paid for bonds on employees who handled money, knowing that those workers could at any time cheat the firm and its customers. All in all, the incident took five months to resolve, expended time and money, and threatened to mar Pacific Mail's reputation.

Frustrated by pervasive personnel problems ranging from turnover to theft, Los Angeles's managerial ranks became keenly sensitive to employee dedication. They searched for ways to make white-collar environments conducive to the interests and needs of young white men. In small businesses, individual figures could personally set the tone of company operations. In large firms, however, leaders had to create more formal structures to achieve the same ends. Most companies engaged in a systematic effort to create company cultures that would bind employees to the enterprise. Such efforts were not new to this period. Industrial firms had encountered the need to build corporate cultures since their widespread formation following the Civil War. These businesses' localized nature and the usually strict demarcation between leaders and workers, however, defined rather narrowly their managerial needs.[4] In contrast, the large bureaucracies that began to appear in most economic sectors around the turn of the century presented more complex challenges. Executives now sought to direct business operations that encompassed thousands of employees spread over wide areas.[5] Directing these vast and diverse workforces was made even more complicated by these companies' reliance on educated, white male employees. The success of these firms often rested on the shoulders of men who had other job options and demanded much in return for their commitment.

The interaction between leaders and the distinctly "empowered" ranks of corporate employees resulted in the construction of complex organizational cultures that represented a settlement in which personnel received certain working conditions and benefits in return for good performance and long, dedicated service. This contract ultimately provided a broad range of rewards, including opportunities for social and recreational activities, promotions, and a generous array of fringe benefits.

At the foundation of corporate cultures lay a very basic interest in fostering good relations with employees—in creating a "company spirit." Such self-conscious efforts to create company cultures dominated corporate management in the early twentieth century. Most large Los Angeles firms engaged in formal campaigns to institutionalize an interest in employee morale and satisfaction and to foster an esprit de corps among their ranks. In a crude but commonplace example, Pacific Electric in 1922 asked its employees to make a New Year's resolution to dedicate themselves to the firm's prosperity. Management cajoled personnel to make the following pledge: "To be loyal each day to our company; to conserve its material and protect its well-being; to strive diligently to better its financial interests and thereby safeguard our own; to be more courteous and considerate of all our patrons and thereby earn their increased respect and good will." PE's New Year's pledge is strikingly similar to mottoes and creeds not only from other local firms but from companies nationwide. The PE resolution, for instance, paralleled a "code of principles" adopted by the Pennsylvania-based Sherwin-Williams Paint Company several years before.[6]

Sherwin-Williams Paint Company Code of Principles, 1919

- To win on our merits . . .
- To be broad and liberal, as well as aggressive, in our policy and methods . . . To take pride in our institution . . .
- To be loyal to the company and to each other . . .
- To foster good fellowship among ourselves, and to take pleasure as well as profit out of our work . . .
- To strive consciously for the improvement and advancement of the business and ourselves . . .
- To be considerate, polite, and courteous within and without the company . . .
- To be high-toned in everything and everywhere . . .
- To grow in knowledge and character as in size.

American corporations clearly read from a similar script; even as they built vast organizations, management teams from throughout the region and nation learned that their efforts to create administrative hierarchies and effective organizations would prove fruitless if they could not secure a dedicated cadre of talented persons to run their daily operations. Technological innovation in business, however, proved easier than personnel innovations. Leaders found their task to be as much a social as an economic process; companies needed to persuade a new generation of young, white men to accept an alternative career ethos and shifting occupational demands.

The Pacific Electric MAGAZINE

ISSUED MONTHLY BY THE EMPLOYES OF THE PACIFIC ELECTRIC RAILWAY

Vol. 6 LOS ANGELES, CAL., JANUARY 10, 1922 No. 8

OUR NEW YEAR'S RESOLUTION

The Pledge

To be loyal each day to Our Company.

To conserve it's material and protect it's well-being.

To strive diligently to better it's financial interests and there-by safe guard our own.

To be more courteous and considerate of all our patrons and there-by earn their increased respect and good-will.

To make the Golden Rule a fact and not merely a precept.

To be a Man, filling a Man's place in a man's game, and prove our's the best manned industry in Southern California.

Signed Every Employee

P.E. RY

1922

Pacific Electric's 1922 Employee New Year's Resolution. Reproduced from the *Pacific Electric Magazine* 6 (January 10, 1922), by permission of the Huntington Library, San Marino, California.

Control through Cooperation

Given the critical and problematic role employees played, it is not surprising that Los Angeles executives waxed eloquent about their subordinates' value. The link between satisfied personnel and corporate success became a self-conscious assertion in many firms' official communications. Pacific Mutual Life Insurance Company leaders, for example, often heralded the benefits of positive employee relations. A publication honoring the firm's sixtieth anniversary summarized its managerial philosophy by saying that the company's actions were prompted "not so much by charitable or kindly considerations as by the feeling that it is always good business for any corporation to take the best possible care of those who are engaged to prosecute their work." Union Oil publications also spoke frequently of the close relationship between employees and the firm: "The enviable position this company holds today is largely due to the thousands of men and women who make up the great Union Oil Company personnel . . . without the corps of loyal workers who have made the Union Oil Company, this development would have been impossible."[7]

Corporate leaders in Los Angeles and throughout the country frequently issued such broad platitudes as they sought to promote an esprit de corps. These efforts occurred amidst a national revolution in business administration. The creation and implementation of a "science of management" had dominated the early development of large firms in the latter half of the nineteenth century. Starting in the 1870s, most companies worked to introduce greater control and efficiency into sprawling operations by implementing "systematic management." This meant the articulation of clearly defined organizational structures with systematized chains of command built on direct reporting and standardized procedures. In these attempts to gain control over large enterprises and to maximize efficiency, leaders continually fine-tuned operating structures and procedures and presented these designs to employees as "natural" and "rational." In the words of one scholar, "systematic management theory suggested that managers acted in completely rational ways, instituting programs dictated by natural laws of efficiency rather than by some system of mutual responsibilities or struggles over power and status." By the early twentieth century, detailed organizational charts and routinized operations were basic elements of corporate life.[8]

Interest in systematic management practices peaked with Frederick Winslow Taylor's efficiency programs in the 1890s. This emphasis on structure and procedure, however, proved largely ineffective in dealing with many of the major dilemmas that plagued American business during the Progressive Era. Systematic management failed to recognize the human component of business structures. In the development of early industrial and white-collar firms, executives often viewed employees as interchangeable and easily replaceable, but early twentieth century business crises mandated a dramatic change in managerial thought. Labor unrest throughout blue-collar ranks, political pressures to regulate business, and high rates of white-collar turnover and alleged apathy pushed employers to engage their employees not as parts but as people. Corporate leaders began to pay heightened attention not only to the structural organization of their firms but also to issues of staff morale. In firms whose success rested on the dedication of salaried white-collar ranks, this importance became a defining element of corporate management. Contented employees were more likely to stay, feel loyal to the company's interests, work hard, and support big business's political agenda.[9]

Between the 1870s and the early twentieth century, corporate management evolved from an emphasis on systematic management to a concurrent preoccupation with personnel management. In this process, the treatment of employees became as important as the delineation of their tasks. This broad scope of corporate administration, which combined an attentiveness to structures, procedures, and employees, testifies to the multifaceted demands on corporate leaders. In the words of one historian, these complex managerial principles "provided a paradigm that seemed to offer hope of managing mushrooming industrialization, a more complicated workforce, the increasingly large business enterprise, and a rapidly expanding hierarchy of local, state, and national government."[10]

In executive offices throughout southern California, business leaders adopted aggressive personnel management programs rooted in the idea that having satisfied employees would result in heightened efficiency, productivity, and thus profits, and would help the firm combat not only business competition but government regulation and other public threats. Under the heading "Stimulation of Employees," a business education author summarized the philosophy: "Getting employees to give their best can only be effected thru the adoption of a definite clear-cut policy which recognizes the fact that the welfare and happiness of the employes are inseparable from the success of the organization."[11]

An increased attention to personnel management characterized the organizational cultures of most large southern California firms during the 1910s and 1920s. In the company's early years, for example, Southern California Edison's leaders set a tone of heavy-handed authority. Frank Balfour, district agent for the company's Pomona office, kept copies of official correspondence received during the years 1903–1908 that exhibited an authoritarian and disciplinary tone. In letter after letter, managers reprimanded district agents for failing to comply exactly with detailed operating procedures. Even executive attempts at goodwill appeared coldly calculated. In his 1907 Christmas letter, president John B. Miller wrote: "To District Agents: Mr. Miller desires to have everybody on the system know how thoroughly he appreciated the loyalty, industry, and integrity of the Edison Men and Women."[12] The detailed instructions employees followed in their daily work, the reprimands for errors, and the stiff formality in contact with distant corporate leaders all contributed to what managerial theorists of later years might term an environment inconducive to generating loyalty and enthusiasm.

By the 1920s, however, the tone of SCE's organizational culture stood in sharp contrast to its early formal and authoritarian style. Though continuing to enforce what employees may well have considered rigid operating rules, top management created a more cooperative spirit and a kinder tone in internal communications. Most employees now received several company newsletters that spoke of SCE as a "family," praised them for their diligent service, and requested their input regarding operations. SCE also sponsored numerous social events, rewarded long-term service, and provided a broad range of fringe benefits.[13]

The shifting managerial philosophies and practices in some local firms reflected a clear desire to counter union activity. Worker-management relations in the nineteenth century had grown increasingly antagonistic, but around the turn-of-the-century, even at the heyday of western labor-capital conflicts, many firms began using less confrontative tactics. Indeed, several Los Angeles railway companies altered their response to worker unrest. In 1893, E. P. Clark, vice president and general manager for the Los Angeles Consolidated Electric Railway, returned home from a business trip to find his employees rather "cold and distant." He learned that they had just received a letter, signed with his name, notifying them of a pay cut. Clark reportedly grew concerned about the possibility of a strike and called in one of the firm's "best" employees, whom management considered a key organizer. In a lengthy meeting, he either persuaded or coerced the employee, depending on one's vantage point, to disavow a strike, although officials refused to rescind the pay cut.[14]

Executives increasingly supplemented such direct and reactive responses to strike threats with efforts to entice employee loyalty through benefits and praise. Positive reinforcement had, of course, always been present in labor relations, but many firms increasingly emphasized such strategies during the era of welfare capitalism in the 1910s and 1920s. The Pacific Electric Railway Corporation, which bought out Los Angeles Consolidated, responded to labor unrest in the 1910s by opening a clubhouse and vacation resort for its employee "family." Company-sponsored picnics, dances, and other social events also began to pervade personnel relations.

Pacific Electric's heightened attention to morale reflected changing responses to union pressures among large companies nationwide. Like many other firms, PE adopted these more ameliorative measures in hopes of quelling labor strife. Yet, as noted above, this new managerial emphasis occurred within a widespread movement towards a more cooperative approach to labor unions. Although increased attention to cooperative personnel management must be recognized as part of a shifting response to worker unrest, the phenomenon was much broader. Efforts to nurture employee satisfaction and a company spirit increasingly occurred in most large blue- and white-collar firms during this period, in significant part as a response to the problems of employee motivation and retention.

In the 1910s and 1920s, Los Angeles business leaders grappled with convincing evidence that satisfied employees increased a firm's productivity and profits. American universities and business organizations began actively studying personnel management and making the case for cultivating employee-friendly cultures. A 1920 personnel administration textbook argued that "a fundamental axiom of personnel management is that progressive labor practices are not only right from a moral and ethical point of view but also more than pay for themselves in the form of increased profit." In 1927, a widely reported study of ten large industrial corporations showed that worker productivity increased when supervisors expressed interest in their work. This finding seemed to apply to all layers of corporate management.[15]

Large firms in every economic sector began to pay careful attention to these new managerial considerations. Even with numerous operating departments already in place, most big companies began to employ specialists in and create departments for various aspects of human and personnel relations. Vice presidents and other high-ranking administrators often headed such new departments. They became responsible for hiring procedures and retention programs, benefits, employee recreational and social activities, and other duties related to monitoring and nurturing morale. In 1928, SCE hired a full-time person to visit ill employees and help with their family's needs. The company also sent flowers to sick employees and hired a full-time chaplain to counsel them when personal crises struck.[16]

Thus, in sharp contrast to the confrontational images of many industrial leaders in the late nineteenth century, personified by Carnegie Steel's notorious manager Henry Frick, the image revealed by many corporate records from the 1910s and 1920s is of a heightened proclivity for cooperation and congeniality. Union Oil records suggest that employees throughout its ranks felt the presence of a personnel-oriented managerial philosophy. The personal correspondence of Union Oil president Lyman Stewart contains numerous letters exhorting managers and department heads to treat employees well and to nurture morale. In one instance, Stewart requested that if retrenchment became necessary, men with families should be given the most protection from cutbacks. He also admonished managers not to purchase expensive personal items when such cutbacks occurred, as it might suggest an insensitivity to employees' plight.

Stewart's interaction with subordinates suggests that he lived up to the ideals he preached. In 1915, when manager C. M. Smith sought to trim the operations of the struggling Union Oil subsidiary Western Gasoline Engine Corporation, Stewart criticized him for layoffs and wage cuts and urged him instead to improve cooperation and enthusiasm among employees as the key to profitable operations. In a series of letters to Smith, Stewart cautioned against worsening employee conditions and urged him to consult with his administrative personnel regularly, to listen to their ideas and concerns, and to address their needs and demands. Following Stewart's advice failed to make the subsidiary profitable, but Smith did gain Stewart's backing. After the subsidiary's dissolution later in 1915, Stewart wrote Union Oil's general manager asking if Smith could possibly be transferred to another position. He at least wanted to ensure that Smith would receive the one month's additional salary and two weeks of unused vacation pay entitled him under company policy, should relocation prove impossible. That same day, Stewart wrote Smith, expressing hope that a new position could be found so that his remaining career would be spent with Union Oil: "I cannot tell you [enough] of my high personal regard for you, and how it grieves me to have any changes made that will hurt you."[17] The interaction between Stewart and Smith suggests that, at least in some cases, Stewart stressed cooperation and kindness and that he worked to carry out these ideals in his own dealings.

The messages in Stewart's correspondence could be dismissed as the congenial philosophy of an individual leader except that even lower-level Union Oil employees believed superiors to be attentive their interests. Perry Chansler, who worked for Union Oil from 1920 to 1960, recalled, "I had a good time working for Union Oil and they were mighty nice to me." Warren Griffith, who worked in the company's transportation department from 1923 to 1958, said, "The management people in the Union Oil Company at the time I went to work were very close to the people in the field. The president of the company, a member of the Stewart family at that time, was probably more interested in the people out in the field than in any other branch, because that was where their income came from." When asked whether she ever felt concerned for the safety of her husband or father, both of whom worked in the production department in the 1920s, Emma Johnson Bennie replied, "No, we never worried about our husbands or our fathers, because the company seemed to take every precaution for the men."[18]

So were Union Oil leaders, managers, and supervisors particularly kind or altruistic? It is difficult to know, and beside the point. While some historians have focused on the personalities of individual leaders as key to understanding company cultures, to do so misses the context in which they and other executives acted. Whether personally kind or cruel, benevolent or vindictive, leaders needed to gain employees' loyalty and dedication. While business contexts and challenges varied among firms, a dedicated workforce could at least partially alleviate most problems. Union Oil, for instance, operated in a highly competitive industry where strikes, turnover, carelessness resulting in accidents, or less than full dedication on the part of employees could only further impair a firm already vulnerable to economic fluctuations. Stewart was wise to pay attention to employee morale. Men who had proven themselves able managers were valuable assets. Warren Griffith astutely equated management's interest in production employees with these employees' central role in the company's raison d'être. While it would have been difficult for company accountants to evaluate the financial result of congenial managerial practices, Union Oil's dramatic growth and profitability brought about no shift in these practices. The kind tone and concern about employees' perceptions and needs seen in Stewart's correspondence and the apparent regard management conveyed to its production workers *may* have reflected the individual personalities of company leaders, but it certainly showed pragmatic considerations, as well.

The existence of a broad spectrum of executive practices suggests that managerial philosophies ultimately emanated from real daily concerns. Union Oil records are not unique in revealing an attentiveness to employee relations at the individual level. In discussing operations and policies, managers invariably discussed specific employees. For instance, an effort to secure better wages for deserving personnel dominated correspondence between Pacific Mail officials. On January 29, 1920, auditor H. E. A. Railton wrote his superior Daulton Mann to ask that six men in his department be granted raises. Most requests were phrased in similar terms: "He has developed to be a very valuable man in freight accounts and deserves this increase"; "He is fast and accurate and should have the encouragement offered by this increase"; "He is a very careful and painstaking man and I think increase is due on account of increased responsibility." In all instances, Railton wrote that his staff performed commendably and *deserved* increased pay. Yet in some cases he also noted that an employee would likely leave if not granted the increase: "I feel that unless he is increased to this rating, we will lose him, which I think would be unfortunate."[19]

These promotion letters testify to the pragmatic considerations behind personnel relations. Comments about an employee becoming "very valuable," or requiring "the encouragement offered by this increase," reveal leaders' awareness of the need to nurture essential employees. This perspective aided in motivating employees generally but became critical when executives considered the possibility of their leaving. Managers knew well that the more talented and valuable an employee, the greater the likelihood that he would receive offers and inducements from other companies.

Pacific Mail officials keenly understood employees' role in the corporation's success. Thus, in addition to efforts to reward the dedication and gain the loyalty of specific individuals, Pacific Mail made broader and more pragmatic efforts to assure employee satisfaction. The company regularly sent inspectors to monitor conditions and attitudes at its various offices and took actions to rectify situations where they could improve morale. In evaluating the Manila office, for example, an inspector wrote: "I found that Mr. Guernesy was very well liked and from what I could see has the confidence and good will of our patrons. The only thing [is,] he seems to be lacking in pep. I am convinced that this is due to the fact that he was through a pretty hard grind when he first took over the agency. It has been so long since he has had a vacation and he should certainly have one as he will be a much better man for the company when he returns." In his report on the company's Japanese offices, the inspector noted the unusually high local cost of living and suggested a pay raise to boost morale. He argued that such would not "encourage extravagance" but would simply put personnel "in a contented frame of mind and thereby keep the morale of our foreign organization up."[20]

Advocates of personnel management would likely have applauded Pacific Mail's efforts. The company willingly incurred costs to monitor workplace conditions and workforce satisfaction, even when those reviews sometimes resulted in calls for greater expenditures on salaries and other matters. Pacific Mail generally accepted personnel management's fundamental axiom that high employee satisfaction would ultimately increase company profits. Those singled out for praise and raises no doubt appreciated the personal attention. In a bureaucratic setting, a sense that one's superiors were aware and appreciative of one's efforts could be a powerful incentive to work hard and feel loyal.

If some concern for morale and satisfaction appeared on all levels of corporate bureaucracies, it usually peaked for employees at the highest rungs. Leaders not only found it imperative to guard the interests of the most valuable personnel but, because of their more similar class and social position, the executives could more easily develop private friendships with these employees. During the 1910s, vice president Jackson Graves of the Farmers and Merchants National Bank in Los Angeles corresponded frequently with the bank's San Francisco–based president, I. W. Hellman. Their letters contained both business and personal news and reflected pragmatic and friendly considerations. In August 1916, for example, upon hearing that construction activity near his office was bothering Graves, Hellman wrote: "[I] am sorry to hear that your hearing has been affected by the noise in the bank. If you feel that it will be for your good to take a vacation, I hope you will do so, but please do not be small about the matter of salary. We can certainly afford to allow a man whose services have been as valuable to the Farmers & Merchants National Bank of Los Angeles as yours have been to take a vacation of a month without talking about cutting off a month's pay." Graves did take a vacation, and after returning in October, Hellman wrote: "I am pleased to learn of the improvement in your hearing and the fine condition of your general health." He closed with the words, "take care of yourself—good people are scarce and far between."[21] So were Hellman and Graves friends or business colleagues? Probably both, and if so, the dual relationship benefited each personally and professionally.

In comparison to his relationship with Hellman, Graves's interactions with subordinates suggests pragmatism. His own descriptions of these encounters reveal a careful attention to assuring subordinates' goodwill in order to keep bank operations running smoothly. For example, he wrote Hellman in October 1914: "You know we have built a building for the Farmers and Merchants National Bank of Redondo. They have made it a little more elaborate than I would have done it, but I hate to be the 'bad man' and quarrel with them all the time, and the bank has been quite a success since its organization."[22]

Securing employee commitment could pay high dividends.[23] Following his promotion to general manager in 1928, SCE executive George Ward received effusive congratulatory letters from employees who had developed loyalties to Ward and the firm. One district manager wrote: "From the bottom of my heart I congratulate you and all I can say is to pledge you a continuance of my loyalty and hearty support of your administration, thereby in small measure repaying the many acts of kindness that the company has conferred on me." Employees, of course, uniformly cherished few leaders, but those who climbed to upper ranks often did so because they showed some ability to manage human resources effectively. Ward's ability to connect personally with colleagues and employees seems to have aided his rise to SCE's leadership ranks. The enormous outpouring of fond remembrances Ward's wife received after his death in 1933 provide another hint of his popularity, and it is interesting to note that all of the pallbearers at his funeral were junior SCE executives.[24]

These examples are not meant to suggest that every firm always acted in its employees' best interests, or that all bosses fought for better pay and conditions for their subordinates, or even that all leaders necessarily wanted to be or were liked. To the contrary, there existed a flip side to managerial concern of which employees were well aware. Employees knew that managerial concern came at a price. In a bureaucratic hierarchy, the potential for reprimand loomed constantly. One report, which also illustrates the corporate leaders' penchant for stereotyping, noted that a Mr. Harrell was "not possibly up on his toes" for he was of the "slow, easy-going Southern type."[25] Employees likely sensed that bosses only expressed concern and offered personal attention in return for dedicated service.

Alongside the ever-present potential for authoritarian oversight in a boss-employee relationship, successful leaders nurtured dedication and engendered loyalty by looking out for those who contributed to company success. The people who staffed corporate bureaucracies needed to "get along" for the firm to succeed. These basic managerial imperatives took on heightened importance as firms grew, and would ultimately require new mechanisms for their fulfillment.

Constructing Community

As large companies came to employ multiple tiers of salaried managers who directed the activities of thousands, corporations could not rely solely on the efforts of individual supervisors to address personnel issues. Attendees at a California Bankers Association meeting in 1908 heard that "it is the duty of an officer, or officers if the institution be a large one, to keep in close touch with the employees and encourage them in their work."[26] Directors of Los Angeles's largest banks only a few years later would have found such advice impractical, given their thousands of employees spread out over many distant offices.

How then to cultivate loyalty on a companywide scale? While always recognizing the importance of nurturing individual employees when possible, most firms began to communicate managerial concern and a company ethos through formalized networks. The early development of American big business had depended on devising internal communications systems through which management could circulate instructions about company operations. Extensive and formal written communication systems gradually replaced personal and primarily oral management networks. In the words of one historian, "quill pens and bound volumes gave way to typewriters, stencil duplicators, and vertical files that aided in creating, copying, storing, and retrieving documents."[27]

The development of elaborate communication networks made possible the implementation of systematic management. Yet while promoting "operating efficiency," these depersonalized and routinized information procedures and pathways amplified the cold and automated feel of bureaucratic employment that personnel management would later arise to combat. Ironically, personnel experts responded by implementing an additional layer of companywide communication networks, but these new initiatives focused on cultivating an esprit de corps. Specifically, big business turned to the creation of company magazines as part of an effort to create corporate cultures. In-house newsletters of various sorts had been around since the earliest days of American big business, but the era of personnel management witnessed much larger and more carefully coordinated efforts. Business leaders seized on companywide magazines, for these publications provided a vehicle with which to combat depersonalization and to humanize the workplace. Management theorists enthusiastically recommended them as "an inspirational means of welding employees into a homogeneous, enthusiastic whole" and "a splendid method of keeping alive the ideals and spirit of the organization as well as making known the activities and achievements of the office workers."[28]

By 1925, at least 539 American firms published some sort of in-house magazine or newspaper. In most companies, a special staff produced a monthly magazine comparable in printing quality to popular journals. While magazines diverged in tone, content, and emphasis based on the managerial needs and operating contexts of individual firms, most shared certain general themes. First, management used them as forums to educate employees about company operations. In some cases, smooth functioning required the dissemination of such information; in other cases, leaders simply wanted personnel to view their individual efforts as part of an important larger enterprise. Second, company magazines became a venue through which executives praised employees. Leaders hoped both to motivate personnel and to cast themselves as supportive and appreciative of workers' efforts. Third, most magazines featured stories and anecdotes about personnel in an effort to give the firm a human face, to make it appear a collection of interesting, caring people rather than a faceless bureaucracy. Fourth, magazines became forums for announcements about and reporting of company social and recreational activities—a sort of companywide bulletin board. Finally, businesses used magazines to try to set a tone for the company's internal culture. Most portrayed the firm as a family, though companies used the family metaphor in imprecise and often differing ways.[29]

In essence, company magazines provided a monthly staff meeting held to accomplish a broad array of tasks that a small business owner could perform in a simple meeting. Leaders carefully orchestrated these propaganda organs, a fact not lost on employees; yet they were more important to the construction of company cultures than historians have often recognized. While leaders sought to use magazines to shape corporate life on their own terms, the resulting format and content were ultimately responses to employee challenges. Large firms willingly spent considerable sums on in-house magazines in hope of offsetting the larger expense of a workforce not adequately trained, motivated, or loyal and to create an esprit de corps in the face of threatened union activity, high turnover, losses stemming from employee apathy, and external public and competitive pressures.

In the inaugural issue of Pacific Electric's company magazine, top executives suggested that the magazine would bring a sense of family into the company's sprawling operations: "We cannot accomplish these views by the good family way of sitting down at dinner together and talking things over. But we can make a family round table out of this magazine, and in spirit get together once a month." Such rhetoric may sound naive, but these words represented officials' genuine efforts to translate their personal understanding of employee management into the context of a large firm's operations. Some historians have suggested perceptively that "the early leaders of American business believed that strong culture brought success," and that "these builders saw their role as creating an environment—in effect, a culture—in their companies." In the minds of most leaders, culture building had significant consequences for company success. Indeed, one historian has suggested that executives' use of simple family images and metaphors was aimed at accomplishing big things, such as stimulating sales, allying public fears of big business, and improving labor relations.[30]

Most major Los Angeles corporations introduced employee magazines during the early decades of the century. Pacific Mutual issued the original *Pacific Mutual News* in 1901. Southern California Edison started *Edison Current Topics* in 1912. Pacific Electric began publication of the *Pacific Electric Magazine* in 1916, and Union Oil created the *Union Oil Bulletin* in 1921. Many local banks published newsletters and magazines by the 1910s, including *The*

Pacific Southwest and *News of the Los Angeles First National. The Security-First News Bulletin* appeared in 1928 following the merger of several local institutions.

A vast international firm with a diverse workforce, Union Oil produced one of the more impressive company magazines. The *Union Oil Bulletin* initially appeared in 1921 as a comptroller's department bulletin, but senior executives were so delighted with the publication that, within eight months, they called for its distribution to all employees. For officials managing a workforce of more than 10,000, whose ranks included large numbers of laborers, young women, professional engineers and geologists, and middle-class men of all ages in salaried positions, the magazine seemed an ideal way of communicating a company spirit. According to Union's vice president: "We desire through this monthly intimacy to develop even closer cooperation and the maximum esprit de corps, to instill throughout the whole of the company's service the requisite enthusiasm, invite friendly rivalry, and fundamentally to stimulate general industrial morale."[31]

Union Oil brass claimed that employees loved the publication. Its executive vice president wrote: "The favorable reception accorded to it by employees and the enthusiasm shown generally indicates that it is filling a long-felt want." Union Oil officials must have believed the publication achieved at least some of its goals, for its continued production evidenced a level of approval. Published monthly, the *Bulletin* averaged more than twenty pages on high-quality paper and had glossy color covers and many photos. One study estimated that publishing a magazine for a workforce the size of Union Oil's, not including the salaries of magazine staff or distribution costs, would have cost over $20,000 a year, a tiny fraction of gross revenues, but not a throw-away expense.[32]

To accommodate its diverse readership, each segment of which presented unique challenges and demands, the *Union Oil Bulletin* became an expansive journal, wide-ranging in scope and topics. Its editors sought to create an aesthetically pleasing and interesting publication—a "good read" in which employees might take pride. The magazine's covers featured fold-out oil paintings of picturesque scenes and events. Most issues contained human interest, adventure, and nature stories—all with some link to the company. In its May and June 1925 issues, for instance, the *Bulletin* ran an extensive feature on the heroic life of Major Frederick Burnham, a decorated British army officer then in the employ of Union Oil. The story, in typical fashion, offered an interesting tale written like a piece that might appear in the *Atlantic Monthly* or *Harper's* but with a Union Oil connection. The *Bulletin* also featured articles on vacation spots and travel guides to these locations, ostensibly part of the company's general effort to promote car travel, which would of course boost the sale of petroleum.[33] Finally, the back page of every issue featured a column entitled "Refined and Crude" that offered amusing anecdotes, jokes, and quotes.

Although the *Union Oil Bulletin* conveyed the image of a general interest magazine, most features in the publication served some obvious company goal. Articles on the petroleum business appeared frequently, as part of an effort to foster a professional identity among the workforce and a sense that they were part of a critically important industry and company.[34] The *Bulletin* occasionally included features on other companies or industries related to Union Oil operations or the petroleum industry, probably to encourage consumption of products from firms that had a stake in petroleum and as a goodwill gesture to potential customers.[35] Technical information pieces designed to address specific operating issues often appeared, as did a continual series of editorials on the importance of thrift, hard work, and loyalty.[36]

Whatever its more practical features, at the *Bulletin's* heart—at the center of every company magazine—lay news and information about employees. Even in a company as large as Union Oil, individual staff members became the focal point of corporate communications. In the magazine's early issues, laudatory stories showcased company executives, yet editors increasingly highlighted those further down the ladder. From executives to the lowest-paid wage earners, members of Union Oil's workforce surfaced in varying ways throughout the magazine.[37] Employee news dominated a column entitled "News of the Month," which began to appear in late 1922. Occupying two or more pages, the section discussed happenings in the lives of individuals and departments. Every issue included news of promotions, awards, and other special achievements, as well as announcements about company social and recreational activities. In one issue, for example, reporters covered a banquet at the company's Vancouver, British Columbia, refinery, announced a professional award won by a company sales manager, touted the head office's basketball team, and told of a district office employee who had been elected to a veteran's organization post. In 1927, the magazine additionally began a feature called "Roll of Honor," which listed the names of men and women receiving length of service awards for ten or more years with the firm. Photos and biographies appeared of those having served the longest periods of time.[38]

Carefully interspersed throughout employee and department news and information were general editorials praising the efforts of all. In a typical comment, the company's executive committee chairman lauded: "The splendid spirit of cooperation and loyalty displayed by the personnel of our company has made a deep impression upon me." He then promised, "The management will not fail to recognize those virtues, and rewards will surely be evidenced to those who persist and follow through."[39] Nearly every issue of the *Union Oil Bulletin* contained glowing messages praising personnel. Equating employee satisfaction with performance, top leadership affirmed exceptional staff in ways they hoped would nurture good feelings toward the company.

Production costs for the *Union Oil Bulletin* make one wonder: Did employees view the firm more fondly because of the publication? Did they act with heightened dedication and loyalty after reading it? Did they read it at all? From management's perspective—did it work? One could easily respond with cynicism. The magazine was, to be sure, managerial propaganda. In the first issue, an editorial asked employees to send in suggestions and to "freely express their opinions and criticisms," but complaints or suggestions never appeared and in fact rarely emerged in any company magazine. Most employees recognized magazines as managerial proclamations and approached them with skepticism. In the words of a 1919 management text, "Employees are prone to judge with considerable shrewdness the motives underlying any move, and no insincere plan can have any lasting effect."[40] Indeed, if a company paid employees poorly and created unpleasant working conditions, no number of laudatory editorials would generate loyalty and dedication. A company magazine could not easily counter an individual's discontent or assuage grievances about pay, treatment, or policies.

Yet the place of magazines in company life and employees' responses to them were more complex than a cynical reading suggests. While personnel at all ranks read the pieces critically, sensitive to the desired intent of each article, they were also human beings with needs for affirmation, identity, and community. Thus, a given staff member might roll his or her eyes or even ignore a piece cataloging the achievements of the company president, yet might feel considerable pride if he or she was the subject of such an article. An employee might pass over if not sneer at the editorial urging personnel to work harder but eagerly search out coverage of his or her department's victory in the city baseball league or look to see if he or she made it into any of the photos. Workers might curse as lies the comptroller's statement listing reasons for reduced profit-sharing bonuses but note with interest an article talking about the company's dominance of the western oil business and feel a sense of pride in its achievement. To the extent that these magazines recognized the important place of employees in the enterprise, they achieved a level of popularity. To the extent that magazines rooted a firm's success in its workforce—and to the extent that leaders acknowledged that debt through material measures—employees took pride in the company's achievement.

Leaders at Union Oil and the hundreds of other large firms with major company publications did not view their magazines as *the* solution to personnel problems, but they did consider them an important component of the hoped-for cure. At best, they helped create an esprit de corps in a large bureaucracy. Their appearance did not result in an end to strikes, high turnover rates, or poor on-the-job performances, but personnel did often greet their issuance with interest. In a 1925 National Industrial Conference Board report, one company magazine editor said: "The magazine has proved very acceptable to our employees and we are all looking for it on the day of issue. It has proved itself a splendid means for uniting the activities of the various departments and we would think a long time before discontinuing it." More realistically, magazines seemed a logical *part* of the solution to personnel problems and in times of prosperity appeared to be a reasonable expense. Another editor put it this way: "As to concrete evidences of the fact that an employee magazine is a positive force in building morale, it is almost impossible to point to any particular accomplishment and truthfully say, 'the magazine did that.' But we have a splendid spirit of cooperation in our plants, and even though our people are scattered in six different sates, they have the 'family' spirit. Naturally our magazine gets credit for part of that accomplishment."[41]

The crafting and context of company magazines became the critical issues in their effectiveness. Because different firms had diverse philosophies and operational natures and faced specific challenges, their magazines portrayed diverse agendas and interests. Yet, while company magazines reflected the widely varying nature of corporate operations, a general interest in humanizing the firm and fostering an esprit de corps became a common theme. All publications that became well-received elements of corporate cultures ultimately recognized employees as the essence of company life and success. Banks, for instance, encompassed a workforce and structure dramatically different from Union Oil, yet their magazines were often remarkably similar. When several mergers created the Security-First National Bank in 1928, a number of individual newsletters merged into the *Security-First News Bulletin*, a semimonthly publication of at least twelve pages. Its structure paralleled the *Union Oil Bulletin* in offering a blend of motivational editorials, news about company operations, and employee features designed to promote loyalty and dedication. A typical editorial read: "This bank, of course, is our own. Every one of us from messenger to director has every reason to be proud of his connection with it."[42] Southern California Edison's company magazine, *Edison Current Topics*, which began publication in 1912, similarly featured photos and biographies of company leaders, articles about employees receiving promotions, editorials praising personnel, technical articles about corporate operations, and notes on office social and recreational activities.

Most issues also featured a section entitled "Heard over the Highline" that printed news about births, marriages, and other personal events of interest.

Pacific Mutual's company magazine reflected well how most companies sought to balance managerial messages with employee news and features. From its beginning in 1901, the *Pacific Mutual News* aimed primarily to motivate employees' sales efforts. Though also intended for its office staff, discussion of agents' sales activities dominated the magazine. The bulk of its pages featured articles urging employees to work harder and rankings of the most productive agents and offices, presumably in an effort to reward leading agents and motivate others through the spirit of competition.

In their frequent use of the phrase "Pacific Mutual family," leaders articulated a very specific message. The creation of a family spirit, and the very metaphor of family, were important to Pacific Mutual's leaders, though in a different way than at Pacific Electric. At Pacific Mutual, *family* implied a close tie between company and employees with the goal of sustained employment. Insurance companies considered employee loyalty crucial, for if an agents abandoned the firm they often took their customers along. The firm relied on distant agents to nurture a close relationship with the local community, meaning that agents were not easily replaced. Thus, alongside the magazine's competitive tint, editors also emphasized the pleasures of an association with the "Pacific Mutual family." In one of the crudest spirit-building efforts, Pacific Mutual in 1912 introduced a company song (sung to the tune of "Marching through Georgia") and urged employees to sing it whenever they "gathered together:"

Hurrah! Hurrah! We sing the Company.
Hurrah! Hurrah! We fear no rivalry.
Hand in hand united we have spread from sea to sea
O'er all the land from California.[43]

Yet, amidst the incessant and at times rather blunt emphasis on sales, the *Pacific Mutual News*, over time, became increasingly devoted to employee features. In 1921, the editors added a column entitled "Just Among Ourselves," after agents reportedly griped that the magazine had become too focused on "shoptalk." According to the editors, agents requested that the journal include more personal information about company employees and activities. While the new column, which featured staff anecdotes and news blurbs, responded specifically to this request, the magazine in general took on a softer and folksier tone. In the issue announcing the new direction, the president wrote: "I like the idea of the Pacific Mutual as a family where all the agents, officers and employees are personally acquainted and feel free to talk."[44] *Pacific Mutual News* subsequently began to feature more photos, biographies, and intimate information about company leaders and employees. In 1927, for example, the magazine began to publish photographs of employees' children. Even at Pacific Mutual, whose corporate culture stressed individualism and competition among employees, nurturing an esprit de corps became a managerial means to achieve individual effort. Employees wanted corporate communications that affirmed their value to the company and recognized their crucial role in its operations.

As with Pacific Mutual, Pacific Electric's magazine made the transition from an abrasive managerial stick to an employee-oriented carrot in the company's culture; it began to articulate employee interests and affirm their valuable roles. The company founded the magazine in the midst of labor tensions during World War I and initially wielded the publication as a paternalistic megaphone in conflicts over unions, wages, and other issues. By the 1920s, however, the magazine broadened its scope, toned down its paternalism, and focused more on simply covering employee life. Following the shift, the publication grew in size and popularity, despite PE's retrenchment.

The *Pacific Electric Magazine* first appeared in June 1916, under the banner, "Our Family Round Table." PE's president proclaimed, "The employees of the Pacific Electric are one large family with many ties and many common interests."[45] Family metaphors appeared frequently in PE communications. In dealing with a large number of workers, who from management's perspective often seemed careless, unruly, and insubordinate, PE leaders sought to create a company culture based on hierarchy and authority. When they used the metaphor of "family," they understood employees to be the children and themselves the parents. Their understanding of "family values" translated into employee deference and obedience. The use of family terminology correspondingly flourished during periods of labor tension. In describing a strike in 1919, executives described the event as a time when many family members left "home," but that "alas, as with the youth leaving home, many will find that it was a siren call that will in the end leave them impoverished."[46]

While initial editions of the *Pacific Electric Magazine* emphasized practical concerns, it quickly became focused on anti-union themes. By the summer of 1918, when PE trainmen struck, the *Pacific Electric Magazine* had become a bully pulpit for leaders.[47] Yet while the magazine became a calculated anti-union tool in the years following the war, it went on to transcend its initial use and to occupy a more acceptable and less contentious spot in the company's culture. The threat of union activity at PE receded in the early 1920s. That, along with increasing financial instability, might presumably have led to the publication's dissolution; if combating unions became less of an issue, and retrenchment instead dominated management, an expensive employee magazine might seem an unjustifiable cost. Nevertheless throughout the 1920s the magazine grew in size and scope.

The *Pacific Electric Magazine* thrived after the war, for it emerged as a chronicle of employees' lives and activities. By the early 1920s, most issues featured sections on various departments, with news and personal happenings of their employees. Editors noted some business activities, but most coverage went to reporting vacations taken, cars purchased, or other news items. In April 1922, for instance, members of the accounting department read reports about five of their colleagues. Among the highlights: "M. Clement Smith of the Disbursements Bureau is the father of a new nine pound baby son, and is wearing a perpetual smile these days." Another hinted at an inside departmental joke: "R. L. Griffith has departed for San Francisco, presumably for a week's vacation, but it is rumored that he is hunting a housekeeper, one who is not afraid to iron. He lays special stress on the ironing, and we are wondering if he is contemplating the opening of a laundry."[48] Pictures and news of other employee activities appeared throughout the rest of this and other issues. By 1926, each issue featured a sports section presenting information about company athletic teams and tournaments, a page entitled "Pacific Electric Club Affairs" that featured news and information about the increasingly popular club's activities, and a section called "Listening In Along The Lines," which comprised columns of news and information about employees from every department.

Company magazines could not counter grievances about material aspects of corporate employment, but if employees generally liked their jobs, magazines that fostered a sense of community, as PE's certainly attempted to do, could be effective in helping to generate loyalty. The magazine's persistence and growth suggests that employees did value the publication, or at least that leaders thought it exerted a positive impact on dedication and loyalty. Even amid all of its financial problems, which only worsened during the Depression, the *Pacific Electric Magazine* appeared, and it continued to be published without interruption until the company's dissolution in 1953.

While some efforts to humanize the firm surfaced in most company publications, few tried more emphatically than the *Security-First News Bulletin.* The publication concentrated more than most on employee news and information, presented as if employees were all close friends, desiring news about others. In the May 1929 issue, the magazine told of bank president Joseph F. Sartori's upcoming family vacation to Europe and discussed the family's tradition of an annual European vacation. Throughout the summer, the magazine charted the course of his trip with updates about his location and activities.[49] Although the bank's staff may well have laughed at this self-promotion or resented the display of wealth, next to coverage of the president they found similar articles on rank and file employees. Readers learned of one employee whose daughter had died, another whose mother was ill, and another who was on a business trip. Articles also appeared noting how and where personnel of all ranks intended to spend their summer vacations. The publication's particularly personal feel likely reflected the firm's smaller organization and more homogeneous workforce. Both characteristics allowed executives to foster an intimate esprit de corps and to produce a magazine that could be selectively read for news and photos of friends and coworkers. Employees likely appreciated the publication, for, while it appeared only months before the onset of the Depression, it remained in print and grew steadily in size and quality throughout the firm's history, ending only in 1989, when the Bank of America acquired Security Pacific National Bank.

Southern California Edison's company magazines differed from those of many other local firms in two ways. First, the firm's earliest major magazine, *Edison Current Topics,* focused on political issues. *Topics* appeared in 1912, one year after passage of the California Public Utilities Act of 1911. The 1911 Act sanctioned SCE's operating monopoly, and the magazine's subsequent appearance reflected the company leaders' newly invigorated charge to manage the vast operation effectively. Because of the critical relationship between state politics and company operations, *Topics* primarily became a political publication. Editorials and articles about public utility matters appeared prominently throughout the magazine. *Topics* aimed to inspire concrete actions by employees on the firm's behalf in the political realm.

SCE's use of company magazines also came to reflect its decentralized administration. Publication of *Topics* ceased abruptly in 1920 and leaders blamed a financial squeeze resulting from construction of a major hydroelectric facility. In fact, however, the firm at the time enjoyed relatively stable finances and became quite prosperous later in the decade, yet no company-wide employee magazine again appeared until the 1940s. Did SCE leaders no longer feel the need to create a company spirit throughout their ranks? Or did they believe a company magazine would not effectively achieve that goal? Evidence suggests they were as attentive to the need to nurture a company culture as their peers in other Los Angeles firms and appreciated the potential value of magazines and newsletters. But SCE's corporate culture paralleled its localized management, centered on a decentralized administrative structure. Because the company essentially comprised many smaller firms taken over through mergers or acquisitions, leaders felt the need to maintain an air of a community firm, in order to stave off municipal ownership. The firm thus allowed its local departments and operating units to act with considerable autonomy. Most of these units assumed responsibility for handling operating issues, and they started newsletters and other communications to deal with personnel matters themselves. Efforts to build corporate culture at SCE subsequently shifted to a local level. By the 1920s, SCE employees received not one companywide magazine but a variety of newspapers and magazines from company clubs, operating departments, and division offices.[50]

Beyond the Company Magazine

At their October 1931 meeting, Southern California Edison's board of directors appointed George C. Ward as new company president and Harry J. Bauer as new board chair. Upon assuming SCE's corporate reins, both figures desired an opportunity to share with employees their plans and aspirations. But directly addressing a nearly 10,000-person workforce spread throughout southern and central California posed a difficult challenge. Ward and Bauer could have simply crafted a letter to be distributed to employees, as previous executives had done, but they instead drew on new technologies to show a "human touch." On October 26, Ward and Bauer spoke to all employees throughout SCE's 55,000-square-mile territory over the company's private telephone system. Ward and Bauer spoke from an office in the firm's downtown headquarters. The company's radiotelephone network then carried the message to a central station in Alhambra which transmitted it to dozens of offices, shops, and yards. SCE's managers were to have employees assembled around speakers at every site to hear their new leaders' greetings. Company officials expressed tremendous excitement about the radio address. Advanced technology, they believed, would allow them to run a great corporation as a smaller, close-knit firm. Such efforts underscored their desire that SCE act as a firm sensitive to its employees' and customers' interests.[51]

SCE's 1931 radio address occurred in the wake of repeated attempts by its leaders and their peers throughout southern California and the nation to find ways to humanize vast corporate operations. The widespread emergence of large firms in the early twentieth century occurred in a society where many people in business esteemed organization, efficiency, and rational planning as national values. The appearance and diffusion of "Taylorism," the flourishing of the social sciences within academia, the professionalization of many occupations, and the interest in rational planning and reform to solve the nation's social and political ills typified the period's organizational and rationalistic dilemmas. The creation of large, managerial corporations drew heavily on those mindsets, as business leaders worked to develop systems and structures to carry out and oversee the production, marketing, and distribution of products and services on an ever-widening scale. In this context, corporate formation progressed as a "rational" and technological process, as if corporate leaders were building mechanical devices.

As business leaders quickly learned, however, they were not building or operating machines, they were directing workforces composed of thousands of human beings. Ultimately, leaders recognized the need for systematic efforts to nurture loyalty and enthusiasm; as a result, they began to construct company cultures designed to humanize and harmonize employee relations. Most firms turned to some sort of in-house company magazine as the most systematic way to create an esprit de corps. While leaders used company magazines as propaganda tools through which to advocate their ideals for good employees, the employees themselves influenced their contents. In many firms they came to be something like a company bulletin board where personnel shared news and information. Magazines became popular and desired elements of corporate employment because they recognized that a large firm ultimately represented thousands of people. In the pages of a company magazine, a firm's human faces came to light.

While employers viewed company magazines as comparatively inexpensive means of heightening employee morale, any hopes that this mechanism would ensure the stable, dedicated workforce they desired were quickly dashed. Company magazines and kindly managerial strategies instead provided merely the outer layer in large Los Angeles firms' employer-employee relations. From the outset most companies continually confronted the need to deal with employees' bottom line: compensation. Many young white men wanted not just secure but lavish futures. Most desired to consume and to accumulate. They continually asked: What would be the material rewards of corporate employment? What would it mean to work for another company instead of this one?

FIVE

PROFIT AND SECURITY

During the past few years a new type of business man has come prominently into being. . . . He is to all intents a merchant, without the merchant's worries.

—*Sunset* magazine, 1919

In May 1921, after completing coursework in a local business school, nineteen-year-old Joseph Benjamin took a position as clerk with the Southern Pacific Railroad. He worked for SP for over a year but quit in the summer of 1922 when the company reduced his pay. The Pacific Mail Steamship Company immediately hired Benjamin as an accounting clerk with a starting salary of $100 a month. Six months later, a promotion earned him a $25-per-month raise. In August of 1923, Benjamin's department head wrote to his superior requesting for him another $25 raise. His letter commended Benjamin's excellent performance and noted that he had accomplished more than his predecessor (who had been promoted). Benjamin's boss clinched the appeal by lauding the young clerk's loyalty. He told of how Benjamin had just turned down an offer of $150 from another firm because he preferred to "take his chances of promotion with this company rather than leave."[1]

Benjamin and his superiors, like all Los Angeles employees and executives, wrestled with what constituted fair and reasonable payment for services. A combination of personal, institutional, social, and cultural factors shaped their perspectives. Most young men, of course, wanted jobs that paid well, and Benjamin's decision to leave Southern Pacific following a pay reduction reminded its managers of this fact. Yet his decision to remain with Pacific Mail, even in the face of a better offer, suggests that factors other than income also shaped his career plans. Like most of his peers, Benjamin struggled with competing desires for maximum income, job security, opportunities for promotion, and a pleasant working environment. In this instance, he declined an immediate salary increase because he believed that Pacific Mail would ultimately prove a better place of employment. Individual Americans like Joseph Benjamin could not mold corporate capitalism to their personal interests, but they could pursue the best opportunities possible among individual firms.

Pacific Mail's response to Benjamin's situation reveals much about managerial strategies. Company leaders could have read this incident as evidence that he would remain with the firm despite a smaller salary. To the contrary, however, they immediately increased his salary to match the offer he had turned down. They most likely did so with ambivalence, given the constant pressures to hold the line on company expenses, but they knew the move would help to secure the loyalty of a worthy employee.

Confronted with numerous managerial dilemmas, most Los Angeles executives recognized that basic material incentives would be necessary to cultivate dedicated corporate ranks. Faced with poaching by rival firms, defection of skilled white-collar workers, new rounds of training costs, the uncertainty of new hires, and their self-imposed limits on what gender and ethnicity they would consider for salaried positions, southern California executives recognized alternative compensatory strategies as an obvious route by which to recruit loyal employees and assure corporate stability. Musing on the delicate subject of employee remuneration in 1912, a Southern California Edison executive likened employees to machinery that would "work better if properly lubricated," and described "an equitable reward for service" as the best kind of lubricant.[2] While corporate executives recognized that an "equitable reward" might be the most effective way to recruit and retain talented men (most men, after all, worked to secure a living) they were uncertain how to define this reward. Leaders wanted to cultivate the highest dedication at the lowest price, but they did not know what that price would be. Employees wanted the maximum reward for their efforts with the fewest strings attached but had to make tough decisions about how vigorously they were willing to pursue their desired payment. Employees, of course, generally saw high salaries as the compensation of choice, but leaders felt this to be a one-sided proposition: it required steady company outlays without any mechanism to assure the desired results. Most firms instead kept wages and salaries low when possible, but raised them if necessary, and continually experimented with various additional compensation programs that could be tied to performance, length of service, or other issues.

Motivated by progressive-appearing self-interest, Los Angeles's corporate leadership experimented with a variety of schemes as they negotiated with workers the rewards of service.[3] By the late 1920s, young men who accepted white-collar posts in major firms could expect modest entry-level salaries that would rise over time as well as a variety of nonsalary bonuses or benefits, including profit-sharing, employee stock ownership, health and life insurance plans, and other perquisites. Benefits like these, which by that time seemed to leaders logical and reasonable compensatory strategies, had been arrived at only through a process of trial and error and only in the presence of a competitive labor market in which rival firms continually honed their programs. While both executives and employees understood who gained and lost from high salaries, they each felt uncertain and tried to determine who benefited the most from what. Interactions over the rewards for service became a fundamental part of the efforts to construct corporate cultures. The matter of compensation required leaders to assess what they needed to give in order to stabilize their company's operations and pressed employees to consider what they expected in return for their long-term commitment.

In most major Los Angeles firms, business officials responded to their personnel challenges by rolling the dice and gambling that the costs of significant compensation initiatives would assure maximum profitability over the long term.[4] This image seems far removed from our traditional understanding of local labor relations. Owners and workers clashed frequently and violently in Los Angeles, a notably open-shop town. The conservative *Los Angeles Times* and the local Merchants and Manufacturers Association led the open-shop crusade against numerous labor organizations and a fledgling socialist movement. Tensions peaked in 1910 when the *Times*' downtown headquarters was bombed. Two labor organizers confessed to the crime, and their lawyer, Clarence Darrow, was accused of jury tampering. After these events, the local union movement lost popular support, but it remained active.[5]

Despite frequent labor-capital strife, however, cooperative personnel relations characterized large sectors of the region's corporate management. It might be easy to read this fact simply as evidence that welfare capitalism, also known as corporate paternalism, occurred in southern California as it did elsewhere. Instead, events in Los Angeles call into question this oft-held understanding's basic premise, that American management introduced expansive compensation packages as anti-union measures to counter working-class activism. The welfare capitalism framework reflects the powerful presence of industrial firms in which worker unrest and union activities were critical concerns, but within this paradigm's common narrative, white-collar workers are nowhere to be found. Their exclusion is significant, for to add them dramatically alters the picture of the local labor relations landscape. As it turns out, welfare capitalism dominated the workings of white-collar firms and, in fact, occurred in most large local companies, affecting blue- and white-collar workers alike.

Incorporating southern California's white-collar employees and companies into the story reveals that Los Angeles's business elite faced a threat more subtle than that posed by unions (and as potentially damaging to their operations)—the significant costs arising from employee turnover and the loss of potential profits resulting from a lack of long-term commitment to the firm's success. Generous benefit programs represented as much a response to the problems of retaining and motivating salaried employees as to the more specific threat of labor and political activism among workers. White-collar and managerial ranks often benefited the most from broad compensation programs in industrial firms, and exclusively white-collar organizations, such as banks and insurance companies, actively developed comprehensive benefit packages.[6]

The "science" of personnel management arose from prevailing Progressive Era impulses toward the bureaucratization and professionalization of business operations. Historians have rightly noted that a sprawling range of concerns and factors affected corporate experiments with supplementary compensation programs. As has been well documented, working-class activism motivated many firms to implement employee benefits as a counter to trade unionism. In some cases, company policies reflected the paternalism of individual leaders. Specific business and industrial crises, most notably the tensions among business, labor, and the state during World War I, also spurred corporate paternalism. Further, welfare capitalism developed as part of a larger process of establishing corporate legitimacy. Growing public hostility to the economic and political power of emerging large-scale industry threatened business leaders with the prospect of state intervention in corporate operations. Gender issues also stirred paternalistic impulses, as executives wrestled with the concerns raised by large numbers of young female employees. Finally, in an effort to stave off the threat of governmental regulation, as well as to blunt cries for legislated reform, business leaders subscribed to the idea of corporate social responsibility, in order to gain public support of large-scale capitalism.[7]

Ultimately, amid this melange of forces and factors, the need to secure a talented, dedicated, and stable workforce underlay all efforts to develop benefit and bonus programs, whatever the specific threats, circumstances, or environments confronting individual firms. Astute corporate leadership maneuvered to assure their firm's maximal efficiency in the face of varying challenges. For example, Chicago's packinghouses acted "to increase efficiency and productivity as well as inculcate a sense of allegiance to the employer." Elsewhere, management understood the costs of labor turnover and labor shortages and worked to increase firm efficiency through promoting employee satisfaction. Indeed, in one southern mill town "corporate paternalism was not the antithesis of hard-nosed management" but, rather, was an integral part of "aggressive corporate strategies. Profits and paternalism went hand in hand."[8]

The desire to increase profits hardly seems congruous with the introduction of fringe benefits, yet the connection actually became fundamental to corporate strategizing in the early twentieth century. Nationally, benefit programs became widespread in firms with over five hundred employees and commonplace in major corporations employing two thousand or more. One might surmise that firms with such packages simply lowered wages or salaries to cover the extra costs. Surveys suggest, however, that companies with nonsalary perquisites typically offered higher salaries than similar firms without them. These programs usually represented an additional layer of remuneration.[9]

The bonus- and benefit-oriented compensation strategies increasingly favored by business leaders reflected not only managerial plotting but also employee concerns and pressures. In many cases, workers demanded such forms of compensation. Company publications rarely noted any requests for specific benefits. They instead gave the benevolence and wisdom of company management full credit for their enactment. But nonsalary benefits became demands of both blue-collar unions and white-collar employees in the early twentieth century, and most programs targeted both sets of employees.[10]

The nature of corporate compensation packages reveals much about employee concerns. Many American men, for example, viewed the loss of control over one's labor to be a major drawback of big business employment. Numerous firms addressed this frustration by announcing bonuses, direct rewards for merit, or stock options to create some sense of ownership within the context of corporate employment. Other compensation programs appealed to very different interests. Many Americans viewed "success" more in terms of security and stability than wealth and status. They sought a secure job and steady income as much as social status.[11] Prior to industrialization, work, for many Americans, entailed producing food or goods for survival or to sell or barter for necessary items. This meant that, barring environmental or agricultural disasters, many Americans had great individual control over their own sustenance. When circumstances threatened them, they found safety nets provided by extended kinship networks, churches, and other local associations.[12] With the emergence of an industrial market economy in the nineteenth century, increasing numbers of Americans in the farm sector began to sell their labor in exchange for wages. Work in urban areas became essentially about money—about procuring the cash necessary to buy needed goods. The nature of family organization also shifted in this process. Families in the new middling classes ceased to operate like rural households. The father's income replaced cooperative activities among all members of the family; his salary became the sole basis for family security.[13] While independent nuclear families in this cash-based market economy had more opportunities for financial accumulation, they also faced greater risks. With the entire family dependent on one source of income, any break in the father's employment could devastate a family. Not only did the threat of illness or death pose great perils, but American men increasingly found themselves small players in a large market where forces beyond their control could result in hardship or ruin. Many middle-class families lacked sustaining personal and community networks to assist them during such a tragedy. In this context, measures of personal security such as medical plans, pensions, and life insurance became items of critical importance.

The development of modern corporate compensation packages occurred largely during the first three decades of the twentieth century, as business leaders experimented with measures to recruit, motivate, and retain employees. Executives wanted programs that would assure long-term dedication at minimal cost, while employees sought the greatest reward for their efforts with the fewest strings attached. Neither group started with any clear idea of what this would eventually mean.

Fostering the Profit Motive

Most southern California businesses had experienced haggling over wages and salaries from their very beginning. In these companies' early years, staff members could individually negotiate their compensation, but as these enterprises grew, remuneration policies had to become more rigid and standardized. Whatever the firm's size, most employees usually saw little need for much discussion of appropriate payment. They wanted high salaries. Executives, however, found this formula distinctly unappealing. Wages and salaries were a significant expense and even small individual raises could bloat the budgets of a company employing hundreds or thousands. Moreover, amid their many expenses, wages and salaries provided one item over which leaders could exert control. The imperative to keep this budget line low preoccupied corporate management, and with an adequate if not excessive supply of labor for lower-level clerical positions, remuneration for these posts suffered.

While most companies believed that they could secure lower-level white-collar employees with, at best, modest salaries, those same firms faced distressingly high turnover rates and sensed a lack of employee dedication. Even among employees in positions with more generous salaries and lower turnover, commitment often seemed lacking. Raising salaries provided one possible strategy to combat these personnel problems, but leaders considered this an expensive proposition that did not guarantee results. Clearly, however, executives had to make some connection between remuneration and performance. They recognized that the nebulous link between an employee's salary and the firm's success thwarted the individual profit-motive which, according to popular lore, lay at the root of small business prosperity. If a company's sales stagnated or even declined, would middle-level managers see their pay cut? Not necessarily. Conversely, if a firm's income soared, would all employees receive corresponding raises? Again, probably not.

Aware of the potential benefits of tying employee income to company performance, but not wanting to raise salaries generally, many firms experimented with profit-sharing and bonus programs as the most "logical" solution to their personnel dilemmas. The strategy of offering profit-sharing bonuses in addition to regular salaries provided an unambiguous mechanism for highlighting employees' direct connection to the firm's success. Profit-sharing plans subsequently became one of the first extra-compensation programs that large firms introduced. At least two dozen major American employers offered some form of profit sharing by the 1890s. The 1892 establishment of the Association for the Promotion of Profit Sharing foreshadowed the popularity these programs would gain among management. In the years prior to World War I, a number of the nation's most visible firms, including Procter and Gamble, United States Steel, and International Harvester, implemented and widely publicized various forms of profit sharing as evidence of their managerial virtuosity. By 1916, at least 250 large firms had enacted profit-sharing plans, a trend mirrored in Los Angeles.[14]

Union Oil commenced a profit-sharing program in 1916 with an annual bonus paid from company profits. Employees received a percentage of their salary based upon their years of service and the extent of the corporate surplus. Leaders believed the program would benefit operations in several ways. First, it would motivate their workforce by making them feel they benefited directly from the firm's success as "fellow members of a business family." Second, the program promised to reduce turnover and retraining costs by providing additional incentives for long-term service. Finally, officials hoped the program would create an environment in which employees would monitor each other's efforts, since all would be aware that poor performance by some would lower the bonus potential. Lest employees not make this connection, Union Oil used its annual profit-sharing reports to spell out the factors that limited company profits. These reports provided a convincing forum through which management could discourage disruptive activities and point out areas where employees had cost the firm profits. In announcing reduced gains for 1921, for instance, Union claimed that two strikes and a reduction in sales efforts had led to smaller year-end bonuses.[15]

Despite profit sharing's early promise, executives viewed such programs with increasing disfavor by the 1920s. They grew suspicious of these schemes because they required firms to make potentially significant cash outlays without any precise way of distinguishing among employee efforts. A management text from 1919 weighed the practice's pros and cons: "In some cases [good] results may be obtained, but if it does occur, the profits, like the rain, fall on both the just and the unjust. In other words, those who do not respond to the incentive presented, share equally with those who do. The fundamental drawback of profit-sharing, however, lies in the fact that the profits which may be earned depend not only upon the individual and collective efficiency, but also on market conditions."[16] In commenting on widespread dissatisfaction among many firms with profit-sharing plans, a 1920 National Industrial Conference Board Study stated that some firm's programs "failed to compensate for the outlay of money." Subsequently, plans that paid cash benefits became "as scarce as hen's teeth."[17]

Employees had their own reservations about profit sharing. If profits were high and their cut generous, it seemed a good deal; but most personnel recognized that many factors outside their control affected company profits, and if profits dwindled, they likely resented the blame. Despite Union Oil's initial enthusiasm for profit sharing, the company abandoned the program in the early 1920s, following a succession of declining bonuses. The program ultimately pleased neither leaders nor employees, who could read their dwindling checks as evidence of the company's frailty.

Rather than implementing blanket profit-sharing programs, some Los Angeles companies experimented with offering cash bonuses for meritorious work. Southern California Edison first announced a cash bonus program in 1905, as part of an effort to "stimulate the obtaining of new power business and to promote a spirit of emulation among the various districts." The program offered a very direct connection between efforts and rewards, with cash bonuses paid to the top three employees in various sales categories. Banks frequently held contests that offered staff prizes or bonuses for bringing in new business. In 1924, for example, the Pacific Southwest Savings Bank announced a competition in which employees would receive points for each account they opened, with additional points given for especially large deposits. At the end of each week, the person with the most points received $25; winners over longer periods could win as much as $500.[18]

Bonuses seemed natural compensation for sales employees and often proved effective. Pacific Mutual, for example, found cash and prizes helpful in motivating its agents.[19] These programs did not work well for all employees, however. While some seized the opportunities for extra income, others resented the added demands. In 1920, the Los Angeles Railway Corporation experimented with a very direct bonus program in which its trainmen received either bonuses or financial demerits based on their performance. Superiors evaluated their employees to determine whether they worked "beyond the call of duty" and performed at "over 100%," or at less than their "capacity." Those rated at over 100 percent received extra cash, while the company docked the wages of those who fell below 100 percent. Employees who fell below 75 percent received termination notices. One month after the program took effect, the company began dismissing employees for poor effort. In December 1920, LA Railway announced that 90 percent of its employees, 2,140 men, would receive merit bonuses of up to $60, totaling $50,000.[20] However, the program disappeared just a few months later when, in the wake of the 1920–21 economic downturn, management would not accept its costs. We can also speculate that trainmen did not like the pressure this kind of compensation package created. Not only did this program threaten their base wages, but it also rendered them vulnerable to their superiors' arguably prejudiced opinions.

If workers such as trainmen resisted such direct incentive programs, they were likely anathema to many white-collar employees, who hoped their salaried status would entail certain, steady incomes. Despite the seeming logic of programs that offered some kind of direct connection between employee or company performance and remuneration, personnel on all rungs of the corporate ladder resisted these schemes. For those at the top, they were often difficult to administer and required giving up a portion of the company's cherished profits. For employees, they often increased job pressures and added new responsibilities.

The Lure of Ownership

With leaders increasingly reluctant to offer employees any additional cash outlays and employees themselves ambivalent about such programs, stock ownership surfaced in the late 1910s and 1920s as an intriguing new compensation option. By 1927, at least 289 American firms had enacted a stock purchase plan for their workforce, 273 of them established after 1916.[21]

Business leaders in Los Angeles turned to stock purchase plans as a way to give employees a feeling of ownership in the firm and to heighten their long-term dedication. These programs also raised needed capital, ingeniously making the firm's payroll an indirect source of company funds. Employee stock ownership further provided an important philosophical salve for existing stockholders, since public concern over the concentration of wealth in big business might be assuaged with the argument that employees were part owners.[22]

At about the same time it abandoned its profit-sharing program, Union Oil introduced an employee stock purchase plan that made stock available to employees at discount prices. Union Oil also placed some of the money in its pension fund investments in company stock and then boasted that all members of the pension fund were indirect stockholders. Pacific Mutual similarly turned to stock ownership as a lure for its salaried employees. Shortly after World War I, the company created a syndicate through which personnel could purchase stock at reduced rates.[23]

Many companies became particularly fond of stock ownership programs because they could be written to include length of service clauses and other items that might reduce turnover. In 1928, for example, the Los Angeles First National Bank announced an ambitious stock plan aimed at lower- and mid-level workers making between $100 and $500 per month. By offering them a stake in company profits, the bank hoped to strengthen their commitment, yet First National constructed the program to achieve additional ends. It contained numerous clauses and provisions to promote long-term loyalty. First, personnel could purchase stock only after three years of service. Second, one could purchase stock only through monthly installments of $2.50 over a five-year period. Employees received dividends starting from the date of their investment, but they only got title to the stock at the end of the period. Finally, the bank required those who quit to sell back their shares.[24]

Southern California Edison leaders also had specific desires for their stock ownership plan. By 1917, the company encouraged its employees to become stockholders and offered them discounts on the purchase of company shares. Beyond its potential motivational effects, SCE officials used the program as a weapon against seizure by holding companies. At the time, SCE was the nation's largest investor-owned utility company not controlled by a holding company. SCE further promoted employee stock ownership as a means to raise desperately needed cash for construction projects. Because leaders felt the benefits of employee stock ownership to be so great, they promoted the programs with exceptional fervor and received an enthusiastic response. By 1920, 1,700 of the firm's 2,500 permanent employees owned some stock. By 1924, nearly all of SCE's "permanent" employees owned shares.[25]

The SCE case suggests that employees responded positively to stock ownership, but the evidence nationally regarding employee interest is mixed. According to a 1927 survey of eighty-nine discontinued stock option plans, only five companies cited a lack of employee participation; only one said that the "plan did not work." Yet by no means did all programs reach capacity. Of 253 companies with stock option programs, only 30 percent of the 2.4 million eligible employees participated. Many employees chose not to purchase stock. For some the cost likely proved prohibitive. Pacific Southwest Savings Bank, for example, announced a plan in 1923 to make most personnel stockholders, but it required a whopping commitment of $375, spread in $15 installments over a twenty-five-month period. In other cases, limited offerings clearly capped the number of employees who could participate. Thirty-seven of the eighty-nine firms in the 1927 survey had discontinued stock programs because they had "no more stock to sell."[26]

Even the most successful stock programs failed to spur employee effort. To top management's disappointment, most stockholders did not necessarily assume the ethos of ownership. Their subscription represented an investment decision and not a judgment about their long-term loyalty to the company. In Chicago, "workers eagerly bought stock at the discounts offered but not because they were making a commitment to their employers. They merely considered it a good way to save and perhaps make a little money on the side."[27] Salaried employees likely held a similar attitude. Few had the funds to acquire a significant amount of stock. No individual could afford more than a tiny share of the firm, and company profits were beyond the control of any individual employee. However diligently an employee might work in hope of increasing the value of his or her stock, larger forces influenced the value of the investment. Thus, while many workers viewed stock ownership as a potential source of extra money—a reasonable gamble—it rarely cemented their interest in the company.

Despite their initial promise, stock ownership programs rarely became critical components of corporate cultures. The 1927 survey found that while some firms argued that they helped reduce turnover, many saw "no change which could be directly attributed to the stock purchase plan."[28] For most firms, stock ownership plans garnered some interest and could benefit the company, but they were not major antidotes to the problems of employee motivation and retention. A significant number of personnel purchased stock when offered discounts, and stock programs provided an important public relations tool in an era of hostility to big business, yet the theoretical benefits of making every employee an owner never materialized. For this reason, most companies increasingly turned to other means of compensation.[29]

A Sense of Security

In their promotion of stock ownership and direct rewards for merit, Los Angeles corporations attempted to reframe individualistic values in the context of bureaucratic employment. Ironically, however, amid their celebration of individual prosperity, executives found that many employees expressed more interest in issues of personal and familial security. Top brass increasingly recognized safety net programs as popular benefits of big business employment.

Turn-of-the-century changes in economic and social organization uprooted many of the mechanisms and institutions American families had traditionally turned to in times of need. In the emerging urban, industrial society, maintaining family security amid rapid economic fluctuations and the ever-present challenges of sickness, old age, and death, became central social and political issues. This created a curious and potentially exploitable paradox for corporate leaders. While many Americans looked upon bureaucratic employment with disdain because of its perceived stifling nature, the very vastness of corporate operations that attracted such criticism provided a high level of economic stability. Business elites recognized and sought to capitalize on these conflicting interests of American men. While touting individualistic lures, they coyly played on desires for security by highlighting the stable and paternalistic nature of corporate employment.

Company publications frequently contrasted the occupational stability possible in a large corporation with the dilemmas of small business ownership. An SCE editorial argued that a corporate manager enjoyed the support of an organization "big enough to sustain a mistake" and, therefore, did not fear "that an error may mean ruin, as in the case with a small business man." To leaders' pleasure, many cultural depictions of white-collar employment stressed occupational security and stability. A 1919 *Sunset* magazine article compared a company manager's life with that of an independent store owner by describing the merchant's annoyance at seeing his neighbor, a "salaried man," working in the garden when he arrived home late each evening. The author noted that the branch manager may have had less independence in running the enterprise but actually enjoyed more personal freedom. "He is to all intents a merchant, without the merchant's worries."[30]

Because images of security and stability seemed to resonate well, many firms introduced compensation packages that provided safety nets against illness, disability, old age, and family poverty resulting from a breadwinner's death.[31] When well crafted, they made one's employer one's basis of personal security and thus strengthened corporate control over employees in a competitive labor market. If leaving a job meant forgoing medical care and perhaps one's investment in life insurance or a pension, an employee might be less likely to abandon the company for a better offer elsewhere.

An insurance package offering coverage against illness and family catastrophes became the first widespread employee benefit in Los Angeles firms as well as those around the nation. These programs initially appeared among industrial firms in the 1870s in response to public concern about the increasingly hazardous nature of factory labor.[32] The enactment of public workman's compensation laws in the 1910s resulted in a declining number of benefit programs among companies that had provided them solely for hazardous accidents. Nevertheless, large corporations in a broad range of industries began to purchase group insurance policies for all their employees, offering death, sickness, and accident benefits. By one account, the number of industrial firms holding such policies grew from 32 in 1916 to 186 in 1926. They tended to be even more common in nonindustrial firms such as insurance companies and large banks. Although only a minority of the country's industrial firms provided such programs, the companies that did "were among the nation's most visible and profitable." This was certainly the case in Los Angeles, where the city's major corporations experimented with insurance provisions.[33]

Pensions ultimately became the most significant of corporate compensation measures. Though the American Express Company discussed establishing a company pension plan as early as 1875, historians credit the Baltimore and Ohio Railroad for enacting the first formal program in 1884. As late as 1900, only about half a dozen companies are known to have joined the B&O in offering pensions, though by that time, such plans were becoming a significant element in the lives of many older Americans. By the last quarter of the nineteenth century, roughly 10 percent of elderly persons depended on pensions for survival; most were veterans or civil servants who received money from government plans. In the 1910s, high rates of poverty among elderly persons began to receive considerable national attention, and as Americans became increasingly concerned about providing for their futures, large firms added pensions to their compensation packages.[34] These programs were popular among company leaders for they seemed to present a simple and powerful tool in reducing labor turnover. If workers knew that lifelong service to the firm would result in financial security during old age, they would presumably be more reluctant to leave. Pension plans could also solve another dilemma, ironically created from other attempts to reduce turnover; they assured the timely retirement of senior employees.[35] The number of American companies with pension plans grew from 50 in 1910 to at least 420 and possibly as many as 700 by 1930. One study argued that by this time, 73 percent of American businesses with more than 1,000 employees offered pensions plans. Most were compulsory contributory plans for salaried employees.[36]

By the 1920s, employees in most large Los Angeles corporations could choose from a smorgasbord of benefits. A casual glance suggests considerable uniformity among these programs, but critical variations existed in their structures and the reasons for their enactment. In some cases, most notably railways, fears of unionization had forced management to implement programs that actually benefited all employees. In other industries, such as oil, both blue- and white-collar issues had yielded across the board programs. In banks and insurance companies, executives had designed packages specifically to combat turnover and weak performance.

At Pacific Electric, blue-collar labor struggles spawned the creation of benefit programs for all employees, though the firm's financial difficulties resulted in leaner offerings. PE's early benefit packages were provided not directly by the company but by the Pacific Electric Club, a company-sponsored employee association started in 1917. Executives founded the club at least partly in response to union efforts among trainmen and other blue-collar workers, but they intended it to attract both blue- and white-collar personnel. Desiring blue-collar workers to identify with the firm and not with their trade, leaders deemphasized status distinctions amongst employees. As a result, perquisites introduced to combat union activity also became available to white-collar employees, who took advantage of the benefits in equal if not greater numbers.[37]

In April 1917, the Pacific Electric Club began offering pool insurance plans for members. Based on the amount of the monthly deductions from employees' paychecks, the company appears to have subsidized the program little if at all. At the same time the Pacific Electric Club asked all PE employees to purchase their fire and life insurance through a company pool plan contracted to an outside firm. In return, the insurance company promised to rebate a percentage of their premiums to the club for a relief fund. The club, in turn, used this fund to provide loans to employees in need. In 1918, the club established a mortuary fund. Members contributed 25¢ a month, and the money in hand went to families of deceased employees.[38]

In 1924 the Pacific Electric Club was able to broaden its various insurance and death benefit plans thanks to added support from its parent company, Southern Pacific. PE employees still had no pension plan, but their insurance program became more comprehensive and now received a company subsidy. All personnel with at least six months of service received a company-paid $250 life insurance policy. Those having served one year received a $500 plan. Staff could purchase additional insurance at a reduced rate, thanks to a corporate subsidy. Employees liked the broadened and more generous packages, no longer so clearly tied to combating union efforts. Within the first week, 90 percent of those eligible bought into the plan. Pacific Electric also offered its employees medical care, but it financed the clinic with automatic deductions from employee paychecks based on total salary. The medical plan initially covered only basic medical care, but in 1924 dental care was added, and beginning in 1927, for employees who had served five years or longer, certain pre-existing conditions were covered under the plan.[39]

Disability insurance became one of the company's most popular benefits. In any given month, *Pacific Electric Magazine* published the names and conditions of roughly thirty to forty employees who had drawn on their benefits to receive amounts ranging from as little as $8 to several hundred dollars. In September 1929, for instance, George Hunter received $16 for missing work because of indigestion, Fred Rollins received $18 for a hemorrhoid-related absence, and M. Livingston took $300 for advanced pneumonia.[40]

The PE case suggests two things about benefit packages. First, while more prosperous companies introduced lucrative compensation packages to lure and retain employees, firms in less enviable positions generally had to settle for scaled-down versions. Their appearance in such a financially strapped business, however, testifies to their popularity.[41] Second, even in cases where blue-collar concerns lay behind company measures, white-collar workers usually benefited as well. In the long run, white-collar employees became the ultimate beneficiaries of such programs, for while labor unrest rose and fell, the challenges posed by office and professional staff never seemed to wane.

Southern California Edison's history exemplifies the evolution of nonsalary compensation programs within American business from small and limited efforts to multifaceted strategies designed to combat a diversity of company and industry-specific challenges. SCE first began to develop a safety net package in 1910 with the establishment of the Edison Benefit Fund. Personnel who participated in the fund, run by men elected from the company's sales agents, agreed to have the firm deduct one dollar from their monthly paychecks. This money would then be placed in an account given to an employee's family in the event of his death. When deaths occurred, the monies would be replenished with an additional dollar contributed from each member. By 1912, 750 workers had joined the fund, but its popularity faltered, because many believed that manual laborers, who encountered more occupational hazards, benefited disproportionately. In 1913 the company addressed these concerns with statistics suggesting that salaried employees received half of the awards. By 1919, 1,600 of the firm's roughly 2,500 permanent staff subscribed.[42]

Mutual benefit associations such as Edison's Benefit Fund represented an early corporate effort to provide some form of catastrophe insurance at no direct cost to the firm. The proliferation and popularity of benefit societies suggests that they addressed a very real need.[43] Yet these plans were only marginally more sophisticated than the social custom of donating money to a fund for a deceased worker's family. They addressed only the most cataclysmic of circumstances and often offered quite modest cash sums. As these schemes' limitations became apparent, employers increasingly offered their personnel access to broader insurance programs, covering illness, disability, and retirement. Unlike mutual aid programs, these plans usually required company subsidies, but in return they gave firms a powerful tool for recruitment and retention.

In the years immediately following World War I, SCE began to enact a wide range of additional compensation measures. These included a group life insurance plan that provided more extensive coverage than the Benefit Fund, a medical department with a full-service medical staff offering employees free basic medical care, and a pension fund to provide income during retirement or in the event of a disability. SCE's compensation package represented substantive measures that required significant company outlays and provided real security to employees. Its pension plan, for instance, stipulated that male employees at the age of 60 and women at the age of 50 could retire with a pension if they had served the company for twenty years. Older employees could retire with fewer years of service. The amount of the monthly pension equaled 2 percent of the employee's monthly salary for the five highest-paying years of employment multiplied by the number of years in service. A person having served the company for twenty-five years would retire at half of his average salary during his last five years. The company also allowed pensioners use of its medical department, so long as they did not engage in any new occupation.[44]

In offering a comprehensive and generous compensation package, SCE leaders were responding to three basic challenges to company interests. First, political battles over potential public ownership embroiled the firm. SCE leaders believed that if its customers felt good about their utility service, a switch to public ownership would have less appeal. Assuring this good service required a very committed workforce, which the company felt it could achieve through measures that made the firm its employees' basis of personal security. Second, in fighting public ownership, SCE officials knew that the company must be perceived as committed to the public good. What better way to do this than through expressing a genuine interest in employees' well being? The firm's executives could not afford to appear stingy, antagonistic, or mean-spirited, factors that often led to public support for employees. Third, like all large firms, SCE strove to increase efficiency by reducing turnover. Because it operated in a very competitive labor market with the state's other major utility firms (San Diego Gas and Electric, and Pacific Gas and Electric) as well as other large companies offering similar benefit programs, SCE's fringe benefits did not ultimately offer employees special inducements but, rather, kept its compensation package viable.[45]

SCE executives acted not simply out of paternal kindness but in clear response to market pressures. They crafted every program to serve the firm's objectives. They based company insurance and pension plans on length of service, thus hoping to mitigate turnover. By keeping employees in the building during lunch, a company cafeteria reduced the time spent away from the office and perhaps increased the likelihood of their eating together and accomplishing some work.[46] The medical department allowed SCE to monitor its employee's health and guard against absenteeism. Regular medical care kept the workforce healthier and reduced costs associated with sickness.

In August 1919, the cover of SCE's company magazine featured a sketch of an entry archway intended to serve as a metaphor for the firm's sound business practices and generosity toward employees. Incorporated in the arch were bricks representing available company benefits—medical care, life insurance, pensions, company stock, and educational opportunities. In this pamphlet and in other company materials, SCE management portrayed its personnel as fortunate to work for a firm that offered such comprehensive rewards for their efforts. Yet while SCE claimed to be unusually generous, its benefit package in fact closely paralleled those of other large American firms.

Despite the widespread implementation of broad compensation measures, most companies claimed to be leaders in these offerings. For example, after enacting an extensive package of employee benefits during the 1910s and 1920s, Union Oil officials applauded themselves for "pioneering in the field of industrial relations" and hailed their employee perquisites as among "the broadest in the West." In fact, Union Oil's programs matched those in other oil firms and typified trends in most oligopolistic industries. Union Oil first enacted a significant benefit package in 1915 with the introduction of the subsidized Employee Benefit Fund. Under this plan, the company deducted one dollar from each employee's monthly earnings after a short period of service. Officials deposited these monthly deductions into a firm-operated fund from which hospital and medical bills up to $250 were paid. Union Oil also established a group life insurance plan for its employees in 1915. The coverage, free

Southern California Edison depicted its personnel benefits and practices as a supportive archway leading to a promising future. Photo courtesy of William Myers, private collection.

to employees, increased in amount from $500 to $2,000 over the course of an employee's tenure. In 1925, Union Oil installed a subsidized contributory life insurance plan that employees with over one year of service were eligible to join. Each year the amount of coverage increased.[47]

Union Oil strengthened its benefit package in 1923 with a pension program known as the Provident Fund, touted in the company magazine as "the most comprehensive and profitable plan divined for any company." Participation in the fund required employees to contribute 3 to 5 percent of their earnings. Union Oil added an equal amount and then paid interest on the total. The money became available as a pension in the cases of disability, death, or retirement, or could be used as collateral for loans from the firm.[48] In 1926, executives placed all of these company-operated programs under the direction of a new insurance and personnel department created to oversee and manage the sprawling measures.

Several factors influenced the establishment of Union Oil's benefit programs. Repeated union efforts and struggles in the early 1920s caused leaders considerable grief.[49] Yet while executives fretted over labor unrest, the major portion of Union Oil's workers—white-collar employees—did not threaten management in these overt ways. Union Oil's benefit programs primarily aimed to cultivate satisfaction, which its leaders associated with productivity, for white- and blue-collar alike. In company correspondence, board chair Lyman Stewart frequently stressed the importance of having managers work closely with personnel to assure full cooperation in their common business venture. While union concerns served as visible sparks motivating company action, leaders designed programs for all employees. Because such programs were tied to length of service and required employee comtributions, they frequently aided salaried personnel the most.

As Union Oil grew and prospered during the 1920s, one could hardly have convinced leaders that its efforts were not working. Warren Griffith, who joined the corporation in 1923, appreciated the steady income and security corporate employment offered. He compared his work there to previous experience in managing dime stores by noting that "the amount of money that you could earn in the Union Oil Company was not comparable," but "you were really happier and you had a better chance for enjoying life."[50] Though Griffith had more potential for personal accumulation in operating a store, Union Oil gave him a more stable and secure future, with less tension and stress about assuring the operation's survival.

Exclusively white-collar firms implemented the most generous compensation measures. Blue-collar unions never threatened banks, for instance, which generally had smaller and more localized workforces to manage. Nevertheless, major Los Angeles firms enacted sweeping benefit programs. Both Security Trust and Savings Bank of Los Angeles and Los Angeles First National introduced pensions and group insurance plans in the 1910s and 1920s. The Pacific Southwest Savings Bank offered employees access to group insurance, a subsidized cafeteria, and a fully-equipped medical facility that provided professional care and medicine at no cost. Bank workers took advantage of the hospital, making over nine thousand visits in 1926.[51]

The appearance of these programs in Los Angeles area banks testifies to their popularity. In examining specific firms' policies, it is easy to find company or industry-specific reasons for their implementation. At Union Oil, for instance, one could argue that leaders established these programs in response to labor unrest or that the programs represented the paternalistic managerial philosophies of chairman Lyman Stewart, yet various local banks with no threat of employee strikes and with different directors created similar programs. In the context of compensation programs, the similarities among SCE, Union Oil, and local banks are more important than their differences. Though facing different challenges, each sought to attract, motivate, and retain employees who would work diligently for the firm's long-term success. These safety nets, when combined with the general stability and security possible in working for a large enterprise rather than running one's own business, promised to make corporate employment an attractive proposition for many Americans.

If businesses carefully designed broad compensation packages to secure long-term, dedicated employees, historians face a simple question—did the gamble work? Prevailing managerial theory in the 1910s and 1920s asserted with little hesitation that generous compensation and good treatment lowered turnover, heightened dedication, and in the long run maximized profits.[52] Arguments equating employee satisfaction with productivity became more widespread and formalized as the field of industrial relations rose to an institutionalized academic and professional discipline. A 1919 management text asserted that it was "getting to be commonly recognized that welfare work pays." It paid because it made employees more content, reduced turnover, and saved "the employer from the losses occasioned his competitors in these days when workers as a rule are lightly anchored."[53] A 1920 text stated, "A fundamental axiom of personnel management is that progressive personnel practices are not only right from a moral and ethical point of view but also more than pay for themselves in the form of increased profit."[54] Many management theorists cited a general decline in turnover rates during the 1920s as compared with prior to the war, as evidence of the effectiveness of broad compensation programs.[55] Whether backed by hard data from their own firms or persuaded by prevailing managerial doctrine, large and successful firms' increasing adoption of these programs reveals that top managers indeed believed them beneficial to achieving their goals.

However, employees had different views. For ambitious white men, bureaucratic employment presented a trade-off in which they sacrificed independence and the potential for significant wealth. In return they came to expect a steady, dependable income and fringe benefits enhancing family security. Although early benefit programs represented managerial tinkering and experimentation, they quickly became the norm for large firms. White, middle-class men increasingly expected that corporate employment would provide a range of perquisites. For major employers in a competitive labor market, the absence of fringe benefits became a barrier to cultivating a dedicated workforce more than their presence became an aid to doing so.

In seeing safety net benefits as a just addition to wage and salary compensation, not something the company generously provided, employees imbued the programs with a very different meaning than employers had intended. Rather than accepting corporate compensation packages with feelings of appreciation and indebtedness, employees began to expect such measures and to become critical when companies handled them poorly. Proposed perquisites received close scrutiny by the rank and file, who did not hesitate to note any perceived flaws or failings. Given such attitudes, leaders usually buried within their self-congratulatory fringe benefit announcements detailed explanations and descriptions that often alluded to employee critiques of earlier proposals. PE personnel, for instance, criticized a company insurance proposal in 1916 and asked that the firm's Insurance Committee consider revisions. Such interactions, typically associated with union-management negotiations, occurred in subtle ways between southern California executives and employees.[56]

As American employees became increasingly aware of and knowledgeable about compensation programs, such benefits became expected elements of corporate life. This process ultimately had unintended consequences for management. While personnel were unhappy when leaders handled programs poorly, they were particularly displeased when executives failed to implement certain measures at all. In Chicago, "welfare capitalists succeeded in having an impact on their workers, although not always in ways they anticipated. Workers took advantage of many of the new programs offered them. They came to expect benefits along with the job. And they judged a good company, in contrast to a bad one, by how close it came to meeting welfare capitalism standards, offered the steady, well-paying decent work that workers could reward with their loyalty."[57] In Georgia, "company paternalism worked too well—indeed, it carried the seeds of its own demise. If the mill families had not come to see themselves as a permanent group of working people whose economic security depended on the industrial system, they would never have looked to unionization to ensure that their needs would be met within that system."[58] Salaried employees were likely to be even more assertive than blue-collar workers in their use of and demand for these programs. By the 1920s, most large American firms offered their salaried ranks a generous array of benefits. A talented, educated, white male in a competitive labor market had good reason to expect them. For the salaried ranks in the nation's leading firms, medical care, life insurance, and pensions did not reflect company benevolence but rather corporate acknowledgment of white-collar workers' rightful due.

Companies had initiated benefit programs to help leaders exert control over the workforce, but they quickly evolved from a bargaining tool to a necessary element of corporate life. In Los Angeles's narrow and empowered white-collar labor pool, executives learned that broad compensation programs would not always guarantee long-term dedicated employees, but without their enactment, they would certainly lose the personnel battle.

Benefits ultimately became a central theme of most corporate cultures because they played on one element of corporate employment Americans seemed to appreciate: the opportunity for a stable and secure livelihood. Ironically, however, southern California executives confronted continual evidence that very different values lay behind many of their personnel challenges. White-collar careers rarely allowed for the expression of individual achievement or the attainment of occupational independence central to prevailing constructions of masculine success, and the increasing presence of women in the clerical workforce did not help. Thus, alongside their efforts to tout security as a theme of corporate life, the region's business elite set out to convince young men that rapid advancement up corporate ladders into leadership positions could be theirs as a reward for meritorious performance.

SIX

WHITE-COLLAR MANHOOD

Only the dull-wits remained behind the counter and at the desk.
—W. W. Robinson, 1942

On December 3, 1921, his twenty-first birthday, George Latham and his father arrived in San Diego, California. These midwestern transplants came in search of good weather, which they found, and work, which they did not find. After several frustrating months, George's father decided to purchase a plot of land in the nearby desert town of El Cajon, in hopes that they could make it on their own; but when George saw the land on "a horribly hot and miserable day," he told his father that he "would rather starve to death than live out there." The two instead headed north to Los Angeles, where after many months of finding only sporadic work, George decided to enroll in a local business college. Within a short time, George's teachers found him a job as bookkeeper for the General Water Heater Corporation. The company soon promoted him into sales, and less than two years later he had become its leading salesman. George's father replied to his son's good news with little enthusiasm, stating tersely, "[You have] been working for someone else long enough." He urged George to quit his position and pursue a more potentially rewarding future. George subsequently went to work as an insurance agent and quickly rose to the rank of manager in the southern California offices of first the New England Life Insurance Company and then Northwestern Mutual Life. Ultimately, many years later, he founded his own insurance firm, one that became enormously successful.[1]

George Latham's career presents an apparent contradiction. Uncertainty and insecurity marked his early life. When, in 1980, an oral historian asked him about the Depression, he replied, "Which depression?" and stated that he and his family had experienced many tough times in the 1910s and 1920s. His early decision to train in bookkeeping seems an understandable effort to find secure, steady work. The desire for stable employment may have dominated his early career, but stability alone did not prove satisfying. Even when he began to find success in seemingly decent positions, his father's prodding moved him from job to job and company to company in a quest for better positions and eventual occupational independence.

For southern California business leaders, George Latham personified the turnover problems that plagued their companies. Talented and ambitious, he was an asset to the firms for which he worked, yet the lure of better positions elsewhere and the desire eventually to run his own business made him a nightmare for personnel directors. Were Latham unique, historians could dismiss his case as that of a rare entrepreneurial individualist misplaced in the emerging corporate world. But Los Angeles executives encountered many men with similar aspirations, and they quickly learned that company spirit and fringe benefits alone would not retain and motivate these employees.

In their search of decent work, tens of thousands of young white men in Los Angeles gladly took office jobs. Initially, such posts promised adequate pay, pleasant working environments, fringe benefits, and conferred a degree of middle-class status. For most, however, clerical posts did not represent the culmination of their career goals; they were instead a starting point on a long journey. As we have seen, low-level and even midlevel white-collar positions proved frustrating for many young men. Meager pay, burdensome regulations, and stifling hierarchies were among the factors that led many to search constantly for better opportunities elsewhere.

Cultural ideals played a major role in pushing men beyond clerical positions. For generations of American men, occupational independence, whether in a small business, a trade, or a profession, had characterized manly success.[2] Andrew Carnegie expressed this traditional (and notably anticorporate) success ethic in a turn-of-the-century speech to students at Cornell University: "Is any would-be businessman before me content in forecasting his future, to figure himself as laboring all his life for a fixed salary? Not one, I am sure."[3] When George Latham's father told him he had "been working for someone else long enough," he explicitly reminded his son that while beginning his career as a bookkeeper in the employ of another was acceptable, he should set his sights higher.

Women's increasing presence in the corporate workplace further dulled young men's enthusiasm for remaining long in clerical posts. Women had been a significant fixture in white-collar positions since the early development of most Los Angeles companies, but leaders initially concentrated them in the positions of stenographer and secretary. By the 1920s, however, women began to hold a broader range of clerical positions, most notably those of bookkeeper and cashier. Responding to young male clerical workers' incessant complaints and high turnover rates, many executives opted to hire young, single women instead. Business officials were more willing to dismiss female grievances about poor conditions and tedious work. They hoped that, with fewer other middle-class work opportunities available, women would ultimately prove more malleable and willing clerical workers.[4]

Unfortunately for leaders, these personnel practices proved to raised new problems even as they solved others. Businessmen attempted to demonstrate white-collar work's masculine nature by careful excluding women from most middle- and upper-level positions, yet the complexity of large corporations' bureaucratic structure stymied executives' efforts to define white-collar work as "manly." While Americans came to view management as distinctly masculine, most firms recruited all new hires into lower-level positions. Companies thus had to convince these young men that entry-level posts offered manly opportunities. The very fact that some women held these jobs, however, called into question the acceptability of such work for men. While firms typically gave men in these jobs higher pay and greater opportunities for advancement than their female counterparts, many men would not long remain in such posts if prevailing wisdom considered them "womanly." And even in mid- and high-level white-collar positions rarely held by women, their very physical proximity in the building led some Americans to view such jobs as somehow effeminate—as "women's work." One scholar has argued that "often, women's presence seemed the most salient fact separating the new corporate workplace from the traditional male office." Seeking to combat such gender-related anxieties, companies physically separated men and women and often retitled positions based on the holder's sex. "The office job structure became gender segregated in such a way that women were neither interchangeable with men nor an economic and socially entitled group." They were instead "a separate 'nation.'"[5]

While elite men held the power within growing corporations, ambitious young men did not always perceive large firms as sites where they could plant their futures. Assuring company men that they indeed worked in a "separate nation" from female coworkers became a high priority in corporate cultures. In fact, the realities of the occupational environment of the time constrained men's ability to pursue other options. Whereas in the early nineteenth-century, 80 percent of the adult white male working populace was in some sense self-employed, by 1870 that proportion had dropped to 33 percent, and by 1940 to barely 20 percent.[6] Some historians imply that, given these facts, white men ultimately acquiesced to the likelihood of white-collar work. As they did so, activities outside the workplace, such as athletics and participation in fraternal organizations, gained importance; physicality became the new realm through which to prove one's manly prowess.[7] While in part correct, such interpretations are incomplete. The corporate workplace itself became contested terrain as leaders and employees sought to create new career paths through which to satisfy male ambitions. The gendered status of a broad range of low- and middle-level white-collar positions remained in flux throughout the 1920s.

Business leaders responded to young men's sensitivities about the long-term prospects of white-collar jobs on several levels. Not only did they try to protect men from the feminization of the corporate workplace through task and spatial segregation; they also constructed within their company cultures a distinct new vision of white-collar manhood. They did this by arguing that white-collar tasks called for the very best attributes of manhood and that their business would provide opportunities to fulfill this noble destiny. To be a corporate employee, most executives argued, meant that one had gained access to a ladder that would allow them to advance over the course of a lifetime in a "manly fashion." Accepting an office job, even a lowly clerkship, meant not that one had agreed to a low-paying routinized assignment. Rather, signing up with a large enterprise meant that a man had tied his future to a major corporation whose grand successes would become his.[8] Historians who have studied the practical structure of white-collar work are well aware of the gulf of experience, power, and authority between lower-level white-collar male workers and senior managers, yet business leaders usually ignored this chasm in their efforts to construct corporate cultures. The corporation provided a ladder, they argued. There were high rungs and low rungs, but they were all part of the same ascension toward a noble, manly identity.

Executives framed the idea of salaried employment in a large firm as an admirable endeavor for young white men; they promised opportunities to rise within corporate ranks to leadership positions. For their part, the young men who searched for work were influenced but not seduced by entrepreneurial or corporate success ideals. They were wary of bureaucratic employment but not unaware of its potential perks. Most ultimately sought their own preferred combination of independence, status, and security. Young men became keenly sensitive to evaluating the nature, status, and long-term prospects of specific jobs, and they continually searched for the post and the company that would assure the brightest future.

Building the Corporate Ladder

In recalling her southern California childhood, Fern Vickery remembered that her father had worked for a nursery for five years after their arrival

This cover from an issue of Union Oil's company magazine portrays white-collar men as strong and dignified, particularly as compared to the nondescript manual workers in the background. Reproduced from *Union Oil Bulletin* 1 (October 1921): 1, by permission of the Huntington Library, San Marino, California.

from Iowa in 1907. In 1912, however, the thirty-year-old man had bought a piece of property and started his own nursery. "He was very anxious to have his own business, as most men are, I think." Fern's assumption that "most men" wanted to own their own business is understandable, for those in her life did. In 1925, she married a man whose father had owned a successful enterprise in North Carolina and who aspired to emulate that success in southern California, despite repeated failures in the 1920s and 1930s.[9]

Fern's family was not alone. Even as large corporations came to dominate the American economy during the early twentieth century, many Americans regarded the corporation as an alien beast on the American landscape. The very year after Fern's father started his own business, President Woodrow Wilson said: "You know what happens when you are the servant of a corporation. You have in no instance access to the men who are really determining the policy of the corporation." According to Wilson, big business "swallowed up" employees and deprived them of individuality.[10]

In Los Angeles, which had a higher proportion of professionals and small business owners than most American cities, the climate seemed particularly ripe for individualistic ambitions. The glamour of Hollywood clashed directly with dreary perceptions of white-collar work. More than a few Angelenos dreamt of becoming a star in "the industry." If not that, even working for a studio carried a certain appeal. Few, of course, considered stardom a likely future, and not every local resident could be an entertainment industry employee. There did seem to be, however, other avenues to independence and wealth. Wild speculation in stocks and bonds briefly captivated middle-class culture in Los Angeles during the 1920s. The prospect of quick wealth and the subsequent easy life flourished among thousands who poured their savings into get-rich schemes.[11] Land speculation presented a particularly intriguing option. During the real estate boom of 1923, more than 12,000 Angelenos engaged in the real estate business, most as independent brokers. This figure represented one third of the total number of California realtors. Writing of this period from the vantage of the 1940s, one historian noted that "in 1922 and 1923 white-collar clerks in southern California everywhere deserted good office jobs to become real estate salesmen. Only the dull-wits remained behind the counter and at the desk."[12]

Within the dominant middle-class idealization of independent businessmen, professionals, and business leaders, Los Angeles executives determined to make white-collar employment in a single company seem an appealing long-term career. The metaphor of the ladder emerged as the nearly universal response among business leaders to the widespread reservations about white-collar positions. Certainly not all corporate jobs offered wealth, autonomy, and glamour, but they did all, at least theoretically, offer the opportunity to advance into jobs with more of these characteristics. If companies provided occupational ladders, then any position in the firm could in the long run prove a good one, since it provided a basis from which to advance.[13] Southern California Edison leaders, for instance, argued that "any Edison Company employee can hope to become its head since the differentiation of tasks is not permanent. There is a constant promotion of those who show ability and who have a capacity for initiative and for making decisions."[14] From this perspective, manly achievement and white-collar careers needed not to be mutually exclusive categories. Rather, large firms could provide dramatic new possibilities for young men to fulfill their highest potentials.

The concept of the company ladder rested on the practice of promotions, which sought to fill all vacancies from within and to allow present employees to advance. For many reasons, promotion systems seemed to make good business sense and received much discussion in management circles. The New York–based Alexander Hamilton Institute, which, beginning in 1917, published a series of management manuals entitled *Modern Business*, offered detailed recommendations. The initial volume, *Business and the Man*, spoke extensively about the benefits of filling vacancies from within: "As it is very important that the organization be kept loyal and enthusiastic, an executive must study the men under him, so that when a new position is to be filled he may promote an employe rather than go outside and bring a new man into the organization." Moreover, "Good business managers will be found almost without exception to have served faithfully in the beginning as rank and file workers." Two years later, a volume entitled *Office Management* spoke more bluntly about the need to utilize promotion systems if a company wanted to retain its best employees: "Concerns who do not adopt the policy of making promotions from the inside cannot hope to maintain a force of ambitious capable workers . . . the lack of opportunity for advancement is a frequent cause for men leaving their jobs just at the time when their experience is becoming a real asset to the firm."[15]

Los Angeles executives listened carefully to such advice and most major corporations implemented well-defined promotion systems. These policies allowed local firms to advertise honestly the possibilities for advancement, since their rapid growth in response to an expanding population and growing economy created a relatively fluid labor market. For instance, such systems flourished in large industrial firms like Union Oil, because of the managerial vacuums created by rapid growth. Between 1893 and 1926, the number of employees swelled from fifteen to over nine thousand. Union Oil's most dramatic growth began in the 1910s. In the midst of this expansion, the company established promotion policies, termed "civil service policies," mandating that vacancies be filled from within in all possible cases. This created an internal labor market based on the very principle of occupational mobility.[16]

Los Angeles banks also instituted policies designed to promote lifelong corporate careers. What it meant to be a career employee in banking had undergone a dramatic change. In turn-of-the-century Los Angeles, most banks were small enterprises with compact managerial hierarchies and few opportunities for advancement. Bank leaders, therefore, initially emphasized job security over promotions. At their first annual convention in 1891, California Bankers Association directors urged members to inspire loyalty with the promise that good performance would guarantee job security. During the 1910s and 1920s, however, as small banks merged with larger enterprises administered by complex chains of command, the prospect of rising through the ranks became an important enticement. By the 1920s, when several local banks had become multibranch businesses with hundreds and sometimes thousands of employees, promotions became an institutionalized aspect of banking operations. When a major bank merger created the Security-First National Bank in 1929, for instance, its employee magazine heralded that promotion from within would be the new firm's organizational rule. The bank quickly announced the creation of a personnel department to seek "young men of the highest quality obtainable, and assist them to advance step by step to the important positions of the bank." That fall, the company magazine printed an article entitled "Making Good a Promise" that listed the names of employees receiving promotions. Los Angeles's Pacific Southwest Savings Bank went so far as to publish a detailed list of advancements its employees could expect should their service be exemplary. Banks became strong advocates of career employees, not only because of the cost benefits of a stable workforce, but also because career personnel helped to gain depositors' confidence. Bank leaders knew that the presence of familiar employees would heighten customer comfort and trust.[17] The lure of promotions became a centerpiece of bank efforts to retain staff.

Internal promotion systems took on a notably familiar character in many banks because banks tended to be smaller, more localized operations than many other corporate businesses. Leaders could become quite familiar with employees and their qualifications for vacant positions. Correspondence between Farmers and Merchants Bank president I. W. Hellman and vice president Jackson A. Graves reveals a continual evaluation of employees' potential for higher positions. In a December 1914 letter, Graves wrote, "Kitchin I think is doing good work here. It may be that he will develop into a big enough man for the presidency in the course of a few years." This same scrutiny, however, could also result in a quick end to an employee's mobility. One month later, Graves again wrote to Hellman, this time to squelch the notion of promoting Kitchin. "Kitchin don't seem to have any faculty for handling men." Graves scored: "The idea of paying a man $5000 a year, who spends most of this time fishing and playing golf! It makes me tired."[18]

As its workforce grew from seven employees in 1895 to nearly three thousand by World War I, Southern California Edison also turned to promotions from within. SCE did not make the practice official policy, but internal mobility became its operational rule. By the 1920s, the company filled nearly all vacancies by promoting lower-level employees and appears to have been sincerely committed to furthering their careers. In 1922, when SCE ceased operations in the city of Los Angeles, the firm rehired most affected people in other branches of company service. In 1927, following the completion of a long-term construction project, SCE promised to rehire those who had occupied "positions of responsibility."[19]

Another public-regulated utility, Pacific Electric, did institutionalize promotion policies. At least by the 1920s, company materials indicate that for agents and other white-collar employees, such strategies became the rule. In response to a 1924 letter from a friend requesting a position, Southern Pacific (Pacific Electric's controlling body) vice president Paul Shoup told him that "your suggestion will receive attention for you are fully qualified," but noted that "it will not be a question of merit, since both he and you are fully qualified, but one of seniority and service." In 1927, Pacific Electric announced a new five-part promotion policy: (1) Station subordinates will be notified of all openings. (2) Employees must request position in writing. (3) If qualified people exist, men from company will fill position. (4) Assuming all else is equal, seniority will be basis of preference. (5) When restructuring results in staff reductions, senior employees will take the posts of juniors if their own job is cut.[20]

The Conservative Life Insurance Company of Los Angeles illustrates how company support for internal promotions increased with bureaucratic growth. Following the company's founding in 1900, its officials initially disputed the idea of careers spent with a single company. In 1903, Wilbur Tupper, vice president and superintendent of agencies, wrote, "Every agent should be loyal to his company; but his first allegiance is to his family and to himself; and that company or agency serves him best which enables him to discharge that great obligation." A young company amidst insurance giants, Conservative Life struggled to recruit agents from other firms during its early years. Not surprisingly, its literature stressed that insurance agents should go to work for the "best company" and not simply remain at one for the sake of loyalty. Within a year, however, the company dropped this idea. Tupper's stance shifted by 1904 when he wrote that "permanent business can be obtained only through permanent agents." When Conservative Life merged with the powerful Pacific Mutual in 1905, an emphasis on lifelong careers with the company became an important theme. In 1913, for instance, Pacific Mutual stated that with regard to the hiring of new agents, "the most important thing is to have permanent staff," because "it is not good to try and bring in quality people from another agency." By the late 1910s, Pacific Mutual had implemented a promotion system in which current employees were given first opportunity for all vacancies.[21]

Promoting Corporate Careers

Cultivating a stable and committed workforce, warding off lures from rival firms, and quelling their employees' own entrepreneurial interests required that large firms not merely institute promotion policies; they had to sell the concept to employees and market the very notion of a corporate career. Los Angeles companies took up this challenge with reckless abandon and touted a new career path appropriate to modern urban society. Discussions of advancement opportunities and the virtual canonization of those who had risen up the company's ranks pervaded the corporate cultures of most every major firm.

Union Oil enthusiastically heralded its "civil service system" in a steady stream of "mobility editorials" that emphasized the promotions possible with long and dedicated service.[22] Some appeared in the form of poems:

Promotion comes to him who sticks
unto his work and never kicks
Who watches neither clock nor sun
to tell him when his task his done
who toils not by a stated chart
defining to a jot his part
But gladly does a little more
than he's remunerated for
The man, in factory or shop,
who rises quickly to the top.[23]

Through such propaganda, Los Angeles business leaders articulated a vision of "white-collar manhood." They continually linked discussions of white-collar occupational norms and ideals with images of successful men. This occurred most often through example. Every local firm vividly recounted the biographies of employees receiving promotions as illustrative models of manly success. At Union Oil, those who advanced into middle- and upper-level management positions might have found their picture, short biography, and praise for their personal qualities featured prominently in the company magazine. In September 1925, for instance, employees read of W. F. Lewis's promotion from cashier of the San Francisco district to assistant district sales manager:

> Mr. Lewis owes his advancement from the ranks to his present position to his energetic application to duty. Coming to the company as a clerk in the Fresno office he was in rapid success appointed credit man and later cashier at that point. In July, 1914, he was transferred to Seattle as cashier, in which capacity he served until March, 1918, when he was transferred to the cashiership at San Francisco. His recent promotion has been received with keen pleasure by his many friends who wish him well in his new endeavor.[24]

This practice of promoting corporate careers with both mobility editorials and real-life accounts of corporate success occurred in most large firms. The Los Angeles First National Bank repeatedly published articles promising promotions for meritorious service, including an adaptation of a Shakespeare line that began, "All The Bank's A Ladder." Banks also actively publicized their executives' mobility and used such stories as a major theme in their employee publications. The Farmers and Merchants National Bank, for instance, noted in 1927 that four of its top officers had risen through the ranks; three had started in the entry-level position of messenger, in the years 1894, 1901, and 1904.[25]

The celebration of promotion policies became a central theme of most corporate cultures. The specific components of a company's promotion policies and the manner in which executives emphasized them, however, varied widely. Firms employed the corporate career ethos according to their own needs and circumstances. While most, like Union Oil and Los Angeles banks, promised promotions as a reward for good performance, others communicated prospects in a more authoritarian manner. Alongside emphases on upward mobility, for example, SCE publications chastised those who fell short of company expectations. SCE's vice president for public relations wrote to employees in 1914 that although "long and faithful service is honorable," it is not enough, for "there must be progress, otherwise the worth of an employee to his company will diminish." SCE frequently framed the mobility ethos in this "produce or perish" manner and stressed not only the prospects for promotion, but also the dismal future for the unsuccessful. In a chapter on occupational mobility from a 1921 public relations textbook, the firm's vice president for public relations noted that lack of application, not ability or ambition, prevented most from rising. Unrewarded employees simply had not tried hard enough. SCE leaders had codified this message in 1919 when company publications began trumpeting a twist on the socialist creed: "From every man according to his ability. To every man according to his worth."[26] This adage well-reflected the dual nature of SCE's emphasis on promotions. The firm promised a bright future for employees, but only after making extensive demands and veiled threats to those whose efforts fell short of expectations.

Companies that struggled and declined, like PE, had a more difficult time celebrating promotion possibilities. Despite its protestations to the contrary, PE's retrenchment during the 1920s limited advancement prospects. As a consequence, news of promotions appeared less frequently. In 1925, the company magazine proposed feature stories about "the lives of employees who through hard work are climbing up the corporate ladder." Such news in fact proved rare in the months and years to come. One hint of employees' discouraging futures came in a 1925 editorial in the magazine of Los Angeles Railway (PE's counterpart serving the city proper): "What Are Your Chances to Get Ahead Here?" The article refuted rumors that trainmen had only one chance in twelve of moving up the company ladder, and asserted that the actual odds were much better. "The man who is determined to advance himself will put just as much energy and study into his job whether there are 11 or 1100 men ahead of him." If climbing the corporate ladder allowed one the opportunity for individual advancement in an otherwise confining occupational environment, then PE's limited promotion opportunities presented a clear problem. As if to combat such concerns, its leaders shrilly emphasized the "manliness" of company employment. In a particularly blatant example, PE's "New Year's pledge" on the cover of their company magazine in 1922 literally accented their employees' manhood: "[I pledge] to be a *Man*, filling a *Man's Place* in a man's game, and prove ours the best manned industry in southern California."[27]

Other efforts were more subtle. Numerous issues of the *Pacific Electric Magazine*, for instance, featured articles or texts that in some way singled out, diminished, or made fun of women. In July 1924, for example, a lengthy poem entitled, "A Wail 'bout the Frail," lamented the difficulty of understanding women, except their perpetual desire to "powder their noses." It opened: "A Woman is queer; there's no doubt about that, she hates to be thin and she

In this official 1932 photo of Southern California Edison president George Ward, the firm sought to convey the essence of the powerful corporate executive. Courtesy of Department of Special Collections, University Libraries, University of Southern California.

hates to be fat; one minute it's laughter—the next it's a cry. You can't understand her however you try. But there's one thing about her that everyone knows. A woman's not dressed till she powders her nose." Jokes at women's expense appeared often in the magazine. In another example, a 1926 article that highlighted how three women had proven themselves extremely capable in the company's engineering drafting department preceded a box with the joke: "It is almost as difficult for a man to live up to his ideals as for a woman to live up to her photographs."[28] Perhaps by continually singling out the difference between male employees and their female counterparts, leaders assured men of their masculine status, even if their careers were not living up to the manly ideal.

Pacific Electric did use what promotions it could to tout the corporate career ethos. None was more important to company leadership than the story of D. W. Pontius, who had truly worked his way up from an entry-level clerical position. In 1929 PE named him president and the firm spared no effort in promoting his career history, regularly reminding employees of his lowly beginnings. In 1928, for instance, the company magazine printed his baby picture and declared: "Know the determined-looking little fellow? Sure you do! Up the ladder to rank and fame he has lost neither the determination nor the see-all piercing eyes that are evidenced in his young childhood." The following year the magazine heralded his appointment as president by noting that Pontius "really ought to be written up for the success magazines, for no man's career more strikingly proves what an average man may accomplish. Thirty-eight years ago he started in about the humblest job a railroad could give him."[29]

Pacific Mutual faced a number of unique challenges and opportunities in its efforts to promote corporate careers. Because the overwhelming majority of insurance employees were agents, with significant managerial departments only at a central headquarters, company organizational pyramids tended to be quite flat, limiting opportunities for upward mobility. As much as possible, executives did highlight advancements as evidence that loyal employees could rise up its ladder. In 1930 leaders announced one such promotion with the words: "His steady advancement has been justified by his work. He is still on the way up." Officials often, however, had to turn to other methods to promote Pacific Mutual careers. Loyalty became one of the central issues in the company's corporate culture. By the 1920s, Pacific Mutual heralded long-term careers as key to an employee's status and actively publicized those with long service records.[30]

Pacific Mutual leaders also defined manly success in terms of sales production. This construction of manliness, based on a sort of entrepreneurial ideal, fit well within a longstanding tradition of manhood based on individual productivity. Pacific Mutual fostered an intensely competitive corporate culture in which leading agents were the subject of glowing articles in the company magazine, and they received vacations, bonuses, and other incentives. An issue of *Pacific Mutual News* in 1911 typified the kinds of messages that dominated Pacific Mutual's corporate culture during the 1910s and 1920s. It included six features: a cover article celebrating the two most productive agents for 1910, a letter from the president in which he noted the company's great success but asserted that "we are confident we can do still better," an article on competition between agencies, an editorial urging employees to "increase their sense of personal responsibility," an article praising the Los Angeles agency for outstanding sales, and last, nine separate rankings of agents in terms of the amount sold.[31]

Amidst Pacific Mutual's frenzied efforts to cultivate a cadre of dedicated agents, affirming male identities was made particularly difficult because the company also hired large numbers of female agents. Throughout the 1910s and 1920s, American insurance companies turned to female agents, believing them more effective in securing women as customers. By 1930, Pacific Mutual's Los Angeles agency employed sixty women, who in 1929 wrote nearly $5 million in new business. While this sales record thrilled company leaders, it put them on the defensive against some male agents, who struggled with the challenge that successful female agents posed to their occupational identity. Pacific Mutual executives responded to this dilemma in several ways. In most agencies the company established separate "women's departments" so that men and women were not technically under the same command, and the company magazine discussed the activities of its female agents in a separate section called "Women and their Activities." Occasionally, Pacific Mutual leaders wrote articles defending the practice of hiring women and trying to reduce resentment toward them. In a March 1930 issue, for instance, they reprinted a newspaper column that argued, "Most working women are working because they have to, not because they want to. The modern world is giving them, not a new freedom, but a new duty."[32]

Pacific Mutual's desire to placate male sensibilities, however, had its limits; and the company granted women equal access to prizes and rewards based on sales, though it had to explicitly defend this policy. One gender distinction it did place on men's and women's participation in sales contests affected the right of employees to hold offices in honorary sales clubs. Male agents with the highest sales held division offices. The highest ranking woman in each sales division, however, assumed the position of secretary-treasurer.[33]

Experiencing Corporate Careers

Major Los Angeles corporations carefully designed promotion systems so that current employees would have priority in filling vacancies. In addition to assuring a ready pool of at least partially trained labor that would lower some of the costs associated with turnover, these systems also promised to reduce turnover itself by encouraging employees to remain with the firm. Persuading young men to adopt such mindsets, however, required getting them to view favorably a career spent climbing the ladder of a single firm. Corporate strategies to transform career ideals raise important questions about the intersection of business structures with social practices and mores. How would American men react to the prospect of corporate employment? Would ambitious young men buy into the corporate career ideal? Would success in white-collar bureaucracies become the new standard of manly achievement?

Changing occupational realities clearly aided corporate efforts. The increasing dominance of big business resulted in declining opportunities for independent entrepreneurs in some sectors of the economy, as small businessmen struggled to compete in the corporate world.[34] The ability to secure an independent livelihood in the United States had, of course, never matched the cultural ideal of a nation of independent farmers and small shopkeepers. Small business proprietorship had never been an easy life: owners certainly knew that, though they could rise to great heights, there existed the ever-present possibility of failure. Large firms readily advertised the struggles of small businesses by way of contrast to the stability of working for a large enterprise. Southern California Edison warned its employees in 1916 that notions of quick riches were unrealistic in comparison to "starting at the bottom of the ladder in some substantial industry and progressing rung by rung to the great things which are at the top."[35]

By the 1910s, many in southern California and throughout the United States began to view corporate ladders as a decent career prospect in a rapidly changing and complicated economy. In correspondence between two brothers in 1914, one consoled the other, a judge, about losing his "faithful secretary," who was leaving to work for the Ford Motor Company: "While you have been good to him and he has a fairly lucrative position, it must be realized that the tenure of a political position is very uncertain and offers very little chances for one in his position to advance. While with a big company, like Ford's, there are many opportunities in front of a good, bright, hustling youngster."[36]

By the early twentieth century, most people knew of someone who worked in a white-collar bureaucracy and likely had at least anecdotal evidence of the opportunities for promotion. For southern Californians, advancement seemed particularly likely in large and heavily bureaucratized firms experiencing rapid growth, such as SCE and Union Oil. These companies not only had multilayered hierarchies with numerous increments but also grew quickly enough that management continually created new positions. Employees knew that when a vacancy occurred, the position would be filled from within. Furthermore, the many small increments on the occupational ladder meant that promotions were common and expected. Finally, rapid corporate growth created a virtual employment vacuum, pulling lower-ranked employees upward. Though managerial hierarchies were pyramid-shaped, meaning that not all employees could advance, the continual turnover at each level resulted in a fluid labor market.

A significant portion, if not the majority, of male Union Oil employees progressed steadily up the company ladder. In a ten-year sample (1927–37) of mid-career Union Oil employees having served at least ten years, roughly 20 percent received at least six promotions; 60 percent received three or more. Only two percent received no major promotions.[37] George Anderson's career exemplifies those of many Union Oil employees. He first worked as a junior clerk in the Union branch accounts department, hired in 1913. Seven years later, the company made Anderson auditor of its San Francisco office. In 1923, Union named him traveling auditor of the station accounts division in Los Angeles and in 1926 put him in charge of forms and printing for the Los Angeles division. Two years later, Anderson became director of the station accounts division and, in 1931, rose to auditor of Union Oil's northern division. In 1933, Union promoted him to accountant of the Seattle District and in 1936 to chief traveling auditor for the Southern division. Although Anderson probably experienced more occupational and geographical changes than the average employee, his career pattern mirrored those of many in its multiple changes and gradual advancement within a complex hierarchy. As was true of the employment history of many white-collar men, it is not always clear to what extent each promotion represented real advancement; yet repeated changes highlighted corporate careers, and over the years most employees advanced in salary and position.

Even in southern California's public transportation sector, where retrenchment dominated in the 1920s, male white-collar employees could reasonably expect some opportunities for advancement. All the managers and supervisors within the Los Angeles Railway Company's transportation department in 1924 had begun their careers with LARC at entry-level positions. A review of employee records at LARC from 1906 to 1920 suggests that the company regularly filled vacancies from within, and that well over half the employees who spent at least five years with the firm received several promotions.[38]

Anderson Borthwick was among those southern Californians who climbed into a corporate leadership position. He migrated from New York in 1914 and started working as a messenger for the First National Bank. Borthwick quickly began to climb the bank's ladder, and by the time he reached a management post, the firm had established a tradition of developing managers from entry-level hires. The bank typically recruited college students for part-time posts and, if they proved desirable, urged them to "centralize on the education that would be effectively used in business." By the 1930s, almost all of the bank's branch managers, in fact, had started out as part-time "after-school" employees.[39]

Advice manuals and career guides written for young men confirmed these realities and proved a consistent ally of corporate efforts. A 1922 book, titled *Choosing Your Life Work,* for instance, presented readers a detailed guide to numerous occupations and told what these jobs entailed and paid, as well as other information. In almost every instance, the author provided an analysis of promotion possibilities; and for white-collar positions, he offered particularly explicit information such as: "Advancement in a bank is usually very slow, but for a man of marked ability there will be much opportunity for rising to a place of trust"; "The Sales Manager is sometimes promoted from a position of salesman or buyer, and at times is drawn from the advertising department"; and "A clerk's work is usually done in pleasant surroundings, is not difficult and generally offers good chances for advancement to the ambitious worker." Another career guide, *I Find My Vocation,* contained numerous drawings of ladders used to illustrate promotion opportunities in different jobs. The book noted, "Many young people have the idea that a man who is now eminent has always been so . . . Most of these higher positions are reached only after a long period in which the worker serves in a series of subordinate positions. And generally speaking, the more desirable the ultimate position, the more numerous are the steps leading to it."[40]

But, of course, the corporate success ideal was also just that, an ideal. Measured against the promises of company rhetoric and selected case studies, opportunities for dramatic success in corporate careers often fell short. Not all employees at Union Oil, for instance, advanced steadily up the ladder. Born in England in 1870, Edward J. Adams moved in 1891 to the United States, where he found a job as bookkeeper at the Standard Oil Company. He worked there twenty years before obtaining a position as clerk in Union Oil's Seattle office, a position he held until 1934, when the company promoted him to assistant agent at the Tacoma, Washington, office. Despite twenty years of service in a semiprofessional position with another oil firm, Union Oil's adherence to promotions from within forced Adams to enter at one of the lowest white-collar positions. Adams worked another twenty years before receiving a promotion. For every story of a rapid corporate advancement, there are others of men like Adams who spent years with a company yet advanced little or not at all.[41]

Few could be assured of reaching the upper rungs on corporate ladders, since the simple arithmetic of business hierarchies dictated that only a few could advance to the top. No doubt there were many like Henry L. Ward who faced rejection in efforts to climb company ladders. Ward came to San Jose at the age of seventeen in 1921 and obtained a position as a clerk for Western Union. He left the firm in 1924 because of "no advancement." The Pacific Mail Steamship Company hired Ward in 1924 as a typist in the accounting department, but he quit three months later. His personnel file stated that Ward's services were "satisfactory" but that he was "not good material for advancement."[42] Ward may have viewed these firms as avenues to success, but he found only disappointment.

Somewhere between the idealized construction of independent business success that flourished in the nineteenth century and the equally idealized corporate mobility ethos large firms advertised in the early twentieth century, most young men tried to negotiate their competing desires for independence, security, and status. Career dreams and aspirations always played within a much more complex array of desires and needs in the lives of individual people. As critics of social mobility studies have pointed out, many other factors often overshadow occupational success ideals; American men clearly had more forces acting on their lives than simply idealized constructions of manliness or their company's urgings.[43] Lloyd McCampbell, for instance, obtained a job as lease clerk for a Texas oil company in 1920, but after a bitterly cold winter, his girlfriend persuaded him to move to southern California. McCampbell quit the position, moved with her, and found employment at Union Oil in 1922. Several years later, when the company tried to transfer him to a different city in southern California, McCampbell quit, preferring to remain at his present residence.[44]

Many employees moved from job to job for reasons that were not obvious. Oliver Palmer worked as a clerk at six different companies between 1913 and 1920. The Pacific Mail Steamship Company hired the thirty-five-year-old Palmer in 1920 as a freight clerk, noting that his letters of recommendation from previous employers were all very positive. Pacific Mail began grooming Palmer for a position in their Hong Kong office. After several months, however, he resigned, obtaining an additional positive recommendation from this most recent firm. For unknown reasons, Palmer moved from city to city around the United States, generally staying less than a year at each location.[45]

Historical scrutiny shatters notions that any corporate career ideal dominated the dreams and experiences of young Americans. But how *did* Americans react to corporate employment? To what extent did they accept and find realistic the goal of some advancement up the ranks of a single company? Evaluating men's reactions to white-collar life is difficult, because it requires analysis from conflicting data. We can find significant numbers of American men who embraced the corporate career ideal and experienced significant advancement, just as we can find significant numbers who either rejected corporate dictates or were unsuccessful by its standards. When faced with the prospect of corporate employment, young men ultimately evaluated positions based on their own potential rank on the corporate ladder. Recognizing that salaried white-collar employment did not offer a monolithic experience, young Americans became keenly sensitive to what kinds of conditions and rewards various positions would offer. A 1926 survey of office workers is significant in revealing that only slightly over half expected promotions. Those that did, already held the highest positions in their departments. Those on the lower rungs expressed the greatest pessimism. As companies grew in size, employment at the lowest rungs became increasingly distasteful; young men recognized the difficulty of advancing from such positions. Yet, as men moved up the corporate ladder, many began to perceive greater opportunities for social mobility, steady income, and good salaries, especially when compared to other career options. The existence of promotion systems and a complex hierarchical network containing minute distinctions in rank in expanding companies meant that many Americans could rise through white-collar ranks to positions of authority.[46]

That employees understood the benefits of promotion systems is evident in the active support many expressed for their establishment. In 1920, Pacific Mutual agents requested the establishment of policies similar to those enacted earlier for the company's office staff. Some Los Angeles bank employees evidenced support for these systems in expressing anger over apparent infractions of routine policies. In 1915, a teller approached Farmers and Merchant president Hellman and, according to Hellman, "called my attention to his many years' service, stating that he thought when we elected the last assistant cashier the place should have been given to him, as he has always done faithful work for the bank and was entitled to the promotion." Hellman saw to it that the teller received the position when it next came available.[47]

The perceptions of those on differing rungs of the corporate ladder become clear when analyzing why most firms experienced high turnover at entry-level positions but less with each step on the ladder. The high turnover in junior posts reflected two factors. First, many companies screened their entry-level employees to eliminate men who seemed ill-suited to serve the firm well.[48] Second, men in these positions were more likely to be young, single, and in a position to shift locations if personal situations changed or better opportunities arose. As these lower-level white-collar positions lost status, and prospects for advancement seemed dubious, the pursuit of better opportunities no doubt took on heightened urgency. The rapid feminization of clerical positions has tended to obscure the fact that, as corporate bureaucracies grew, management increasingly stripped entry-level positions of status and authority. As promotion opportunities from these positions decreased, fewer men sought them and those who did often remained only a short time. They transferred frequently in search of better opportunities.[49]

In sharp contrast to the high turnover in entry-level positions, employee rosters at many companies showed greater stability in midlevel positions. At Pacific Mail, loyalists staffed managerial positions. Among the ten general officers at its San Francisco office in 1922, only two had served fewer than ten years with the company; five had served more than twenty years, one thirty-eight years, and another forty-six years. At Pacific Mutual, the twenty-nine leading agents in 1928 had held their positions for an average of eleven and a half years, and most of them probably had served the company even longer in junior positions. At SCE by the 1920s, most departments reported little turnover. The Dispatching Department, for instance, employed on average between thirteen and nineteen people from 1923 to 1927, but it lost no more than two employees per year and generally only experienced the departure of one employee per year.[50]

If many lower-level employees felt doubts about just how far they could climb, midlevel and senior managers perceived greater chances for promotion and, thus, were more attached to their positions. J. E. Brick Elliott, mentioned earlier as one who transferred from company to company, finally started his own drilling company in the early 1920s. Elliott found it difficult to lure men from large companies to help manage his operation. He did ultimately find a superintendent, but only at the whopping price of $750 a month, an unusually high salary for the position.[51] Elliott's difficulty in recruiting managers from established firms reflected the extent to which they enjoyed secure positions with good salaries, benefits, and promotion opportunities. Middle-aged men with families to care for and relatively good opportunities for promotion demanded greater inducements. While few corporate employees advanced to high-level positions, most men in senior management had climbed through company ranks.[52]

A 1926 article in *Atlantic Monthly* reported on a survey of college men suggesting that corporate employment continued to rank low among occupational preferences. According to the author, college graduates expressed resentment when not promoted quickly and often considered corporate employment too restricting.[53] And yet, at each higher rung on the ladder, men found heightened status, pay, and opportunities to advance. At some point, most men who advanced out of entry-level posts came to believe that a career with one firm offered adequate personal and material compensation. Personnel stability increased as one progressed up corporate hierarchies.

Manhood Redefined?

Ambiguity characterized the way in which young white men in Los Angeles viewed chances of "success" in white-collar employment. While some came to view office work as a stable and secure job with some opportunities for eventual promotion, others continued to view the corporate workplace as little more than a dungeon where "dull-wits" spent their lives in servitude. Images in popular culture only underscored these divisions. Throughout the 1920s, sharply conflicting representations of company men surfaced in books, magazines, and films, as lingering nineteenth-century constructions clashed with the new corporate ideal.

Sometimes, competing images collided in the same article. In the summer of 1925, *Sunset* magazine published an essay titled "Making $5 Grow to Millions," which chronicled the story of retail magnate George Pepperdine. The author effusively described how Pepperdine, with "little formal education and in poor health," initially became a bookkeeper but had "no intention of working for someone else all his life." In 1909 Pepperdine started a mail-order accessory catalog for auto parts, and by the mid 1920s it had grown into a lucrative chain of 125 stores. The tale of Pepperdine's dramatic rise to independent wealth resonated as a mythic archetype in middle-class culture. Though faced with challenging circumstances, he determined to achieve independent business success, and in doing so, epitomized the manly ideal for ambitious white men. Yet, in the midst of praising this "self-made" entrepreneur, the writer discussed the benefits of working as an employee in Pepperdine's company. He reported that it was "not easy to get into the Pepperdine organization," but then stressed that if an employee "passes the test and is accepted as one of the family, the salaries and bonuses are attractive and the opportunities for promotion extraordinary."[54] In celebrating both Pepperdine's business achievements and the rewards of working for his firm, the author attempted to straddle a growing chasm between the lingering nineteenth-century construction of middle-class manhood grounded in individual autonomy and the realities of the twentieth century.

Leaders promoted the ideal of a single-company career, and young white men evaluated their employment opportunities in a cultural milieu that offered deeply conflicting interpretations of corporate employment. The pattern that began to emerge, however, suggested that, just as a collar line evolved to distinguish between working- and middle-class status, an equally powerful pecking order developed among the various steps on the corporate ladder to define acceptable variants of white male identity. Senior figures in corporate hierarchies increasingly appeared in films and literature as strong-willed individuals with considerable power. Such characterizations hinted that corporate ladders, as promised by leadership, did in fact offer ambitious and talented men opportunities for individualistic achievement. Cultural depictions of employees farther down the ladder, however, were less flattering. Books, magazines, and films more often showed middle- and lower-level workers as faceless pawns with no initiative or control, and no hint of masculinity. The antibureaucratic tradition in earlier constructions of American masculinity lingered as those working in subservient positions appeared pitiful and effeminate.

Safety Last, a popular 1923 Harold Lloyd film, captured the varying degrees of status and respect on the white-collar ladder. The movie opens with Lloyd at a small-town train station leaving for the big city. His fiancée tells him at the depot, "It would break my heart if you failed." Once in the city, the best position Lloyd can find is as a lowly sales clerk in a fabric store. Embarrassed by the job, he seeks to make his fiancée believe he is "making it big." He sends her jewelry and writes false notes about his prosperity. Ironically, all the talk of Harold's success leads his fiancée's mother to worry about his being all alone with so much money, so the fiancée decides to visit. When she arrives, she first spots him working behind the sales desk and gasps in horror. Yet Lloyd, seeing her panic-stricken face, pretends to be helping to train other clerks. His quick thinking provided her considerable relief. Harold then receives a note to see the general manager about a complaint, and coyly excuses himself. Several minutes later, however, his fiancée sees him coming out of the general manager's office and assumes *he* is the manager. This makes her deliriously happy and proud. Lloyd ultimately escapes the predicament by gaining his fiancée's love and approval through scaling a twelve-story building in a heroic act.

Safety Last offers a powerful commentary on the precarious status of bureaucratic employment. Although nonmanual work gained middle-class status during the nineteenth century, by the period of corporate emergence, it alone did not assure a healthy, masculine identity. Senior management became esteemed figures, yet according to both the employee and his fiancée, the lowest clerks within the company occupied positions of near shame. Notably, Lloyd only wins his fiancée's approval through an act of physical prowess, a clear reversion to notions of physical masculinity.[55]

If corporate interests did not rewrite constructions of masculinity, the emergence of corporate capitalism did affect representations of employment in popular culture. Surveys suggested that the common nineteenth-century derision of "hirelings" and dependent employees in American literature faded somewhat. During the Progressive era, American authors and playwrights sometimes, though not always, gave corporate employment greater recognition and status.[56] The mere fact of changing occupational realities no doubt led to shifting cultural understandings. As corporations came to dominate American business, executives became key players in the nation's economy and public life, and writers increasingly drew on business themes in their work. The increasing representation of corporate life in American literature had the reciprocal effect of granting it heightened cultural legitimacy.[57]

The individual white-collar employee played an increasingly important role in the works of many American writers as well. In turn-of-the-century popular literature, heroes increasingly were white-collar employees, men who achieved business success by rising through corporate hierarchies. Famously, all of Horatio Alger's heroes were male employees who rose through the ranks; no one was an entrepreneur. And, as one scholar notes, "the riches Alger's heroes achieved were jobs in offices at good salaries."[58]

Many middle-class publications celebrated the white-collar career ideal. Los Angelenos read of the merits of corporate advancement not only in company publications, but in various local journals and magazines. *The Graphic*, a Los Angeles progressive journal, had, since its beginning in the late nineteenth century, highlighted business leaders in a column entitled "Prominent Personalities." By the 1910s, these personalities frequently included men who had climbed company ladders. In the 1920s, *Sunset* began to feature essays by corporate personnel directors and career counselors that not only affirmed corporate careers but offered tips on how to get promoted.[59]

Numerous other local publications joined in promoting the white-collar mobility ethos. *Southern California Business*, the magazine of Los Angeles's Chamber of Commerce, editorialized frequently about corporate careers in the 1920s. In an essay entitled "Chance to Climb," the magazine counseled junior employees on how to impress their superiors and secure advancement. Popular literature affirmed corporate careers by echoing the mobility ethos as a success ideal. *Saturday Night*, which catered to affluent southern Californians, reported regularly on significant promotions within local companies. With descriptions similar to those in company magazines, it highlighted recent promotions as symbols of regional pride and heralded corporate executives as role models for young men.[60]

While advancement up bureaucratic ranks became a promising route to a successful masculine identity, powerful critiques of bureaucratic employment offered steady challenges to the voice of corporate interests in middle-class culture. For every representation celebrating one who had advanced to a leadership position, critical indictments of corporate employment focused on the plight of men who had not. In 1912, *Atlantic Monthly* ran an article titled "The Man Who Failed," which chronicled the story of a washed-up thirty-five-year-old former manager. Fired after failing to gain a big promotion, the man could not obtain a new position because no one trusted him. He overheard one personnel director say, "I want young men in my business. By the time a man's thirty-five he ought to be fixed so that he doesn't have to come to me for a job if he's any good." In a later article in *Century* magazine, readers learned of a senior executive who, dissatisfied with new management, quit his job but could not find another position. Believing his situation more difficult than that of unemployed laborers, he said that "in the larger organizations there is usually an oversupply of executive talent, and almost never a chance for one who has not grown up with the business."[61] While companies promised that promotion systems would provide new pathways to success, these policies presented hardships to people who, for whatever reason, found themselves in middle age looking for mid-career positions. Readers learned that in the white-collar world, opportunities wasted could mean an early end to hopes for "success."

Representations of men in middle- and lower-level white-collar positions suggest that the ideal of the "self-made man," characterized by some professionals, small businessmen, and entrepreneurs, continued to influence images of success long after large corporations began to overshadow small businesses.[62] A 1923 *Sunset* article depicted the plight of a man whose wife left him after twenty-three years of marriage, giving as one of her reasons that she felt "ashamed" of her husband's position as a clerk. The man noted that "he had no intention of remaining a clerk always," and he went on to start a successful business of his own.[63]

Perhaps no stronger critique of white-collar employment ever appeared in American popular culture than King Vidor's 1928 film, *The Crowd*, seen by hundreds of thousands of American moviegoers. Released at a time when big business seemed to reign supreme, the two-hour silent movie presented evidence of the continued challenge facing corporate leaders in their efforts to lure young men into white-collar employment. The story began on July 4, 1900, with the birth of Johnny Sims in an idyllic small town. Upon seeing his new son, Johnny's father triumphantly announced, "There's a little man the world is going to hear from all right . . . I'm going to give him every opportunity." Twenty-one years later, however, Johnny Sims was working as #137 in a New York City insurance company, toiling away in what can only be described as white-collar hell. His desk was in a vast room where hundreds of identically dressed young men sat in evenly spaced rows turning page after page of documents in perfect unison. Johnny's home life proves equally stifling, as his wife and in-laws grow bitter over his inability to climb in the firm. When he finally gets a break and wins $100 in an advertising jingle contest, an automobile strikes and kills his youngest child during the celebration. Despondent with grief, Johnny then quits before being fired for poor performance. The film closes with Johnny and his wife escaping to the movies. He sits in the theater having a great time, but as the camera fades, viewers see him watching amidst a crowd of thousands who appear and act exactly as he. Even in this brief moment of pleasure, he remains immersed in the crowd.[64]

The Crowd offered Americans a bleak appraisal of urban life in the 1920s. Small-town kids moved to cities, only to find themselves enveloped in urban jungles where opportunities for personal autonomy and individual achievement were at best rare. If a young man already leery of white-collar work saw the film, it likely reinforced his fear of "working for someone else" any longer than necessary. Executives no doubt winced at its depiction of company life as well, recognizing the message it sent to young men searching for promising ways to start their careers. Yet these leaders may also have seen a silver lining in the film, in that several in the cast expressed frustration at Johnny Sims's inability to rise up the firm's ladder. At one point, Sims mocked a friend who was willing to grovel in order to receive promotions, yet grudgingly acknowledged his friend's advancement. *The Crowd* revealed a crack in the pervasive loathing of dependent employment. Working in a large firm might not be intolerable if the firm allowed one to rise to a leadership position.

Executives found popular culture an inconsistent ally in their efforts to promote new standards of careers and success. On the positive side, corporate employment increasingly became the setting for stories and plays that featured executives as heroes. Yet while literary and other cultural depictions endowed major figures in big business with a virile, masculine identity, most white-collar men served in middle- or lower-level positions with less autonomy, power, and income. Cultural representations of these figures noted their disempowered standing. Negative depictions of white-collar employment rooted in the lingering nineteenth-century ideal of economic self-determination also persisted. The dream of entrepreneurial success did not give way to corporate ideals. Rather, both themes came to coexist in American popular culture.

Half Empty or Half Full?

In 1910, the *American Globe*, a Los Angeles business magazine, trumpeted Harry Rodgers's career history as the ideal model for young men to follow. Rodgers moved to Los Angeles in 1905 at the age of twenty-four. He came with some experience in the insurance business but accepted a humble position as "general utility man" for the Los Angeles Investment Company. According to the author, Rodgers devoted himself to the firm: "He did anything he could do. Why he even did the janitor work. Some young men who would be too proud to do this kind of work are today either living on their people, or occupying positions offering no possibilities for the future." So what did five years of such loyal service earn Rodgers? It garnered him, readers learned, the position of "main purchasing agent" in this, the "greatest financial institution in Los Angeles." The story is curious, for it seems to idolize a man who worked slavishly for five years simply to receive a modest white-collar post. Such a reading, however, misses the point. In *only* five years, Rodgers rose *within an important business* from a menial post to a position of some significance. The biography articulates two critical themes echoing throughout corporate cultures during the early twentieth century. First, white-collar firms provided opportunities for a man from his first days in the firm throughout the course of his career to ascend into high-status managerial positions. Second, white-collar careers allowed individuals to identify themselves with major business institutions and to share in their stature and prestige. Corporate offices, according to this perspective, were thus ideal sites for ambitious and aggressive young men to prove their worth and bask in well-deserved status.[65]

Similar stories reverberated through corporate Los Angeles during the 1910s and 1920s, the frequency of which suggests business insecurities. In heralding white-collar careers with such fervor, executives seemed to protest too much. Though large businesses pervaded American life by the 1910s, young white men's career expectations and occupational ideals continued to reflect entrepreneurial and small business mindsets more appropriate to an earlier era. While office jobs in powerful urban corporations appealed to many young men as starting points in their careers, they expected to move rapidly and far beyond such bureaucratic posts. Few set their sites on being middle-managers.

Social mobility and corporate employment studies suggest that large numbers of Americans did indeed cast their lots with white-collar interests. Once employees began to move up the ladder they were likely to sign on for the long haul. Popular culture increasingly sanctioned such decisions by celebrating corporate leaders' virility and powerful standing in American life. Corporate career ideals did not replace entrepreneurial and individualistic desires; indeed, they continue to flourish today. But white-collar mobility did become an accepted alternative. By the 1920s, constructions of manhood had expanded to encompass both entrepreneurial and professional independence and ascendance up company ladders as legitimate avenues to success.

The fusion of reasonable opportunities for promotion with fringe benefit packages providing familial security motivated hundreds of thousands of young southern Californians to explore corporate careers during the early twentieth century. These men did not, however, determine any particular job's merits solely based on these components. Once hired, employees valued benefits and took advantage of promotion opportunities, but such things alone did not define a job. Far more personal factors worked to make a job a good job, or a source of drudgery. No material reward could fully negate an unpleasant or hostile workplace environment. Conversely, deficiencies in salary or advancement could in part be tolerated if one derived other benefits from the work. The degree of workplace community continually loomed as a nebulous but critical element in the formation of successful corporate cultures.

SEVEN

THE CORPORATION AS COMMUNITY

> We try to make the feeling in our organization as close and loyal as that of a college fraternity. "Me and the prez" is a term which most aptly expresses the feeling of relationship which should exist between the employee and the firm.
>
> —R. H. Ballard, president, Southern California Edison, 1915

On a June evening in 1927, one of the Pacific Southwest Savings Bank's senior executives treated fifteen employees to dinner at the posh downtown California Club, and then to a show at the Orpheum Theater. Bank executives had entertained this particular group several times previously with dinners at a vice president's home. One might expect executives and employees to meet occasionally over dinner: informational briefings, motivational seminars, and banquets to celebrate promotions or retirements all provided occasions that might call for such collegial gatherings. These dinners, however, represented none of the above. The guest list comprised the bank's Pasadena division baseball team roster, and it was bank vice president John Willis Baer, one of the cohort's most ardent boosters, who hosted most of the meals. At the June dinner and show, the group celebrated its championship in the Pasadena Playground Community Baseball League.[1]

While Pacific Southwest Savings Bank existed to make a profit, company records often portrayed an organization more closely resembling an athletic league, social club, or fraternal order. Social and recreational activities played an integral part in the bank's corporate culture. In this, Pacific Southwest enjoyed much company; most Los Angeles firms became the site of active social networks. Officially a transportation company, Pacific Electric became a community in the lives of its employees. In the most dramatic example, on

September 18, 1929, PE opened a new five-story employee clubhouse adjacent to its downtown Los Angeles headquarters for its increasingly popular employee club, which had begun in 1916. The building housed a 900-seat movie theater, ballroom, dance floor, library, restaurant, barber shop, and lounge, as well as various sports facilities, including a swimming pool, handball gym, and rooftop tennis court. For thirty-five cents each month, employees gained access to the building and its almost nightly menu of movies, plays, athletic tournaments, and other attractions.

In their efforts to construct effective company cultures, local business leaders promoted one of two themes, and often both. They promised to provide employees and their families lifelong security, and they promoted their companies as sites where ambitious young men could rise to important positions. While both issues were critical in employees' career decisions, many sought more from work than just promotions, paychecks, or a pension. If employees did use these criteria for evaluating a job, they also asked other more intangible questions: Did they like being at work? Did they have friends there? Could they combine their family life with work? Such questions were central to the building of corporate cultures, and the development of internal social networks became critical to the growth of large firms.

Given the centrality of recreation and leisure to modern American culture, and to southern California in particular, it should be no surprise that they became important elements within the region's corporations. Yet understanding this phenomenon requires one to reverse historians' frequent reification of the spheres of work and leisure and to recognize the significance of social and recreational activities within corporate histories. Because work and leisure became increasingly distinct components of daily experience in industrial societies, it is easy to overplay their separation and downplay the blurred zone between the two.[2] Viewing companies solely in terms of their "business" functions, however, precludes fully understanding how Americans came to terms with the corporate order, or how corporate leaders came to terms with their employees. When one thinks of a large firm, one generally envisions offices, shops, and factories filled with people working. As the nation's largest electric railway company in the 1920s, PE certainly matched this image. Its six thousand employees worked in scattered offices, stations, and train yards to provide transportation services to hundreds of thousands of southern Californians. But if PE existed to carry passengers, how does one explain among its assets an employee baseball diamond, mountain resort, and clubhouse? And what is one to make of its annual company picnic attended by nearly fifteen thousand employees and their families, or the firm's baseball team, Masonic lodge, bowling league, or rod and gun club?

To be sure, PE leaders, like their peers throughout the nation, promoted social and recreational activities as anti-union tools, but this was only a small part of a much larger story. Executives in all economic sectors, blue- and white-collar alike, sought to foster community at the workplace. Surveys of department and other large retail stores in the 1920s, for example, showed that a higher percentage of them as opposed to industrial firms sponsored social programs for workers.[3] Companies hoped these programs would harmonize employee relations, heighten morale, and link employees more closely and permanently to the enterprise. Personnel problems would have disappeared had this proven a solution, for internal communities flourished in most firms beyond what leaders ever tried to nurture. Social networks emerged in many forms, among all levels of a company's workforce, and grew from employee as well as employer interest. Indeed, in the words of one historian, "corporate leisure filled in the interstices of organizational charts and office spaces with ties of consanguinity and competitive play."[4]

Company picnics, baseball teams, and social clubs represented more than either simply the workings of management or employees having a "good time." They were instead evidence of Americans' efforts to integrate their personal lives with the occupational milieu of urban big business. Social networks helped employees adjust to bureaucratic cultures and, in fact, made the corporate workplace palatable for many otherwise disgruntled workers. Through office friendships, employees could counteract many of big business employment's cold and impersonal aspects. Social and recreational interaction not only made life within corporate walls more amicable and humane; it allowed male employees expressions of individual personality and masculine identity in an often faceless and seemingly emasculating environment.

Of course, community could be double-edged. Some employees may well have appreciated the impersonal elements of bureaucratic life, and found the workplace to be a refuge from other stifling or burdensome communities. Also, events that allowed for demonstrations of masculinity could further marginalize and exclude female coworkers. Such factors and dynamics contributed to making occupational communities both as vibrant and fragmented as any social group.

King Vidor's 1928 film, *The Crowd*, offered a subtle hint of big business employment's social dimensions. Buried within the film's harsh and dehumanizing caricature of corporate life, the audience found that oppressed clerical worker Johnny Sims's best friend is a colleague with whom he goes out after work. The audience also watches Johnny delay telling his wife when he quits, because she so eagerly anticipated the next day's company picnic. Even in a carefully constructed "worst-case scenario," corporate employment could not be completely stripped of social and personal interaction. Contested, varied, and multilayered social networks gradually emerged in large Los Angeles firms as they came of age in the 1910s and 1920s. Originating from above and below, the networks reflected both managerial strategies and employees' own efforts to mold the workplace into a more tolerable environment. In these interactions, work and leisure commingled in corporate cultures and, for many employees, softened the least pleasant elements of bureaucratic life.

Work, Community, and Leisure

In November 1915, Southern California Edison executive R. H. Ballard commended his employees, saying, "Their love for the company and their loyalty to it is something inspiring. It is like the comradeship of veterans of many campaigns." Such enthusiasm, he stated, derived from the firm's genuine devotion to them: "We try to make the feeling in our organization as close and loyal as that of a college fraternity. 'Me and the prez' is a term which most aptly expresses the feeling of relationship which should exist between the employee and the firm." Ballard's carefully crafted imagery, though likely causing more than a few smirks among employees, echoed that of many southern California business leaders who believed that workplace community would heighten loyalty. Discussions about how to promote personal relationships between company leaders and employees pervaded managerial circles in Los Angeles and throughout the nation. One contemporary authority recommended that leaders send employees birthday cards, because "the fact that the executive is thinking of the employee aside from the actual work he or she may be doing cannot help but indicate that the employee is not a mere machine."[5]

The gradual separation of most Americans' daily experience into distinct spheres of work and leisure, which had come about in the course of the nineteenth century, and the shifting nature of community in an urban society molded leaders' and employees' personal and familial interests and their efforts to shape corporate life. Few transformations were as critical to the origins of modern social experience as the increasing division between work and "private time" and the subsequent formalized rise of "leisure."[6] As growing numbers of Americans found themselves in urbanizing settings with both "free time" and a cash income, mass cultures emphasizing commercialized recreation and leisure gained in popularity. Urban-based clubs and voluntary organizations similarly thrived among new city dwellers.[7]

However, business leaders feared and fought the idea of a strict demarcation between working and private life and sought to counteract attitudes distinguishing a supposedly dreary corporate workplace from a happier home life. Not only did they want personnel to be continually attentive to the firm's interests when away from work, they believed that social cohesion among employees could heighten morale and engender increased occupational loyalty and enthusiasm. Employees who based their social community at the workplace might not only be less likely to leave but also more likely to identify with the firm and support its interests.

At the Los Angeles Railway Company, John Jay Akin exemplified this ideal. In 1913, Akin retired from his position as superintendent of the claims department after twenty-four years of service. In his farewell address to his staff, he said, "My association with you has been the most agreeable and enjoyable of my business experience and while heretofore I have been your boss and friend, after January 1st, I will not do any bossing but will continue to be your friend."[8] Most leaders hoped to nurture exactly such feelings of camaraderie. Yet as the LARC and other local firms grew during the 1910s and 1920s, promoting such community seemed increasingly difficult and required more deliberate mechanisms.

Los Angeles executives believed so strongly in the benefits of employee social cohesion that they invested considerable money and effort toward achieving it. Across the nation, leadership-sponsored social and recreational activities had appeared in many large firms by the turn of the century, and they grew more popular through the 1920s. Seventy-three percent of four hundred firms surveyed in 1926 hosted some variety of social or recreational activities.[9]

Though often instigated as managerial tools, social groups emerged within large firms quite independently. To the extent that corporations became communities, employees played the critical role in this process. The workplace could, of course, easily become a source of friendships; the office seemed a logical place to make friends and derive identity, and many Americans anchored their own community at work. For white-collar employees, the nature of corporate operations allowed, and in fact required, much personal interaction. Midlevel and upper-level white-collar workers did not typically experience the close supervision and grueling environment characteristic of manual and clerical labor. Instead, they generally worked with little direct oversight or supervision in environments conducive to collegial interaction. This contact could prove particularly meaningful for those who found themselves in a rapidly emerging city like Los Angeles, where one might feel isolated and alone. Social and recreational outlets not only helped to personalize the corporate office but also gave many thousands of men, newly arrived to Los Angeles, a sense of community.[10]

Although both leaders and employees had an interest in establishing workplace communities, there were limits to their development. Personnel often differed over the meaning of social interaction. Relationships could turn sour upon managerial intrusion or manipulation. Other employees might resent social demands at what they perceived to be simply their place of work. They wondered whether superiors would notice if one missed a company barbecue. Would opting out of the department's baseball team limit opportunities for promotion? Would it be smart to let the general manager win the company tennis tournament? Leaders, by contrast, struggled to understand at what point social interaction between employees become disruptive rather than a sign of company spirit. They also speculated whether or not employee interaction could impair office efficiency and whether one could one maintain control, authority, and respect while nurturing camaraderie. Any examination of social life within corporations must be additionally tempered by an awareness that employees participated in numerous other communities. Corporate personnel did not necessarily live near their coworkers or share their religion, politics, or other personal values. Industrial "company towns" provided at least a partially "natural" social community, but big companies in large urban centers enjoyed no such circumstances. The workplace provided but one venue in which Americans could root friendships and identity.

In Los Angeles, where a Mediterranean climate could combine with innumerable opportunities for recreation to make the office a comparatively dull place, the fragmentation between work and leisure seemed especially great. Yet even in southern California, work and leisure intertwined in complex ways. The nature of community within individual companies became more complicated than simply leaders hosting parties or individual employees developing friendships. Employees of all ranks interacted during the day while working, at staff and business meetings, over lunch, at company parties and socials, and after hours away from work. These contacts, like those between members of any community, ranged from closely personal to hostile. The nature and extent of these interactions were not distinct from or secondary to the firm's business activities but, rather, represented an important part of white-collar cultures.

Business with Pleasure

In the mid 1920s, when a rash of industrial accidents marred operations at several Union Oil facilities, leaders started holding "safety meetings" to discuss new policies with workers and managers. Far from dry workplace lectures at drab company offices, the meetings followed a lavish evening dinner. In December 1926, for example, the company invited employees to a safety dinner in Fullerton at which precautions and regulations would be discussed during a "perfect meal."[11] Most Los Angeles firms held similar working dinners where business meetings became social occasions. The mere gathering of employees, for whatever purpose, created a social opportunity as they mingled with friends and colleagues. Rather than fret over attentiveness and order, as a school teacher might in a classroom, leaders played on this phenomenon by adding social outlets to business meetings in order to heighten employee interest and nurture an esprit de corps. This intersection of business and pleasure became a distinct characteristic of corporate meetings, conferences, and conventions.

Few employee gatherings passed without some degree of social activity. Personal interactions emerged spontaneously from employee initiative, but leaders often formalized and bolstered such encounters; executives believed that business meetings would benefit if employees attended with interest. At Union Oil, most offices held annual meetings for their sales and marketing staffs. These provided an occasion to educate new personnel about policies and procedures, to update current employees on any changes, to reward those with outstanding sales records, and to encourage future performance. Whatever the meetings' formal design, they were by no means all business, and the social events often became the most popular features. Union Oil's San Francisco office, for example, hosted an annual meeting for agents, salesmen, and district sales managers. The conference featured speeches by company leaders as well as question and answer sessions. The occasion's most popular element, however, was the banquet. At the 1922 meeting, eighty employees gathered in formal attire in a posh hotel banquet room adorned with American flags and Union Oil banners. Over dinner, they joined in "an informal discussion of marketing problems," and then, following the meal, enjoyed a program of music and motion pictures. According to company reports attendance increased steadily each year, and the annual banquet always received the most publicity in news releases.[12]

The presence of social affairs at company meetings may not have made them yearned-for events, but they did likely increase interest in what might otherwise have been boring or tedious sessions. Social interaction became a carefully planned component of even the most official parts of corporate life. The Los Angeles Conservative Life Insurance Company made this mixing of business and pleasure a specific part of its corporate culture. During its first years, early in the century, the firm began hosting a yearly convention for employees and agents that featured an array of business and informational meetings. Company magazine reports hinted that entertainment took precedence over business, however, noting that the numerous parties were extremely well attended, particularly one described as a "theater party." These annual gatherings continued after the merger with Pacific Mutual in 1906 and drew growing crowds. By the 1910s, the conference had become so popular that the company could use attendance as a bonus for high sales. Meritorious employees would now go at company expense. Needing to bring its widespread agents together periodically for business meetings, Pacific Mutual leaders became adept at hosting sessions that would lure employees. Its semiannual conference of leading agents known as the "Big-Tree Club" became an elaborate affair held at places such as Colorado Springs and Yosemite National Park and attracted both agents and their families. In a process well known to professionals today, conferences could become social reunions and family vacations.[13]

Executives hoped the mixing of business and pleasure would turn coworkers into colleagues. The distinction became important, because colleagues shared a sense of camaraderie and purpose, elements necessary to fashioning a cohesive and cooperative team. In its continual acquisition of smaller firms, Southern California Edison needed to integrate the activities and personnel of new firms into its operations. SCE leaders came to see this integration as requiring more than simply the relocation of personnel and reorganization of operations. The company increasingly planned social galas to celebrate the "mergers" and to provide a forum in which employees could meet. In 1917, the company held a large ball and reception at Los Angeles's Shrine Auditorium following the company's merger with Henry Huntington's Pacific Light and Power Corporation. Hundreds jammed the facility for a ritzy gala.[14]

Company Events

While mixing business and pleasure at company meetings became a consistent component of most corporate cultures, such activities represented but a small segment of the diverse interactions taking place. Annual company-sponsored events for employees and their families illustrate another manifestation of business efforts to build community. Typically, leaders planned them, firms paid for them, and public relations offices actively publicized them. In some cases these events flopped, whether for lack of employee involvement or because of tensions within the firm's ranks. More often, however, workers molded these occasions to suit their interests, and the events became central features of company lore.

Much like the contemporary, generic office holiday party, annual parties, picnics, and dances took on an institutionalized role in many Los Angeles firms. Nationally, a 1927 Department of Labor Survey of 170 industrial firms showed that approximately half hosted an annual picnic or field day. Had the survey been broadened to include dances, holiday parties, and other affairs, as did the 1926 survey, or included companies in the service sector, the percentage would have been higher.[15]

If many firms mixed business and pleasure for pragmatic ends, explicit company socials furthered these efforts. Evidencing the prevailing managerial interest in such activities, many resorts and recreation centers explicitly cultivated corporate functions. In 1922, for example, a Venice Beach resort near Los Angeles advertised in *Southern California Business*, telling executives that if they really wanted "to get the best cooperation out of those whose ser-

One of the popular dances at the Pacific Electric Club had a Japanese theme. Reproduced by permission of the Huntington Library, San Marino, California.

vice makes your business a success," then "the way to do this is to stimulate them to new activity and exhilaration by planning their recreation in the same manner you assign their work." The resort urged leaders to "plan a big evening for them, a private dancing party." Pacific Electric, which itself hosted an employee picnic, actively and explicitly marketed its Redondo Beach resort to other companies for similar events.[16]

Even if key managers or leaders directed major annual company events, these activities were by no means solely management's idea. Rather, long-running company socials usually reflected employee support. While executives offered official and financial support for these endeavors, their impetus came from and their organization was often assumed by the middle and lower ranks, and they could become memorable parts of employees' careers. When, for instance, Ronald Health looked back on his career as a natural gas industry employee, he recalled how each year he and his colleagues spent a day at the Rio Hondo Country Club in Downey for a company picnic. He spoke fondly of an annual barbecue and vaudeville show, and especially remembered the much-anticipated and very competitive golf tournaments that captivated employees' attention. A golf contest in which employees had to tee off with the ball atop an eight-inch piece of garden hose became a particularly popular tradition.[17]

Union Oil's experience illustrates the prominence of annual socials and the ways in which they reflected employee interests. The company employed too many people to host a single occasion, so most offices or districts held their own events, usually summer picnics. Attendance and the nature of activities varied from region to region, suggesting that various employees and leaders had unique interests and divergent levels of enthusiasm. Union Oil's Orange district held an elaborate picnic every June that by the late 1920s attracted as many as 4,000. The picnics began with lunch, which was followed by an afternoon of athletic events. An annual baseball game between the company's Stearns and Richmond departments became the most popular attraction. In the evening, employee families attended a barbecue, watched their colleagues perform in a talent show, and then danced late into the night.

Attendance figures, photographs, and the elaborate program of activities each year suggest that employees enthusiastically enjoyed the picnic. The baseball game became the subject of a major rivalry, much discussed during the succeeding months.[18] The picnic's success may have stemmed from an unusual degree of personal interaction and friendship among employees there. Orange district personnel also engaged in many worker-led social clubs, which imply the presence of after-hours social networks. If employees had good friends at work, an annual event at company expense could well be an enjoyable occasion.

Similar festivities occurred throughout Union Oil's workforce. The almost uniform presence of summer picnics throughout the organization suggests that they became a key element of the company's culture.[19] Leaders, no doubt, felt a certain amount of pressure to hold these events. If some offices and districts hosted them and received acclaim from either executives or employees for doing so, others likely felt pushed to emulate their actions. Yet the events would not likely have continued year after year if they had not generated significant employee interest. Moreover, individual offices or districts developed their own popular traditions. Whether it was the Orange division's baseball game or the Valley division's tug-of-war contest, most picnics featured a unique format and a special event. A basketball game between the men and women in which the men had to play left-handed became the most popular activity at the Sacramento main station's annual "wiener roast" on the American River.[20]

Yearly picnics, dances, and parties also flourished within the southern California banking business. Each summer during the 1920s, Security-First National Bank's Santa Barbara branch manager hosted a barbecue and all-day picnic for employees and families. Two hundred persons gathered in 1928 and enjoyed swimming, movies, and an orchestra. Southern California Edison employees participated in a similar array of annual socials. Its steam plant began hosting an employee Christmas party in 1921. That first year, 150 guests experienced an evening of dancing, food, and games. At decade's end, nearly 800 persons attended.[21]

Annual socials became institutionalized features of many corporate cultures because they provided a casual social forum for leaders and employees. Leaders found these events excellent venues through which to promote their vision of a harmonious workforce and to give evidence of their recognition and appreciation of employees. These occasions offered employees a pleasant occasion at which to mingle with coworkers and bosses in a relaxed and often less hierarchical setting. Those whose community of friends sprung from the workplace enjoyed the events as an inexpensive occasion to be with them. For employees who felt less, but still some, community at the workplace, they offered a chance to take family and friends to often posh and elaborate social affairs. Subsidized company events provided opportunities for many to engage in activities which they otherwise could not afford.

As widespread and popular as corporate social events became, they were by no means universally appreciated. Employees who viewed the workplace as a poor site for social interaction may have felt pressured to attend and resented the events. Or, they may have simply chosen to stay home. These occasions became particularly problematic if workplace tensions existed. As a company with significant blue- and white-collar ranks, Pacific Electric struggled to host activities that would engage a broad spectrum of workers. When labor strife arose, all employees, not to mention executives, found these occasions difficult. PE's annual picnic, for example, alternated between tremendous popularity and cancellation. The company began hosting the event sometime around 1910, and within several years it had become an elaborate and well-attended affair. The festivities usually began at mid-morning on a day during August or September. PE trains would carry employees and their families, free of charge, to a company-affiliated Redondo Beach resort. At 11:30, PE's president gave a speech thanking personnel for their efforts, urging them to work even harder, and outlining challenges facing the company (usually those that would make wage increases impossible). Following the address, employees spent the remainder of the day with their families and friends engaged in numerous social and recreational activities. Many enjoyed the beach or swimming pools, while others participated in a broad schedule of competitive events, such as tug-of-war contests between departments, children's wheelbarrow races, and other contests. By 1917, estimated attendance had reached 11,000 and local newspapers provided extensive coverage. The *Pacific Electric Magazine* covered the picnic in detail. In departmental news sections, editors featured employees who had won contests.[22]

Labor turmoil in 1918 and 1919 dampened the spirit of PE's picnic as its trainmen struck on at least two occasions. Union activity among PE platform workers did more than pit these ranks against management. The strikes also polarized blue- and white-collar ranks when office staff filled in for striking trainmen. The relationship between a company's social life and such tensions in its business operations became evident in 1919 and 1920 when leaders canceled the picnic, citing "war-time conditions" and "other reasons familiar to all of our employees." The latter factors certainly included the rash of strikes and subsequent company turmoil. Large company social gatherings likely had little appeal to leaders, office staff, or platform men during this period of tense conflict. PE officials effectively quashed the union activity in 1919, but tensions lingered. In 1920, in lieu of the company picnic, PE opened its Redondo Beach resort for an "employee's day," when staff members could use the facilities for free; but only 1,400 turned out, a third of the attendance at earlier company gatherings.[23]

The popularity of Pacific Electric social events rebounded in the early 1920s, once passions cooled, and after the firm replaced 80 percent of those who had struck with "more loyal" workers. A spirited employee culture emerged at PE during the 1920s despite the earlier bitterness. Executives reactivated the company's annual picnic in 1921 and described turnout as high, though reports hinted that it remained well below earlier years' attendance. Each year thereafter, however, the event grew in scope and popularity. By 1929, the estimated attendance had surpassed 15,000, with employees from all ranks represented.[24]

Corporate social events were not universally popular. Some employees viewed the workplace as an inappropriate site for social interaction or felt pressured to attend; many did not attend. Some leaders may have been uninterested in the concept or felt the expense a waste of money. Beginning in the early 1910s the Pacific Mutual Life Insurance Company hosted a June picnic for its headquarters employees at a Long Beach resort. The event traditionally included "a golf tournament and a variety of other games and amusements" as well as lunch and dinner. The company canceled the picnic in the early 1920s, however, at the very time when similar events in other local firms were soaring in popularity. According to leaders, they did so because the staff's size had grown "to unwieldy proportions."[25]

Pacific Mutual's explanation seems unconvincing, given the size of such events in other firms. The 1926 Department of Labor survey found one midwestern company with 17,000 employees whose picnic attendance surpassed 50,000. A more likely explanation has to do with the changing composition of Pacific Mutual's headquarters staff, its unique structure, and the company's managerial demands. The headquarters staff performed clerical tasks for agents and offices scattered nationwide. Also, its personnel were more stratified than most and largely comprised two distinct blocks: an all-male cadre of executives and managers and a large and rapidly growing segment of lower-level clerical workers, a significant number of whom by the 1920s were female. In light of this polarized office force, split by rank and sex, a company picnic especially suited for family interaction may not have seemed a logical idea. Perhaps hosting an event at which its largely male and often married salaried managers would mingle with its distinct corps of young, unmarried women seemed less than a comfortable occasion, particularly given prevailing beliefs that some young women had come to view the corporate office as a place to find and meet respectable men.[26] We know from the popularity of clubs, teams, and other social organizations of Pacific Mutual employees that social networks did exist and that management encouraged them. An annual picnic, however, likely seemed a less than ideal venue for nurturing community within this firm. Upon canceling the picnic, the company instead gave its staff an extra day off, likely pleasing employees who could now use the free time as they pleased.

As the Pacific Electric case illustrates, the kind of workplace collegiality and bonding encouraged by company socials could fail to materialize in the face of tension or turmoil regarding workplace issues. As the Pacific Mutual case illustrates, some enterprises, by virtue of their unique workforce dynamics, found that such events met the interests of neither leaders nor employees. Despite such limiting factors, annual events gained considerable popularity in many firms because they provided a convenient and relatively easy opportunity for leaders to exhibit their interest in employees, who correspondingly enjoyed the social and recreational opportunities events afforded.

Community from Above and Below

Rooted in more personal interaction between employees, other forms of community emerged within large firms. Although few sources comment directly on such interactions, one can detect a wide diversity of social activities throughout corporate ranks. While management nurtured interaction amongst them, many employees themselves actively formed friendships and networks with their colleagues. These encounters varied greatly, from formal company events to private employee parties.[27]

At Union Oil, social life emerged from above and below, and on every rung of the corporate ladder. In addition to the major annual events, local offices hosted frequent activities. Many departments gave employees bonuses in the form of social events. In June 1925, for instance, after the Arizona district reported the most profitable single month in its history, leaders invited district personnel to a barbecue and picnic to celebrate their accomplishment. In April 1927, the Insurance and Personnel Department made arrangements for employees to see productions of "Applesauce" and "So This Is London" at the Belmont and Egan theaters at reduced rates. Executives viewed social and leisure activities as legitimate rewards for good performance and inducements for dedication and loyalty.[28]

Managerial interest in social relations occurred on a more personal level as well. Whatever the hierarchical structure of corporate bureaucracies, many managers and supervisors developed personal friendships with employees, often as they ascended the ladder. Union Oil's San Diego district sales manager periodically invited a small group of agents and salesmen to his mountain cabin for weekend getaways where "business worries and competitive conditions" were forgotten.[29] The dynamics of such interactions are difficult to determine, but one can hypothesize that they reflected a complicated mixture of personal and pragmatic interests. On a personal level, corporate employees, even of differing ranks, likely often came to be friends, both at the workplace and after hours. A weekend of camping might have reflected a genuine camaraderie among friends that had originated but did not end at work. Workplace concerns and interests were probably not entirely forgotten, however. Even in the mountains, few employees could completely forget the power structure of the workplace. Making friends with one's boss was often a good idea. Managers may have similarly become genuine friends with those under their direction but could hardly have been oblivious to the loyalty that could arise from such friendships and the potential benefits to be gained from cultivating loyal employees.

There were, of course, always potential tensions in social activities when people on different rungs of the corporate ladder interacted. Social intimacy between leaders and employees challenged hierarchies of power important to many managers. One Los Angeles department store executive said of such relationships: "I don't think executives and employees should be familiar with each other, or friends. It is bad for the business. The employee loses his respect for the employer. He should think of the one above him with respect. I think the executive should hold himself aloof." Equally, some employees resented it when friendships between managers and employees seemed to influence "company politics." An assistant buyer in a Los Angeles department store complained: "You don't get noticed for what you do. You have to have pull to get anywhere. It's wrong."[30]

Management and employees did not necessarily attend the same social events. Reports and photographs from office dances suggest that personnel of similar rank attended them. Such homogeneity made these events comfortable venues for social interaction, hence their general popularity. Even when management and staff were both present, executives rarely fox-trotted with stenographers. In an analysis of company outings, one scholar has noted that corporate leisure did not operate free from workplace structures: "Class, status, and gender differences between groups thus were reinforced at outings, even as they seemed to bridge those differences." In fact, company outings "simultaneously reinforced the corporate ideal of harmonious familial relations and extruded corporate organization into real family and leisure relations."[31]

While management often hosted, subsidized, or promoted social occasions, workers usually made the events their own, particularly dances, which were among the most frequent and popular events in Los Angeles companies. Employees themselves often planned and held dances, such as a June 1924 outdoor occasion staged by Union Oil's Los Angeles pipeline staff which drew 150 persons. Dances assumed such popularity because they offered an intriguing venue for all concerned. Leaders could reap the potential morale and good will benefits available from providing a well-received evening. Dances also succeeded among employees because they offered an enjoyable occasion at company expense in which sponsorship did not necessarily mean control. In April 1926, for example, the Field Department and the Geological and Land Departments in Union Oil's Los Angeles district sponsored a "Hard Times Dance." While departmental management paid for the event, it was rank-and-file employees who took advantage of and enjoyed it most. At least sixty attended, most of whom had spent considerable effort dressing up in "hard times" garb.[32]

Many social networks also emerged outside of leadership-sponsored events. By the mid 1920s, employees in most Union Oil districts had created musical organizations as well as hunting, camping, Masonic, and other clubs. Most had significant memberships with active schedules. Union Oil's Los Angeles Masonic Club, for example, counted 250 members by 1924. Within local SCE offices, employees nurtured a similar range of social clubs and organizations. At the Pacific Southwest Savings Bank, staff members formed several associations, including a pistol club, glee clubs, and orchestra.[33]

The widespread presence of employee social clubs suggests that the corporate workplace became more than a site of business activity with occasional company-sponsored social activities. Rather, it became a diverse arena in which employees made friendships and built associations that transcended their occupational identities and workplace hours. Company social events and organizations remained just as popular in the 1930s.[34]

Given what we know about public hostility to big business and middle-class aversion to long-term bureaucratic employment, such camaraderie suggests an important conclusion: corporate employment became more palatable to individual employees who rooted their social lives at the workplace. In contrast to the harsh public caricatures of big business, many employees found significant personal rewards in their work. Sherman Denny, for instance, worked for the Huntington Beach Company from 1923 to 1962, serving his last fifteen years in a managerial capacity. Years after his retirement he noted: "I'm very happy that I had a part in it during that early period. I still am in touch with [colleagues] almost daily, though I'm retired."[35]

The extent and popularity of social groupings within Los Angeles firms suggest that their ranks encompassed many personal friendships on all rungs of the company ladder, like Isaias Hellman and Jackson Graves of the Farmers and Merchants National Bank. Similarly, employees at Union Oil's Mateo Street office became close friends. Initiated at work, these relationships extended far beyond the office. In June 1921, a group of Mateo Street employees joined together to build a cabin in the La Crescenta Valley north of Los Angeles. By the following year, the group had paid off the mortgage on the property and owned the cabin outright as a personal retreat.[36]

The history of the Pacific Electric Club offers a collage that illustrates the complicated nature of social communities within large firms. Leaders organized the club in 1916 as part of an effort to battle the unionization of workers, but by the end of the 1920s it had emerged as a popular social and recreational organization that met many different needs.[37] Departmental representatives first proposed the idea of a company club at a meeting of the picnic committee in September 1916. The suggestion did not represent a sudden creative vision. Social, recreational, religious, and service clubs flourished among all classes and both sexes in urban centers during the early twentieth century; and many companies found that in forming clubs they could exert some control over employees' leisure time and the influences acting upon them, perhaps engendering greater loyalty. The Los Angeles Railway Corporation had founded an employees' club in 1913 with five clubhouses scattered around the city. PE management had likely been aware of the option at least since then. Nearly 20 percent of 430 industrial firms surveyed nationally in 1926 had separate employee clubhouses and just under half had recreation or clubrooms within their plants.[38] Such facilities became at least equally popular among exclusively white-collar and service-sector firms.[39]

Early announcements about the Pacific Electric Club picture a corporate leadership intent on providing a lavish space for social and recreational activities. The company first gave employees an abandoned Masonic temple but quickly started work on a new clubhouse, which opened the following year. For dues of twenty-five cents each month, personnel could enjoy free use of the clubhouse and its billiard room, library, music room, card room, and other features. The company paid for the construction, maintenance, and upkeep of the building and helped subsidize programs and amusements that the dues could not cover.[40]

One might think employees would be enthusiastic about a subsidized clubhouse for their enjoyment, but announcements imploring them to join appeared in almost every issue of the company magazine for several years. Initial interest may have been dampened as workers learned why the idea of an employees' club so enthralled management: Executives intended it to be more than a social organization, and they expected membership to entail more than simply monthly dues. Leaders wanted the club to serve as an internal employees' association, negating interest in outside unions. The company centered its benefit programs in the PE Club, made it the official mouthpiece of employee concerns, and held meetings at the clubhouse at which leaders spoke on company issues.[41]

Most employees probably sensed the added expectations of membership when, upon entering the new "employee" clubhouse on January 1, 1917, they found a large portrait of the company president hanging in the main lobby. The appearance of an almost apologetic editorial in the company magazine which noted that officials had hung the picture without the president's knowledge and that its presence completely surprised him suggests that some workers expressed displeasure over its presence.[42] Those still uncertain about the club found their fears confirmed as they encountered pressure to join the "voluntary association." Leaders repeatedly insisted on "100 percent participation." The strength of their calls may have precipitated resistance and resentment among some employees, for in the club's opening month, the company president issued several statements noting that membership was voluntary.

By 1918, two years after the club's founding, only half of all employees had joined. That November, PE issued a statement noting the number and percentage of employees in each department who had joined, most likely to pressure departments with low enrollment. The report revealed that at least a third of every department's staff were members but also that the percentages were lowest among trainmen and mechanics, which is not surprising given their engagement in labor strikes at the time.[43] By late 1920, when internal tensions stemming from the 1918–19 strike had cooled, nearly 75 percent of employees had become members, but leaders continued to push aggressively for greater involvement. While the percentage of enrollees may have surpassed this figure, the company's continued call for greater participation throughout the 1920s suggests that "total membership" never materialized.[44]

If executives hoped that the PE Club would function as a companywide employee association and would thwart worker organizing, they were disappointed. The clubhouse eliminated neither the union activity in 1918 or 1919 nor sporadic collective bargaining efforts in subsequent years. PE leadership learned that expending large sums of money toward providing employees with social and recreational facilities could not dampen employee grievances about pay and workplace conditions. So, did the firm abandon the club as a failure? To the contrary, it grew steadily in popularity among blue- and white-collar employees throughout the 1920s. By mid-decade, the company subsidized club activities with over $10,000 a year, and in 1929 built an elaborate new clubhouse.

Most members selectively drew on the Pacific Electric Club when it suited their interests and needs. While records suggest that during times of labor strife attendance at the clubhouse dipped, some activities usually attracted large crowds, and the club's social functions increased throughout the 1920s.[45] By mid-decade the club was printing a monthly calendar of events that featured some kind of activity or program at least every second or third night. The club's first movie night occurred on a Tuesday evening in August

1919, when four pictures were shown, including a five-reel main feature starring George Beban, *One More American.* By the fall of that year, movie nights had become weekly events, drawing capacity crowds of several hundred persons. In the spring of 1920, the club made every other movie night "amateur night"; before, between, and after the films, employees performed musical, theatrical, or dance numbers on stage. Movie nights remained popular throughout the 1920s; when the company built the new clubhouse in 1929, it included a posh 900-seat movie theater. The movie house proved the most cherished feature of the new facility, and by the fall of that year, club officers were hosting film nights twice each week.[46] Significant levels of clubhouse interaction promoted social networks outside company confines. Indeed, PE employees formed several major social organizations of their own, including a Rod and Gun Club (1916) with fifty-five charter members and a Masonic Club (1920) that had over 500 members by 1922.[47]

If the PE Club's history displayed the subtle but ever-present tensions surrounding issues of managerial control and intent, another of the company's efforts at building community received a nearly universally enthusiastic response. In 1917, PE opened an employee vacation camp in the nearby San Bernardino Mountains. The property featured cottages, dining halls, swimming pools, and other recreational facilities available to employees and their families at subsidized rates. Employees booked nearly every room on every weekend during its first summer. In following years, PE steadily enlarged and upgraded the facility to accommodate ever-increasing reservation requests.[48]

Many companies matched PE's elaborate infrastructure of social activities. Most large firms comprised a variety of social networks that included interaction around company-sponsored events and employee-initiated activities. By no means did all personnel root their personal friendships in the workplace, but for many, the office took on more meaning than simply a job. The grim and foreboding corporation of popular lore became a warm, social community in many employees' lives.

Corporate Athletics

In no realm did the relationship between corporate employment and social life become more intimate than in athletics. Sporting events and employee teams emerged as institutionalized features of many corporate cultures, highlighted by golf, bowling, tennis, and other tournaments. Employees also initiated such contests and formed baseball, basketball, and other teams for play in company and city leagues. In a 1926 national survey of industrial establishments, 319 out of approximately 400 firms reported employee athletic programs. Over half of all firms queried sponsored employee baseball teams and nearly half had some kind of athletic facility on company property, such as a baseball diamond, athletic field, or tennis court. Thirty-three firms even reported summer camps and thirteen had golf courses.[49]

Competitive sports flourished throughout the United States during the Progressive Era, and, for the same reasons they emerged nationally, sports became an important part of company life. Far from simply reflecting new interests and the desire for "fun," the rise of twentieth-century athletic and recreational practices represented a fusion of assertive leisure with new cultural and business values. One useful perspective suggests that six characteristics defined American competitive sports: secularism; equality of opportunity for players wishing to compete; specialization of different sports and, within each sport, rationalization of rules and training; quantification of athletic performances; and an obsession with establishing and breaking performance records. Most of these characteristics, if thought of in business terms, could apply to the building of modern corporate structures.[50]

Athletics also gained popularity because they provided an opportunity for masculine self-identification in an environment lacking earlier avenues through which to exhibit virility and creativity. The rise of large corporations challenged traditional male roles based on independent achievement and economic autonomy and, according to some historians, led many men to enact their masculinity through activities outside the workplace.[51] Competitive sports, one of the primary of these activities, however, flourished as much within corporate offices as outside. Company sporting events became prominent features of corporate cultures. Employees who spent their days in subordinate positions, devoid of personal authority or status, could become manly heroes after hours on the company ballfield, and those who did received considerable attention in in-house communications. The Los Angeles First National Bank's magazine, for instance, frequently carried elaborate front page articles about employees' athletic prowess. Those who hit winning home runs, pitched superb games, or shot notably low golf scores could anticipate glowing and often illustrated accounts of their exploits.[52]

Just as the rise of modern sports was a complex process with diverse causes and consequences, so too were company recreational activities. As they did with social activities, leaders used corporate athletics for managerial ends. Sports did not solve managerial dilemmas, but recreational activities touched many personal chords among leaders and employees; as a result, company athletics flourished beyond what leaders ever intended. Company teams and tournaments aroused enthusiasm because they provided broad ranks of salaried men opportunities for individual achievement in front of their peers, as well as outlets for aggressive activity rarely allowed at the workplace. Executives found little evidence that their sponsorship of athletics reduced turnover or increased profitability, yet they enthusiastically underwrote company sports programs and events.

Union Oil illustrates the variety of athletic subcultures extant in large firms. By the early 1920s, tennis, bowling, golf, baseball, and basketball had become important to its company life. The Los Angeles district instituted an annual tennis tournament in 1919. The company rented courts, provided a trophy known as the President's Cup, and actively promoted the contest in the company magazine. One hundred employees signed up for the first tournament and the number increased steadily thereafter. Leaders had to reschedule the event during its third year because so many employees complained that their vacations prevented them from entering. By this time a number of other districts held similar tournaments. While no companywide contests materialized, a match between the champions of the Los Angeles and San Francisco district tournaments became a cherished annual event.[53]

Union Oil's tennis tournaments became popular traditions but paled in comparison to the success of the company's bowling leagues. By the 1920s, most district and divisional office employees engaged in some sort of athletic competition. Head office personnel, for example, competed in a league with ten teams, including three from the engineering department as well as squads representing the transportation, comptrollers, traffic, gas, and lubricating departments, and the Los Angeles branch office. Meanwhile, the Union Oil Bowling League (1920) welcomed teams from offices and departments throughout the Los Angeles metropolitan area. By 1928, eighteen groups competed.[54]

Bowling, a less elitist sport with broader interest than tennis, may have been more popular. Golf, considered an upper-middle-class sport, flourished in many corporate cultures. Golf's popularity among Union Oil employees is an indicator of the number of middle- and upper-class men within its ranks. Many local offices and departments held formal tournaments by the early 1920s, when Union Oil employees operated at least three golf courses. In 1923, for example, Orange district office personnel as well as those in surrounding departments organized the Unoco Golf Club and constructed an eighteen-hole course and clubhouse on company land. The firm split the $3,000 tab with employees. Within several months, 333 staff members had joined the club, which required a $5 initiation fee and monthly dues of $1.10. By 1924, as many as 800 people attended club socials.[55]

With golf leagues and tournaments throughout Union Oil's organization, management launched an elaborate companywide competition in 1926. The contest began at the district level with a local tournament or a number of smaller events leading to a main showdown to determine that district's sixteen best players. Those players then met in district championships with the winners playing in a final match for the President's Cup. Following the tournament, leaders developed a ranking of Union Oil golfers from which they later picked teams to compete in matches with other companies. Rosters suggest that as many as 1,000 men, nearly 10 percent of Union Oil's workforce, ultimately participated.[56]

Individualized athletics provided a countervailing influence on the corporate hierarchy of the workplace. The strict chain of command and lines of authority that employees followed at work might be lessened when they met on the tennis court or golf course. The assistant freight clerk and district sales manager found their relationship changed when pitted against each other in a company tournament. Victors often represented a cross-section of employees in terms of rank and department. Underlings could both challenge and become partners with superiors. In 1921, for instance, a young-looking man from the field department won the tennis singles tournament, while the Los Angeles office's chief accountant and a clerk in the purchasing department, both middle-aged, won the doubles. For all but the few employees who felt no sense of subordination at work, company athletics could be a liberating and empowering arena, full of opportunities for independent achievement, revenge, or partnership.[57] Simultaneously, however, workplace superiors held subtle power. While the tennis court might seem a neutral environment, the vanquished superior would again be boss back at the office. Young personnel had to ponder whether athletic dominance would result in a backlash back at the firm the next workday. Furthermore, some employees probably resented managerial participation in sporting contests. One detailed study of corporate athletics found that in team sports, higher-ranking employees served as team captains, and that "when officers or managers joined in the general games . . . they joined as privileged players."[58]

The potentially disturbing effects of athletics in corporate hierarchies may explain why executives often resisted direct involvement in athletic subcultures. Many held memberships at private golf and tennis clubs and preferred playing with friends to being embarrassingly defeated by an upstart clerk. In a survey from the mid 1940s that likely had parallels with corporate cultures in the 1920s, recreation directors from seventy-five Los Angeles companies reported their primary difficulty was getting management to become involved. Conversely, fewer than two percent claimed to have trouble obtaining employee participation.[59]

Company basketball and baseball leagues also flourished, but they re-

Union Oil's company magazine caricatured its executives following the annual golf tournament. Reproduced from *Union Oil Bulletin* 1 (September 1921): 23, by permission of the Huntington Library, San Marino, California.

flected different social dynamics. Employees formed squads with little managerial coaxing, though executives expressed pleasure with such activities and often paid for uniforms as well as provided coverage in corporate communications.[60] Few offices in Union Oil's organization did not have employee teams. They were particularly popular in San Francisco and Los Angeles, where business leagues abounded. Pacific Electric employees formed several teams, including the PE Trainmen's Ball Club, PE Office Club, and the PE Baseball Club. In 1920, the firm constructed a baseball field on company grounds for the Pacific Electric Club baseball team. It achieved considerable popularity among employees after gaining entry into the Los Angeles Industrial League. Banking employees showed no less interest. By 1927, employees of the Pacific Southwest Savings Bank had organized baseball, basketball, tennis, and golf programs. Insurance company personnel played alongside bank and industrial teams. Employees at Pacific Mutual's Los Angeles headquarters as well as its agencies around the country had been forming athletic teams to participate in local leagues since at least 1910.[61]

So popular were corporate athletics that baseball and basketball leagues composed solely of company employees existed in many urban centers and played teams from other industries. Union Oil's San Francisco personnel, for example, often played against teams from Union Pacific, Anglo-American Bank, and the Bank of Italy. The firm's Los Angeles employees often competed in the city's Petroleum Athletic Association, which matched groups from the city's various oil companies.[62] It is a testimony to the strength of workplace athletics that so many people chose to play in company leagues rather than or in addition to church, neighborhood, or other leagues.

A 1926 survey of industrial establishments testifies to the fervor of corporate athletics. The report found two problems troubling management in many firms. First, some discovered animosities on the ballfield spilling over into work relations. This may explain why leagues that pitted teams from different companies against each other attracted more interest than intracompany leagues. Second, some executives reported that athletic programs had to be carefully monitored, since certain offices or departments made athletic ability a factor in hiring. The Bureau of Labor Statistics 1926 survey noted that a small number of companies had actually abolished sporting events because of the severity of such problems. Both problems remained in the mid 1940s when Los Angeles recreation directors complained that "ringers" brought in by management in hope of a win fomented anger among the regular players.[63]

If tennis, bowling, and golf tournaments thrived in part because they allowed opportunities for individual achievement and challenge to workplace hierarchies, why were team sports popular, given that they presented less opportunity for individual effort and often provided competition outside the firm? Clearly, significant numbers of employees chose their coworkers as friends. Employees could and no doubt did play in church, neighborhood, and other leagues, but the vitality of company teams and business leagues suggests that many employees found team sports based at the workplace not only convenient but personally rewarding. Business teams provided a strong sense of identity in an increasingly fragmented society. For American men, who derived much of their public identity from their jobs, participation in an athletic team with coworkers on behalf of the company could become a particularly strong element in their corporate identification. When playing for a company team, the workplace could very dramatically and graphically move from job to community.

The Firm as Family

During the summer of 1927, the Pacific Southwest Savings Bank's golf committee fervently publicized its annual fall tournament. They provided employees plenty of time to prepare for the event, which occupied a central place in the firm's corporate culture. The festivities began on the weekend of August 28 when bank staff played in a qualifying tournament. Admission proved rather easy; anyone who shot under 350 for eighteen holes gained entrance. Declared the golf committee chairman, "As this is a family affair we want everyone to participate." Successful entrants next gathered on the evening of September 8 for a "get together dinner" featuring an address by a national golf authority. The men then reassembled the following day at the San Fernando Valley's St. Andrew's Country Club. The top 128 golfers played a special round for the Flint Trophy. The remaining participants played a consolation round for "a trophy presented by the Iowa Miners League." Company officers awarded these and other prizes, including both serious and gag honors, at a post-tournament banquet.[64]

The enthusiastic participation in Pacific Southwest's annual golf tournament clashes with many popular depictions of corporate life during the 1920s and 1930s which show dreary images of homogeneous gray-suited armies revolving through monotonous rows of skyscrapers. Most southern California firms' corporate cultures exuded more vibrancy than popular characterizations suggested. While historians write of the turn of the century as a time of increasing demarcation between work and leisure, and the rise of mass, commercialized leisure and recreational cultures distinct from employment, those working in early corporations did not perceive the separation so clearly.

For many the company became not only one's employer, but also a source of friends and a community in which to root identity and professional associations. Company outings, athletic tournaments, social gatherings, and personal friendships with coworkers became cherished components of corporate life.

Few employees saw the workplace as simply a place for work. Most developed at least some friendships with colleagues which transcended the office and office hours. Many people made the workplace an important source of community, if not their primary social network. Social interaction among employees became a critical element in the construction of company cultures upon which the stability and success of many large firms rested. In a business whose size and hierarchy might seem oppressive and confining even to one raised in a modern, urban setting, and downright intimidating and stifling to young men recently arrived from the rural hinterlands, the formation of company social networks made corporate employment more humane and palatable. Through social and recreational interaction employees expressed their personalities, asserted their masculinity, and formed esprit de corps. By the late 1920s, corporate leisure joined company magazines, internal promotion systems, and fringe benefit programs as central to white-collar life.

EIGHT

THE WHITE-COLLAR DEPRESSION

Now is the Time for Teamwork!
—*Pacific Electric Magazine*, 1930

On August 29, 1933, twenty-five-year-old Dan Strebel wrote the California State National Recovery Administration Board (NRA) to plead for a job. A native-born American, lifelong resident of southern California, and holder of a baccalaureate from the University of Southern California (USC) in business administration, Strebel probably never expected to have trouble finding work. Yet his impressive resume and long list of references, whose fifteen names included everyone from a police lieutenant to USC's president, failed to open any doors. Strebel's letter was not the only such appeal the Los Angeles NRA office received in the fall of 1933. Each week the bureau logged dozens of letters from southern Californians desperate for work. Another came from thirty-nine-year-old A. O. Tench, who had arrived in Glendale in November 1932, having been laid off after twelve years work in the Chicago Western Electric Company's engineering department. Tench hoped to find a job in the supposedly still strong southern California economy, but Los Angeles proved a great disappointment. Within several months, he had applied, without success, for at least fourteen positions, including that of clerk, engineer, and mechanic. Seven companies flatly rejected him, seven others never even responded. The following November, Tench wrote the local NRA office to complain. Bitter and desperate, he asked for a job, any job.[1]

While the "Okie" migration of poor southwesterners to California has dominated popular images of the Great Depression in the state, the economic downturn seared the region's middle class as well. A majority of the job requests that Los Angeles's NRA office received were from displaced young and middle-aged white-collar men. William Bjerke had worked as a secretary for the Santa Fe and Union Pacific Railroads but wrote to say that he was "willing to accept a minimum wage, and could report to work at once." Forty-one-year-old W. S. Briggs, who had twelve years experience as a sales manager, wrote to plead for help, as he had a wife and three children to support. W. W. Riedel, who had served as an accountant for three local banks, implored, "I am greatly in need of some source of income." M. T. Coogan, who sent a lengthy resume listing accounting positions held with railroads, department stores, and the National Cash Register Company, bluntly stated, "Salary is not a consideration. I want a job."[2]

Whatever their specific circumstances, white-collar men's employment requests shared a common desperation. One wrote, "Please, please give this consideration—what I want is a job and I will not fall down on you no matter what it is. I must go to work." Unemployed petitioners relied on a variety of tactics to secure a positive response. Some sent multiple letters. P. M. W. Becker wrote eight times in a three-month period. Others recounted stories of their hungry children or elderly parents. Some sent long lists of references, copies of diplomas or awards, or gushed effusively about their love of Franklin Roosevelt, the Democratic party, or the NRA. In his plea, Dan Strebel noted that he fully supported President Roosevelt's National Recovery Act and realized its "tremendous importance to the people of this country." Whatever their case, all received quick and disappointing replies. Some responses noted that as many as five hundred job requests deluged the state's NRA office each week.[3]

Popular opinion, ironically fueled by the region's own boosterism, held that the Depression had struck the west coast with less force than it had other areas of the country. That prevailing wisdom was wrong. Southern California's economy recovered more quickly than most in the nation, but it did not escape the painful dislocations that followed the stock market crash in 1929. In summer 1931, a Los Angeles relief organization surveyed 1,500 businesses employing fifteen or more persons and found that thirty-three of every one hundred workers employed in the fall of 1929 had been laid off, and that a majority of the remaining employees had experienced either pay cuts or time reductions, or both. One historian argues that the West may have been even worse off in the early years of the Depression and that Los Angeles, in particular, suffered greatly. The city's economy crashed as hard if not harder than any in the West. Between 1929 and 1933, per capita wages fell by one half, bank debits decreased 71 percent, retail sales declined 56 percent, and southern California led the nation in bankruptcies. Half of the state's 344,000 unemployed lived in Los Angeles. A New Deal administrator touring the area to study relief efforts recounted that some people were calling Los Angeles "the blackest spot in the United States from the relief angle"; he noted, "There are too many people in Los Angeles for the amount of employment that its many industries, even under the most favorable circumstances, can provide."[4]

That Los Angeles's unemployed included large numbers of white-collar men made the Depression especially horrifying to middle-class residents. White-collar unemployment attracted considerable attention, for it seemed a new problem and one that aroused many status anxieties. The scope of economic peril placed Anglo-Saxon manhood in a state of crisis. One eyewitness to the situation observed a relief agency employee agonizing over "able-bodied, well-educated men of the finest sort who came into his office and simply cried because they could not find a job." Nationally, white-collar unemployment rose significantly during the Depression, though it always lagged behind blue-collar unemployment. In 1937, for instance, when national unemployment stood at 15 percent, white-collar male unemployment was at 8.8 percent. But Los Angeles's white-collar workers may have fared more poorly. In the San Francisco Bay area, more clerks and skilled workers than unskilled workers were unemployed in the early years of the Depression. Because Los Angeles had a similarly large commercial and service economy, white-collar positions were more vulnerable there as well. In the late 1930s, the infusion of federal monies into southern California's fledgling aviation industry fueled the local recovery, but manufacturing benefited ahead of service industries.[5]

For Los Angeles executives, white-collar unemployment would seem to have provided a slight silver lining during what were otherwise extremely painful times. For years they had struggled to cultivate a corps of dedicated company men. Now, with so many "good men" looking for work, their problems appeared over. For one thing, local firms could now recruit from an even larger labor pool. The Depression temporarily retarded women's progress toward obtaining white-collar jobs, as more men became willing to take low-level positions. The 1930s saw a reversal of the decline in the number of men in lower-level white-collar work. By 1940, men had again become a slight majority of clerical workers in Los Angeles, holding 57 percent of such positions. When one removes receptionists, telephone operators, and stenographers from the roster, men held 70 percent of the remaining clerical jobs. Additionally, turnover rates in many firms dropped dramatically as those with jobs clung to them tightly. At the Security-First National Bank, turnover plunged nearly 80 percent between 1929 and 1933. Despite these conditions, business leaders felt little easing of their workforce dilemmas. The economic crisis led most to try even harder to cultivate dedicated employees and to create effective corporate cultures. Top management had never viewed personnel relations as a simple act of finding and retaining men. Rather, effective management required nurturing a loyal and enthusiastic workforce. Few executives could remember a time when their firms were not facing difficult problems. The downturn that appeared so horrifyingly in the early 1930s was just one more such challenge, albeit the most extreme most had yet faced.[6]

Los Angeles's business community responded to the Great Depression by seeking even better employees and demanding even more from them. The case of Security-First illustrates that process. When the economic downturn began in 1929, executives devised methods to attract employees who would be more talented and committed. The bank established contacts with local high schools, colleges, and universities to forward names of promising students. Security-First officials helped to persuade the Los Angeles Junior College to inaugurate a banking course from which they could draw recruits. The firm also began to hire a pool of young men who would rotate as interns through the bank's operations. When an opening appeared, the most talented of these men would receive the job. These programs, combined with high regional unemployment rates, allowed the bank to secure higher-quality employees. The percentage of new employees who were college graduates grew from 7 percent to 28 percent between 1930 and 1934. Annual turnover also dropped significantly, dropping from 35 percent to 20 percent between 1928 and 1930, and to approximately 10 percent by 1933. Yet even as banks hired better-qualified employees and as turnover declined, economic conditions worsened. Leaders, thus, had no time to gloat about improvements in personnel, but instead remained preoccupied with finding ways to stabilize the firm. Getting their employees to work harder and serve the company more effectively overshadowed all their actions. In 1934, when bank fortunes began to improve, turnover rose again to roughly 25 percent, the highest level since 1929, and reminded Security-First leaders that the "better" the employee, the more hard-earned the loyalty.[7]

The Depression presented a paradox for company men. As fewer and fewer white-collar positions became available, men sought them with greater urgency but were less empowered to press their demands. Companies, in turn, responded to the crisis by laying off marginal employees and cutting the salaries and hours of those that remained. Yet even as they did so, Los Angeles businesses believed that they could best overcome the economic slump by increasing sales, and to do this they turned to employees. A Pacific Electric editorial in the fall of 1930 noted that "possibly one of the best things that has happened to us during the past year is a definite realization of a fundamental principle, that we cannot individually prosper unless business is prosperous, and to you and me business is the Pacific Electric Railway."[8] Most firms ultimately relied on the same strategies they had carefully honed during the 1920s—promising mobility, security, and community to those who would adopt the firm's interests as their own. Those who did hold their jobs during the Depression had a comparatively good deal, and the emerging white-collar corporate culture within the nation's growing middle class not only survived the Depression but grew stronger and more pervasive.

The Worst of Times

In July 1930, *Southern California Business,* the mouthpiece of the Los Angeles Chamber of Commerce, gleefully featured a letter to the editor that downplayed the nation's apparent economic crisis. Emory Smith, an engineering firm executive, wrote to announce that his company refused to let the alleged problems worry them. "Personally," he stated, "we are taking advantage of this slack period to spruce up generally around our establishment. Nobody has been discharged, nobody's salary has been cut, and the payment of bills has not been unduly delayed." Furthermore, Smith noted, "While we believe careful consideration should be given to major expenditures, we do not believe it is a time for penuriousness or narrowness in thought or act." Chamber of Commerce officials proudly displayed Smith's letter, for it fit well with their argument that the region's supposed economic difficulties were more a state of mind than anything else and could be overcome quickly once confidence returned. As the months went by, however, the Chamber's campaign against pessimism became more difficult to sell. Between 1929 and 1931, the rate of business failures in Los Angeles climbed 28 percent. Southern California hit rock bottom during the winter of 1932–33, by which time no one disputed the situation's seriousness.[9]

From the crash on Wall Street throughout the turbulent 1930s, southern California business leaders struggled to guide their firms amid economic chaos. Although in retrospect one can view the Depression as a national calamity with distinct cycles of decline and recovery, individual businesses in urban economies perceived no such order. The Pacific Mutual Life Insurance Company actually enjoyed its best year ever in 1930, while across town, the Richfield Oil Company plunged into receivership. Whereas the film industry began to recover from the Depression in 1933 and enjoyed relative prosperity thereafter, Pacific Mutual and other insurance firms faced their greatest challenges later in the decade.

Individual firms faced unique storms during the 1930s and weathered them in different ways. Pacific Electric, for instance, may well have traced the origins of its depression to 1924, when a natural disaster joined with changing transportation habits to deal a blow from which the company never recovered. In that year, a severe drought reduced electric power supplies and forced the closure of some of the company's operations. Yet the reduction in PE service did not seem to concern southern Californians, who were rapidly abandoning the trolleys for automobiles. When the company later resumed some of its routes, its trains sat empty amid the traffic jams new drivers created. PE never regained its lost business and stagnated throughout the rest of the 1920s.

The Great Depression exacerbated PE's problems. The region's economic difficulties thwarted any opportunities for service expansion. While some southern Californians opted for electric railways as a cheaper form of personal transportation than automobile ownership, overall the company steadily lost riders. At its height in the early 1920s, PE employed more than 6,500 people and its railway service carried more than 110 million passengers each year over 1,200 miles of track. Although the region's population soared throughout the 1920s and would grow by nearly 600,000 during the 1930s, PE's ridership dropped to 80 million passengers, 27 percent below its peak in 1923. By 1932, PE employed only 4,000 people, a 38 percent cut from its high point a decade earlier. In 1936, the firm experienced a growth in ridership for the first time in years and raised its employee roster to 4,800, but the company still hit the 1940s limping badly.[10]

Like Pacific Electric, Union Oil entered the 1930s already in trouble. Wild speculation in oil drilling during the 1920s had resulted in an enormous production glut. California oil wells pumped sixteen million barrels in 1930, but the market could absorb only eleven million. This surplus had devastating effects on prices, and as the Depression further reduced demand, Union Oil's income plummeted. Company sales dropped from $89 million in 1929 to $51 million in 1932, when Union Oil cut annual production from 878,000 to 675,000 barrels. Amidst the company's adjustment to the changing business climate, one leader commented that the oil business was "entering a new era." He observed, "Conditions and practices under which we have been operating have gone, never to return."[11]

Union Oil executives turned to cost-cutting as the primary solution to their financial woes. Within the decade's first three years, the company halted virtually all new capital expenditures, shut down five hundred wells, reduced its drilling teams from forty-six to six, and authorized only the barest maintenance of plants and equipment. These measures shrank the company's workforce by 20 percent to eight thousand employees, but most layoffs affected blue-collar production workers. The firm sought to keep white-collar layoffs to a minimum, and it accomplished this partly by wage cuts and partly by the implementation of shortened work weeks for all employees. Even these measures did not keep Union Oil in the black, but the company balanced its books by drawing on cash reserves, a luxury few companies enjoyed.[12]

Union Oil's business began to improve in the mid 1930s. Alongside proud declarations about how the firm had weathered the stormiest years and never missed a dividend, leaders in 1935 introduced a new motor oil with great expectations. Triton Motor Oil did well, and in 1937 production surpassed that of 1929. Booming demand bolstered by a swelling population, industrial growth, and heightened automobile and aviation markets propelled Union Oil profitably into the 1940s.

Security-First also weathered the 1930s well, though it too faced many challenges. Having created the company in 1928 from two large branch banking networks, its officers knew much about consolidation by the time the Depression hit. During the merger, leaders had promised that the bank would seek to avoid layoffs, but this proved difficult once the Depression took its toll. Between 1929 and 1933, assets fell from $624 million to $506 million. Deposits during this period dropped from $534 to $438 million. To cope with declining income, the bank streamlined operations by cutting salaries and expenses, closing branches, not filling vacant positions, and laying off some employees. Security-First had employed more than 3,500 people in 154 branches in 1929, but by 1934 it had pared its roster to 3,000 in approximately 120 offices. Desperate to trim expenses further, in 1934 the firm began soliciting cost-cutting tips from its employees. The company magazine featured their suggestions, which included efficiency items (unlikely to save much money companywide) such as: immediately correct wrong phone numbers, recycle rubber bands and envelopes; don't take messages requiring a return call but help the person yourself; and wait to mail correction notices with other standard mailings. Such hard times proved relatively short-lived. By 1935, business began to pick up, and, at the end of the decade, assets, deposits, and income far surpassed pre-Depression levels.[13] Security-First entered the 1940s with a streamlined operation, having nearly 40 percent fewer branches than in 1929, and as a profitable business.

Southern California Edison opened the 1930s in style when on March 20, 1931, it threw a public gala unveiling its new $4 million downtown Los Angeles headquarters. Hailed as the world's first "all-electric building," the stunning art deco structure remains a downtown landmark. Despite the company's best efforts, however, the economic crisis marred the grand opening. From 1929 to 1933, SCE's net earnings dropped from $27.1 to $18.4 million. To cope, the company halted construction projects, consolidated some departments, implemented a five-day work week and salary reductions, and dismissed personnel. Its roster dropped from 5,400 in 1929 to approximately 4,000 in 1933. Much of this reduction represented a decline in construction jobs.[14]

SCE suffered additional blows when, just as its sales started to recover in the mid 1930s, New Deal initiatives such as the development of rural electric cooperatives, began to tap into company business. Federal loans financed these cooperatives, which received energy from electric power plants built with government dollars. New Deal programs put Southern California Edison on the political hot seat throughout the 1930s, and the company did lose some of its outlying areas in rural California deserts.[15] By decade's end, gross earnings had surpassed 1929 levels, but SCE remained a smaller company with fewer employees and lower profits than it had previously enjoyed.

The 1930s proved an especially bitter period for Pacific Mutual Life, which had opened the decade with the best performance in its history. That year the firm created eighteen new agencies, and 64 percent of all agencies showed a gain in business. In the spring of 1931, company president George Cochran attributed Pacific Mutual's success to the fact that people wanted more insurance in hard times, but such claims proved premature. Between 1930 and 1933, company income declined from $48.3 to $43.9 million and the amount of insurance in force fell by more than $100 million. The worst drop occurred during 1932 and 1933, when business fell 18 percent.[16]

A bad situation turned worse in 1935 when Pacific Mutual announced that ill-conceived insurance packages were bankrupting the firm. In 1918, Pacific Mutual had become the first insurance company in the nation to issue a "non-cancelable disability income policy." Under this program, the firm could not nullify policies "when the holder ceased to be insurable." As policyholders began to cash in during the 1930s, these "liberal terms" sapped company reserves. In July 1936, Samuel L. Carpenter, California state insurance commissioner, initiated proceedings to seize and reorganize Pacific Mutual. Many board members, stockholders, and policy owners filed suit to block the move, but state courts ultimately approved dissolution of the old entity and the creation of the new Pacific Mutual Life Insurance Company (previously, "of California"). By 1938, the firm had implemented revised noncancelable policies that would protect company reserves, and had successfully fought off many legal challenges to the changes.[17]

Pacific Mutual's financial woes and contested reorganization proved a public relations nightmare in an already difficult business climate. Nationally, new life insurance volume in 1938 totaled only 63 percent of that purchased in 1929. Pacific Mutual's new business dropped 40 percent in 1937. The company lost money through 1938, despite cost-cutting measures that included staff reductions and pay cuts. Only in 1940 did Pacific Mutual see a real increase in the total amount of insurance in force, though this figure still represented only 80 percent of the company's 1930 policy base.[18]

When the Going Gets Tough . . .

Not long after the stock market crash in October 1929, Pacific Mutual agents began to report greater difficulty selling insurance as potential customers attempted to cut their own expenses. Company leaders responded to such news by asking agents to make a resolution for the year 1930: "I am going to fight to maintain the circle of confidence unbroken. As far as it is within my power, I will fight—any movement to lower wages, any attack on living standards, any slowing up of production, any retrenchment in selling effort . . . By harder work, by more aggressive selling, I am going to maintain my own normal growth in 1930, and thus contribute to the soundness of the whole business structure.[19] Agents met this pledge by making 1930 the most successful year in company history. A positive selling attitude clearly had its limits, however, and business began to slip late in the year. Executives responded to the decline by urging even greater effort. One announcement stated that "Everyone in the Company's service, from the President down, should be a salesman of the Pacific Mutual, and if he is not he is not measuring up to all that is expected of him." Such admonitions could not counter a national economic tragedy, and business plummeted even further. By late 1931, some agents began quitting, finding it impossible to sell insurance in the midst of a Depression. Leaders responded angrily to this news, declaring, "Why a life underwriter should ever want to give up his job, we have never been able to explain satisfactorily." They argued that an insurance agent was engaged in the "greatest business in the world, for he can succeed both in good times and in bad. But it is always up to him."[20] In hindsight it is easy to sympathize with agents' plight, but executives at the time believed that efforts should yield results and wrung their hands over employees' apparent resignation.

With times worsening and agents leaving, Pacific Mutual sought ways to improve the performance of those still in its ranks. Leaders introduced new sales manuals with extensive strategies and high expectations. The company announced that the 200 top-selling agents would be given a trip to Chicago, and they continually promoted the contest alongside detailed rankings of how agents and agencies were doing. A 1932 issue of the *Pacific Mutual News* featured twelve such lists.[21] In frustration, many underwriters grew bitter over the company's insistence and rose in protest. In reaction to the argument that the firm's sales manual set unrealistic expectations, top management published a letter, scripted as if penned by the manual itself:

> To avoid debate (because debate has no place in a sale) let me again concede everything you have claimed as to present economic conditions. The fact remains that you must still provide food, clothing and shelter (today and tomorrow) for yourself and your loved ones. I have presented a plan, not an easy one but—A PLAN. It has been proved. Have you a better one? If not, then you are welcome to the use of mine and I urge you to USE IT HARD. Does that FIX THE PROBLEM ON YOU?[22]

Even as executives presented this less than sympathetic response, they removed rankings of agents and agencies from the company magazine for the rest of the year. Only when business picked up slightly in 1934 did the rankings return.

Events at Pacific Mutual illustrated the difficult, Depression-era relationship between corporate executives and white-collar employees. As company incomes declined, most firms tightened their belts, often in ways that hurt employees. And yet even as they did so, leaders believed that those very employees were key to the company's survival and success. Executives walked a fine line between cutting expenses and maintaining a satisfied and effective workforce. No firm assumed personnel would act with total dedication simply because they were thankful for their jobs. To the contrary, leaders believed it more imperative than ever that they motivate their employees to act as if the company were their very own, though in Pacific Mutual's case, they edged toward more authoritarian strategies. Company officials, in fact, frequently devised motivational campaigns that many employees likely considered odd if not irritating. On June 29, 1935, for instance, Pacific Mutual president George Cochran celebrated his twenty-ninth year with the firm, not with cakes or parties in company offices, but by asking all agents to break their single-day sales records.[23]

Most large firms continued to produce company magazines during the Depression. Executives considered these productions vital to maintaining morale, fostering company spirit, and reminding employees of their obligations. In an effort to economize, Union Oil stopped producing color covers on its magazine in 1931 and in 1935 made the magazine bimonthly instead of monthly. The firm never discontinued the *Bulletin*, however, and the magazine again began to appear monthly in 1937. Security-First reduced its magazine to a bimonthly publication in 1932 but kept it in print throughout the decade. Even amidst its greatest crises, in 1933 and 1935, Pacific Mutual never missed an issue of its monthly, the *Pacific Mutual News*.[24]

Pacific Electric, one of the region's most embattled major firms, broke ranks by discontinuing its magazine between 1932 and 1936. Executives struggled with the decision, for they viewed the publication as their best means to motivate employees and used it precisely for this purpose in the Depression's early years. As in the 1910s and 1920s, the *Pacific Electric Magazine* routinely printed editorials urging employee dedication, with titles such as "Are You Pacific-Electric Minded?", "Service Is Our Stock in Trade," and "Courtesy Makes Everyone Happier." In 1930, the magazine became particularly preoccupied with urging employee activism on several political measures of interest to the company. By 1931, editorials pled with personnel to secure new business and goodwill: "All of us can do something to improve our position in the public mind, and it is well to constantly remember that whatever advances this railway's interest is of direct benefit to employees." By summer 1931, however, budget shortfalls forced Pacific Electric to make its magazine bimonthly; and the next summer, even as it launched a new "Went over the Top" campaign to inspire employees to solicit new business, leaders suspended the magazine's production. In 1936, with the first signs of PE's recovery, the magazine reappeared, filled once again with editorials about employee loyalty, proddings to heighten sales efforts, and discussions of political measures.[25]

Attempts to motivate employees to secure new business, create goodwill toward the company, and promote its political interests had been central to the corporate cultures of Los Angeles firms throughout the early twentieth century. As local firms struggled to survive in depressed economic conditions, however, these efforts reached a fevered pitch. In November 1933, Southern California Edison announced the most ambitious "load-building" campaign in its history. SCE aimed to secure $3,000,000 of new business by the end of 1934, and it sought to reach this goal by making all employees solicitors for the firm.[26] Union Oil sales managers throughout the 1930s similarly worked to design motivational sales competitions. In 1937, one sales district held a contest in which what an employee wore to the monthly staff banquet depended upon how much he had sold (no women were a part of this competition). If "clothes make the man," the magazine story reported, then unsuccessful agents found themselves stripped of both their clothing and manhood. Some were able to attend fully clothed, but others had to pose with no shirt, jacket, or tie, and still others sat in their boxers. The magazine reported: "Nobody actually had to come in a barrel, and the meeting was obviously not a nudist conference, but one might readily have been pardoned for assuming that the men had decided to join a nudist colony, and were preparing themselves for acceptance. There were delegates in every stage of attire, and a few had even won back their pants, but hadn't earned suspenders in time for the banquet, so were both uncomfortable and embarrassed."[27]

Union Oil sought, by any means possible, to convince employees of their role in helping the business survive. In 1931, the company magazine printed a letter from two stockholders apologizing for using non–Union Oil products: "We plead 'guilty' to having been a bit careless at times going to the most convenient oil station for gas and oil: — but, in the future we have both resolved to GO OUT OF OUR WAY to seek Union products . . . It has always been a PLEASURE (in the past) to patronize a UNION station but now we make it a **DUTY**." This letter became one of the many examples from which leaders expected employees to learn. In 1937 the company published a letter received from a grateful man whose car had broken down but who had been rescued by two Union Oil employees. The firm made its expectations for employee ambassadorship particularly explicit each year when it continued to insist that its Los Angeles personnel contribute to the local Community Chest, a private charitable fund whose directors established quotas for local firms. The company generally succeeded in meeting its share, thanks to nearly unanimous employee participation.[28]

Desperation to increase sales led some Union Oil offices to resort to unusual tactics. One department equated strong sales records with manly strength and lobbed attacks on the masculinity of those with poor showings. Leaders made this point by creating a sales chart on an office wall on which each agent's picture appeared in a ranking according to his performance. Searching for ways to energize employees, a pair of "pink unmentionables" (women's underwear) was tacked underneath the pictures of those with the lowest sales record.[29]

Few Los Angeles firms as consistently made demands on employees as did Security-First. Bank executives continually urged them to recognize their importance to business success. In 1931, leaders announced, "No group or organization is better than its personnel, whether that group be a football team or bank, or any department or branch of a bank." The following year the company magazine declared: "There is a hidden asset in this Bank, never to be expressed in terms of dollars and cents because it is precious beyond any monetary computation. That asset is loyalty." Time after time, leaders reminded employees that Security-First's ability to prosper during the economic crisis rested on its ability to both secure and retain customers. But what exactly did this mean for bank staff? Top management left nothing to the imagination. Reifying elements of a corporate culture they had been crafting for years, leaders asked staff members to become the company: "In the minds of those who know you or hear about you, you are linked up with this Bank. To them you are not just Mr. Blank, but Mr. Blank of the Security-First National Bank." Management expected employees to take this principle to heart should they anticipate careers with the bank. In a typical object lesson, personnel in 1933 learned that a colleague had earned a recent promotion because he lived by the rule: "I try to make my customers' problems MY problems."[30]

Throughout the 1930s, Security-First intensified the common bank practice of sponsoring competitions for employees to bring in new business. In a 1933 contest, personnel received points for bringing in new safe deposit box accounts. The winning man received a pair of tickets to the Rose Bowl, while the winning woman won tickets to a Hollywood premiere. In the few hours they were not soliciting the business of their friends and neighbors, Security-First employees were expected to campaign for political causes. Whether it was for the 1932 measure to abolish the trust deed form of lending, the 1938 proposition known as "$30 every Thursday," or the 1939 "Ham and Eggs" initiative, political support for or in opposition to measures affecting the banking industry remained a distinct part of job descriptions.[31]

The need to reinforce employees' awareness of their broad duties remained an ever-present theme of Los Angeles corporate cultures throughout the 1930s. Even if widespread unemployment lowered turnover, it did not ensure enthusiasm. In 1937, Union Oil leaders published an angry editorial clearly reflecting a belief that not all employees were acting with the desired dedication: "Do you really like your job? Do you get a kick out of working?" leaders demanded. They urged each worker to "sit down some time and talk it over," and argued that after doing so, it would become clear that the "job is fine" and that it is the employee's own attitude which is at fault.[32] Despite these words, executives knew that the loyalty of educated and ambitious white men would not be gained by appealing to their attitudes, even in the wake of a horrific depression. As always, management would need to devise more tangible means to motivate their company men.

Profit and Security

Throughout the Great Depression, many Americans found relief from their economic woes by going to movie houses, which, unlike most industries, witnessed a steady rise in business. While many films offered an escape from daily worries, some forced audiences to confront painful realities. In 1935, for instance, RKO Pictures' *Alice Adams* told the story of a young woman's efforts to overcome her modest upbringing and compete in local society circles. Unable to dress properly, invite suitors home, or benefit from the standing that wealthy parents might provide, Alice Adams (portrayed by a young Katherine Hepburn) suffered indignity upon indignity, all of which her desperation exacerbated. In the end, however, Alice won the heart of a dashing young man, displacing one of the town's debutantes. Although moviegoers learned that ultimately, love triumphs over wealth, the road to this destination passed through many difficult scenes. Even though Alice finally succeeded, the film presented harsh evidence that poor Americans suffered painful social and economic inequities.[33]

In addition, *Alice Adams* captured a painful contradiction in American social experience during the 1930s. While most in the audience could identify with the Adams family's financial struggles, they were aware that many elite Americans, like the families who snubbed Alice, were largely oblivious to the Depression's sting. For young white-collar workers, this dichotomy hit particularly close to home, for they worked in environments where earnings varied widely. Clerks and stenographers, with the most meager of incomes, worked next door to the offices of executives who commanded enormous salaries. While all personnel saw their incomes decline during the Depression, the reductions were particularly difficult for already poorly paid low-level white-collar workers.

Of course, Los Angeles corporations had never viewed high salaries as their core tactic for rewarding employees. As corporate incomes and national per capita wages declined precipitously during the early 1930s, most firms did not hesitate to cut white-collar salaries, though the reductions were generally less than for blue-collar employees. While declines in blue-collar wages slightly exceeded national wholesale price deflation, white-collar incomes nationally fell less than consumer prices, and rose more quickly than prices during the recovery.[34] The general fluctuations in Los Angeles's white-collar incomes paralleled national trends, though the degree of cuts may have been greater in Los Angeles. As Table 8.1 shows, national white-collar incomes dropped significantly during the early 1930s, began to rise later in the decade, and, by 1939, neared 1929 levels. Security-First mirrored these trends. The bank lowered salaries steadily following the stock market crash in October 1929. Leaders did not slash payrolls without great hesitation and apology, however, and they continually adjusted salaries as the economy rose and fell. In January 1933, for instance, Security-First announced a new 5 percent reduction in salaries but rescinded this action in August when business seemed to improve. Yet despite such fluctuations, the bank reduced its work week, and overall salaries fell approximately 23 percent percent between 1929 and 1936 (surpassing a national deflation rate of 16 percent between those years). Leaders finally reversed the decline in 1936, after the first year of inflation since 1926. Bank wages reached parity with 1929 levels in 1940. Southern California Edison followed a similar course. SCE began to shorten its employees' work week and to scale back salaries as the Depression hit and intensified. Executives began to reverse cuts only in 1937.[35]

While most employees preferred high salaries over other compensation options, corporate leaders had long sought to create alternative inducements more favorable to the company. These efforts continued during the Depression. Though employee stock ownership programs, for instance, had never proven particularly effective and seemed especially dubious to employees after 1929, many firms continued or renewed such efforts. In 1931, Security-First began a new plan, whereby employees could purchase bank stock through payroll deduction. By 1935, 64 percent of the bank's staff had enrolled.[36]

When business incomes began to recover in the late 1930s, leaders, albeit often reluctantly, started raising salaries; profits still seemed tenuous and executives wanted to keep expenses trimmed. In this context, annual or Christmas bonus programs appealed to executives as a middle ground. Leaders liked such "gifts," for while ultimately a form of salary increase, they were not "official" and could be decided on from year to year. Bonuses also carried the aura of a special "present" from top management, which could imply that employees would feel grateful. Security-First began to enact an annual Christmas bonus in 1936, the same year salaries began to rise. The bonus, which continued for the rest of the decade, provided employees one-half of one month's income, up to $75. Southern California Edison also began an annual bonus program in 1936, just as its revenues started to expand, providing a direct per-

Table 8.1 Average weekly earnings of blue- and white-collar workers

Year	*Blue-Collar*	*White-Collar*
1929	$27.14	$34.78
1933	18.59	29.42
1937	25.25	32.57
1939	25.44	33.04

Source: Jürgen Kocka, *White Collar Workers in America, 1890–1940: A Social-Political History in International Perspective* (London: Sage Publications, 1980), 232.

centage of yearly salaries. In 1939, the company began issuing monthly "bonus charts" to show employees how much they might receive given the company's performance that month. Leaders informed personnel that each month's bonus chart was "not only informative but it encourages each employee to make whatever contribution he can toward the success of the bonus plan."[37]

Throughout the 1910s and 1920s, the heart of most compensation programs had been benefits designed to provide employees and their families measures of personal security. Executives favored these perquisites, for they were more difficult for small businessmen and independent professionals to acquire and, thus, represented one of the more enticing rewards for white-collar work. In the Depression-era climate, those benefits took on heightened significance and remained central to most corporate cultures. In 1930 Security-First introduced a new mandatory savings and pension program that built on the plans from the two banks that had merged in 1928. Under the new program, all employees contributed 3 percent of their salaries to the fund. This money, combined with a company subsidy, would be available for medical emergencies and in time would provide a pension. Retiring employees would receive a stipend based on 2 percent of the average maximum annual income received for any five-year period multiplied by the number of years in service. No pension could exceed $2,400 per year. Employees who resigned prior to retiring would be refunded their contribution with 4 percent interest.[38]

Union Oil also upgraded its employee benefit programs during the 1930s. Since 1919 the company had had a contributory Employees Benefit Fund that paid both life insurance and medical care. In 1930, Union Oil divided the plan and established a separate life insurance program which gave employees policies, paid for by the company, based on their length of service. The remaining employee-subsidized Benefit Fund then became devoted to covering expenses incurred during illnesses and hospitalizations. Throughout the 1930s, just over two-thirds of all personnel participated in the fund, which, for approximately $2 a month, provided up to $500 for medical emergencies. In 1936, the company enlarged the plan to include dental care.[39]

Union Oil continued its Provident Fund during the Depression. Created with equal contributions from employees and the company, the fund established retirement pensions for every employee, as well as a savings account for emergencies. Retrieving contributions became a matter of debate in 1934, when executives reported that many employees were drawing on their monies, not for "emergencies," but to pay taxes and insurance premiums and to purchase cars, radios, and other personal items. Although Union Oil sought to limit access to the Provident Fund, it remained in force until 1939, when leaders decided that the $11,000,000 program had become too large for the company to monitor and turned it over to the Equitable Life Assurance Company. Southern California Edison, which had started a pension program in 1919, increased its policy in 1934. More than 95 percent of SCE employees signed up for the enlarged program, which combined employee contributions with a company subsidy.[40]

Not surprisingly, given the transit industry's steady decline, Pacific Electric struggled more than other local firms to maintain its benefit programs during the Depression. In 1924 it had instituted a life insurance plan that provided death payments ranging from $250 to $500 based on length of service, free of charge. In the fall of 1931, the company began charging a monthly fee to continue the policy, though its terms were now enlarged. PE's workforce could now secure insurance for contributions of sixty to seventy cents per month per $1,000 of coverage. The firm continued its contributory medical insurance throughout the 1930s. By 1913, it had established a "hospital department" where enrolled employees and their families could receive medical care. In 1936, Pacific Electric significantly enlarged and improved this facility with the establishment of a new fifteen-person medical office occupying the entire ninth floor of its downtown headquarters.[41]

Pacific Electric had offered employees "retirement gratuities" prior to the Depression but had to enlarge and systematize its program following passage of the federal Railroad Retirement Act of 1937. Pacific Electric enacted a pension plan slightly more generous than the statute mandated. Employees over the age of sixty who had worked for thirty years received an annual annuity based on length of service, but not to exceed $300 per month. Those who had worked fewer than thirty years were still eligible for the program but at reduced payment levels. Employees who worked in departments related to its bus service were not eligible for the railway plan, but they received a "gratuity" that, when combined with their social security pensions, equaled the amount other employees received.[42]

Corporate employment generally provided white-collar men not only greater job security and a more stable income but also other opportunities to enhance personal and familial security that could be derived only by pooling the resources of a large number of people. Although company life insurance, medical programs, and pensions were the most notable supplements to corporate employment, white-collar employees enjoyed other benefits as well. In the mid 1930s, for instance, Union Oil began establishing credit unions for personnel—fourteen by 1936, covering more than two thousand employees. By summer 1936, these credit unions had extended loans to nearly nine hundred employees, more than a third of whom used their accounts to consolidate bills and clear other debts. In the midst of a national Depression, this proved to be a popular benefit.[43]

Paid vacations were continued and often expanded during the 1930s. Security-First allowed employees who had served over four months two weeks paid vacation, to be taken between March 1 and October 31. Those who had worked between two and four months were entitled to one week sometime late in the summer, to be scheduled by management. In 1939, Security-First enhanced its vacation package for long-term employees. The company gave those who had served more than twenty years two additional weeks of paid annual leave.[44]

Finally, corporate employees continued to benefit from a variety of group discounts. In some cases, companies secured the special prices, while other times local businesses extended them directly. Ironically, Pacific Electric, though hurt by increasing automobile usage, arranged a group rate for employees' auto insurance in 1929, yielding savings of 30 percent off general market prices.[45] Local businesses continually courted PE employees. In the early 1930s, before PE's medical plan included dental care, dentists routinely offered its staff specially priced services. Local optical companies also vied for PE customers, since they knew that each employee had a company subsidy for glasses. Furniture, sporting goods, tire, suit, and watch stores were among the business that advertised employee discounts in the *Pacific Electric Magazine*.[46]

Depression-Era Manhood

In a 1932 Paramount Pictures film entitled *If I Had a Million*, a business magnate decided to give one million dollars to eight persons randomly selected from the telephone book rather than pass his wealth on to ungrateful relatives. After initially turning to the name of John D. Rockefeller, the millionaire drew up a list of eight persons whom the audience then observed receiving and reacting to their newfound wealth. Most vignettes were complex stories ten to twenty minutes in length, yet the film portrayed the tale of one recipient without dialogue and in barely a minute's time. The scene opened with a shot of a huge room in which dozens of clerks toiled away at identical tasks at identical desks. Among them was Phineas Lambert, a pudgy, meek, and timid middle-aged man. After receiving the million dollar check, Lambert quietly got up and walked to the stairwell where he ascended to the firm's executive offices. One by one he walked through managerial suites until he finally arrived at the president's office. Lambert then opened the door and gave the startled man a loud raspberry. The scene's brevity, simplicity, and lack of dialogue suggest that there was little need to provide much context or explain the point. Audiences understood exactly the situation. Lambert held a lousy, degrading job; and when given independent wealth, he immediately assailed the ultimate source of his hellish circumstance.[47]

If I Had a Million was not unusual among contemporary American films in lamenting the plight of company men. Such debasement, set during the Depression when any job might be thought to be a good job, underscored the fragility of white-collar manhood. The segment's structure suggests that its producers believed many viewers would readily identify with the pent-up frustration of a lower-level company man. Phineas Lambert's plight seemed even more grave to white American men in 1932 than it would have in the 1920s. While one might be grateful simply to have a job when so many did not, the status of positions low on the corporate ladder continued to decline. Popular culture suggested that those who could not rise above low-level office jobs were hardly men at all. This was certainly a message presented in *Alice Adams.* Throughout the story, Alice's father convalesced at home, too weak from an illness to go to work. The wholesale drug company that employed him, however, continued his salary in appreciation for his many years of good service. The father, Virgil, repeatedly told his family of their good fortune in working for a firm that cared for him, but his wife would hear none of it. She persistently blamed him for her daughter's difficulties in competing with local society girls: "The men in those families went right on up the ladder, while you are still a clerk." The mother lambasted her meek husband and left no doubt as to her impression of his masculinity: "If only she had a father who had the gumption *to be a man.*"[48]

Throughout their companies' early growth, Los Angeles executives had sought to construct an understanding of corporate employment based on the metaphor of the ladder. Every position could lead to the highest rungs. Thus, ambitious young white men need not feel embarrassed or embittered by taking entry-level white-collar jobs, for they were appropriate starting points for successful business careers. This strategy continued during the Depression. In December 1932, amidst massive retrenchment, Security-First leaders promised employees that their advancement would come in due time: "In every pay envelope in this bank is a hidden and intangible asset—a claim to a position of greater power, responsibility and influence, if we can prove in our present work that we qualify for the job."[49]

Convincing white-collar men that realistic potential to climb the ladder existed presented leaders a considerable challenge, for in a time of declining profits and retrenchment, promotions proved rare. Pacific Electric had always striven to provide advancement opportunities for its employees, but the Depression did not help. When promotions did occur, however, officials widely touted them as examples of where loyal service could lead. In 1937, the company magazine printed a glowing biography of its new president, O. A. Smith, that enthusiastically recounted his rise up the corporate ladder. Interestingly enough, a company editorial that appeared that same year attacked the idea of municipal bus ownership in part with the argument that private companies could provide more advancement opportunities.[50]

Throughout the 1930s, Union Oil celebrated promotions as evidence of continued opportunities to climb the ladder. Having made advancement such a central feature of its corporate culture, leaders were sensitive to insinuations that the company was not delivering on its pledges. At the end of the decade, for instance, top managers responded to charges that "important positions" were being filled by men from outside the firm:

> It is our policy, whenever possible, to fill executive positions with men from within the Company. As a matter of fact, in only one case has such a position been filled by an outsider during the past year. That was the highly specialized position of Director of Advertising and Public Relations, and even in this case the man, whom we brought in from Lord & Thomas, our advertising agents, had worked with our organization for many years. We believe this policy of promoting from within is a sound one.[51]

Security-First employees also pressured executives to maintain internal promotion systems. Leaders responded by continually reporting advancement rates. In 1934, for instance, they announced that since the bank's creation in 1928, management had filled 98 percent of all vacancies above the entry-level from within. More than most local firms, Security-First officials discussed the extent of promotions in unusual detail. In January 1931, they reported that four hundred employees (out of approximately three thousand) had been assigned new positions during 1930, and that almost all of those represented significant steps upward. In addition, leaders noted that forty-eight promotions involved "staff" becoming officers, or officers rising to higher posts. In 1932 and 1933, as retrenchment set in, management repeatedly reminded its workers that in the "better times just around the corner" meritorious employees would be rewarded for their Depression-era service. Security-First's personnel director reported pleasure in the fact that "a large number of personnel members are preparing themselves for advancement in the post-depression era."[52] That era started in 1936, and the bank indeed began heralding successful climbers with unbridled vigor. Photos of promoted employees dominated the company magazine and in the late 1930s became part of a regular column entitled, "Up The Ladder." Security-First also began to recycle the mobility editorials that had been standard fare in corporate circles during the 1910s and 1920s:

> In the diplomatic service of certain nations there are individuals known as "career men." They are the men who enter the service at an early age and devote the rest of their lives to it, spending approximately the first ten years in preparing for their life work by assignments in minor functions and consistent study . . . There are approximately 350 officers in the SFNB. They are the career men who have been willing to make minor sacrifices for a major cause.[53]

Pacific Mutual similarly advertised promotions as evidence that loyal employees could still reach the upper echelons. One such promotion announcement from 1930 noted: "His steady advancement has been justified by his work. He is still on the way up." As had long been the case, however, Pacific Mutual leaders defined success largely in terms of sales production. With the majority of its male employees being agents with few chances to advance, individual achievement through sales remained a hallmark of Pacific Mutual manhood. This construction of manliness continued to reverberate in the firm's corporate culture during the Depression. A 1936 issue of *Pacific Mutual News* echoed this familiar theme in describing the aggressive nature of several new agents: "Men are like that. They enlist for an ideal. They fight for a future."[54]

Appeals to manhood at Pacific Mutual proved ironic, given the firm's policy, fully in place by the 1920s, of hiring women as agents. Executives had to defend this practice to some male employees who struggled with the challenge successful female agents posed to their occupational identity. These men's grievances intensified in the 1930s with arguments that the nation's unemployment problem would be solved if women stopped "taking" men's jobs.[55] Pacific Mutual leaders rejected these concerns by explicitly defending the policy of hiring women. In one instance they reprinted a newspaper column that argued that women's work supported their families, that most women were working because they had to, not because they wanted to. Such explanations may have received a tepid reception among men, for in 1931 the *Pacific Mutual News* stopped featuring a special women's section and throughout the rest of the 1930s rarely printed stories specifically discussing female agents.[56]

Community

In July 1930, Pacific Electric executives canceled the company's annual Redondo Beach Picnic, scheduled for the following month. Financial constraints did not allow for such a luxury.[57] As Los Angeles corporations tightened their budgets, recreational expenditures would seem to have been an easy target, but, in fact, PE was one of the few major local firms to alter longstanding social traditions. The Great Depression did little to dampen the many forms of community that flourished within large firms. Sporting contests, employee clubs, and social galas remained prominent features of most corporate cultures. Clearly, employees themselves instigated and organized many manifestations of community; many such activities occurred outside the reach of company policy or control. Yet firms rarely suspended even those activities that demanded financial outlays, for leaders and employees alike considered them an established feature of company life. To cease them would have been more than simply an act of cost-cutting, but rather a blow to the corporate culture's carefully woven fabric.

By the 1930s, most local firms had established longstanding social rituals. The minimal expenses they involved rarely triggered any serious scrutiny. To the contrary, while some employees might have wondered why the company would fund parties while it cut salaries, executives usually considered such events money well spent, for these socials affirmed the very sense of "corporate family" they hoped would yield dedicated workers. Pacific Mutual banquets, for instance, bolstered the firm's aggressive sales culture. Following sales campaigns in which management pitted employees against each other, competing for individual prizes, the firm often held banquets that did more than honor top sellers. Held in posh downtown hotels, they provided an elegant opportunity for successful agents and their spouses to dine and socialize at company expense, and for executives to affirm their personnel's efforts.[58]

By the time the Depression struck, Union Oil's Orange District had a longstanding tradition of a fall barbecue and picnic. A national economic crisis did nothing to mar the event, which continued to attract large numbers through the 1930s. In 1935 the barbecue drew approximately 5,200 people to Orange County Park, where they enjoyed "one of the best arranged and most enjoyable picnics that has ever been organized for their entertainment." The theme chosen for that year's picnic was "whiskers," meaning that male employees were supposed to sport facial hair. According to the company magazine, most did: "we doubt if in the entire history of facial landscaping there has ever been gathered in one spot such a complete and diversified assortment of fungus. To render the shrubbery more attractive, the owners in most cases donned appropriate costumes, and the whole scene was not only highly amusing but was also decidedly picturesque." The *Union Oil Bulletin* featured the picnic in a comprehensive four-page spread that showed pictures of the many games, athletic contests, dances, and eating opportunities.[59]

Office parties similarly continued as established fixtures in large companies. Even as its accountants worried over plummeting deposits in December 1932, Security-First's downtown trust office held its elaborate annual Christmas Eve fête. The event commenced in midafternoon, when a bank vice president dressed as Santa Claus entered the lobby surrounded by a group of "Security Trust women" dressed as "maidens." They escorted Santa to a throne from which he delivered an address highlighting meritorious bank personnel. The entourage then presented a box of red roses and holly to each female staff member, and a red boutonniere to each man. All received candy and cigarettes. Following the presentations, the bank's Trust Counsel, sporting green knickers and a feather in his hat, led a company-formed German oompah band into the office. An employee octet leading Christmas carols followed a short band concert. Finally, gathered around a Christmas tree, personnel exchanged gifts.[60]

That active social communities continued within most of these corporations throughout the Depression reveals much about the ways in which corporate cultures transcended the dictates of company balance sheets. Fluctuating profits might depress wages, downsize workforces, and tighten operating budgets; but they did not prevent friendships among personnel, result in the cancellation of employee-led games and activities, or end most social traditions. Sporting events flourished throughout the 1930s. Dozens of bowling, baseball, and basketball leagues existed in Los Angeles, featuring both intra- and intercompany play. Even though PE leaders canceled the annual picnic, which likely cost thousands of dollars, their longstanding bowling league, needing a scant subsidy, continued to run from October through March of each year and attracted as many as one hundred entrants. Throughout the season, PE's company magazine featured lengthy reports on the league, listing scores and showcasing winners.[61]

Union Oil also continued to hold its annual bowling tournament, in which offices and districts throughout California competed for the Major Burnham Trophy. The annual Comptroller's Golf Tournament, held in March at ritzy locales such as the Brentwood Country Club, became the company's most celebrated sporting event. Few male members of the firm's "adding machine brigade" failed to compete. Participants enthusiastically recounted the event throughout the year. While the better golfers competed for a variety of championship trophies, the real fun came in the awarding of less distinguished honors. In 1938, for instance, G. S. Kelly won an enormous cellophane-wrapped sucker for having the highest (worst) score. Elmer Rogers won a pair of lady's undergarments for never having won a prize. And Bert Mason, not known for his prodigious play, won a box of smashed and chipped golf balls, resembling prunes, for making the longest drive of his career. Officials gave out the awards during a lengthy banquet filled with comedic speeches and roasts, including one aimed at the company's worst golfers, labeled "divot lofters."[62]

Numerous accounts in company magazines provide ample evidence that sporting leagues, clubs, and social organizations flourished throughout the Depression. However, for every employee that participated in a company bowling tournament or joined a company club, many more went out with friends after work or engaged in social life with colleagues far outside the scope of any managerial oversight. One can observe the faintest glimmer of this world in the human interest stories that permeated company magazines. Readers who ignored the editorials telling them to work harder likely read stories and carefully examined photos of themselves and their friends. Magazine editors continually struggled to balance the demands of executives, who wanted certain kinds of content, with the desires of employees, who had a different view of what constituted news. In 1932, editors of the *Security-First News Bulletin* responded to apparent criticisms by employees who wanted more personal items in the magazine. The editors wrote that while they intended the magazine to help employees get acquainted, its contents would have to be restricted to "what may be termed the public rather than the home connections of its readers. After all is said and done, the latter are only vitally interesting to those who will hear about them anyway through other and more natural channels."[63] In the latter 1930s, when bank executives felt more freedom to ease off on their incessant motivational articles, they allowed for the inclusion of more and more personal news about employees.

Amid their official pronouncements and carefully screened news features, employee magazines remained filled with information about employee activities, suggesting that even in a world of business peril, friendships and social interactions pervaded corporate cultures. The *Pacific Mutual News* published a column entitled "Sundry and Personal," which often reported employee obituaries, news about company agents' vacations or trips, or announcements of marriages between personnel. Union Oil included similar material in a column entitled "Here and There with Union Oil Employees." At Pacific Electric, employees read personal news about their coworkers in a feature entitled "News of the P. E. Family." In any given issue, one could read of medical crises, visits from relatives, parties, and other events in the lives of

PE employees, all of which revealed levels of interaction that far surpassed lines on an organizational chart. Why else, even as the firm retrenched and cut wages, would PE employees push for the publication of a magazine that printed news such as: "Mr. Gould, who is recuperating at Banning, says he will appreciate a couple of yards of letters any time any of his friends feel like it! Those who have called on him report him as sassy as ever to his visitors and still as interested in football."[64] In the midst of declining sales, executives viewed employee loyalty and dedication as even more important, and thus felt in no position to water down the corporate cultures which they had come to believe promoted business success.

The basic structures of most corporate cultures remained intact throughout the 1930s. We see this in a 1935 book entitled *Los Angeles: City of Dreams*, in which journalist Harry Carr celebrated the high quality of life he believed the city afforded its residents. "It is the manner of life out here," he wrote, "that gives our pueblo individuality." In a chapter called "Mr. and Mrs. Los Angeles," Carr tried to capture that "manner of life" by describing a couple he believed representative of the region's populace. He chose a husband and wife in their mid fifties who had previously lived in both San Francisco and New York City (apparently finding Los Angeles to be a superior place to reside). The man worked as "a newspaper artist on a good salary" and the woman held memberships in the Friday Morning Club and the Women's Athletic Club. The respectable middle-class couple belonged "neither to the Hollywood night life nor to the prayer-meeting" crowd but did enjoy their English Georgian cottage on the outkirts of Hollywood as well as their Sunset Beach summer cottage. According to Carr, they frequently attended theater, traveled often, spent considerable time in athletic pursuits, and loved USC football.[65]

Harry Carr's 1935 idealized portrait of Mr. and Mrs. Los Angeles hardly provides a documentary account of Depression-era southern California. Far more local families struggled to pay the rent and put food on the table than enjoyed summer cottages, expensive club memberships, or world travel. However, his representation of affluent middle-class residents tells us much about the world of corporate Los Angeles. Carr chose an artist as Mr. Los Angeles, but not one who owned his own business, worked freelance, or lived off other revenues. He instead worked for a major local firm (all hints suggest the *Los Angeles Times*) that provided him a good salary—Mr. Los Angeles was a "company man." The occupational choice could hardly have been accidental, for in choosing a salaried corporate professional, Carr presented a figure believable to readers. The Depression pummeled Los Angeles's economy, and no company or segment of the workforce escaped unscathed. Major Los

Angeles firms trimmed white-collar ranks, lowered salaries, limited promotion opportunities, and capped expenses as much as possible. Yet amidst such retrenchment, those company men who held on to their jobs escaped the calamity's fiercest blows. Their wages fell less sharply than prices and recovered quickly in the late 1930s. They continued to enjoy most company-supplied nonsalary benefits. And by the mid 1930s, when local business fortunes began to improve significantly, opportunities for advancement, raises, and new perquisites again became a fact of life for many mid- and upper-level white-collar men in large firms.

CONCLUSION

> The enviable position this company holds today is largely due to the thousands of men and women who make up the great Union Oil Company personnel. They are the Union Oil Company to the Public.
>
> —*Union Oil Bulletin*, 1927

On a foggy June morning in 1900, a crowd of students, families, and friends gathered for commencement exercises at Los Angeles High School. In a special ceremony for graduates of the school's commercial department, George H. Stewart took to the podium to deliver the commencement address. A prominent and wealthy local entrepreneur, Stewart seemed a fitting speaker. With their business degrees now in hand, the crowd of largely white men no doubt looked to the new century as the dawning of their own bright futures. Yet in this environment of eager anticipation, Stewart's speech may well have disappointed. Near the close of his address, at a point where most graduation speakers reach heights of optimistic platitudes, Stewart declared: "Boys! It is probably not one of you who has the ghost of a chance to be President of the United States, or even a member of Congress. Very few in our broad land, with its teeming millions, can ever become statesmen, millionaires, heroes or heroines. The most of you are destined to form the rank and file in the struggles of peace."[1]

Stewart's less than dreamy declaration came at the end of a lengthy address in which he extolled the virtues of conscientious, diligent service as an office employee. He had opened with the line: "Perhaps you are under the impression that to wave one of these documents [diplomas] in the face of prospective employers will at once call forth urgent invitations to accept reasonable positions at lucrative salaries. But alas! A strict regard for the truth will not encourage such a notion, nor can our most ardent wishes cause it to be realized." Stewart went on to speak about the importance of following instructions, being punctual and attentive to detail, and never sitting idly or pestering a boss for instructions. And he cautioned them against optimism, even if they encountered hopeful moments: "No matter how great the promotion, Men, circumstances and conditions will still be above and control you, and to accept this with ecunimity [equanimity] will prove your common sense." Stewart concluded by telling the students that they would be better off "having learned to obey."[2]

In retrospect, Stewart's advice seems prescient given the way southern California's economy developed in the early twentieth century. The realities of a region dominated by big businesses increasingly checked dreams of independent business ownership and entrepreneurial success. Growing numbers of Los Angeles's young white men spent their careers in white-collar offices. Yet, however prophetic, Stewart's words may have met a frosty reception. Few graduates probably felt gratitude to Stewart for his candor and insight, or sat up straighter and grinned at the thought of dutiful obedience to an office supervisor. Most young business students aspired to greater heights than Stewart anticipated for them. While they and many thousands of others in following years would sign on with Los Angeles firms in entry-level jobs, their desires for more pay, authority, and autonomy would plague local companies in the years to come. Many of these young men viewed office work as a necessary starting point in their careers, not a lifelong endeavor.

During the early decades of the twentieth century, Los Angeles companies struggled to win the loyalty of ambitious young white men like those who heard Stewart's commencement talk. This process played out as a series of negotiations between employees and executives over the nature, structure, and meaning of corporate employment. The region's white-collar men were neither pathetic dupes disempowered by the irreversible tide of bureaucracy nor the fortunate victors of the country's second business revolution. They instead represented a relatively privileged population who came to approach white-collar work as a set of trade-offs. Young men carefully negotiated this terrain with calculating eyes toward what they hoped to gain and what they were willing to give.

The needs, attitudes, and interests of these young white men shaped the designs and affected the success of individual firms. Although historians today clearly demarcate the roles of owner, employee, small businessman, and white-collar manager, the leaders and employees in emerging firms at the time still often thought in terms of nineteenth-century occupational cultures and struggled to weld those understandings into the framework of corporate employment. The first national generation of white-collar employees wrestled with what a position within a large enterprise entailed, the extent and nature of their connection to the firm, the level and degree of their responsibility to the company, and the advantages of this new kind of employment. If, from afar, corporations seemed cold and impersonal, individual employees made friends with coworkers and transformed offices into vibrant social networks. If bureaucratic employment countered traditional definitions of masculine success, young men still looked for opportunities to advance on corporate ladders and seized higher titles and control over subordinates as symbols of status and success. And if corporate employment did not offer the independence and opportunities for significant financial accumulation that many independent businessmen and professionals found, employees nevertheless grabbed large firms' steady, stable incomes and demanded additional perquisites offering greater personal and familial security.

That salaried employees ultimately shaped the corporate workplace in ways that dulled its roughest edges did not mean that all or even most American men came to terms with big business employment practices. In fact, loyal personnel gained as much control and as many benefits as they did largely because so many men refused the dictates of such posts, or at least refused to play by the rules in any single firm, that leaders became especially sensitive to courting those who did. Talented and dedicated men became valuable capital for large firms and could command a decent price for their services.

The rise of large firms was thus a profoundly human process; American men negotiated the corporate workplace with individual desires for community, status, and security. Were the "American dream" a simple matter of money, many could claim to have achieved it, for most firms could afford to pay employees well. But the complexity of corporate cultures hint that most employees saw more at stake. Did they feel valued by the firm? Did they have friends at work? Were they proud of their job? Did their families feel secure?

Corporate employees perceived their fate in complex ways, so they asked complicated questions. As president of the Farmers and Merchants National Bank during the 1920s, for instance, Jackson Graves ranked among the nation's business elite; he received most of the benefits to be accrued from corporate capitalism. In 1930, however, he reflected on his career in a book that, at times, lapsed into almost regretful commentary:

> The very character of people has changed. Man is now considered merely as a cog in the machinery necessary to keep the wheels going round. When all his resistance is worn off, he is discarded and thrown aside. Where once we were all like one great happy family, where everybody knew everybody else,

> rejoiced in their jobs and sympathized in their distresses, formality has entered, castes have been created and cordiality has disappeared.[3]

Even the winners had some doubts about the corporate order.

Warren Griffith, by contrast, might be thought to be one who had lost out in the world of big business. Among Union Oil's ten thousand employees, he served on the bottom rungs, working as a wage-laborer in the company's oil fields. Yet, though Griffith's position ranked low on middle-class status and income charts, he felt no inclination to advance, even when given the opportunity:

> We had several chances to leave here. I had a chance to go to Hawaii for the Union Oil Company, and to go to Los Angeles and work uptown, but I figured we'd rather stay. We had this superintendent who was a very fine person. He was an Englishman and it puzzled him. He'd say, "After all, Grif, these are the best years of your life. If you're ever going to get any place, you'll have to get out of Brea.

Griffith's wife also commented:

> Well, we would rather take the cut in wages and live in Brea raising four children than to live in Los Angeles, because Los Angeles is a bigger town and we figured that a small town was better.[4]

Such statements reveal that corporate history is more than company balance sheets, personnel directories, or annual reports. These personal comments suggest how, within the rise of big business, different groups of Americans achieved personal identity, community, and security in changing social and economic contexts. This process occurred in surprising places, such as on the shores of Lake Arrowhead in the San Bernardino mountains, eighty miles east of downtown Los Angeles. There, in 1915, the Pacific Electric Railway Company purchased property for a company vacation resort. The Pacific Electric Camp opened in the spring of 1917, offering cottages, dining halls, swimming pools, and other recreational facilities to employees and their families at subsidized rates. The camp reached full capacity that July. In following years, the company steadily enlarged and upgraded the facility to accommodate increasing requests for reservations.[5] A mountain resort might seem an odd place to study the workings of a downtown Los Angeles corporation, but leaders considered the camp vital to company operations. Why? PE leaders learned that building rail lines, creating operating systems, and designing company policies were the easy parts of business management. Dealing with personnel needs presented a much more difficult challenge. Executives realized that they could not simply hire and then direct a workforce; instead, they had to go to elaborate lengths to secure and motivate loyal employees. With their presence and level of effort as bargaining tools, white, middle-class men demanded that their work provide status, community, and security. In envi-

Pacific Electric Railway employees and their families pour out of the company's mountain resort at Lake Arrowhead. Reproduced by permission of the Huntington Library, San Marino, California.

ronments such as the PE camp at Lake Arrowhead, many Americans transformed bureaucratic employment into a more rewarding venture.

Ultimately, no aspect of big business employment became more important than the promise of cradle-to-grave security. However much American men fought the stifling components of bureaucratic cultures, those who accepted the order often did so because of the stable income and measures of personal security white-collar work offered. Leaders and employees ultimately arrived at a pact by which, in return for faithful service and good performance, companies would assure employees a lifelong career with some opportunity for advancement and a generous package of safety-net benefits such as health care and pensions.

American business leaders and employees forged the nation's modern corporate cultures in the early twentieth century, but the Depression solidified their place in middle-class life. In spring 1938, for instance, seemingly irritated Security-First bank leaders lectured employees on the benefits of working for the firm and attacked those who would "grouch and criticize" and picture themselves as "being unfortunate because of the conditions of [their] job." Executives used the column titled "Loyalty and Happiness" to lay out explicitly the advantages of Security-First employment:

> Anyone will agree that a person who works for a bank which is loyal to its staff, carries a surplus of personnel through depression times, promotes education and pays for tuition, provides and pays for group insurance, fills practically all vacancies by line promotions, continues salaries during sickness, and loans its employees money in emergencies—anyone will concede that such a person is better off than if working for an institution less conscious of its responsibilities to the rank and file.
>
> Anyone will agree that working for a bank with recognized standards of management, with established policies of correct and courteous service in every department and banking function—a bank whose customers like it and respect it—is better than working for an institution which doesn't stand quite so well in the general esteem . . . Anyone will agree that working in a bank which maintains a high-class staff, and which provides comfortable working conditions with the best of mechanical equipment is better than working for a concern which does not insist on these conditions.[6]

One might think that by the late 1930s, southern California executives would not have to work so hard to secure the loyalty of employees. After years of turbulent economic conditions and high unemployment rates, a white-collar job with Security-First would seem a good deal. The Depression taught

Los Angeles businessmen otherwise. The need to simultaneously cut expenses and heighten productivity made the cultivation of dedicated company men more imperative than ever. Even as officials trimmed expenses in ways that hurt personnel, they expected energetic performance. The employees whom companies most wanted to keep were the ones most likely to have other opportunities should their jobs prove wanting. Business leaders thus found themselves in no position to weaken the basic structures undergirding corporate cultures, which not only survived the 1930s, but also, in the case of many firms, grew stronger.

Neither the Depression, the Second World War, nor the innumerable crises of the postwar era weakened the urban corporate cultures negotiated in the 1910s and 1920s. The commitment to providing steady incomes and personal security remained central to employee retention and motivation. The building of corporate cultures continued to dominate big business, because the fundamental managerial imperatives that called for an esprit de corps never waned. Corporations always struggled to secure the talents of employees who would act as if the firm was their very own. In most firms this meant persuading young men that faithful service would result in a secure career marked by a rising salary, generous perquisites, steady advancement, and pleasant working conditions.

Tom Hotchkiss was one who took advantage of this offer. He joined Southern California Edison as an engineer around 1927, after graduating from Caltech. Highly educated and skilled, he looked forward to a promising career, but like many Americans of his generation the Depression threatened that future. SCE, however, struggled determinedly to avoid layoffs of salaried employees throughout the Depression. Hotchkiss found his rank and pay cut, but he retained his job. When the Depression subsided, he regained his position on the ladder and enjoyed a long career of secure income and steady advancement. When he retired in the 1960s, people in the company with less than twenty-five years of service were considered "junior."[7]

Of course, not all company men exhibited Hotchkiss's loyalty, nor did that loyalty come cheap. In the crowded and competitive world of corporate Los Angeles, executives wrestled with each other over the best employees, and they never felt entirely confident about their personnel. Business leaders had learned long before that, ultimately, employees were the company, and that making them act accordingly would be a never-ending challenge in good times and especially in bad. Efforts to cultivate dedicated company men—and, increasingly, women—dominated southern California business executives throughout the twentieth century.

NOTES

Preface

1. Allan Sloan, *Newsweek* (February 26, 1996), 44.

2. "AT&T Lays Out Bold Plan for the Future," *Los Angeles Times* (January 27, 1998), D1.

3. Angel Kwolek-Folland, *Engendering Business: Men and Women in the Corporate Office, 1870–1930* (Baltimore: Johns Hopkins University Press, 1994), 71.

Introduction

Epigraph: George Hart, "California," address given at the Los Angeles Chamber of Commerce annual banquet, February 22, 1905, *The Members' Annual* (Los Angeles: Chamber of Commerce, 1905): 58.

1. James F. Crank with E. L. Lewis, "Memories of the Pacific Slope by a Pasadena Pioneer," and Mary Agnes Crank, "Ranch Life Fifty Years Ago," unpublished manuscripts, James Crank Collection, box 10, Huntington Library, San Marino, Calif.

2. William A. Myers, "An Engineer's Life: A Brief Biography of George Clinton Ward," unpublished manuscript, Southern California Edison Corporate Communications Department, 1983; William B. Friedricks, *Henry E. Huntington and the Creation of Southern California* (Columbus: Ohio State University Press, 1992), 94–95.

3. Bureau of the Census, U.S. Department of Commerce, *Historical Statistics of the United States from Colonial Times to the Present, Part 1* (Washington, D.C.: U.S. Government Printing Office, 1975), 139–140. Jürgen Kocka, *White Collar Workers in America, 1890–1940: A Social-Political History in International Perspective* (London: Sage Publications, 1980), 94–95.

4. Robert S. and Helen Merrell Lynd, *Middletown: A Study in Modern American Culture* (New York: Harcourt Brace Jovanovich, 1929), 22–23; C. Wright Mills, *The Power Elite* (New York: Oxford University Press, 1959); David Riesman, *The Lonely Crowd: A Study of the Changing American Character* (New Haven, Conn.: Yale University Press, 1961); William Whyte, *The Organization Man* (New York: Simon and Schuster, 1956); Sloan Wilson, *The Man in the Gray Flannel Suit* (Cambridge, Mass.: R. Bentley, 1955).

5. Olivier Zunz emphasizes the role of corporate employees in shaping the new business structures: "Middle-level managers and white-collar workers were largely independent actors who brought about much social and cultural change." Olivier Zunz, *Making America Corporate, 1870–1920* (Chicago: University of Chicago Press, 1990), 9.

6. The 1910 and 1920 census samples used in this research comprise 588 and 651 gainfully employed men, respectively, and come from Steven Ruggles and Matthew Sobek, *Integrated Public Use Microdata Series: Version 1.0* (Minneapolis: Social History Research Laboratory, University of Minnesota, 1995) (hereafter referred to as IPUMS-95).

7. Albert Broussard, *Black San Francisco: The Struggle for Racial Equality in the West, 1900–1954* (Lawrence: University of Kansas Press, 1993), 51. I am indebted to Doug Flamming for his insights on this history.

8. "Introducing A. B. Nordling," *Security-First News Bulletin* 5 (July 1, 1933): 4.

9. "Introducing C. C. Bowerman," *Security-First News Bulletin* 5 (April 15, 1933): 4.

10. "President's Report to the Board of Directors of the Alfred Dodge Felt Company for the Year 1908," Henry E. Huntington Personal and Corporate Papers, box 3, Huntington Library; Kocka, *White Collar Workers*, 100–101, 291. Angel Kwolek-Folland, *Engendering Business: Men and Women in the Corporate Office, 1870–1930* (Baltimore: Johns Hopkins University Press, 1994), 30, 42; *Clerical Salaries in the United States, 1926* (New York: National Industrial Conference Board, 1926), 32.

11. IPUMS-95; Kocka, *White Collar Workers*, 100; Zunz, *Making America Corporate*, 132–144.

12. Sharon Hartman Strom, *Beyond the Typewriter: Gender, Class, and the Origins of Modern American Office Work, 1900–1930* (Urbana: University of Illinois Press, 1992), 192.

13. Angel Kwolek-Folland offers this interpretation in *Engendering Business*, 12.

14. In her study of turn-of-the-century Pittsburgh, Eileen A. DeVault argues that white-collar workers comprised three different tiers of corporate employees: male managers, male clerical workers, and female clerical workers. Sharon Strom conceptualizes three main strata: employers, midlevel and low-level managers, and clerks or clerical workers. Marxist scholars also argue for a distinction between white-collar and clerical employees, in order to emphasize the proletarianization of the latter. Eileen A. DeVault, *Sons and Daughters of Labor: Class and Clerical Work in Turn-of-the-Century Pittsburgh* (Ithaca: Cornell University Press, 1990), 174; Strom, *Beyond the Typewriter*, 11, 235; Harry Braverman, *Labor and Monopoly Capital: The Degradation of Work in the Twentieth Century* (New York: Monthly Review Press, 1974), 298–299; Kocka, *White Collar Workers*, 101; *Clerical Salaries, 1926*, 25–39.

15. Kwolek-Folland, *Engendering Business*, 197.

16. I chose not to focus on any major film companies, despite the industry's prominence as the leading employer in Los Angeles by the 1920s, because its employees exhibited more of a professional mentality than those in other sectors. In other

words, many people likely chose to work in the industry because of the glamour associated with Hollywood, rather than of any rewards from their specific jobs. I believe this attitude prevailed less in most other white-collar industries.

17. For portraits of the city at mid-century, see Robert Glass Cleland and Frank Putnam, *Isaias W. Hellman and the Farmers and Merchants Bank* (San Marino, Calif.: Huntington Library, 1980, 2nd printing); Michael Gonzalez, "Searching for the Feathered Serpent: Exploring the Origins of Mexican Culture in Los Angeles, 1830–1850," (Ph.D. diss., University of California, Berkeley, 1993).

18. John Russell McCarthy, *Joseph Francis Sartori, 1856–1946* (Los Angeles: Ward Ritchie Press, 1948), 41. A "gee string" was the slang term Anglos used for loin cloths and was generally employed in descriptions of native American attire.

19. W. C. Patterson, presidential address printed in *The Member's Annual: Los Angeles Chamber of Commerce, 1895* (Los Angeles: Los Angeles Chamber of Commerce, 1895), 22.

20. John M. Findlay, "Far Western Cityscapes and American Culture since 1940," *Western Historical Quarterly* 22 (1991): 42.

21. Glenn S. Dumke, "Advertising Southern California before the Boom of 1887," *Quarterly of the Historical Society of Southern California* 24 (March 1942): 15–16; Tom Zimmerman, "Paradise Promoted: Boosterism and the Los Angeles Chamber of Commerce," *California History* 64 (winter 1985): 22–33; Clark Davis, "From Oasis to Metropolis: Southern California and the Changing Context of American Leisure," *Pacific Historical Review* 61 (August 1992): 357–386.

22. Note, for instance, the recent MacArthur Foundation "genius awards" given to western historians William Cronon, Richard White, Patricia Limerick, and Mike Davis.

23. James Clifford Findley, "The Economic Boom of the Twenties in Los Angeles," (Ph.D. diss., Claremont Graduate School, 1958), 29; Margaret S. Gordon, *Employment Expansion and Population Growth: The California Experience, 1900–1950* (Los Angeles: University of California Press, 1954). Various factors have been put forward to explain the unusually high proportion of service-sector employment in California, including the presence of the entertainment industry, the presence of the regional offices of many federal government agencies, and a heavy volume of immigration, each of which creates needs for expanded services.

24. Robert Fogelson, *The Fragmented Metropolis: Los Angeles, 1850–1930* (Cambridge: Harvard University Press, 1967), 75–84.

25. Quoted in John Gunther's, *Inside U.S.A.* (New York: Harper and Brothers, 1947), 43.

Chapter 1 The Rise of Corporate Los Angeles

Epigraph: "March of Progress," *Southern California Business* 4 (June 1925).

1. "Review of Business for April," *Southern California Business* 5 (May 1926): 40–44; "Review of Business for May," *Southern California Business* 5 (June 1926): 41–

45; "Disaster on the Los Angeles Pipe Line," *Union Oil Bulletin* 6 (June 1926): safety insert.

2. "Memorandum," ca. January 1927, H. A. Burgess Collection, University of Southern California Regional History Center, 52–2.

3. Widney, R. M., in Hawley, *The Present Condition*, 93–94; William Spalding, "Autobiography of an Ordinary Man," unpublished manuscript, p. 11, Spalding Collection, Huntington Library; Frederic Cople Jaher, *The Urban Establishment: Upper Strata in Boston, New York, Charleston, Chicago, and Los Angeles* (Urbana: University of Illinois Press, 1982), 582.

4. Kevin Starr, *Material Dreams: Southern California through the 1920s* (New York: Oxford University Press, 1990), 69.

5. Starr, *Material Dreams*, 78; Robert Fogelson, *The Fragmented Metropolis: Los Angeles, 1850–1930* (Cambridge: Harvard University Press, 1967), 151.

6. William B. Friedricks, *Henry E. Huntington and the Creation of Southern California* (Columbus: Ohio State University Press, 1992), 2–3. Morrow Mayo, *Los Angeles* (New York: Alfred A. Knopf, 1932), 310.

7. Art Seidenbaum, *Los Angeles 200: A Bicentennial Celebration* (New York: Harry N. Abrams, 1980), 175; Kevin Starr, *Inventing the Dream: California through the Progressive Era* (New York: Oxford University Press, 1990), 163–164.

8. Harris Newmark, *Sixty Years in Southern California, 1853–1913* (New York: Houghton Mifflin, 1930), 346–347, 603; "The Story of Oil in California," Union Oil Company of California museum brochure, ca. 1954, Union Oil File, UCLA Special Collection Department; Robert Glass Cleland, *March of Industry* (Los Angeles: Powell Publishing, 1929), 148; J. R. Douglas, *The Bank and the Community; A History of the Security Trust and Savings Bank, 1889–1929* (Los Angeles: Security Trust and Savings Bank, 1929), 34–36; Seidenbaum, *Los Angeles 200*, 175; *Facts about Industrial Los Angeles: Nature's Workshop* (Los Angeles: Los Angeles Chamber of Commerce, 1922); Lary May, *Screening out the Past: The Birth of Mass Culture and the Motion Picture Industry* (New York: Oxford University Press, 1980), 183–199; Starr, *Material Dreams*, 98.

9. James Clifford Findley, "The Economic Boom of the Twenties in Los Angeles," (Ph.D. diss., Claremont Graduate School, 1958), 399–401; *Facts about Industrial Los Angeles;* May, *Screening out the Past*, 183–199; Starr, *Material Dreams*, 98.

10. William F. Deverell, *Railroad Crossing: Californians and the Railroad, 1850–1910* (Berkeley: University of California Press, 1994), chapter 4. Findley, "Boom of the Twenties," chapter 3; Ernest Marquez, *Port of Los Angeles: A Phenomenon of the Railroad Era* (San Marino, Calif.: Golden West Books, 1975); Ella A. Ludwig, *A History of the Harbor District of Los Angeles* (Los Angeles: Los Angeles Historical Record Co., 1927); Charles F. Queenan, *The Port of Los Angeles: From Wilderness to World Port* (Los Angeles: Los Angeles Harbor Dept., 1983); Starr, *Material Dreams*, 90.

11. Michael Kazin, "The Great Exception Revisited: Organized Labor in San Francisco and Los Angeles, 1870–1940," *Pacific Historical Review* 55 (August 1986): 371–402; Douglas, *The Bank and the Community;* 34–35; "March of Events, in Figures," *Southern California Business* 6 (January 1928): 36, 40; Starr, *Material Dreams*,

94. In adjusting industrial output figures for inflation I used the U.S. Department of Commerce, Bureau of the Census, *Historical Statistics of the United States: Volume 1* (Washington, D.C.,: U.S. Government Printing Office, 1975), series E, 87–89, 203.

12. David M. Gordon, "Capitalist Development and the History of American Cities," in William K. Tabb and Larry Sauers, eds., *Marxism and the Metropolis: New Perspectives in Urban Political Economy* (New York: Oxford University Press, 1978), 21–53.

13. John Haskell Kemble, *A Hundred Years of the Pacific Mail* (Newport News, Va.: Mariner's Museum Publication no. 19, 1950. (Extract from the *American Neptune* 10 [1950]: 5–16.)

14. Ibid., 18–24.

15. Findley, "Boom of the Twenties," 268–270; Cecilia Rasmussen, "The Cattle Baron and the Curse," *Los Angeles Times* (February 16, 1996), B3.

16. Harris Hanshue, "History of Western Air," 1932. Unpublished manuscript, H. A. Burgess Collection, box 3.

17. Rasmussen, "The Cattle Baron," B3; H. A. Burgess, "Comments and Suggestions inspired by trips over W.A.E. and competing Air Lines," November 5, 1929. H. A. Burgess Collection, box 2.

18. U.S. Department of Commerce, Bureau of the Census, *Fifteenth Census of the United States, Volume 14, Population, 1930, Occupation Statistics* (Washington, D.C.: U.S. Government Printing Office), 173.

19. Jules Tygiel offers an excellent portrayal of this oil frenzy in *The Great Los Angeles Swindle: Oil, Stocks, and Scandal during the Roaring Twenties* (New York: Oxford University Press, 1994).

20. Findley, "Boom of the Twenties," 250, 285.

21. Union Oil Company of California annual reports to stockholders, Thomas Bard Collection, Huntington Library, San Marino, Calif.

22. Earl M. Welty and Frank J. Taylor. *The 76 Bonanza: The Fabulous Life and Times of the Union Oil Company* (Menlo Park, Calif.: Lane Magazine and Book Company, 1966), 338–340.

23. Union Oil Company of California budget statement for quarter ending July 31, 1893, Thomas Bard Collection; "Story of Oil in California" ; Lyman Stewart to Thomas Bard, July 18, 1895, Thomas Bard Collection.

24. *Union Oil Bulletin* 6 (September 1926): 14.

25. Fred L. Hartley, *The Spirit of 76; The Story of the Union Oil Company of California* (New York: Newcomen Society in North America, 1977), 11; *Union Oil Bulletin*, 10 (October 1930): 2.

26. *Union Oil Company of California Bulletin* 2 (August 1922): 15.

27. *Union Oil Company of California Bulletin* 1 (February 1922): 5; "Annual Report, Union Oil Company of California 1926,"; H. S. Reavis, "Properties and Prospects of the Union Oil Company of California," reprint article from the *Oil Trade Journal* 1916, Thomas Bard Collection, box 4.

28. Pacific Mutual's history is recorded in two works: C. I. D. Moore, *The Pacific*

Mutual Life Insurance Company of California: A History of the Company and the Development of Its Organization, the Sixtieth Anniversary, 1928–1969 (Los Angeles: Pacific Mutual Life Insurance: 1928) and Doyce Blackman Nunis, Jr., *Past Is Prologue: A Centennial Profile of the Pacific Mutual Life Insurance Company* (Los Angeles: Pacific Mutual Life Insurance, 1968).

29. Moore, *Pacific Mutual*, 107.

30. Ibid., 116.

31. Ibid., 107, 117, 123–158, 180.

32. The firm had five branch offices by 1927: Chicago (1906), New York (1913), San Francisco (1922), New Orleans (1925), and St. Louis (1927). Ibid., 156–157.

33. "Our Friends the Enemy," *Conservative News* 1 (May 1903): 2; Wilbur Tupper, "Story of Conservative," *Conservative News* 3 (February and March 1905): 8–10; "California Leadership for 1905," *Pacific Conservative News* 4 (January 1906): 1.

34. Moore, *Pacific Mutual*, 124, 181–250.

35. Harold C. Passer, *The Electrical Manufacturers, 1875–1900: A Study in Competition, Entrepreneurship, Technical Change, and Economic Growth* (Cambridge: Harvard University Press, 1953), 213–215, 341–342; Richard F. Hirsch, *Technology and Transformation in the American Electric Utility Industry* (New York: Cambridge University Press, 1989), 37.

36. The development of regional monopolies like Southern California Edison (SCE) would become the power industry's norm. The nationwide consolidation of utility companies into large, nearly monopolistic enterprises by the 1910s and 1920s reflected the industry's unique economic and political situation. Because they considered electrical service a vital resource, many towns and cities feared the instability possible in a competitive market. Furthermore, many communities felt that the capital investment required to operate a utility made it wasteful to have several firms competing. National sentiment subsequently favored municipal ownership of utilities, and numerous cities and communities built and operated power companies alongside water, sewer, and other public services. Some regions, however, allowed closely regulated commercial monopolies. Californians adopted a compromise situation with the passage of the California Public Utilities Act of 1911, which allowed regional monopolies in the utility industry in exchange for state regulation of rates and policies. Passer, *Electrical Manufacturers*, 21–25; R. H. Ballard, "Concentration Brings Efficiency and Low Rates," *Edison Current Topics* 4 (October 1915): 190. William A. Myers, "Electricity in Orange County, California, 1890–1940: A Case Study of the Socioeconomic Impact of Technology" (master's thesis, California State University at Fullerton, 1991; Jaher, *The Urban Establishment*, 598.

37. William A. Myers, *Iron Men and Copper Wires: A Centennial History of the Southern California Edison Company* (Glendale, Calif.: Trans-Anglo Books, 1983), 12–47.

38. "Statement of the Southern California Edison Company of its Claims for the Charles A. Coffin Medal Effort of the Year 1922," unpublished manuscript, Southern California Edison archives, Rosemead, Calif.

39. "A Review of 1923 Progress," *Edison Facts*, 2 (January 1924): 1.

40. "Charles A. Coffin Medal Effort of the Year 1922"; "Review of 1923 Progress," 1; Myers, *Iron Men and Copper Wires*, 166–167; Myers, "Electricity in Orange County," 27–29.

41. "Charles A. Coffin Medal Effort for the Year 1922."

42. "Jacob Maier Long-Term Medal Holder: Records of the Fifteen- and Twenty-Year Medal Men," *Edison Current Topics* 3 (July 1914): 525; list of officers in *Edison Current Topics* 4 (August 1915); "A Bright Future Ahead for Edison Employees," *Edison Current Topics* 1 (October 1923): 3; "Three New Districts to Be Established," 1 (December 1923): 3; "Rosters of the Jacob Maier Long-Term Medal Holders," *Edison Current Topics* (1928, 1929).

43. John Russell McCarthy, *Joseph Francis Sartori, 1856–1946* (Los Angeles: Ward Ritchie Press, 1948); Douglas, *The Bank and the Community*; Tom Furlong, "Security Pacific: A History," *Los Angeles Times* (April 22, 1992), D1; Lynne Pierson Doti and Larry Schweikart, *Banking in the American West: From the Gold Rush to Deregulation* (Norman: University of Oklahoma Press, 1991), 78–79; Jaher, *The Urban Establishment*, 595–601.

44. Hawley, *The Present Condition*, 97–98.

45. The new bank merged as the Farmers and Merchants Bank in 1871 and remained the city's largest until 1905. Jaher, *The Urban Establishment*, 601; *Fifty Years of Banking Service under Conservative Management; Farmers and Merchants National Bank of Los Angeles* (Los Angeles: Farmers and Merchants National Bank, 1921), 8; Michael F. Konig, "Isaias W. Hellman," in Larry Schweikart, ed., *Banking and Finance to 1913*, (New York: Facts on File, 1990), 249–259.

46. Jaher, *The Urban Establishment*, 625; J. Henry Wood, *Banks and Bankers in Southern California* (Pasadena: n.p., 1908); "March of Events," 40; "Pocket Book Los Angeles," *Southern California Business* 10 (January 1931): 36.

47. Findley, "Boom of the Twenties," 299–300; Rockwell Hereford, A *Whole Man—Henry Mauris Robinson—and a Half Century—1890–1940* (Pacific Grove, Calif.: Boxwood Press, 1985).

48. Furlong, "Security Pacific," D1.

49. George H. Hilton and John F. Due, *The Electric Interurban Railways in America* (Stanford, Calif.: Stanford University Press, 1960), 1–90, 197.

50. Hilton and Due, *Electric Interurban Railways*, 406–413; Jaher, *The Urban Establishment*, 598.

51. Edwin L. Lewis, "Spring and West Sixth Street RR Line," unpublished manuscript, Los Angeles Railway Corporation Collection, Huntington Library, 1931; Gordon DeMarco, *A Short History of Los Angeles* (San Francisco: Lexikos, 1988), 94.

52. Randolph Karr, "Rail Passenger Service History of the Pacific Electric," unpublished mimeograph, 1973, Huntington Library, 12; Friedricks, *Henry E. Huntington*, 48–58, 98–100; Thomas H. Shanks, *From Horse Car to Red Car to Mass Rapid Transit: A Century of Progress* (Virginia Beach, Va.: Donning Co., 1991), 72–73; Starr, *Material Dreams*, 79.

53. "Number of Employees: Pacific Electric Railway Co., January 12, 1903," Pacific Electric Collection, Huntington Library; "Department Personnel in General Passenger Department," *Pacific Electric Magazine* 5 (December 10, 1920).

54. "Autos Still Climbing Hill of Death," *Pacific Electric Magazine* 11 (November 10, 1926): 7; Shanks, *From Horse to Mass Transit*, 75; Starr, *Material Dreams*, 106–110.

Chapter 2 Defining Corporate Employment

Epigraph: Paul Lupke, "Expanded Loyalty," *Edison Current Topics* (July 1912): 1.

1. *Los Angeles Saturday Night* 2 (December 10, 1921): 1; *Los Angeles Saturday Night* 2 (August 6, 1921): 1; *Coast Banker* (Los Angeles: 1910): 7.

2. "One's Impression of a Corporation," *Union Oil Bulletin* 3 (September 1923): 5.

3. "Advertising and Clerical Efficiency," *Los Angeles Saturday Night* 2 (December 24, 1921): 1.

4. On the ways in which public opposition shaped big business, see Louis Galambos, *The Public Image of Big Business in America, 1880–1940: A Quantitative Study in Social Change* (Baltimore: Johns Hopkins University Press, 1975); Neil J. Mitchell, *The Generous Corporation: A Political Analysis of Economic Power* (New Haven, Conn.: Yale University Press, 1989); James Livingston, *Origins of the Federal Reserve System: Money, Class, and Corporate Capitalism: 1890–1913* (Ithaca, N.Y.: Cornell University Press, 1986)

5. H. A. Burgess, "Comments and Suggestions inspired by trips over W.A.E. and Competing Airlines," November 5, 1929. Unpublished manuscript, H. A. Burgess Collection, box 32; Walter E. Davis, letter to Charles F. McManus, 17 March, 1931. Burgess Collection, box 32.

6. H. A. Burgess, "Comments and Suggestions inspired by trips over W.A.E. and Competing Airlines," November 5, 1929. Unpublished manuscript, H. A. Burgess Collection, box 32; Walter E. Davis, letter to Charles F. McManus, 17 March, 1931. Burgess Collection, box 32.

7. S. M. Kennedy, *Winning the Public* (New York: McGraw-Hill, 1921), 6.

8. "Every Driver a Salesman," *Union Oil Bulletin* 8 (June 1928): 22.

9. For an understanding of the cultural milieu of small business, see Mansel G. Blackford, *A History of Small Business in America* (New York: Twayne Publishers, 1991); Stuart Bruchey, ed., *Small Business in American Life* (New York: Columbia University Press, 1980). On professional cultures, see Burton J. Bledstein, *The Culture of Professionalism: The Middle Class and the Development of Higher Education in America* (New York: W. W. Norton, 1978), chapter 3; for a discussion of these issues within a specific profession, see Paul Starr, *The Social Transformation of American Medicine: The Rise of a Sovereign Profession and the Making of a Vast Industry* (New York: Basic Books, 1982). On nineteenth-century farming cultures, see Jeremy Atack and Fred Bateman, *To Their Own Soil: Agriculture in the Antebellum North* (Ames: Iowa State University Press, 1987); Paul Gates, *The Farmers' Age: Agriculture, 1815–1860* (New York: Harper and Row, 1960).

10. Address by Frank Miller, *Proceedings of the First Annual Convention of the California Bankers Association held at San Francisco, October 14–16, 1891* (Los Angeles: Times-Mirror, 1891): 38–40; *Proceedings, Eighteenth Convention, California Bankers Association, Long Beach, 1912* (San Francisco: Hicks-Judd Co., 1912).

11. Olivier Zunz charts American responses to the lost autonomy wrought by corporate capitalism in *Making America Corporate, 1870–1920* (Chicago: University of Chicago Press, 1990), chapter 1.

12. Lois Ritchie, "Social Status of Department Store Salespersons among Certain Groups in Los Angeles" (master's thesis, University of Southern California, 1932), 22.

13. T. A. Graham, "Tardy Reports," memorandum of April 1, 1922, Pacific Mail Steamship Company (PMSC) collection, box 6A, file 439, Huntington Library, San Marino, Calif.

14. "How Big Is Your Job," *Security-First News Bulletin* 1 (July 1, 1929): 2.

15. Lupke, "Expanded Loyalty," 1.

16. Angel Kwolek-Folland, *Engendering Business: Men and Women in the Corporate Office, 1870–1930* (Baltimore: Johns Hopkins University Press, 1994), 52.

17. Harry Dexter Kitson, *I Find My Vocation* (New York: McGraw-Hill, 1931), 173, 174.

18. William G. McAdoo, "The Soul of a Corporation," pamphlet reprinted from *World's Work* (New York: Doubleday, Page, 1912), 3, 4, 5. In Huntington Library General Scrapbook 42.1.

19. "Employes Who Climb," *Pacific Electric Magazine* 4 (September 10, 1919): 5.

20. Ernest G. Bishop, "Loyalty," *Pacific Mutual News* 24 (September 1925): 314.

21. Roland Marchand, *Advertising the American Dream: Making Way for Modernity, 1920–1940* (Los Angeles: University of California Press, 1985); Stuart Ewen, *Captains of Consciousness: Advertising and the Social Roots of the Consumer Culture* (New York: McGraw Hill, 1976); Kwolek-Folland, *Engendering Business*, chapter 3; Zunz, *Making America Corporate*, chapter 7.

22. Robert O'Hair, "Commercial Development Department," *The Pacific Southwest* 5 (July 1927): 4.

23. "Sixth Anniversary Tribute Campaign Successful," *The Pacific Southwest* 5 (July 1927): 1, 8.

24. "Statement of the Southern California Edison Company of Its Claims for the Charles A. Coffin Medal Effort, the Year 1922," unpublished manuscript, Southern California Edison archives, Rosemead, Calif.

25. "Electrical Christmas Campaign," *Edison Energy* 2 (December 1928): 5; "Better Home Lighting: A Textbook for Power Company Employees and Their Families," pamphlet issued by Southern California Edison in 1930, SCE archives; "Statement by Southern California Edison Company in Respect of Its Accomplishment during the Year 1928 for Consideration in the Award of the Charles A. Coffin Medal for That Year," unpublished manuscript, 1929, SCE archives.

26. From the *Union Oil Bulletion:* "Visiting Ten County Seats in Twenty-four Hours," 7 (June 1927): 12–13; "Our Interest in Aviation," 7 (August 1927): 1; "Western

Asphalt Association," 6 (February 1927): 18; "Riding on Rubber," 5 (June 1925): 4; George H. Woodhams, "Oil Sprays for Insect Pest Control," 8 (April 1928): 11.

27. Don Francisco, "Are You Enlisted in Your Firm's Army of Recommenders?" *Union Oil Bulletin* 3 (March 1923): 1.

28. "Grows Like a Snowball," *Union Oil Bulletin* 3 (June 1923): 25.

29. From *Pacific Electric Magazine*: "Are You Pacific Electric–Minded?" 14 (December 10, 1929): 3; "Wanted!—5,000 Business Getters," 9 (January 10, 1925):7; "Are You Helping to Increase PE Revenues?" 3 (December 10, 1918): 4–5; "Cooperation of Every Factor the Backbone of Company Success," 3 (January 10, 1919): 5; "Selling Transportation," 3 (December 10, 1918): 5; "Travel Tip Campaign Begins," 12 (June 10, 1927): 10; "Freight Solicitation by Employees," 1 (June 10, 1916): 6.

30. F. E. Billhardt, "Over Thousand Passengers from 4 Employees Tips," *Pacific Electric Magazine* 11 (August 10, 1926): 15; "Many Employees Active in Freight Solicitation," *Pacific Electric Magazine* 9 (March 10, 1925): 10.

31. Pacific Mutual had systematic training programs designed to help its agents become more effective salesmen. Beginning in 1914, for instance, the firm began a correspondence school in sales for all agents. See "Pacific Mutual School for Salesmen: An Important Announcement," *Pacific Mutual News* 13 (May 1914): 108.

32. John F. Forrester, "Life Insurance as a Business: Its Scope and Possibilities," *Pacific Mutual News* 10 (February 1911): 5–6; "Insure Your Friends," *Pacific Mutual News* 22 (October 1923): 320; "Leisure Hours," *Pacific Mutual News* 9 (June 1910): 5.

33. Key points of government involvement in business activities included the creation of the Interstate Commerce Commission in 1887, the passage of the Sherman Antitrust Act in 1890, and the Supreme Court's dissolution of the Standard Oil Company in 1911. Although these events mark high points in government intervention in business, the activities and interests of government and big business intersected continually throughout this period.

34. Louis B. Perry and Richard S. Perry, *A History of the Los Angeles Labor Movement, 1911–1941* (Berkeley: University of California Press, 1963), 82. White-collar workers appeared not only more resistant to unions but more conservative politically than their blue-collar counterparts. Franklin Roosevelt never captured as high a percentage of white-collar workers as he did of blue-collar ranks. In 1936, he garnered 74% of the manual workers' vote, but only 61% of white-collar employees. In 1940, Roosevelt took 66% of the blue-collar vote but only 48% of white-collar employees. Jürgen Kocka, *White Collar Workers in America, 1890–1940: A Social-Political History in International Perspective* (London: Sage Publications, 1980), 206–243; Martin Oppenheimer, *White Collar Politics* (New York: Monthly Review Press, 1985).

35. R. H. Ballard, "Concentration Brings Efficiency and Low Rates," *Edison Current Topics* 4 (October 1915): 190; William A. Myers, "Electricity in Orange County, California, 1890–1940: A Case Study of the Socioeconomic Impact of Technology," (master's thesis, California State University, Fullerton, 1991); See Mansel G. Blackford, *The Politics of Business in California, 1890–1920* (Columbus: Ohio State University Press, 1977), chapter 5.

36. "Employe's Manual," handbook issued by Southern California Edison Company, early 1920s, SCE archives.

37. George Walker, "Capital," *Edison Current Topics* 5 (April 1916): 61; see also "Public Interests and Private Interests Synonymous," *Edison Current Topics* 5 (June 1916): 108.

38. A. W. Childs, "Great Banquet of Employees," *Edison Current Topics* 2 (April 1913): 12.

39. "Charles A. Coffin Medal Effort for the Year 1922," SCE archives.

40. See Paul Shoup, "Our Financial Condition," *Pacific Electric Magazine* 1 (August 10, 1916); see also: "Taxes and the Jitney," *Pacific Electric Magazine* 1 (October 10, 1916): 4; "Taxes One of Greatest Burdens of Nation and State," *Pacific Electric Magazine* 9 (November 1924): 12.

41. "Increased Taxation versus Economy," *Pacific Electric Magazine* 5 (February 10, 1921): 1; "To All Employees of This Company," *Pacific Electric Magazine* 7 (April 10, 1923): 1; "Are You a Good Citizen?" *Pacific Electric Magazine* 9 (October 10, 1924): 2; "Vice-President Pontius Points Out Election Importance and Urges All to Vote," *Pacific Electric Magazine* 10 (April 10, 1926): 4; "Employees Rally to Own Company's Cause in Opposing Territory Invasion," *Pacific Electric Magazine* 14 (June 10, 1929): 11.

42. Lynne Pierson Doti and Larry Schweikart, *Banking in the American West: From the Gold Rush to Deregulation* (Norman: University of Oklahoma Press, 1991), chapters 2, 3.

43. "Senate Passes Bill: Elliott on Return from Sacramento Reports Progress on California Bank Act Amendments," *Security-First News Bulletin* 1 (April 15, 1929): 4; "Elliott Discusses New Tax Decision of Supreme Court in Convention Report: Head Office Vice President in Opening Address at CBA Conclave Declares Verdict of High Tribunal Regrettable Set-back," *Security-First News Bulletin* 1 (June 15, 1929): 1. Another example of the relationship between larger political concerns and bank operations is seen in the frequent correspondence about national and international matters between bank officers. Farmers and Merchants National Bank's president and vice president corresponded regularly during the 1910s on issues ranging from railroad regulation to the effect of the war on trade, to railroad policies, noting how these issues might affect bank operations. See, for example, series of letters regarding war issues: I. W. Hellman, letter to Jackson A. Graves, March 17, 1915, July 10, 1915, September 17, 1915. Jackson A. Graves Collection, Huntington Library.

44. Blackford, *The Politics of Business*, 40–59; "Overproduction," *Union Oil Bulletin* 7 (May 1927): 1; "Conservation of Gas," *Union Oil Bulletin* 7 (July 1927): 1; E. W. Clark, "Good Business," *Union Oil Bulletin* 8 (November 1928): 1.

45. Jerry H. Powell, "Taxing the Motorist," *Union Oil Bulletin* 4 (February 1925): 1–3.

46. Francis P. Smith, "Getting the Most for the Highway Dollar," *Union Oil Bulletin* 5 (November 1925): 13.

47. C. C. Mallory correspondence to Mr. T. A. Graham, August 12, 1924, PMSC collection, box 4.

48. "Public Appreciation Expressed: Service and Courtesy Bring Their Reward," *Pacific Electric Magazine* 13 (August 10, 1928): 13.

49. From *Pacific Electric Magazine* see: "Over the Top," 2 (May 10, 1918): 1; "Our Red Cross Auxiliary," 3 (July 10, 1918): 5; "Riverside Trainmen Go over Top," 3 (July 10, 1918): 5; "Still a Few Openings in Company B," 5 (August 10, 1920); "Employees Exceed Quota in Charity Drive," 10 (December 10, 1925): 11; and "Community Chest Drive Begins," 11 (November 10, 1926): 4.

50. W. R. Neelands, "Relations to Consumers Discussed by Neelands," *Edison Current Topics* 5 (May 1916): 92–93.

51. S. C. Haver, "Uses of the Little Red Book," *Edison Current Topics* (June 1912): 15–16; These pamphlets are housed in SCE archives.

52. See for instance, "Edison Men Make Big Red Cross Drive," *Edison Current Topics* 6 (June 1917): 111–113.

53. Kennedy, *Winning the Public*, 136; "Charles A. Coffin Medal Effort for the Year 1922"; minutes, Management Committee meeting, Southern California Edison, April 12, 1923, SCE archives.

54. Kennedy, *Winning the Public*, 51.

55. "Your Responsibility," *Pacific Mutual News* 23 (April 1924): 168; Danford Baker, "The Need of New Men," *Pacific Mutual News* 23 (May 1924): 206; Viviana A. Rotman Zelizer, *Morals and Markets: The Development of Life Insurance in the United States* (New Brunswick: Transaction Books, 1983), chapters 6 and 7.

56. Jackson A. Graves, letter to I. W. Hellman, July 20, 1918, Jackson A. Graves Collection.

57. William H. Wallace, "Personality as an Asset in Banking," *Proceedings of Eighteenth Convention of California Bankers Association, 1912*, 184–197; On the matter of sensitivity toward branch banking, see Barney Goss, "Business and Financial Review," *Saturday Night* (September 22, 1922), 21.

58. The company used this system at least through 1910. Jess Stoddard, untitled speech, *Proceedings of the Sixteenth Annual Convention of the California Bankers Association, Los Angeles, 1910* (Los Angeles: Time-Mirror, 1910), 71–74.

59. "Personality Is an Asset in Trust Relations," *News of the Los Angeles First National* 5 (February 12, 1928), 4; "The Boss," *Security-First News Bulletin* 1 (September 1, 1929): 2.

60. In the first two weeks of April 1929, bank employees spoke to ten different groups including the Arnama Club, the Vermont Avenue Presbyterian Church, the Bell Flower Real Estate Board, the Los Angeles Chapter of the League of American Pen Women, and classes at Venice High School and Sentous Junior High School. "Speakers Division Promotes Good Will: MacLennan in Charge of Bureau Providing Security-First National Men and Women for Organization and Club Programs," *Security-First News Bulletin* 1 (August 1, 1929): 3; "Security-First National Speakers," *Security-First News Bulletin* 1 (April 15, 1929): 3.

61. In the spring of 1929, for instance, bank president Joseph Sartori began contributing a weekly column about matters of local business and economic needs to the

Los Angeles Examiner. "Our Greatest Need: President Starts Unique Series of Weekly Articles in *Examiner* on Civic Necessities," *Security-First News Bulletin* 1 (May 1, 1929): 4. Like most large corporations, banks also believed participation in charities would boost their image. Security-First even organized its own charity fund, the Los Angeles Community Foundation. Evidencing the bank's public relations ambitions for the foundation, the booklet given to employees read: "Perhaps nothing can build more general good will for our institution." "Read the Foundation Booklet," *Security-First News Bulletin* 1 (June 15, 1929): 2.

62. "Courtesy in Business," *Union Oil Bulletin* 3 (January 1924): 17.

63. "Courtesy in Business," 17; 1926 issues of *Union Oil Bulletin* contain numerous articles devoted to the firm's "Outdoor Campaign for Safety and Courtesy on the Highways." As an example, see L. P. St. Clair, "Be Careful," *Union Oil Bulletin* 5 (February 1926): 3–6.

64. "An Interview with Carl Eichenlaub, Sr., June 4, 1975," Robert Wright, interviewer, San Diego Historical Society Oral History Program.

65. Sam Grinsfelder, "The Story of Lindsay Buford Little as Related by Richard Sneddon, October 1963," in "Transcribed Interviews Collected, 1963–1973, by the Petroleum Production Pioneers Folklore Committee," bound volume at Huntington Library, p. 322.

Chapter 3 Company Men

Epigraph: "An Interview with Charles K. Fletcher, April 11, 1984 (1902–1985), Sylvia Arden, interviewer," San Diego Historical Society Oral History Program.

1. "Personnel File for Mr. Leo James Devlin," Pacific Mail Steamship Company (PMSC) collection, box 34A, Los Angeles file; *Los Angeles City Directory* (Los Angeles: Los Angeles Directory Company, 1923–1931).

2. This term appeared frequently in the speech and writing of Los Angeles elites. For an early reference, see J. S. Slauson's introduction of Senator Stephen White, *The Members' Annual* (Los Angeles: Los Angeles Chamber of Commerce, 1895), 32.

3. Bureau of the Census, U.S. Department of Commerce, *Fifteenth Census of the United States: 1930. Population, Part 1* (Washington, D.C.: U.S. Government Printing Office, 1931), 18–19; Bureau of the Census, *Historical Statistics of the United States from Colonial Times to the Present, Part 1* (Washington, D. C., 1975), 11–12.

4. Carey McWilliams, *Southern California: An Island on the Land* (1946; reprint, Salt Lake City: Peregrine Smith Books, 1990), 114, 135.

5. Robert Fogelson, *The Fragmented Metropolis: Los Angeles, 1850–1930* (Cambridge: Harvard University Press, 1967), 78; Oscar Osburn Winther, "The Rise of Metropolitan Los Angeles, 1870–1900," *Huntington Library Quarterly* 10 (1947): 391–405; *Facts about Industrial Los Angeles: Nature's Workshop* (Los Angeles: Los Angeles Chamber of Commerce, 1922); Reyner Banham, *Los Angeles: The Architecture of Four Ecologies* (New York, 1971), 203; Kevin Starr, *Material Dreams: Southern California through the 1920s* (New York: Oxford University Press, 1990), 69; Glenn S. Dumke,

The Boom of the Eighties in Southern California (San Marino, Calif.: Huntington Library, 1944); Laurance L. Hill, *La Reina: Los Angeles in Three Centuries* (Los Angeles: Security Trust and Savings Bank, 1929), 71; McWilliams, *Southern California*, 113–125. On the history of California railraods see William F. Deverell, *Railroad Crossing: Californians and the Railroad, 1850–1910* (Berkeley: University of California Press, 1994).

6. Bureau of the Census, *Fifteenth Census, Volume IV, Occupations, by States*, 172.

7. "Introducing J. A. H. Kerr," *Security-First News Bulletin* 2 (May 15, 1930): 6.

8. Joseph French Johnson et al., *Modern Business Volume 19: Office Management* (New York: Alexander Hamilton Institute, 1919), 85–86.

9. D. Freeman, "Outgoing Presidential Address," *The Members' Annual: Los Angeles Chamber of Commerce, 1895* (Los Angeles: Chamber of Commerce, 1895), 21; James C. Kays, "Report of Committee on Immigration," *Members' Annual: Los Angeles Chamber of Commerce, 1904* (Los Angeles: Chamber of Commerce, 1904), 41; *Los Angeles—Nature's Workshop: Home of Efficient Labor* (Los Angeles: Chamber of Commerce, 1921), 3.

10. *Facts about Industrial Los Angeles—Nature's Workshop* (Los Angeles: Chamber of Commerce, 1924), 10.

11. Slauson, introduction of Sen. White, *Members' Annual* (1895), 32.

12. "Mr White's Address," *Members' Annual* (Los Angeles: Chamber of Commerce, 1900), 33; Burt Estes Howard, "The Greater Republic," *Members' Annual* (Los Angeles: Chamber of Commerce, 1902), 35–40. For an analysis of such rhetoric in national political culture, see Gail Bederman, *Manliness and Civilization: A Cultural History of Gender and Race in the United States, 1880–1917* (Chicago: University of Chicago Press, 1995).

13. Clarence Matson, "The Los Angeles of Tomorrow," *Southern California Business* 3 (November 1924): 37.

14. In his study of migration to California from the Dust Bowl during the 1930s, for instance, James Gregory notes that "those hoping to gain access to white-collar jobs and middle-class social circles realized that it was important to shed behaviors that identified them as Okies." James N. Gregory, *American Exodus: The Dust Bowl Migration and Okie Culture in California* (New York: Oxford University Press, 1989), 121–122.

15. John Russell McCarthy, *Joseph Francis Sartori, 1856–1946* (Los Angeles: Ward Ritchie Press, 1948), 45. Photographs of Pacific Electric employees in blackface are in the E. L. Lewis/Pacific Electric photo files at the Huntington Library. On the racialized nature of minstrel performance and images consult Kenneth Goings, *Mammy and Uncle Mose: Black Collectibles and American Stereotyping* (Bloomington: Indiana University Press, 1994); Patricia A. Turner, *Ceramic Uncles and Celluloid Mammies: Black Images and Their Influence on Culture* (New York: Anchor Books, 1994).

16. Fogelson, *Fragmented Metropolis*, chapter 4; Louis Adamic, *Laughing in the Jungle: The Autobiography of an Immigrant in America* (New York: Harper and Brothers, 1932), 217–218.

17. The 1910 and 1920 census samples used in this research comprise 588 and 651 gainfully employed men, respectively, and come from Steven Ruggles and Matthew Sobek, *Integrated Public Use Microdata Series: Version 1.0* (IPUMS-95) (Minneapolis: Social History Research Laboratory, University of Minnesota, 1995).

18. These numbers are based on a randomly selected population of 4,223 white men who registered for the draft from the city of Los Angeles in 1917, from draft registration records housed in federal archives in Atlanta, Georgia. Hereafter referred to as "1917 sample."

19. This argument is made in Stuart Blumin, *The Emergence of the Middle Class: Social Experience in the American City*, 1760–1900 (New York: Cambridge University Press, 1989). See also Olivier Zunz, *Making America Corporate*, 1870–1920 (Chicago: University of Chicago Press, 1990), chapter 5. On the "collar line," see Sanford M. Jacoby, *Employing Bureaucracy: Managers, Unions, and the Transformation of Work in American Industry* (New York: Columbia University Press, 1985), 278–280.

20. Mansel G. Blackford, *A History of Small Business in America* (New York: Twayne Publishers, 1991); Stuart Bruchey, *Small Business in American Life* (New York: Columbia University Press, 1980).

21. Cindy Sondik Aron, *Ladies and Gentlemen of the Civil Service; Middle-Class Workers in Victorian America* (New York: Oxford University Press, 1987), 34–35; C. Wright Mills discusses the degrading nature of white-collar work in *White Collar: The American Middle Classes* (New York: Oxford University Press, 1956), 227. See also Harry Braverman, *Labor and Monopoly Capital: The Degradation of Work in the Twentieth Century* (New York: Monthly Review Press, 1974).

22. On southern California boosterism, which played into these impressions, see: Glenn S. Dumke, "Advertising Southern California before the Boom of 1887," *Quarterly of the Historical Society of Southern California* 24 (March 1942): 15–16; Tom Zimmerman, "Paradise Promoted: Boosterism and the Los Angeles Chamber of Commerce," *California History* 64 (winter 1985): 22–33; and Clark Davis, "From Oasis to Metropolis: Southern California and the Changing Context of American Leisure," *Pacific Historical Review* 61 (August 1992): 357–386.

23. Ken Beko et al., eds., *Pipelines to the Past: An Oral History of Olinda, California* (Fullerton: California State University-Fullerton Oral History Program, 1978), 1; interview with Elmer Wilson, by Ollie Prickett, Pasadena Oral History Project, Pasadena Public Library Special Collections.

24. These groups kept Los Angeles's "official" nonwhite population proportionally stable, shifting from 6.3% to 5.2% in the period between 1890 and 1920. Given the general underreporting of minority groups in the United States census, Los Angeles probably had a more heterogeneous population than these numbers indicate. This is particularly true given the problematic status assigned to peoples from Mexico and Central American countries by the U.S. census. In each census until 1930, Mexican Americans were counted as "white." Only in 1930 would the census categories match the perception of most Euro-American Los Angelenos in classifying Latinos as "nonwhite." Largely because of this, the conservatively calculated census estimate of Los

Angeles's nonwhite population increased suddenly from 5.2% in 1920 to 14.2% in 1930. Even when Mexicans and Mexican Americans were counted as whites, Los Angeles ranked among the highest American cities in the proportion of its population who were not white. Fogelson, *Fragmented Metropolis*, 75–84.

25. As would become increasingly evident throughout the twentieth century, race and class interacted in complex ways in multiracial and multiethnic urban centers, often resulting in patterns of social, residential, and occupational segregation that worked to the economic benefit of whites. See Lisbeth Haas, *Conquests and Historical Identities in California, 1769–1936* (Berkeley: University of California Press, 1995). Tomás Almaguer, *Racial Fault Lines: The Historical Origins of White Supremacy in California* (Berkeley: University of California Press, 1994).

26. Gail B. Johnson, "Side Talks to the Agents," *Pacific Mutual News* 12 (August 1913): 170; "How the Pacific Mutual Is Helping the Agent to Organize His Time," *Pacific Mutual News* 25 (September 1926): 328; C. C. Mallory to Mr. T. A. Graham, August 12, 1924, PMSC collection, box 4.

27. Eugene C. Walsh, personnel file, PMSC collection, box 30; Pacific Mail, letter to Mr. Clifton S. Wardell, February 27, 1926; Daulton Mann, letter to Mr. Albert Walker, freight clerk, June 1925, PMSC collection, box 30.

28. Unpublished manuscript, January 18, 1912, Los Angeles Railway Collection, identification number 8618; "Personnel Plan and Policy Outlined," *Security-First News Bulletin* 3 (January 1, 1931): 6. Salaries of most white-collar men declined in comparison with blue-collar workers during this period, because white-collar workers did not experience the rise in pay enjoyed by blue-collar workers during World War I. In 1903 white-collar workers in industrial firms made, on average, 2.5 times the income of blue-collar employees. By 1920, however, the gap had shrunk considerably, with white-collar workers making only 1.65 times what blue-collar industrial workers made. Jürgen Kocka, *White Collar Workers in America, 1890–1940: A Social-Political History in International Perspective* (London: Sage Publications, 1980), 77–83, 156. IPUMS-95; *Clerical Salaries in the United States, 1926* (New York: National Industrial Conference Board, 24–33.

29. Kocka, *White Collar Workers*, 82–83.

30. "How Did He Do It?" *American Globe* 7 (November 1909): 13.

31. "An Interview with Raymond S. Hindman, September 14, 1988, by Craig Carter," San Diego Historical Society Oral History Program.

32. Edward King Isaacs, "An Important Message to Ambitious Young People and to Those Interested in Them." *American Globe* 9 (January 1912): 15; "Better Than Salary," *American Globe* 11 (February 1914): 7; "Are You Bottled Up?" *American Globe* 7 (January 1910): 2; Edward King Isaacs, "Promotion to Subordinate Employees and to All Young People Generally," *American Globe* 9 (April 1912): 16.

33. "Fred Herr Becomes Agent," *American Globe* 7 (February 1910): 15.

34. 1917 sample; Eshref Shevky and Marilyn Williams, *The Social Areas of Los Angeles: Analysis and Typology* (Berkeley: University of California Press, 1949): fig. 11.

For a description of white-collar boarding practices in Chicago, see Zunz, *Making America Corporate*, 130–132.

35. U.S. Department of Commerce, Bureau of the Census, microfilm copy of 1920 census manuscripts for California, enumeration district 206, reel 108, precinct 187.

36. Ibid., enumeration district 478, precinct 248.

37. U.S. Department of Commerce, Bureau of the Census, *Fourteenth Census of the United States, 1920, California: Volume* 58, enumeration district 356, reel 113.

38. White-collar and salaried employees never organized unions in large numbers. There was only slight and sporadic activity during the 1910s and virtually none in the 1920s. The Depression aroused great organizing. By 1935, there were twenty-six white-collar unions with 588,000 members. See: Martin Oppenheimer, *White Collar Politics* (New York: Monthly Review Press, 1985); Joseph McCartin, "Labor's Great War: Workers, Unions, and the State, 1916–1920," (Ph.D. diss., State University of New York at Binghamton, 1990); A. Sturmthal, ed., *White-Collar Trade Unions* (Urbana: University of Illinois, 1967); Marjorie Murphy, *Blackboard Unions: The AFT and the NEA, 1900–1980* (Ithaca, N.Y.: Cornell University Press, 1990); and David Ziskind, *One Thousand Strikes of Government Employees* (1940; New York: Arno, 1971).

39. J. F. Johnson et al., *Office Management*, 109–110; Sharon Hartman Strom, *Beyond the Typewriter: Gender, Class, and the Origins of Modern American Office Work, 1900–1930* (Urbana: University of Illinois Press, 1992), 188–189.

40. Sam Grinsfelder, "J. E. Brick Elliott," in *Transcribed Interviews Collected 1963–1973: Petroleum Production Pioneers Folklore Committee*, unpublished bound volume at the Huntington Library, 279.

41. Fred Pearson personnel file, PMSC collection, box 30.

42. "Minutes, Board of Directors, Union Oil Company of California, June 5, 1894." Thomas Bard Collection, box 4; Susan Strasser, "'The Smile that Pays': The Culture of Traveling Salesmen, 1880–1920," in James Gilbert et al., eds., *The Mythmaking Frame of Mind: Social Imagination and American Culture* (Belmont, Calif.: Wadsworth, 1993), 169; Angel Kwolek-Folland, *Engendering Business: Men and Women in the Corporate Office, 1870–1930* (Baltimore: Johns Hopkins University Press, 1994), 79.

43. "Salaried and Registered Expenses, 1904–1909," PMSC collection, box 30.

44. "Personnel Plan and Policy Outlined," *Security-First News Bulletin* 3 (January 1931): 6.

45. Walter Licht, *Getting Work: Philadelphia, 1840–1950* (Cambridge: Harvard University Press, 1992), 229; J. F. Johnson et al., *Office Management*, 109–110; *Proceedings of the Northwestern University Conference on Business Education*, June 16–17, 1927 (Chicago: Northwestern University, 1927), 42, 63–68.

46. "An Interview with Lester G. Bradley, March 14, 1961," Edgar Hastings, interviewer, San Diego Historical Society Oral History Program.

47. "Introducing Lewis I. Pierce," *Security-First National News Bulletin* 5 (October 15, 1933): 4.

Chapter 4 Creating an Esprit de Corps

Epigraph: Joseph French Johnson et al., *Modern Business Volume 19: Office Management* (New York: Alexander Hamilton Institute, 1919), 130.

1. "Employees Give Loving Cup to H. E. Huntington," Los Angeles newspaper clipping dated 1910, Los Angeles Railway Corporation Scrapbook.

2. Marrow Mayo, *Los Angeles* (New York: Alfred A. Knopf, 1932), 293–303.

3. Innumerable letters and memoranda surrounding this incident are filed in Pacific Mail Steamship Company (PMSC) collection, box 51.

4. On early industrial management and nineteenth-century managerial strategies, see: Daniel Wren, *The Evolution of Management Thought* (New York: John Wiley and Sons 1987, 3rd ed.); Thomas Dublin, *Women at Work: The Transformation of Work and Community in Lowell, Massachusetts, 1826–1860* (New York: Columbia University Press, 1979); Jacquelyn Dowd Hall et al., *Like a Family: The Making of a Southern Cotton Mill World* (Chapel Hill: University of North Carolina Press, 1987); Richard M. Candee, "Early New England Mill Towns of the Piscataqua River Valley," in John S. Garner, ed., *The Company Town: Architecture and Society in the Early Industrial Age* (New York: Oxford University Press, 1992), 111–138; Jonathan Prude, "The Social System of Early New England Textile Mills: A Case Study, 1812–1840," in Herbert Gutman and Donald Bell, eds., *The New England Working Class and the New Labor History* (Urbana: University of Illinois Press, 1987), 90–127; and Thomas C. Cochran, *Frontiers of Change: Early Industrialization in America* (New York: Oxford University Press, 1981).

5. Railroads are usually cited as the first national big business to emerge in the United States. See Alfred D. Chandler, Jr., "The Railroads: Pioneers in Modern Corporate Management," *Business History Review* 34 (spring 1965); Alfred D. Chandler, Jr., *The Railroads: The Nation's First Big Business* (New York: Harcourt, Brace, and World, 1965); Thomas Cochran, *Railroad Leaders, 1845–1890: The Business Mind in Action* (Cambridge: Harvard University Press, 1953); Walter Licht, *Working for the Railroad: The Organization of Work in the Nineteenth Century* (Princeton, N.J.: Princeton University Press, 1983).

6. "Our New Years Resolution," *Pacific Electric Magazine* 6 (January 10, 1922): 1; J. F. Johnson et al., *Office Management*, 196–97.

7. C. I. D. Moore, *The Pacific Mutual Life Insurance Company of California: A History of the Company and the Development of Its Organization: The Sixtieth Anniversary, 1868–1968* (Los Angeles, 1928), 167–168; "Loyal Service," *Union Oil Bulletin* 7 (October 1927), 1.

8. Joseph Litterer, "Systematic Management: The Search for Order and Integration," *Business History Review* 24 (winter 1961): 461–76; Angel Kwolek-Folland, *Engendering Business: Men and Women in the Corporate Office, 1870–1930* (Baltimore: Johns Hopkins University Press, 1994), 74.

9. Bruce E. Kaufman, *The Origins and Evolution of the Field of Industrial Relations in the United States*, Cornell Studies in Industrial and Labor Relations, no. 25

(Ithaca, N.Y.: ILR Press, 1993), 7, 26. An interest in personnel management did not appear spontaneously in the midst of corporate emergence but grew from an interest in "impressionistic management" dating back at least to the Civil War, when executives began to note that "people skills" were important traits for managers. According to one historian, most businessmen recognized that "good managers were 'noble men' who were patient, kind, not pompous or officious, and generous." Concern with managers would ultimately turn to concern with employees. Kwolek-Folland, *Engendering Business*, 76.

10. Sharon Hartman Strom, *Beyond the Typewriter: Gender, Class, and the Origins of Modern American Office Work, 1900–1930* (Urbana: University of Illinois Press, 1992), 21.

11. J. F. Johnson et al., *Office Management*, 130; Strom, *Beyond the Typewriter*, 112.

12. A. M. Kennedy, letter to Frank Balfour, January 20, 1904; ibid., October 3, 1904; John B. Miller, letter to district agents, December 24, 1907; Pomona Scrapbook: Frank Balfour's Files of Official Communications Received, 1903–1908. Southern California Edison Company Vault Document No. 142351.

13. "Statement by the Southern California Edison Company in Respect to Its Accomplishments during the Year 1928 for Consideration in the Award of the Charles A. Coffin Medal for That Year," unpublished manuscript, 1929, Southern California Edison archives, Rosemead, Calif.

14. "E. P. Clark," photo file 232 in Los Angeles Railway Collection, photo album 58, Huntington Library.

15. In 1920, industrial relations became a professional field of study when the University of Wisconsin opened a program. That same year, the Industrial Relations Association of American was founded. Kaufman, *Origins and Evolution of Industrial Relations*, 19. Ordway Tead and Henry C. Metcalf, *Personnel Administration: Its Principles and Practice* (New York: Mcgraw-Hill, 1920), quoted in Kaufman, *Origins and Evolution of Industrial Relations*, 39; Alan Dawley, *Struggles for Justice: Social Responsibility and the Liberal State* (Cambridge: Harvard University Press, 1991), 299; Richard Gillespie, *Manufacturing Knowledge: A History of the Hawthorne Experiments* (New York: Cambridge University Press, 1991).

16. Kaufman, *Origins and Evolution of Industrial Relations*, chapters 4 and 5; Jürgen Kocka, *White Collar Workers in America, 1890–1940: A Social-Political History in International Perspective* (London: Sage Publications, 1980), 171; "Statement in Respect to Coffin Medal" for 1928.

17. Lyman Stewart to C. M. Smith, May 28, 1915; also see June 30, 1915, Lyman Stewart Collection, Biola University, La Mirada, Calif.; Lyman Stewart to A. C. Stewart, July 28, 1915; Lyman Stewart to C. M. Smith, July 28, 1915.

18. Oral history given by Perry Chansler, taken by Gail Norman-Bilby, May 18, 1982 (O.H. [oral history] 1728); and oral history given by Warren E. Griffith, taken by Beverly E. Schmidt, April 5 and 25, 1968, and May 2, 1968 (O.H. 31), both in the Brea Community History Project of the California State University, Fullerton, Oral History Program. Oral history of Emma Johnson Bennie from Ken Beko et al., eds., *Pipelines*

to the Past: An Oral History of Olinda, California (Fullerton: California State University, 1978), 1.

19. H. E. A. Railton, letter to Daulton Mann, January 29, 1920, PMSC collection, box 34.

20. C. C. Mallory, letter to T. A. Graham, August 12, 1924, PMSC collection, box 4.

21. I. W. Hellman, letters to Jackson A. Graves, August 22 and November 25, 1916. Jackson A. Graves Collection.

22. Jackson A. Graves, letter to I. W. Hellman, October 2, 1914. Graves also dealt gently with employees whom he criticized, so as to assure good feelings and respect. In 1914, Hellman complained to Graves about a bank employee who had been less than successful in managing some of Hellman's properties. Graves acknowledged that the man had a reputation for being rather gruff but defended him and promised to deal with the matter firmly yet gently: "Regarding Whitaker, he means well, is a faithful and energetic employee, and I do not know how you could better him. The first time he is in, when we are talking about the difficulty of retaining tenants, I will take the matter up and put it to him just as nicely as I can, and I think it will do him some good." Jackson Graves, letters to I. W. Hellman, October 10, 1914, and October 15, 1914.

23. For a contemporary discussion of the relationship between trust and productivity, see Ronald Wintrobe and Albert Breton, "Organizational Structure and Productivity," *American Economic Review* 76 (June 1986): 530–538.

24. SCE company district manager, letter to George C. Ward, March 17, 1928, George C. Ward Collection, Huntington Library; "Ward Funeral Plan Arranged," *Los Angeles Times* (September 12, 1933), 3.

25. C. C. Mallory, letter to T. A. Graham, August 12, 1924, PMSC collection, box 4.

26. E. A. Brown, "Efficiency in Banking," *Proceedings of the Eighteenth Annual Convention of the California Bankers Association, Long Beach, 1912 (San Francisco: Hicks-Judd Co., 1912)*, 234.

27. JoAnne Yates, *Control through Communication: The Rise of System in American Management* (Baltimore: Johns Hopkins University Press, 1989), xv.

28. J. F. Johnson et al., *Office Management*, 134. In the words of one scholar, the introduction of such efforts "cannot be dismissed as a secondary or tertiary institution but must be studied as the principal instrument in coordinating and harmonizing the corporation's activities." David Nye, *Image Worlds: Corporate Identities at General Electric, 1890–1930* (Cambridge: Massachusetts Institute of Technology Press, 1985), 5.

29. National Industrial Conference Board, *Employee Magazines in the United States* (New York: National Industrial Conference Board, 1925), 27; Kwolek-Folland, *Engendering Business*, 135.

30. Paul Shoup, "Our Family Round Table," *Pacific Electric Magazine* 1 (June 10, 1916): 1; Terrence E. Deal and Allan A. Kennedy, *Corporate Cultures: The Rites and Rituals of Corporate Capitalism* (Reading, Mass.: Addison-Wesley, 1982), 5.

31. E. W. Clark, "To My Fellow Employees," *Union Oil Bulletin* 1 (November 1921): 1.

32. Ibid.; National Industrial Conference Board, *Employee Magazines*, 34–35.

33. V. L. Ehrenclou, "Major Burnham—The Scout," *Union Oil Bulletin* 5 (May 1925): 1–7; (continuation of previous article) *Union Oil Bulletin* 5 (June 1925): 8–11, 19; H. D. Seeley, "A Canadian Travelogue," *Union Oil Bulletin* 8 (October 1928): 15–17; "Death Valley," *Union Oil Bulletin* 8 (December 1928): 16–18. Such articles were steady features of the company magazine.

34. See diverse articles such as: "Romance of Gasoline: The Names and Uses of Petroleum," *Union Oil Bulletin* 5 (July 1925): 17, 22; A. E. Fowks, "A Petroleum Industry of the Sixteenth Century," *Union Oil Bulletin* 8 (March 1928): 8–9; L. P. Stockman, "California Oil: A Glimpse of an Ever-Changing Picture," *Union Oil Bulletin* 8 (May 1928): 4–9. In the early 1920s, for the "real professionals" among Union Oil's ranks, the company frequently published "Current Petroleum Literature Abstracts."

35. "The Gasoline Malemute," *Union Oil Bulletin* 6 (March 1926): 7; E. H. Weaver, "Supply and Transportation of Lumber," *Union Oil Bulletin* 6 (July 1926): 14–15; C. F. Lienesch, "The Air Era Dawns," *Union Oil Bulletin* 7 (July 1927): 2–7; Morris L. Boxell, "Gas Bags," *Union Oil Bulletin* 7 (November 1927): 13–16; Al D. Macleod, "Speed in Pacific Coast Waters," *Union Oil Bulletin* 7 (January 1928): 2–5.

36. See: E. H. Jones "Evaporation Losses—How to Combat Them," *Union Oil Bulletin* 5 (March 1925): 4–8; American Petroleum Institute, "Standardization in the Oil Fields," *Union Oil Bulletin* 5 (June 1925): 1–3; "Ten Rules for Running Casing; or, The Ten Commandments for Casing Crews," *Union Oil Bulletin* 7 (May 1927): 16–18; Philip Subkow, "More About the Patent Policy Plan," *Union Oil Bulletin* 7 (August 1927): 14–17; and Hubert C. Ferry, "Handling Waste Water and Oil," *Union Oil Bulletin* 8 (October 1928): 7–14. For company editorials, see: "Promotion," *Union Oil Bulletin* 3 (December 1923): 25; "Courtesy in Business," *Union Oil Bulletin* 3 (January 1924): 17; and "I Like Business," *Union Oil Bulletin* 7 (July 1927): 11.

37. The opening piece of the first issue highlighted Lyman Stewart, one of the company's founders and its board chair: "The remarkable growth of our Company has been made possible by the faith and tenacity of one man, who risked his fortune and name, when bankers flatly refused to loan money to finance the oil industry, characterizing all oil men as a wildcat crowd." "Mr. Lyman Stewart," *Union Oil Bulletin* 1 (March 1921): 2. In the December 1921 issue, the magazine presented a four-page spread on the company's treasury department highlighting five of its members, including the assistant treasurer, company cashier, credit manager, credit division attorney, and his assistant attorney. "Treasury Department," *Union Oil Bulletin* 1 (December 1921): 18–21. In the March 1925 issue, an article appeared entitled "The Men Behind the Gun," which presented a photo of thirty-two service station operators in the company's Seattle district, each immaculately groomed in white uniforms and bow ties, standing in front of a Union Oil advertising backdrop. "The Men Behind the Gun," *Union Oil Bulletin* 5 (March 1925): 9.

38. "News of the Month," *Union Oil Bulletin* 5 (March 1925): 24–26; "Service Pins for Employees," *Union Oil Bulletin* 7 (August 1927): 10.

39. "Message from Nelson A. Howard," *Union Oil Bulletin* 1 (June 1921): 3.

40. "Announcement," *Union Oil Bulletin* 1 (March 1921): 1; J. F. Johnson et al., *Office Management*, 131.

41. National Industrial Conference Board, *Employee Magazines*, 42–43.

42. "Our New Birthday," *Security-First News Bulletin* 1 (April 15, 1929): 2.

43. "Pacific Mutual Prize Song," *Pacific Mutual News* 11 (September 1912): 185.

44. C. I. D. Moore, "Just Among Ourselves," *Pacific Mutual News* 20 (September 1921): 285.

45. Shoup, "Our Family Round Table," 1.

46. "New Faces in the Big Family," *Pacific Electric Magazine* 4 (September 10, 1919): 5. Further drawing on the metaphor, an editorial discussing the strike's end noted happily that the company, now rid of disloyal workers (1,500 out of 4,800 went on strike) was again a "family." "The Family Spirit Returning," *Pacific Electric Magazine* 4 (October 1919): 2.

47. In a front-page editorial in June 1918, the company president claimed surprise in hearing of efforts to "coerce men into joining unions." He proclaimed, "It is hard to believe any of our employees would do this, but reports make it necessary for me to say that any attempt made to coerce any employee into joining the union by another employee, is sufficient ground for dismissal from our service." The next issue featured another front-page editorial in which the president declared, "My very positive view is that our troubles are our own and should be ironed out inside our own family and there is no room for outsiders to take a hand." "Message from President Shoup," *Pacific Electric Magazine* 3 (June 10, 1918): 2; "A Statement from President Shoup," *Pacific Electric Magazine* 3 (July 10, 1918): 1. On the strike itself, see Louis B. Perry and Richard S. Perry, *A History of the Los Angeles Labor Movement, 1911–1941* (Berkeley: University of California Press, 1963), 78–93.

48. Mary A. Blackburn, "Departmental Brevities — Accounting Department," *Pacific Electric Magazine* 6 (April 10, 1922): 13.

49. See for instance, "President to Leave Saturday on Outing: Sartori Party to Take Trip Across Ocean," *Security-First News Bulletin* 1 (May 15, 1929): 1.

50. The more prominent publications included *Edison Partners* (for employee and other stockholders), *The General Office Torch* (for company headquarters staff), *Edison Facts*, *Edison Era* (for members of the general office Edison Club), *Edison Energy* (for employees of the Steam Generation Department), and the *Edison News Service Bulletin*.

51. George C. Ward file, Herald-Examiner Collection, USC Regional History Center.

Chapter 5 Profit and Security

Epigraph: J. R. Sprague, "The Easiest Way: We All Have Moments When Some Other Business Looks Better Than Our Own," *Sunset* 42 (March 1919): 44.

1. Joseph Benjamin Personnel File, Pacific Mail Steamship Company (PMSC) collection, box 34D.

2. George Damon, "Public Regulation," *Edison Current Topics* (May 1912): 6–8.

3. H. M. Gitelman describes benefit programs as "discretionary" yet "consistent with profit maximizing behavior." "Welfare Capitalism Reconsidered," *Labor History* 33 (winter 1992): 21

4. In his empirical account of welfare capitalism, Stuart Brandes defines benefit programs as "any service provided for the comfort or improvement of employees which was neither a necessity of the industry nor required by law." Stuart Brandes, *American Welfare Capitalism, 1880–1940* (Chicago: University of Chicago Press, 1970), 5–6. While Brandes's definition is correct in that corporate operations did not require employee compensation programs per se, he obscures the central role they played in many firms' strategic planning. Most corporations viewed benefit programs as critical elements in securing a workforce that would ensure long-term profitable operations. From the perspective of a firm that was losing money because of strikes, employee turnover, or antagonistic government regulations, certain benefit programs might indeed have seemed important to assuring corporate stability.

5. Grace Heilman Stimson, *The Rise of the Labor Movement in Los Angeles* (Berkeley: University of California Press, 1955), 366–391; Robert M. Fogelson, *The Fragmented Metropolis: Los Angeles, 1850–1930* (1967; reprinted, Berkeley: University of California Press, 1993), chapter 10; Morrow Mayo, *Los Angeles* (New York: Alfred A. Knopf, 1932), 139–155; Paul Greenstein, Nigey Lennon, and Lionel Rolfe, *Bread and Hyacinths: The Rise and Fall of Utopian Los Angeles* (Los Angeles: California Classic Books, 1992); Louis B. Perry and Richard Perry, *A History of the Los Angeles Labor Movement, 1911–1941* (Los Angeles: University of California Press, 1963).

6. Jürgen Kocka, *White Collar Workers in America, 1890–1940: A Social-Political History in International Perspective* (London: Sage Publications, 1980), 123–124. David Montgomery's comments on welfare capitalism typify the difficulties of examining these programs only in the context of working-class issues: "There was little advance in corporate welfare practice anywhere in American industry after 1921. The creative years for mutual-benefit societies, pension plans, stock options, company newspapers, and sporting clubs were the years of labor militancy, 1916–1922." While perhaps this was true for blue-collar workers, broad compensation programs were, in fact, major themes of white-collar corporate employment before this period and throughout the 1920s. David Montgomery, *The Fall of the House of Labor: The Workplace, the State, and American Labor Activism, 1865–1925* (New York: Cambridge University Press, 1987), 455.

7. The historical literature on welfare capitalism is vast and diverse. Critical studies include Andrea Tone, *The Business of Benevolence: Industrial Paternalism in the Progressive Era* (Ithaca, N.Y.: Cornell University Press, 1997); Sanford M. Jacoby, *Modern Manors: Welfare Capitalism since the New Deal* (Princeton, N.J.: Princeton University Press, 1997); Sharon Hartman Strom, *Beyond the Typewriter: Gender, Class, and the Origins of Modern American Office Work, 1900–1930* (Urbana: University of Illinois Press, 1992); Brandes, *American Welfare Capitalism*. For a more complete review, see Essay on Sources.

8. Rick Halpern, "The Iron Fist and the Velvet Glove: Welfare Capitalism in Chicago's Packinghouses, 1921–33," *Journal of American Studies* 26 (1992): 171; Douglas Flamming, *Creating the Modern South: Millhands and Managers in Dalton, Georgia, 1884–1984* (Chapel Hill: University of North Carolina Press, 1992), 135–146.

9. Most surveys of corporate payrolls suggest that firms with benefit programs actually paid similar if not higher wages than firms without such programs. Sanford M. Jacoby, *Employing Bureaucracy: Managers, Unions, and the Transformation of Work in American Industry* (New York: Columbia University Press, 1985), 199; and Gitelman, "Welfare Capitalism Reconsidered," 23. A well-noted example of this pattern is the Kodak Company, which in addition to offering very generous benefits that received national attention for their scope, was known to pay the highest wages in the city of Rochester. Sanford Jacoby, "Employers and the Welfare State: The Role of Marion B. Folsom," *Journal of American History* 80 (September 1993): 525–556.

10. Martin Oppenheimer, *White Collar Politics* (New York: Monthly Review Press, 1985), chapter 8. Kocka, *White Collar Workers*, 90–124.

11. See Howard P. Chudacoff, "Success and Security: The Meaning of Social Mobility in America," *Reviews in American History* 10 (December 1982): 101–111; see also James Henretta, "The Study of Social Mobility: Ideological Assumptions and Conceptual Bias," *Labor History* 18 (1977): 165–178.

12. An excellent study depicting the changing nature of family security and priorities over the course of the nation's history is Gerald W. McFarland, *A Scattered People: An American Family Moves West* (Amherst: University of Massachusetts Press, 1985).

13. Mary Ryan explores this process in *Cradle of the Middle Class: The Family in Oneida County, New York, 1790–1865* (New York: Cambridge University Press, 1981).

14. Brandes, *American Welfare Capitalism*, 83–84.

15. Earl M. Welty and Frank Taylor, *The 76 Bonanza: The Fabulous Life and Times of the Union Oil Company of California* (Menlo Park, Calif.: Lane Magazine and Book Co., 1966), 169; "General Comment," *Union Oil Bulletin* 1 (April 1921): 23; "Employees' Share of Profits," *Union Oil Bulletin* (February 1922): 15; "Annual Report of the Union Oil Company of California, for the Year Ending on December 31, 1916." Thomas Bard Collection, box 4, Huntington Library, San Marino, Calif.

16. Joseph French Johnson et al. *Modern Business Volume 19: Office Management* (New York: Alexander Hamilton Institute, 1919), 211.

17. *Practical Experience with Profit Sharing in Industrial Establishments: Research Report Number 29* (Boston: National Industrial Conference Board, 1920), 22; Daniel Nelson, *Workers and Managers: Origins of the New Factory System in the United States, 1880–1920* (Madison: University of Wisconsin Press, 1975), 105–106; Alan Dawley, *Struggles for Justice: Social Responsibility and the Liberal State* (Cambridge: Harvard University Press, 1991), 302.

18. S. M. Kennedy, letter to district agents, January 2, 1905, Pomona Scrapbook, private collection; "Frank Balfour's Files of Official Communications Received, 1903–1908," Southern California Edison Company Vault Document no. 142351; "Most Successful Contest Ever Held," *The Pacific Southwest* 1 (May 1, 1924), 1.

19. Pacific Mutual introduced a steady stream of material inducements based on sales. In a 1912 sales campaign, for instance, leading agents received cash bonuses of $300 and gold watches. "Two Attractive Prize Propositions for Fall Campaign," *Pacific Mutual News* 11 (September 1912): 163.

20. "LARC Establishes a Merit System," *Two Bells* 1 (June 7, 1920): 1; "First Automatic Dismissal Recorded," *Two Bells* 1 (July 26, 1920), 1; "$50,000 Bonus Will Be Given Trainmen," *Two Bells* 1 (December 13, 1920), 1.

21. *Employee Stock Purchase Plans in the United States* (New York: National Industrial Conference Board, 1928), 2.

22. "Profit-Sharing Plan Grows," *Saturday Night* 2 (January 1926): 3.

23. "The Provident Fund," *Union Oil Bulletin* 7 (February 1926); C. I. D. Moore, *The Pacific Mutual Life Insurance Company of California: A History of the Company and the Development of Its Organization: The 60th Anniversary, 1968–1928* (Los Angeles: Pacific Mutual Life Insurance, 1928), 173–175.

24. "Employee-Partner Plan for L.A.—First," *News of the Los Angeles First National* 5 (June 1928): 1; "Employee-Partner Plan for LA First: Bank Stock at $85; Details of Plan," *News of the Los Angeles First National* 5 (June 1, 1928): 1.

25. "Employees of Edison Profit-Sharing Partners," *Edison Current Topics* 6 (August 1917): 143–146; *Edison Current Topics* 9 (January 1920); Charles Heston Peirson, "The Great Development of the SCE Company," *The Central Station* 23 (June 1924): 377. Because during the 1910s and 1920s SCE was continually involved in construction projects for which it hired large numbers of temporary workers, supervisors, and engineers, the company always distinguished between its temporary and permanent employees.

26. *Employee Stock Purchase Plans*, 32–35; John E. Barber, "Want Everybody as Stockholders Under New Plan," *The Pacific Southwest* 1 (July 1, 1923), 1.

27. Lizbeth Cohen, *Making a New Deal: Industrial Workers in Chicago, 1919–1939* (New York: Cambridge University Press, 1990), 195. For a critical review of the practical effect of stock ownership on company success, see Jack W. Duncan, *Great Ideas in Management: Lessons from the Founders and Foundations of Managerial Practice* (San Francisco: Jossey-Bass, 1989), 142.

28. *Employee Stock Purchase Plans*, 129; for a contemporary discussion of stock ownership plans, see Richard Reichler, ed., *Employee Stock Ownership Plans: Problems and Potentials* (New York: Law Journal Press, 1977).

29. In his study of the Du Pont Corporation, historian John Landry found that, in the spirit of the company's tradition as a "family firm," owners and leaders experimented with direct individual rewards for merit as the key to company success. Yet, according to Landry, Du Pont leaders over time recognized that incentives based on security and promotions would be more effective for lower and middle management. The company thus increasingly implemented policies that rewarded employees as members of the firm, not as individuals. John Theodore Landry, "Corporate Incentives for Managers in American Industry, 1900–1940," (Ph.D. diss., Brown University, 1995), chapter 5. A modern discussion of the limited effects of stock ownership as an

incentive for managers is found in, Gary Miller, *Managerial Dilemmas: The Political Economy of Hierarchy* (New York: Cambridge University Press, 1992), 167–171.

30. The Human Factor," *Edison Current Topics* 5 (January 1916): 17; Sprague, "The Easiest Way," 44–45, 56.

31. Thomas Cochran has speculated that "the logical motivation for men at the top was not profit as such; often they were not large stockholders in the company, but rather the long-run welfare of the organization, that would guarantee good salaries and pensions." *Social Change in America: The Twentieth Century* (New York: Harper and Row, 1972), 104; see also Mansel Blackford, *The Politics of Business in California, 1890–1920* (Columbus: Ohio State University, 1977), 161.

32. Robert Asher, "The Limits of Big Business Paternalism: Relief for Insured Workers in the Years before Workman's Compensation," in David Rosner and Gerald Markowitz, eds., *Dying for Work: Workers' Safety and Health in Twentieth-Century America* (Bloomington: Indiana University Press, 1987), 19–33.

33. Brandes, *American Welfare Capitalism*, 97; Jacoby, "Employers and the Welfare State," 526.

34. Carole Haber, *Beyond Sixty-Five: The Dilemma of Old Age in America's Past* (New York: Cambridge University Press, 1983), 110–113; David Hackett Fischer, *Growing Old in America: The Bland-Lee Lectures Delivered at Clark University* (New York: Oxford University Press, 1977), 157–163; W. Andrew Achenbaum, *Old Age in the New Land: The American Experience since 1790* (Baltimore: Johns Hopkins University Press, 1978), 109; William Graebner, *A History of Retirement: The Meaning and Function of an American Institution, 1885–1978* (New Haven, Conn.: Yale University Press, 1980); Joyce D. Goodfriend, "The Struggle for Survival: Widows in Denver 1880–1912," in Arlene Scadron, ed., *On Their Own: Widows and Widowhood in the American Southwest, 1848–1939* (Urbana: University of Illinois Press, 1988), 166–194; Donna J. Guy, "The Economics of Widowhood in Arizona, 1880–1940," in Scadron, *On Their Own*, 195–223.

35. Sanford Jacoby found in his study of Kodak that low turnover became a problem if employees stayed on the job for too long, because in doing so, they kept upper positions filled, denying younger employees advancement opportunities. Jacoby, "Employers and the Welfare State," 535. A 1931 study by the National Industrial Conference Board found conflicting data about the benefits of pension plans. The survey suggested that pensions did promote long-term service, but more so among older employees who were, for other reasons, perhaps less likely to leave. Younger men seemed less interested in pensions. *Elements of Industrial Pension Plans* (New York: National Industrial Conference Board, 1931), 10–14.

36. *Elements of Industrial Pension Plans*, 1; *Industrial Pensions in the United States* (New York: National Industrial Conference Board, 1925); Jill Quadagno, *The Transformation of Old Age Security: Class and Politics in the American Welfare State* (Chicago: University of Chicago Press, 1988), 77–96; Fischer, *Growing Old*, 166; Haber, *Beyond Sixty-Five*, 113; Brandes, *American Welfare Capitalism*, 105–106; Kocka, *White Collar Workers*, 322.

37. "The Employees Insurance and Mutual Aid Proposition," *Pacific Electric Magazine* 1 (June 10, 1916); "The Magazine's Club Number," *Pacific Electric Magazine* 4 (January 20, 1920): 2–4.

38. "Accident Insurance," *Pacific Electric Magazine* 1 (10 April 1917): 1; "Relief Fund," *Pacific Electric Magazine* 2 (April 10, 1917): 8; "The Mortuary Fund," *Pacific Electric Magazine* 3 (August 10, 1918): 11.

39. "Group Insurance Plan Now Effective," *Pacific Electric Magazine* 8 (January 1924): 4. "Our Modern Equipped Hospital Department Unsurpassed," *Pacific Electric Magazine* 7 (April 10, 1923): 4; "New Ruling Is Made by Medical Department," *Pacific Electric Magazine* 12 (August 10, 1927): 4.

40. "During the Month of September the Pacific Mutual Life Insurance Company Paid the Following P.E. Employees Daily Benefits Through the William T. Thomas Agency," *Pacific Electric Magazine* 14 (October 10, 1929): 25.

41. Pacific Electric did offer other benefits in areas where out-of-pocket costs were minimal, including free Pacific Electric passes for employees and their families as well as special access to resorts and camps operated by PE. "Privileges and Advantages of PE Employment," *Pacific Electric Magazine* 9 (May 10, 1925): 2.

42. Charles S. Walton, "The Edison Benefit Fund," *Edison Current Topics* (May 1912): 9–10; William Lawler Clark, "How the Edison Benefit Fund Is Helping," *Edison Current Topics* 2 (May 1913); *The Edison Benefit Fund: History and Rules* (Southern California Edison, 1928); benefit associations were found in 214 out of 430 (59%) of firms surveyed by the U.S. Bureau of Labor Statistics in 1919. *Bulletin of the U.S. Bureau of Labor Statistics*, no. 458 (February 1928), 59–61.

43. See Brandes, *American Welfare Capitalism*, 92–97; *Experience with Mutual Benefit Associations in the United States: Research Report* 65 (New York: National Industrial Conference Board, 1923).

44. "Pension Authorized for Edison Employees," *Edison Current Topics* 13 (August 1919): 2; minutes of Management Committee meeting, Southern California Edison, April 12, 1923. During the 1910s and 1920s, SCE introduced a number of other programs that offered various material benefits, including a subsidized cafeteria for employee lunches, a commissary department offering subsidized food and goods for employees, special allowances during times of sickness, and loans for buying stock.

45. See a similar account of this issue at the San Diego Gas and Electric Company: R. Bert Tallman, "How an Employees' Association Grew," *The Central Station* 23 (October 1923): 107.

46. Sharon Strom makes this argument in *Beyond the Typewriter*, 121–122.

47. Welty, *The 76 Bonanza*, 169, 186–187; from *Union Oil Bulletin:* W. L. Stewart, "The President's Letter" 5 (July 1925): 9; "Group Insurance Benefits Increased" 12 (September 1931): 1; "The Human Element in Industry" 7 (July 1927), 8–11; and "Employee Benefit Fund: An Employee-Managed Organization" 12 (January 1931): 11–12.

48. R. D. Matthews, "The Provident Fund," *Union Oil Bulletin* 3 (May 1923): 1–5.

49. Union Oil's leaders were deeply troubled by the threat of labor unions. Concern over worker organization appears in the personal correspondence of the com-

pany's leadership as well as in its publications. In a 1920 letter, board chair Lyman Stewart wrote the company's president about the possibility of building a church at its refinery as "no man with the opened Bible in his hand can ever become a Bolshevist." The church, Stewart wrote, could be part of a "campaign of education among our employees, and thus get them onto a higher [meaning capitalist] plane of thinking." In 1921, Union Oil endured two strikes by blue-collar workers which the company newsletter quickly labeled major reasons for the decline in profits and, consequently, profit-sharing bonuses. Lyman Stewart, letter to E. W. Clark, 1920, Lyman Stewart Collection. The two strikes were a marine engineers strike from May–July 1921 and an oil workers strike in the San Joaquin Valley fields, September–November 1921. *Union Oil Company of California Bulletin* 1 (February 1922), 15.

50. Oral history of Warren E. Griffith, 5, 25 April, and 2 May 1968. Beverly E. Schmidt, interviewer. California State University, Fullerton, Oral History Program.

51. J. R. Douglas, *The Bank and the Community: A History of the Security Trust and Savings Bank of Los Angeles, 1889–1929* (Los Angeles: Security Trust and Savings Bank, 1929), 26; "Employee-Partner Plan for L.A.—First," *News of the Los Angeles First National* 5 (June 1928): 1; A. H. Nieter, "Personnel," *The Pacific Southwest* 5 (July 1927): 2.

52. See, for example, a 1913 article in the *American Economic Review* that discussed how pensions could reduce turnover. Albert deRoode, "Pensions as Wages," *American Economic Review* 3 (June 1913): 290.

53. J. F. Johnson et al., *Office Management*, 216–217. The University of Wisconsin began to teach industrial relations in 1920, the same year the Industrial Relations Association of America was founded. Bruce F. Kaufman, *The Origins and Evolution of the Field of Industrial Relations in the United States*, Cornell Studies in Industrial and Labor Relations, no. 25 (Ithaca, N.Y.: ILR Press, 1993), 19; Dawley, *Struggles for Justice*, 326.

54. Ordway Tead and Henry C. Metcalf, *Personnel Administration: Its Principles and Practice* (New York: McGraw-Hill, 1920), quoted in Kaufman, *Origins and Evolution of Industrial Relations*, 39. For a more recent discussion of these issues, see Ronald G. Ehrenberg, *Do Compensation Policies Matter?* (Ithaca, N.Y.: Cornell University Press, 1990).

55. Jacoby, *Employing Bureaucracy*, 275–278.

56. Untitled article, *Pacific Electric Magazine* 1 (July 20, 1916): 8.

57. Cohen, *Making a New Deal*, 208.

58. Flamming, *Creating the Modern South*, 140.

Chapter 6 White-Collar Manhood

Epigraph: W. W. Robinson, "The Southern California Real Estate Boom of the Twenties," *Historical Society of Southern California Quarterly* 24 (March 1942), 25.

1. "An Interview with George D. Latham," February 23, 1980, Pauline Wray, interviewer, San Diego Historical Society Oral History Program.

2. Anthony Rotundo explores this history in *American Manhood: Transformations in Masculinity from the Revolution to the Modern Era* (New York: Basic Books, 1993), chapter 8.

3. Quoted in Thomas C. Cochran, *Challenges to American Values: Society, Business, and Religion* (New York: Oxford University Press, 1985), 64–65. For an excellent study of corporate response to emasculating qualities of factory work, see Wayne A. Lewchuk, "Men and Monotony: Fraternalism as a Managerial Strategy at the Ford Motor Company," *Journal of Economic History* 53 (December 1993): 824–856.

4. See Sharon Hartman Strom, *Beyond the Typewriter: Gender, Class, and the Origins of Modern American Office Work, 1900–1930* (Urbana: University of Illinois Press, 1992), 188–189; and Olivier Zunz, *Making America Corporate, 1870–1920* (Chicago: University of Chicago Press, 1990), 132–148. The feminization of clerical work has been the subject of several excellent studies, which are outlined in the Essay on Sources.

5. Angel Kwolek-Folland, *Engendering Business: Men and Women in the Corporate Office, 1870–1930* (Baltimore: Johns Hopkins University Press, 1994), 11, 42–69.

6. C. Wright Mills, *White Collar: The American Middle Classes* (New York: Oxford University Press, 1956), 63.

7. See, for instance, Rotundo, *American Manhood,* chapter 10; and Mark C. Carnes, *Secret Ritual and Manhood in Victorian America* (New Haven, Conn.: Yale University Press, 1989).

8. Corporate efforts to instill such an ethos required a subtle repositioning of cultural mores. Leaders openly struggled to adapt earlier gender constructions by assuring young men that white-collar employment in big firms was not only "masculine," that is, acceptable for men, but argued that it was also "manly," that is "synonymous with the highest conceptions of manhood." The histories and significance of these terms are explored in Gail Bederman, *Manliness and Civilization: A Cultural History of Gender and Race in the United States, 1880–1917* (Chicago: University of Chicago Press, 1995), 10; and Kwolek-Folland, *Engendering Business,* 51–52.

9. "An Interview with Fern Lee McClammy by Robert Wright, October 1, 1988," San Diego Historical Society Oral History Program.

10. Woodrow Wilson, *The New Freedom: A Call for the Emancipation of the Generous Energies of a People* (New York: Doubleday, 1913), quoted in Anthony Sampson, *Company Man: The Rise and Fall of Corporate Life* (London: Harper Collins, 1995), 37.

11. Jules Tygiel, *The Great Los Angeles Swindle: Oil, Stocks, and Scandal during the Roaring Twenties* (New York: Oxford University Press, 1994), chapter 3.

12. James Clifford Findley, "The Economic Boom of the Twenties in Los Angeles" (Ph.D. diss., Claremont Graduate School, 1958), 175.; Robinson, "Southern California Real Estate," 25.

13. For an argument on the centrality of promotions in managerial theory, see William Lazonick, "Strategy, Structure, and Management Development in the United States and Britain," in Kesaji Kobayashi and Hidemasa Morikawa, eds., *Development of Managerial Enterprise* (Tokyo: University of Tokyo Press, 1986) 104, 115.

14. "The Edison Organization," *Edison Facts* 2 (February 1924): 1.

15. Joseph French Johnson, ed., *Modern Business, Volume 1: Business and The Man* (New York: Alexander Hamilton Institute, 1917), 216, 234; Joseph French Johnson, et al., *Modern Business, Volume 19: Office Management* (New York: Alexander Hamilton Institute, 1919), 126, 146.

16. Lyman Stewart, letter to Mr. H. P. Lane, February 5, 1918, Biola University Archives.

17. *Proceedings of the First Annual Convention of the California Bankers Association, San Francisco, October 14–16, 1891* (Los Angeles: Times-Mirror, 1891), 38–40, 42–44; "Smock Establishes Personnel Department: Cashier Creates New and Much Needed Division," *Security-First News Bulletin* 1 (July 1, 1929): 3; "New Personnel Program Outlined," *Security-First News Bulletin* 1 (November 1, 1929): 1; "Making Good a Promise," *Security-First News Bulletin* 1 (November 15, 1929): 2; A. H. Nieter, "Personnel," *The Pacific Southwest* 5 (July 1927): 2; Lynne Pierson Doti and Larry Schweikart, *Banking in the American West: From the Gold Rush to Deregulation* (Norman: University of Oklahoma Press, 1991), 4.

18. Jackson A. Graves, letters to I. W. Hellman, 29 December 1914, and 7 January 1915, Jackson A. Graves Collection, Huntington Library, San Marino, Calif.

19. "Statement of the Southern California Edison Company of Its Claims for the Charles A. Coffin Medal Effort for the Year 1922," unpublished manuscript, 1923, 59; "Statement by the Southern California Edison Company in Respect of Its Accomplishments during the Year 1928 for Consideration in the Award of the Charles A. Coffin Medal for That Year," unpublished manuscript, 1929, 158, SCE Archives, Rosemead, Calif.

20. Paul Shoup, letter to Mulford Wade, 16 June 1924, Los Angeles Railway Collection; "Method of Filling Station Vacancies Is Announced," *Pacific Electric Magazine* 12 (June 10, 1927): 12.

21. Wilbur Tupper, "The Agent's Position," *Conservative News* 1 (May 1903): 2; Wilbur Tupper, "The Permanent Agent," *Conservative News* 3 (October 1904): 2; Lindsay Forbes, "Some Suggestions on Conducting a General Agency," *Pacific Mutual News* 12 (December 1913): 260; C. I. D. Moore, *The Pacific Mutual Life Insurance Company of California: A History of the Company and the Development of Its Organization: The Sixtieth Anniversary, 1868–1928* (Los Angeles: Pacific Mutual Life, 1928).

22. Gerald G. Blue, "The Human Element in Industry," *Union Oil Bulletin* 7 (July 1927): 10.

23. "Promotion," *Union Oil Bulletin* 3 (December 1923): 25.

24. "San Francisco Cashier Promoted," *Union Oil Bulletin* 5 (September 1925): 20. Lest the reader view promotion features as mere public information pieces and miss the deeper meaning, they often concluded with words such as: "In the promotion of the three above mentioned men, the company has maintained its policy of taking ability as the criterion of advancement. Seniority alone has not earned them progress, but greater responsibility has become theirs through consistent development of whatever ability they first possessed." *Union Oil Bulletin* 8 (July 1928): 18.

25. T. W. Johnson, "All the World's a Stage," *News of the Los Angeles First National* 5 (November 1927): 2; Ira B. Cross, *Financing an Empire: History of Banking in California* (Los Angeles: S. J. Clarke Publishing, 1927). The practice of promoting from within continues in recent times; Security Pacific National Bank (now merged with Bank of America) boasted as recently as 1989 that all its presidents had climbed the corporate ladder. Another recent example of the twentieth-century prevalence of internal promotion systems was revealed when IBM hired RJR Nabisco CEO Louis V. Gerstner, Jr., as its new CEO in March 1993, the first time in seventy-nine years that the company had hired its top executive from outside its own ranks.

26. S. M. Kennedy, "The Road Ahead," *Edison Current Topics* 3 (July 1914): 539; S. M. Kennedy, *Winning the Public* (New York: McGraw-Hill, 1921), 32–37; *Edison Current Topics* 13 (August 1919): 2.

27. "Ready for Promotion," *Pacific Electric Magazine* 10 (December 10, 1925): 8; "Employees up Ladder Chosen from Ranks," *Pacific Electric Magazine* 10 (October 10, 1925): 18; "What Are Your Chances to Get Ahead Here?" *Two Bells* 6 (September 14, 1925): 21; "Our New Year's Resolution," *Pacific Electric Magazine* 6 (January 1922): 1.

28. J. M. Mills, "A Wail 'bout the Frail," *Pacific Electric Magazine* 9 (July 10, 1924): 13; "The Feminine in Engineering," *Pacific Electric Magazine* 10 (March 10, 1926): 15.

29. Clipping from D. W. Pontius Scrapbook, General Scrapbook Collection 55, Huntington Library.

30. "New Appointments and Promotions," *Pacific Mutual News* 29 (March 1930): 365; "Service Pins," *Pacific Mutual News* 22 (April 1923): 136; Moore, *Pacific Mutual,* 172–173.

31. *Pacific Mutual News* 10 (February 1911).

32. "Women Forced into Employment by Increased Responsibilities," *Pacific Mutual News* 29 (March 1930): 95.

33. "Opportunities for Women," *Pacific Mutual News* 29 (February 1930): 54.

34. Mansel G. Blackford, *A History of Small Business in America* (New York: Twayne Publishers, 1991), chapter 2.

35. Cindy Sondik Aron, *Ladies and Gentlemen of the Civil Service: Middle-Class Workers in Victorian America* (New York: Oxford University Press, 1987), 3; Charles Heston Peirson, "More than Service," *Edison Current Topics* 5 (August 1916): 159.

36. Charles Lindsay, letter to Benjamin Lindsay, August 14, 1914,Benjamin Lindsay Papers, box 139, Library of Congress. Robyn Muncy directed me to this source.

37. This sample was taken from promotion and service award notices in the company's magazine. Such lists did not always mention all promotions, and many employees' careers were far from over when these lists appeared.

38. "Promotions Won by Men Who Stick with Job," *Two Bells* 5 (June 1924): 1; Los Angeles Railway Company collection.

39. "An Interview with Anderson Borthwick, February 28, 1979," Bob Wright, interviewer, San Diego Historical Society Oral History Program.

40. William Rosengarten, *Choosing Your Life Work* (New York: McGraw-Hill, 1922), 125, 133, 135; Harry Dexter Kitson, *I Find My Vocation* (New York: McGraw-Hill, 1931), 97–100. See also, Franklin Stewart Harris, *The Young Man and His Vocation* (Boston: Richard G. Badger, 1916).

41. Adams's career can be pieced together from a series of service award chronicles appearing sporadically in the *Union Oil Bulletin* during the latter 1920s.

42. Henry L. Ward, personnel file, Pacific Mail Steamship Company (PMSC) collection, box 30, Huntington Library.

43. See Howard P. Chudacoff, "Success and Security: The Meaning of Social Mobility in America," *Reviews in American History* 10 (December 1982): 101–111; and James Henretta, "The Study of Social Mobility: Ideological Assumptions and Conceptual Bias," *Labor History* 18 (1977): 165–178.

44. Oral history of Lloyd McCampbell by Evelyn F. Scott, April 18, 1980, Ventura County Historical Society.

45. Oliver Palmer Personnel File, PMSC collection, box 30.

46. Jürgen Kocka, *White Collar Workers in America, 1890–1940; A Social-Political History in International Perspective* (London: Sage Publications, 1980), 184.

47. "Agents Association," *Pacific Magazine* 4 (March 10, 1920); I. W. Hellman, letter to Jackson A. Graves, April 9, 1915; Jackson A. Graves, letter to I. W. Hellman, April 10, 1915.

48. The ability of many firms to screen out numerous people at the lower levels often indicates that they encountered vast pools of applicants. For instance, in 1922 SCE received 24,769 applicants for "ordinary positions" in technical and clerical areas and 1,500 applicants for "better" (defined as positions with an income of over $150 per month) positions. Of these applicants, 2,282 were hired for the ordinary positions and 121 for the better positions. "Charles A. Coffin Medal Effort for the Year 1922."

49. In Philadelphia between 1870 and 1936, 42% of both blue- and white-collar workers left their first job for a better position elsewhere. With each job change, the percentage who left for a still better position decreased, but it remained as high as 18% for a given position. Conversely, the number being promoted from the first job was only 9%. Walter Licht, *Getting Work: Philadelphia, 1840–1950* (Cambridge: Harvard University Press, 1992), 229.

50. H. E. A. Railton, memo to Mr. Graham, January 20, 1922, PMSC collection, box 4; Moore, *Pacific Mutual*, 163–165; Superintendent of Dispatching, "Yearly Report, 1927, SCE Annual Operating Report, 1927," SCE Archives.

51. San Grinsfelder, "J. E. Brick Elliot," *Transcribed Interviews Collected, 1963–1973: Petroleum Production Pioneers Folklore Committee,* unpublished bound volume at the Huntington Library, 298.

52. Other historians have found similar patterns, see: Walter Licht, *Working for the Railroad: The Organization of Work in the Nineteenth Century* (Princeton, N.J.: Princeton University Press, 1983), 26; Mabel Newcomer, *The Big Business Executive* (New York: Columbia University Press, 1955), 80, 90, 112; Suzanne Keller, *The Social Origins and Career Lives of Three Generations of American Business Leaders* (New

York: Arno, 1980), 98; C. Wright Mills, *The Power Elite* (New York: Oxford University Press, 1956), 132; W. Lloyd Warner, *Occupational Mobility in American Business and Industry* (Minneapolis: University of Minnesota Press, 1955), 116.

53. A. W. Armstrong, "Are College Men Wanted?" *Atlantic Monthly* 138 (July 1926): 12–20.

54. Victor Willard, "Making $5 Grow to Millions: How the Pepperdines, with Team Work and Courage, Have Built a Chain of Stores," *Sunset* (August 1925): 30–31, 56.

55. For an interesting reference to this, see Melissa Dabakis, "Douglas Tilden's *Mechanics Fountain*: Labor and the 'Crisis of Masculinity' in the 1890s," *American Quarterly* 47 (June 1995): 204–205.

56. See: Theodore P. Green, *America's Heroes: Changing Models of Success in American Magazines* (New York, 1970); Daniel T. Rogers, *The Work Ethic in Industrial America: 1850–1920* (Chicago: University of Chicago Press), 38–39; Kocka, *White Collar Workers*, 150; Morrell Heald, *The Social Responsibilities of Business: Company and Community, 1900–1960* (Cleveland, Ohio: Press of Case Western Reserve University, 1970), 69; and Jay Cohn, "The Business Ethic for Boys: The Saturday Evening Post and the Post Boys," *Business History Review* 61 (1987): 185–215.

57. Christopher P. Wilson, *White-Collar Fiction: Class and Social Representation in American Literature, 1885–1925* (Athens: University of Georgia Press, 1992).

58. James Oliver Robertson, *America's Business* (New York: Hill and Wang, 1985), 175–176; Mills, *White Collar*, 263.

59. "Prominent Personalities," *The Graphic* 53 (October 10, 1918): 8; Harold J. Fitzgerald, "Room at the Top: What the Retail Business Has to Offer the Ambitious Young Man," *Sunset* 48 (January 1922): 43–45; Lyle M. Spencer, "Going Up! Traffic Rules for Those Who Want to Get Where There's Abundant Room—the Top," *Sunset* 49 (December 1922): 24–26, 68–70; Eddy Elford, "Has Your Job a Future? The Story of a Musical Youth Who Abandoned Harmonics for the Gas Business," *Sunset* (July 1923): 40, 81.

60. "Chance to Climb," *Southern California Business* 1 (November 1922): 18; "Business Review—Thomas Is Promoted," *Saturday Night* (January 7, 1922): 5.

61. Helen Ormsbee, "The Man Who Failed," *Atlantic Monthly* 109 (April 1912): 508–517; "The Executive Looks for a Job; and What He Encounters in the Search," *Century Magazine* 117 (1928–29): 484–490.

62. These contradictory images and realities are studied in Eyal Naveh, "The Transformation of the 'Rags to Riches' Stories: Business Biographies of Success in the Progressive Era and the 1920s," *American Studies International* 29 (April 1991): 60–80; see also Richard Weiss, *The American Myth of Success: From Horatio Alger to Norman Vincent Peale* (Urbana: University of Illinois Press, 1969), 3–15.

63. "The End of the Trail; Why Does a Woman Leave Home and Faithful Mate After Twenty Years," *Sunset* 50 (March 1923): 30–33; Part II, 50 (April 1923): 40–43.

64. King Vidor, *The Crowd* (MGM, 1928).

65. "The Man Who Buys," *American Globe* 7 (April 1910): 14.

Chapter 7 The Corporation as Community

Epigraph: R. H. Ballard, "Corporation Employees Most Loyal Workers," *Edison Current Topics* 9 (November 1915): 205.

1. "Pasadena P. S. W. Team Champs," *The Pacific Southwest* 5 (July 1, 1927): 7.

2. Many historians have traced the histories of recreation, leisure, and other non-work elements of popular and mass culture. They have found these activities to be complex and to involve contentiousness, for in the larger context of social experience, sports, movies, and vacations are more than simply "fun"—they are important cultural traditions with profound implications for broad realms of American life. See, for instance, Roy Rosenzweig, *Eight Hours for What We Will: Workers and Leisure in an Industrial City, 1870–1920* (New York: Cambridge University Press, 1983); and Kathy Peiss, *Cheap Amusements: Working Women and Leisure in Turn-of-the-Century New York* (Philadelphia: Temple University Press, 1986).

3. Jürgen Kocka, *White Collar Workers in America, 1890–1940: A Social-Political History in International Perspective* (London: Sage Publications, 1980), 171–172.

4. Angel Kwolek-Folland, *Engendering Business: Men and Women of the Corporate Office, 1870–1930* (Baltimore: Johns Hopkins University Press, 1994), 163.

5. R. H. Ballard, "Corporation Employees," 205; Joseph French Johnson et al., *Modern Business Volume 19: Office Management* (New York: Alexander Hamilton Institute, 1919), 133.

6. E. P. Thompson, "Time, Work-Discipline, and Industrial Capitalism," *Past and Present* 38 (1967): 56–97; Herbert G. Gutman, *Work, Culture, and Society in Industrializing America* (New York: Vintage, 5th ed., 1977), chapter 1.

7. John Gilkeson, *Middle-Class Providence, 1820–1940* (Princeton, N.J.: Princeton University Press, 1986); Jeff Charles, *Service Clubs in American Society: Rotary, Kiwanis, and Lions* (Urbana: University of Illinois Press, 1993); Thomas Bender, *Community and Social Change in America* (Baltimore: Johns Hopkins University Press, 1978), 108–120; Gerald W. McFarland, *A Scattered People: An American Family Moves West* (Amherst: University of Massachusetts Press, 1985), 241–242.

8. "Division No. 5 Is Dedicated to Retiring Superintendent John J. Akin," *Southern California Trolley* (January 1913): 15–17.

9. "Employers' Welfare Work," *U.S. Bureau of Labor Statistics Bulletin* (*BLS Bulletin*), 123 (Washington, D.C.: U.S. Government Printing Office, 1913); "Welfare Work for Employees in Industrial Establishments in the United States," *BLS Bulletin*, 250 (GPO, 1919); "Health and Recreation Activities in Industrial Establishments," *BLS Bulletin*, 458 (GPO, 1926); Jackson M. Anderson, *Industrial Recreation: A Guide to Its Organization and Administration* (New York: McGraw Hill, 1955): 52–60.

10. The issue of community at the workplace within salaried ranks has received little historical attention, but many excellent works explore this issue for nonsalaried workers. See Essay on Sources. Three works that show the diversity and variety of social experience for working, middle-, and upper-class Americans in the 1920s are Becky Nicolaides, "In Search of the Good Life: Community and Politics in Working-

Class Los Angeles, 1920–1955" (Ph.D. diss., Columbia University, 1993); Margaret Marsh, *Suburban Lives* (New Brunswick, N.J.: Rutgers University Press, 1990); Frederic Cople Jaher, *The Urban Establishment: Upper Strata in Boston, New York, Charleston, Chicago, and Los Angeles* (Urbana: University of Illinois Press, 1982), 612–685.

11. "Safety Dinner at Fullerton," *Union Oil Bulletin* 6 (December 1926): "Safety in the Union" insert, 1.

12. (Employee sales banquet photo feature), *Union Oil Bulletin* 1 (January 1922): 21; "Annual San Francisco Banquet," *Union Oil Bulletin* 3 (March 1923): 21.

13. "Convention Program," *Conservative News* 2 (February and March 1904): 8; C. I. D. Moore, *The Pacific Mutual Life Insurance Company of California: A History of the Company and the Development of Its Organization, 1868–1928* (Los Angeles: Pacific Mutual Life Insurance, 1928), 158–161.

14. "First Big Reception Held for Greater Edison Family," *Edison Current Topics* 6 (November 1917): 203–204. Union Oil held an annual social gala that similarly provided a personal dimension to a business event. In connection with its announcement of profit-sharing bonuses during the 1920s, the company held a "profit-sharing dance." In 1923, 1,200 persons attended the event, which was held at the Ambassador hotel. "Profit-Sharing Dance," *Union Oil Bulletin* 2 (February 1923): 19.

15. "Health and Recreation Activities," *BLS Bulletin*, 458: 51.

16. "The Spirit of Good Fellowship—Employers," *Southern California Business* 1 (November 1922): 32. See Pacific Electric advertisement clippings in General Scrapbook Collection, 42, Huntington Library, San Marino, Calif.

17. Richard Sneddon, "Reminiscences of Early California Natural Gas and Gasoline Processing by Pioneers of the Industry," found in "Transcribed Interviews Collected 1963–1973" (unpublished manuscript compiled by the Petroleum Production Pioneers, Folklore Committee, ed. Sam Grinsfelder), 38–39.

18. For accounts of the picnic, see: H. A. Brett, "Orange District Barbecue," *Union Oil Bulletin* 7 (June 1927): 17; and "Orange Park Picnic," *Union Oil Bulletin* 8 (July 1928): 17.

19. The company's Valley division, for example, began in 1923 holding an annual picnic that also featured a luncheon, talent show, dancing, and other events. The highlight of the picnic came to be an annual tug-of-war among field, sales, and pipeline employees. The producers pipeline department at Santa Margarita held a similar annual picnic and barbecue for employees, families, and guests beginning in 1923. The San Francisco office held an annual picnic at the estate of a local business elite. The Bay District held an annual gathering at Neptune Beach in Alameda. See the following from *Union Oil Bulletin*: "Valley Division Barbecue" 4 (August 1924): 21; "Annual Valley Picnic" 6 (June 1926): 20; "Pipe Line Barbecue" 3 (July 1923): 19; "News of the Month" 4 (July 1924): 21; "San Francisco Office Picnic" 3 (August 1923): 22; "Union Oil Day at Neptune Beach" 8 (July 1928): 20.

20. "Sacramento Outing," *Union Oil Bulletin* 7 (October 1927): 18.

21. "Edwards to Entertain: Santa Barbara Vice President to Be Host to Staff at

Unique Barbecue at His Huge Ranch," *Security-First News Bulletin* 1 (May 1, 1929): 3; "The First Christmas Party," *Edison Energy* 4 (December 1929): 4.

22. "Our Great Family Re-Union Picnic," *Pacific Electric Magazine* 1 (October 10, 1916): 1–2; "Our Annual Picnic," *Pacific Electric Magazine* 2 (September 10, 1917): 1–2; "1917 Tug-of-War Champions—Electric Department Team," *Pacific Electric Magazine* 2 (October 10, 1917): 3. For an example of how company picnics were covered in local papers, see "L.A. Railway Men Make Merry at Redondo," *Los Angeles Examiner* (August 26, 1913).

23. From *Pacific Electric Magazine*: "Annual Employees' Picnic at Redondo Beach" 6 (August 1921): 2; "Pacific Electric Picnic" 6 (September 10, 1921): 8–10; "New Business" 5 (August 10, 1920): 15; C. M. Stuart, "Membership," 5 (November 10, 1920): 2.

24. Louis B. Perry and Richard S. Perry, *A History of the Los Angeles Labor Movement, 1911–1941* (Berkeley: University of California Press, 1963), 78–93. From *Pacific Electric Magazine*: "Pacific Electric Employee's Annual Picnic and Re-Union" 7 (August 10, 1922): 2–3; "Annual Picnic Number for 1922" 7 (September 10, 1922); "Best Time Ever Verdict of 1923 Reunion" 8 (September 10, 1923): 3–5; "Annual Redondo Beach Picnic a Gala Event; Immense Throng Enjoys Yearly Gathering at Beach City Where All Joined in Fine Program of Sports and Amusements" 10 (September 10, 1925): 4, 5; "Annual Picnic Gathering Is Another Classic" 12 (September 10, 1927): 3–4. "Picnic Lures Largest Crowd," 14 (September 10, 1929): 7; "Our Annual Ball at Redondo" 6 (February 10, 1922): 8.

25. Moore, *Pacific Mutual*, 169–171.

26. "Health and Recreation Activities," *BLS Bulletin*, 458: 52; Eileen DeVault, *Sons and Daughters of Labor: Class and Clerical Work in Turn-of-the-Century Pittsburgh* (Ithaca, N.Y.: Cornell University Press, 1990), 148, 162.

27. The range of these activities is discussed in "Health and Recreation Activities," *BLS Bulletin* 458.

28. "Entertainments," *Union Oil Bulletin* 7 (May 1927): 19; "Arizona Employees Celebrate," *Union Oil Bulletin* 5 (August 1925): 22. In 1926, Union Oil leaders proclaimed: "the modern corporation has a soul and sometimes a musical soul was clearly demonstrated when the company recently arranged for two concert parties for its employees at the Hollywood Bowl." *Union Oil Bulletin* 6 (September 1926): 20.

29. "Migratory Fish and His Breed," *Union Oil Bulletin* 5 (October 1925): 18.

30. Lois Meyer Ritchie, "Social Status of Department Store Salespersons Among Certain Groups in Los Angeles" (master's thesis, University of Southern California, 1932), 11, 22.

31. Kwolek-Folland, *Engendering Business*, 154–155.

32. "News of the Month," *Union Oil Bulletin* 4 (July 1924): 21; "Shades of Micawber!" *Union Oil Bulletin* 6 (May 1926): 21. On the important place of dancing in working-class and lower-middle-class culture during this period, see Peiss, *Cheap Amusements*, chapter 4.

33. "News of the Month," *Union Oil Bulletin* 4 (July 1924): 21. Other examples of these organizations included the Seattle office's employee orchestra, the San Jose of-

fice's Aristo Club (a social club named after a Union Oil gasoline), and the L.A. office's vocal, orchestral, and dramatic clubs. "Seattle Employees Orchestra," *Union Oil Bulletin* 6 (July 1926): 21; "Aristo Club Meets," *Union Oil Bulletin* 5 (March 1925): 24; "San Jose Club Holds Big Affair," *Union Oil Bulletin* 6 (March 1926): 21; "Musical Club Organized," *Union Oil Bulletin* 6 (April 1926): 21; "Statement of the Southern California Edison Company of Its Claims for the Charles A. Coffin Medal Effort the Year 1922," unpublished manuscript, 1923, SCE Archives, Rosemead, Calif.; A. H. Nieter, "Personnel," *The Pacific Southwest* 5 (July 1927): 2.

34. John William Shaw, "The Social Phases of Industrial Recreation as They Affect Employer-Employee Relations in the Los Angeles Area" (Ph.D. diss., University of Southern California, 1948).

35. Oral history of J. Sherman Denny, taken by Harry Henslick, May 15, 22, and June 1, 1968, California State University, Fullerton, Oral History Program, Huntington Beach Community History Project.

36. "Comradeship that Counts," *Union Oil Bulletin* 1 (July 1921): 7; "Comradeship that Counts," *Union Oil Bulletin* 2 (April 1922): 13.

37. On company unions, see Daniel Nelson, "The Company Union Movement, 1900–1937: A Reexamination," *Business History Review* 56 (autumn 1982): 202–224. Southern California Edison made similar attempts at internal employee associations under the guise of employee clubs known as "Edison Clubs." See: B. F. Pearson, "War a Failure," *Edison Era* (May 1923); "Statement of the Southern California Edison Company of Its Claims for the Charles A. Coffin Medal Effort, the Year 1923," 36–40.

38. "The New Club Proposal," *Pacific Electric Magazine* 1 (September 10, 1916): 2. On the Los Angeles Railway's employee clubs, see: "Trainmen Enjoy Exclusive Clubs," *Los Angeles Express* (3 September 1913); and "Health and Recreation Activities," *BLS Bulletin*, 458: 30–33.

39. One indication that companywide employee clubs and clubhouses were more than just ways to thwart unions is their presence in wholly white-collar firms. New York's Metropolitan Life Insurance Company operated a sanitorium and athletic facilities for its employees by the late 1920s, and the Equitable Life Insurance Company opened an employee vacation camp at about the same time. In 1918, Pacific Mutual built an annex onto its headquarters for the Home Office Association, an organization of its Los Angeles–based employees. The annex included an auditorium and social hall where the company and association frequently sponsored social and cultural gatherings for employees. The annex was expanded in 1920 to include an employee recreation room, dance floor, and park. Angel Kwolek-Folland, "Gender, Self, and Work in the Life Insurance Industry, 1880–1930," in Ava Baron, ed., *Work Engendered: Toward a New History of American Labor* (Ithaca, N.Y.: Cornell University Press, 1991), 172; Kwolek-Folland, *Engendering Business*, chapter 5. On Pacific Mutual Life, see: Lindsay Forbes, "Our Completed Home Office," *Pacific Mutual News* 17 (January 1918): 3–6; and C. I. D. Moore, "The Bigger Pacific Mutual Building," *Pacific Mutual News* 19 (October 1920): 383–341.

40. "Pacific Electric Club," *Pacific Electric Magazine* 1 (October 10, 1916): 3;

"Our Fondest Hopes Are More than Realized," *Pacific Electric Magazine* 14 (October 10, 1929): 3–6.

41. Several years after its founding, PE leaders would explicitly define the club in terms that employees had likely sensed in 1917. The company announced that union interests outside the company were working to organize a citywide railway employee club known as the Carmen's Club and that any employees joining would be fired, since it would represent a rejection of the PE Club: "The Pacific Electric club is organized, maintained, and operated by the employees of this Company, affords at a less cost many more advantages than can possibly be given by the Carmen's Club. It is YOUR Club and is run for YOUR benefit." D. W. Pontius (vice president and general manager), "Circular No. 54," reprinted in *Pacific Electric Magazine* 7 (June 10, 1922): 4. The Clubhouse became the site of managerial addresses and sessions with employees. See, for instance, "Employees' Meeting at the Pacific Electric Club," *Pacific Electric Magazine* 3 (June 10, 1918): 12.

42. General reports, *Pacific Electric Magazine* 1 (January 10, 1917): 1–3.

43. One could surmise that company efforts to generate interest in company events or activities would be difficult during these periods. During this period, Los Angeles Railway Corporation trainmen voted against wearing badges announcing how many years an employee had been with the company. "Service Stripes Rejected," *Two Bells* 1 (April 18, 1921): 1.

44. From *Pacific Electric Magazine*: "Our Club Continues to Grow Lustily," 1 (November 10, 1916): 1; "Club Membership Statement," 3 (November 10, 1918): 2; "The Magazine's Club Number," 4 (January 20, 1920); C. M. Stuart, "Membership," 5 (November 10, 1920): 2.

45. "PE Club Affairs," *Pacific Electric Magazine* 5 (June 10, 1920).

46. From *Pacific Electric Magazine*: "Moving Picture Night at Club," 4 (August 10, 1919): 9; "The Magazine's Club Number," 4 (January 20, 1920): 7; C. M. Stuart, "Pacific Electric Club Affairs," 5 (June 10, 1920): 8; "Movie Shows Now Twice Weekly," 14 (November 10, 1929): 11. The integration of movies into corporate cultures represented an attempt at co-opting one of the most popular urban amusements in the 1920s. On the rise of motion pictures to mass and cross-class appeal in this decade, see: Lary May, *Screening out the Past: The Birth of Mass Culture and the Motion Picture Industry* (Chicago: University of Chicago Press, 1980), chapter 6; and Robert Sklar, *Movie-Made America: A Cultural History of American Movies* (New York: Random House, 1975), chapters 8, 9.

47. "The P.E. Masonic Club Is Notable in Southland," *Pacific Electric Magazine* 13 (August 10, 1928): 11.

48. From *Pacific Electric Magazine*: "Our Summer Vacation Home in the Mountains," 2 (June 10, 1917): 9–10; "Vacation Camp Closed for the Season," 2 (October 10, 1917): 1; "Alluring Vacation Camp Awaits Employees," 7 (June 10, 1923): 3–6; "Many Improvements to Greet Camp Visitors," 9 (June 10, 1924): 3–4; "June Camp Attendance Largest Yet Recorded," 11 (July 10, 1926): 12; "Camp Reservations Insure Banner Season," 13 (June 10, 1928): 3–4.

49. "Health and Recreation Activities," *BLD Bulletin* 458, 45–50.

50. Alan Guttmann, *A Whole New Ball Game: An Interpretation of American Sports* (Chapel Hill: University of North Carolina Press, 1988), 55. In his comparison of workplace culture and baseball in the late nineteenth century, Steven Gelber argues: "The integrated organization of work patterns and the kinds of success and failure found in the workplace reappear on the ball field as a replication of the work experience." Steven M. Gelber, "Working at Playing: The Culture of the Workplace and the Rise of Baseball," *Journal of Social History* 16 (summer 1983): 15.

51. E. Anthony Rotundo, *American Manhood: Transformations in Masculinity from the Revolution to the Modern Era* (New York: Basic Books, 1993), 168, 176, 238–251; Peter Filene, *Him/Her/Self: Sex Roles in Modern America* (Baltimore: Johns Hopkins University Press, 1986, 2nd ed.), 70, 72, 138–142; Michael Messner, "The Meaning of Success: The Athletic Experience and the Development of Male Identity," in Harry Brod, ed., *The Making of Masculinities: The New Men's Studies* (Boston: Unwin Hyman, 1987); Elliott J. Gorn, *The Manly Art: Bare-Knuckle Prize Fighting in America* (Ithaca, N.Y.: Cornell University Press, 1986); Mark C. Carnes, *Secret Ritual and Manhood in Victorian America* (New Haven, Conn.: Yale University Press, 1989); Michael C. C. Adams, *The Great Adventure: Male Desire and the Coming of World War I* (Bloomington: Indiana University Press, 1990).

52. See, for instance, Charles Von Belfont, "Bookkeepers Beat Tellers—at Baseball," *News of the Los Angeles First National* 5 (November 1, 1927): 1–3.

53. See: "Tennis," *Union Oil Bulletin* 1 (September 1921): 19; "Fourth Annual Tennis Tournament," *Union Oil Bulletin* 2 (July 1922): 14; and "Tennis Tournament Postponed," *Union Oil Bulletin* 3 (July 1923): 18.

54. "Manufacturers Take Bowling Honors," *Union Oil Bulletin* 6 (February 1927): 19; "Bacon Wins E. W. Clark Cup," *Union Oil Bulletin* 3 (March 1925): 17; "Bowlers Cease Hostilities," *Union Oil Bulletin* 6 (April 1926): 21.

55. "Mount Solomon Golf Club Dance," *Union Oil Bulletin* 3 (November 1923): 19; "Open Brea Golf Course," *Union Oil Bulletin* 3 (April 1923): 17; M. F. Robertson, "Playtime Hours," *Union Oil Bulletin* 4 (November 1924): 6; "Field Men at Play," *Union Oil Bulletin* 4 (June 1924): 21.

56. "Union Oil Company Golf Tournament," *Union Oil Bulletin* 6 (October 1926): 19; "Inter Company Golf Matches," *Union Oil Bulletin* 7 (April 1927): 19.

57. "Tennis Champs" (photo), *Union Oil Bulletin* 1 (November 1021): 17; "Spokane Championship Baseball Team," *Union Oil Bulletin* 8 (September 1928): 19.

58. Kwolek-Folland, *Engendering Business*, 154.

59. Shaw, "The Social Phases of Industrial Recreation," 74.

60. By 1926, sports had become such an intricate part of Union Oil's corporate culture that the company magazine began to feature a separate sports section, containing stories about company athletic events, listings of standings, and photos of winning teams and individuals. "Sports," *Union Oil Bulletin* 6 (December 1926): 19.

61. "Baseball," *Union Oil Bulletin* 1 (July 1921): 17; "Baseball," *Union Oil Bulletin* 1 (August 1921): 10; "Union Oil Baseball Team—Champions Intercity League," *Union*

Oil Bulletin 1 (September 1921): 9; "Lining 'em Out," *Pacific Electric Magazine* 1 (July 10, 1916): 5; "Baseball," *Pacific Electric Magazine* 1 (August 10, 1916): 2; "Pacific Electric Club Baseball Team," *Pacific Electric Magazine* 4 (April 10, 1920): 13; "Pacific Electric Club Baseball Team," *Pacific Electric Magazine* 4 (March 10, 1920): 12; "PE Ball Club Joins League," *Pacific Electric Magazine* 7 (April 10, 1923): 15; Nieter, "Personnel," 2; Moore, *Pacific Mutual*, 171; "Mutual at the Bat," *Pacific Mutual News* 12 (July 1913): 143.

62. "San Francisco Main Station Baseball Team," *Union Oil Bulletin* 1 (May 1921): 22; "San Francisco Industrial League Champions," *Union Oil Bulletin* 6 (August 1926): 21; "Union Wins Industrial Meet," *Union Oil Bulletin* 8 (July 1928): 20; "Petroleum League Basketball," *Union Oil Bulletin* 6 (October 1926): 20.

63. "Health and Recreation Activities," *BLS Bulletin*, 458: 46; Shaw, "Industrial Recreation," 84.

64. J. E. Morris, "Stage All Set for Big Golf Handicap," *News of the Los Angeles First National* 5 (September 1, 1927): 7.

Chapter 8 The White-Collar Depression

Epigraph: D. W. Pontius, "Now Is the Time for Teamwork," 15 (July 10, 1930): 2.

1. Don G. Strebel, letter to Campbell MacCullough, August 29, 1933; and A. O. Tench, letter to Jack Warner, chairman, District Recovery Board, November 1, 1933. Both in National Labor Relations Board (NLRB) collection, National Archives, Pacific Region, Laguna Niguel Office, RG 25, box 13.

2. William Bjerke, letter to Campbell MacCulloch, November 13, 1933; W. S. Briggs, letter to National Recovery Administration, August 22, 1933; W. W. Reidel, letter to Mr. McCullough, August 23, 1933; and M. T. Coogan, letter to George Rogers, August 3, 1933. NLRB collection.

3. Ralph Baker, letter to Jack Warner, Los Angeles National Recovery Administration office, October 18, 1933; "Employment Requests" file, P. M. W. Becker letters; Don G. Strebel, letter to Campbell MacCullough, August 29, 1933; and George Creel, letter to William Bjerke, November 7, 1933. NLRB collection.

4. Unemployment Suffering If Aid Is Not Forthcoming," *Pacific Electric Magazine* 16 (September–October 1931): 6; William H. Mullins, *The Depression and the Urban West Coast, 1929–1933* (Bloomington: Indiana University Press, 1991), 1–5; Richard Lowitt, *The New Deal and the West* (Bloomington: Indiana University Press, 1984), 24; Leonard Leader, *Los Angeles and the Great Depression* (New York: Garland Publishing, 1991), 10–16. Following the Depression's early ferocity in southern California, the region recovered more quickly than most, thanks in part to the film industry's strength, a steadily booming population, and the infusion of federal defense dollars.

5. Jürgen Kocka, *White Collar Workers in America: A Social-Political History in International Perspective* (London: Sage Publications, 1980), 195–196, 200; Mullins, *The Depression*, 54, 91.

6. U.S. Department of Commerce, Bureau of the Census, *Sixteenth Census of*

the United States: Population; Volume III, The Labor Force, Part II (Washington, D.C.: U.S. Government Printing Office, 1943): 244–248; "Commends Bank Staff," *Security-First News Bulletin* 6 (January 17, 1934): 2.

7. "Personnel Plan and Policy Outlined," *Security-First News Bulletin* 3 (January 1, 1931): 6; "Putting It into Practice," *Security-First News Bulletin* 3 (January 21, 1931): 6; "Personnel Department Reports Activities of Past Year," *Security-First News Bulletin* 7 (January 8, 1935): 4.

8. "The Agent's Field of Endeavor," *Pacific Electric Magazine* 15 (October 10, 1930): 10.

9. Emory E. Smith, "An Open Letter—Re: Hard Times," *Southern California Business* 9 (July 1930): 15; Mullins, *The Depression*, 48.

10. "Gain in Employee Activity," *Pacific Electric Magazine* 16 (May–June 1932): 12; "Christmas Greetings," *Pacific Electric Magazine* 17 (December 1936): 2; "Railway Facts That You Should Know," *Pacific Electric Magazine* 17 (December 1936): 6.

11. This cut reflected, in part, new state limits on production. Frank J. Taylor and Earl M. Welty, *Black Bonanza: How an Oil Hunt Grew into the Union Oil Company of California* (New York: McGraw-Hill, 1950), 184–186; "Annual Meeting," *Union Oil Bulletin* 12 (March 1931): 6–7.

12. Earl M. Welty and Frank J. Taylor, *The 76 Bonanza: The Fabulous Life and Times of the Union Oil Company* (Menlo Park: Lane Magazine and Book Company, 1966), 210, 30; Taylor and Welty, *Black Bonanza*, 184–186; "Our First Fifty Years, *Union Oil Bulletin* 20 (fourth quarter 1939): 15; "350,000 Users in 4 Months," *Union Oil Bulletin* 16 (March–April 1935): 19; "Five-Day Week," *Union Oil Bulletin* 12 (April 1931): 4.

13. From *Security-First News Bulletin:* "Unit Consolidation Process Is Continued," 2 (February 1, 1930): 1; "Employees Submit Economy Suggestions," 6 (November 21, 1934): 3; "Competent Staffs," 4 (January 20, 1932): 5; "Clearinghouse of Data on Personnel," 6 (August 1, 1934): 2; "Year of 1934 in the Bank Reviewed by President Wallace," 7 (January 8, 1935): 3; "President Wallace Presents Annual Report for 1936," 9 (January 12, 1937): 3. See annual reports of bank activity presented in January issues of *Security-First News Bulletin*. California banking fared better than most states during the Depression. See Rockwell Hereford, *A Whole Man—Henry Mauris Robinson—and a Half Century—1890–1940* (Pacific Grove, Calif.: Boxwood Press, 1985).

14. William A. Myers, *Iron Men and Copper Wires: A Centennial History of the Southern California Edison Company* (Glendale, Calif.: Trans-Anglo Books, 1983), 166–169; Southern California Edison, *Annual Report to the Stockholders of Southern California Edison Company for the Year 1931* (Los Angeles: Southern California Edison, 1932), 6. For earnings, see the company's annual reports in the collections of the Huntington Library, San Marino, Calif.

15. Myers, *Iron Men and Copper Wires*, 131.

16. *Pacific Mutual News* 30 (January 1931): 49; George Cochran, "A Personal Message from President Cochran," *Pacific Mutual News* 30 (May 1931): 168–169; Earnings statements for Pacific Mutual were printed in the March issue of the *Pacific Mutual News* each year. "The Year's Work," *Pacific Mutual News* 33 (March 1934): 38.

17. Doyce Blackman Nunis, Jr., *Past Is Prologue: A Centennial Profile of Pacific Mutual Life Insurance Company* (Los Angeles: Pacific Mutual Life Insurance, 1968), 42–52.

18. Ibid. See also Pacific Mutual's annual reports.

19. "I Am Going to Fight," *Pacific Mutual News* 29 (February 1930): 65.

20. "We Should All Be Salesmen," *Pacific Mutual News* 30 (January 1931): 18; "The Best Business," *Pacific Mutual News* 31 (May 1932): 194.

21. "Big Tree Club: Can You Afford to Miss Chicago in 1933?" *Pacific Mutual News* 31 (April 1932): 134; *Pacific Mutual News* 31 (April 1932): 135–144.

22. *Pacific Mutual News* 32 (May 1933): 140. See also "Depression Objections and How to Answer Them," *Pacific Mutual News* 31 (March 1932): 94.

23. Untitled article, *Pacific Mutual News* 34 (August 1935): 158.

24. On the issue of the magazine's covers, see "Photographic Covers," *Union Oil Bulletin* 12 (August 1931): 4.

25. *Pacific Electric Magazine* 14 (December 10, 1929): 3, 4, 17; "Register and Vote," *Pacific Electric Magazine* 14 (April 10, 1930): 2. In other issues of *Pacific Electric Magazine,* see: entire issue of September 10, 1930; "How to Gain More Business," 16 (July–August 10, 1931): 2; "Gains in Employee Activity," 16 (May–June 10, 1932): 12; "Value of Good Will," 17 (August 1936): 2; "Our Parent Company Thanks Us," 17 (July 1936): 4; "Sales Means Jobs" and "Campaign for Business," 19 (October 1938): 2; and "Municipal Busses or Not?" 18 (April 1937): 3.

26. Southern California Edison, *Annual Report to the Stockholders of Southern California Edison Company for the Year 1933* (Los Angeles: Southern California Edison, 1934).

27. "Clothes Make the Man," *Union Oil Bulletin* 19 (January 1937): 19.

28. George Hanna and Edward Warren, letter to John McPeak, printed in *Union Oil Bulletin* 12 (October 1931): 3; John Riegle, letter to Ralph Rosborough, superintendent, Union Oil Company, *Union Oil Bulletin* 19 (January 1937): 22; "Employees Over-Subscribe Community Chest," *Union Oil Bulletin* 16 (January 1935): 6.

29. "Not for Me, Thanks!," *Union Oil Bulletin* 19 (January 1938): 21.

30. Personnel Plan and Policy Outlined," *Security-First News Bulletin* 3 (January 1, 1931): 6; "Loyalty," *Security-First News Bulletin* 4 (May 1, 1932): 2; *Security-First News Bulletin* 8 (May 20, 1936): 2; "Factors of Success," 5 (May 15, 1933): 2.

31. "Individual Prize Winners Announced," *Security-First News Bulletin* 5 (December 15, 1933): 1; "Trust Deed Measure Defeated by a Margin of Nearly a Million Votes," *Security-First News Bulletin* 4 (November 15, 1932): 1; "Proposition 20—The Single Tax," *Security-First News Bulletin* 10 (September 21, 1938): 1; "Register Now," *Security-First News Bulletin* 11 (July 1, 1939): 1.

32. Untitled editorial, *Union Oil Bulletin* 19 (October 1937): 13.

33. *Alice Adams,* RKO Radio Pictures, 1935.

34. Kocka, *White Collar Workers,* 194. U.S. Department of Commerce, Bureau of the Census, *Historical Statistics of the United States: Volume 1* (Washington, D.C.,: U.S. Government Printing Office, 1975), table E, 40–51, 200.

35. "Staff Will Receive Increase in Salary," *Security-First News Bulletin* 5 (August 1, 1933); "Eleventh Anniversary of the Security-First National Merger," *Security-First News Bulletin* 12 (April 1940): 1, 4; "Year 1934 in the Bank Reviewed by President Wallace," *Security-First News Bulletin* 7 (January 8, 1935): 3; Southern California Edison, *Annual Report for 1931*, 6; Southern California Edison, *Annual Report to the Stockholders of Southern California Edison Company for the Year 1937* (Los Angeles: Southern California Edison, 1938), 3.

36. "Staff May Purchase Stock on Terms," *Security-First News Bulletin* 3 (April 1, 1931): 1; "Year of 1934 in the Bank Reviewed by President Wallace," *Security-First News Bulletin* 7 (January 8, 1935): 3.

37. "Group Life Insurance," *Security-First News Bulletin* 9 (January 12, 1937): 2; "Christmas Bonus Voted by Directors," *Security-First News Bulletin* 10 (November 21, 1939): 1; Southern California Edison, *Annual Report to the Stockholders of Southern California Edison Company for the Year 1939* (Los Angeles: Southern California Edison, 1940), 15.

38. Sanford Jacoby, *Modern Manors: Welfare Capitalism since the New Deal* (Princeton, N.J.: Princeton University Press, 1997), 31–34; "Savings and Pension Plan Announced," *Security-First News Bulletin* 2 (April 15, 1930): 1; "Savings and Pension Plan Clarified," *Security-First News Bulletin* 2 (June 15, 1930): 1.

39. "The Employees' Benefit Fund," *Union Oil Bulletin* 12 (January 1931): 11–12; "Group Insurance Benefits Increased," *Union Oil Bulletin* 12 (September 12, 1931): 1; "Employees' Benefit Plan," *Union Oil Bulletin* 16 (September–October 1935): 5; "Employees' Benefit Plan," *Union Oil Bulletin* 17 (March–April 1936): 6.

40. "Provident Fund Loans," *Union Oil Bulletin* 15 (October 1934): 1–2; "A New Retirement Plan for Employees," *Union Oil Bulletin* 21 (first quarter 1940): 4; Southern California Edison, *Annual Report to the Stockholders of Southern Califronia Edison Company for the Year 1934* (Los Angeles: Southern California Edison, 1935), 18.

41. "Largest Year's Insurance Paid," *Pacific Electric Magazine* 14 (February 10, 1930): 10; "Revise Group Insurance," *Pacific Electric Magazine* 16 (November-December 1931): 6; "Medical Department Offers Latest and Best," *Pacific Electric Magazine* 17 (August 1936): 3; "Membership Campaign," *Pacific Electric Magazine* 18 (March 1937): 2.

42. "Prospective Change in Gratuity Payments," *Pacific Electric Magazine* 18 (June 1937): 2; "New Governmental R.R. Retirement Plan Is Now in Effect," *Pacific Electric Magazine* 18 (July 1937): 3; "Company's Pension Plan Is Announced," *Pacific Electric Magazine* 18 (September 1937): 4.

43. "Credit Union Movement in the Union Oil Company," *Union Oil Bulletin* 17 (September–October 1936): 5–7.

44. "Vacations," *Security-First News Bulletin* 3 (February 15, 1931): 6; "Extra Vacation for Forty-Two," *Security-First News Bulletin* 11 (February 1939): 1.

45. "Savings for Employees in Auto Insurance," *Pacific Electric Magazine* 14 (January 10, 1930).

46. Ibid. See, for instance, advertisements in the following issues of *Pacific Electric Magazine*: 16 (May–June 1932); 18 (March 10, 1938).

47. *If I Had a Million*, Paramount Pictures, 1932.

48. *Alice Adams*, RKO Radio Pictures, 1935.

49. "Promotions," *Security-First News Bulletin* 4 (December 1, 1932): 2.

50. "Our Two Ranking Executives Advanced to Higher Posts," *Pacific Electric Magazine* 18 (April 1937): 3–4; "More Municipal Busses or Not," *Pacific Electric Magazine* 18 (April 1937): 3.

51. "Changes in Personnel," *Union Oil Bulletin* 21 (first quarter 1940): 5.

52. "Commends Bank Staff," *Security-First News Bulletin* 6 (January 17, 1934): 2; "Putting It into Practice," *Security-First News Bulletin* 3 (January 21, 1931): 6; "Praises Personnel," *Security-First National Bank* 5 (January 18, 1933): 1.

53. "The Career Man," *Security-First News Bulletin* 9 (March 18, 1937): 2.

54. "New Appointments and Promotions," *Pacific Mutual News* 29 (March 1930): 365; *Pacific Mutual News* 35 (March 1936): 70–71.

55. See Alice Kessler-Harris, "Gender Ideology in Historical Reconstruction: A Case Study from the 1930s," *Gender and History* 1 (spring 1989): 31–44.

56. "Women Forced into Employment by Increased Responsibilities," *Pacific Mutual News* 29 (March 1930): 95. Most insurance companies had gradually developed women's departments between the 1890s and the 1920s but often limited or closed them in the early years of the Depression. Sharon Hartman Strom, *Beyond the Typewriter: Gender, Class, and the Origins of Modern American Office Work, 1900–1930* (Urbana: University of Illinois Press, 1992), 93–94; Angel Kwolek-Folland, *Engendering Business: Men and Women in the Corporate Office, 1870–1930* (Baltimore: Johns Hopkins University Press, 1994), 172.

57. "Decide to Forego Annual Employees' Picnic," *Pacific Electric Magazine* 15 (July 10, 1930): 4.

58. For an illustration of such banquets, see "An All-Pacific Mutual Evening," *Pacific Mutual Field News* 1 (October 1937): 267.

59. "Operating Department Barbecue and Picnic," *Union Oil Bulletin* 16 (November–December 1935): 11–15.

60. "Holiday Spirit Reigns at Yule Affairs," *Security-First News Bulletin* 4 (January 1, 1932): 3.

61. "Bowling News," *Pacific Electric Magazine* (March–April, 1932): 10.

62. "Comptroller's Golf Tournament," *Union Oil Bulletin* 19 (March 1938): 22–23.

63. "How Do You Like the News Bulletin?" *Security-First News Bulletin* 4 (January 15, 1932): 2.

64. "Sundry and Personal," *Pacific Mutual News* 30 (May 1931): 214; Thelma Meighan, "News of the P.E. Family," *Pacific Electric Magazine* 16 (September–October 1931): 20.

65. Harry Carr, *Los Angeles: City of Dreams* (New York: D. Appleton-Century, 1935).

Conclusion

Epigraph: "Loyal Service," *Union Oil Bulletin* 7 (October 1927): 1.

1. George H. Stewart, "For You and You and You," manuscript copy of commencement address delivered at the Commercial Department of the Los Angeles High School, June 1900. George H. Stewart collection, USC Regional History Center.

2. Ibid.

3. Jackson A. Graves, *California Memories, 1857–1930* (Los Angeles: Times-Mirror Press, 1930), 6.

4. Oral history of Warren E. Griffith, interviewed by Beverly E. Schmidt, April 5 and 25, 1968, May 2, 1968, California State University, Fullerton, Oral History Program, O.H. 31.

5. From *Pacific Electric Magazine:* "Our Summer Vacation Home in the Mountains," 2 (June 10, 1917): 9–10; "Vacation Camp Closed for the Season," 2 (October 10, 1917): 1; "Alluring Vacation Camp Awaits Employees," 7 (June 10, 1923): 3–6; "Many Improvements to Greet Camp Visitors," 9 (June 10, 1924): 3–4; "June Camp Attendance Largest Yet Recorded," 11 (July 10, 1926): 12; "Camp Reservations Insure Banner Season," 13 (June 10, 1928): 3–4.

6. "Loyalty and Happiness," *Security-First News Bulletin* 10 (May 18, 1938): 2.

7. This story told to SCE corporate historian William Myers. Oral history of Tom Hotchkiss, taken January 23, 1994, private collection.

ESSAY ON SOURCES

I am grateful for the existence of rich sources and scholarship in business, labor, social, and cultural history. The following essay is not exhaustive but does outline some of the materials I found most helpful in understanding white-collar and middle-class experience, corporate formation, and the history of southern California.

Primary Sources and Period Publications

The Huntington Library in San Marino, California, is the most important site for scholars of corporate Los Angeles. Its holdings thoroughly cover the region's late-nineteenth and early-twentieth-century social and economic history. The library serves as the de facto corporate archives for the Pacific Electric Railway, the Los Angeles Railway, and the Pacific Mail Steamship Company, and contains extensive ephemeral materials for all the major firms in this study. Outside the Huntington, numerous sites hold local corporate archives. Pacific Mutual Life Insurance Company and Southern California Edison both provide historians limited access to public historical materials at their corporate archives in Newport Beach and Rosemead, California, respectively. Bank of America's corporate archives in San Francisco houses employee magazines and records from the Los Angeles First National Bank and the Security-First National Bank of Los Angeles. The H. A. Burgess Collection at the Regional History Center of the University of Southern California (USC) has records from the Western Air Express Company. The Long Beach Public Library houses a local petroleum industry history collection. Biola University in La Mirada, California, keeps the papers of Union Oil founder and early president, Lyman Stewart; and the Department of Special Collections at the University of California, Los Angeles, has some collections of ephemera from regional corporations, particularly Union Oil.

Company magazines used in this study include: *Conservative News, Edison Current Topics, Edison Energy, Edison Facts, News of the Los Angeles First National, Pacific Electric Magazine, P. G. and E. Progress, Pacific Mutual News, Security-First National News Bulletin, Southern California Trolley, The Central Station, The Pacific Southwest, Two Bells*, and the *Union Oil Bulletin*.

The Los Angeles Chamber of Commerce Collection at USC's Regional History

Center is one of the best sources for tracking the area's economic growth as well as its business boosterism. Of particular value are the Chamber's monthly magazine, *Southern California Business*, and its yearly, *Members' Annual*. The annual proceedings from the California Bankers Association, as well as its monthly *Coast Banker*, provide rich insights into banking employment and history. Important business memoirs and histories from the period include: H. James Boswell, editor, *Men of Achievement* (Los Angeles: 1930); Robert Glass Cleland, *March of Industry* (Los Angeles: Powell Publishing, 1929); Ira B. Cross, *Financing an Empire: History of Banking in California* (Los Angeles: S. J. Clarke Publishing, 1927); J. R. Douglas, *The Bank and the Community: A History of the Security Trust and Savings Bank* (Los Angeles: Security Trust and Savings Bank, 1929); *Facts about Industrial Los Angeles: Nature's Workshop* (Los Angeles: Los Angeles Chamber of Commerce, 1922); Laurance L. Hill, *La Reina: Los Angeles in Three Centuries* (Los Angeles: Security Trust and Savings Bank, 1929); Marrow Mayo, *Los Angeles* (New York: Alfred A. Knopf, 1932); John Russell McCarthy, *Joseph Francis Sartori, 1856–1946* (Los Angeles: Ward Ritchie Press, 1948); *Fifty Years of Banking Service under Conservative Management: Farmers and Merchants National Bank of Los Angeles* (Los Angeles: Farmers and Merchants National Bank, 1921); J. Henry Wood, *Banks and Bankers in Southern California* (Pasadena, Calif.: 1908); *Milestones in History: The Citizens National Bank of Los Angeles* (Los Angeles: Citizens National Bank, 1915).

Governmental and private agencies devoted considerable effort in the 1910s and 1920s to studying personnel relations. These surveys offer extensive statistical evidence about specific programs and packages, as well as much qualitative discussion and analysis. Of particular value are *Employee Magazines in the United States* (New York: National Industrial Conference Board, 1925); *Practical Experience with Profit Sharing in Industrial Establishments: Research Report Number 29* (Boston: National Industrial Conference Board, 1920); *Employee Stock Purchase Plans in the United States* (New York: National Industrial Conference Board, 1928); *Industrial Pensions in the United States* (New York: National Industrial Conference Board, 1925); *Elements of Industrial Pension Plans* (New York: National Industrial Conference Board, 1931); "Employers' Welfare Work," *U.S. Bureau of Labor Statistics Bulletin* #123 (1913); "Welfare Work for Employees in Industrial Establishments in the United States," *U.S. Bureau of Labor Statistics Bulletin* #250 (1919); "Health and Recreation Activities in Industrial Establishments," *U.S. Bureau of Labor Statistics Bulletin* #458, (Washington, D.C..: U.S. Government Printing Office, 1926); and *Clerical Salaries in the United States, 1926* (New York: National Industrial Conference Board, 1926). Other useful studies include Herbert Feis, *Labor Relations: A Study Made in the Procter and Gamble Company* (New York: Adelphi Company Publishers, 1928); John William Shaw, "The Social Phases of Industrial Recreation as They Affect Employer-Employee Relations in the Los Angeles Area" (Ph.D. diss., University of Southern California, 1948); Jack Petrill, *After the Whistle Blows: A Guide to the Field of Recreation in Industry* (New York: William Frederick Press, 1949); Lois Meyer Ritchie, "Social Status of Department Store Salespersons among Certain Groups in Los Angeles" (master's thesis, University of Southern California, 1932); and Margaret Macgowan, "An Investigation of Factors Influencing Choice of Occupation as Revealed in Ninety-five Selected Biographies and Autobiographies of Americans Published 1925 to 1930" (master's thesis, University of Southern California, 1934).

For examples of early-twentieth-century management texts, see Joseph French Johnson et al., *Modern Business, Volume 1: Business and The Man* (New York: Alexander Hamilton Institute, 1917); idem, *Modern Business, Volume 19: Office Management* (New York: Alexander Hamilton Institute, 1919); and S. M. Kennedy, *Winning the Public* (New York: McGraw-Hill, 1921). Typical career guidance texts for young adults include Franklin Stewart Harris, *The Young Man and his Vocation* (Boston: Richard G. Badger, 1916); William Rosengarten, *Choosing Your Life Work* (New York: McGraw-Hill, 1922); Harry Dexter Kitson, *I Find My Vocation* (New York: McGraw-Hill, 1931); J. J. Davis and J. C. Wright, *You and Your Job* (New York: John Wiley and Sons, 1930); C. M. Ernst and T. M. White, *Opportunities Ahead* (New York: D. Appleton, 1929).

The rich oral history collections at the Pasadena Public Library, the Ventura County Historical Society, the San Diego Historical Society, and California State University at Fullerton's Oral History Program all house personal reflections on corporate experience. Helpful manuscript collections include those of James Crank, Thomas Bard, Donald Marr Nelson, Jackson A. Graves, George C. Ward, and William Spalding at the Huntington Library, and the George Stewart Scrapbook at USC's Regional History Center. Related memoirs include Jackson S. Graves's, *California Memories, 1857–1930* (Los Angeles: Times-Mirror Press, 1930), as well as his *My Seventy Years in California* (Los Angeles: Times-Mirror Press, 1927); Harris Newmark, *Sixty Years in Southern California, 1853–1913* (New York: Houghton Mifflin, 1930); Mary Logan Orcutt, editor, *Memorabilia of William Warren Orcutt, 1869–1942* (Los Angeles: Fred S. Lang Press, 1945); William Russel Swigart, *Biography of Spring Street in Los Angeles* (Los Angeles: Parker and Company, 1945); and Louis Adamic, *The Truth About Los Angeles* (Girard, Kans.: Haldeman-Julius Publications, 1927). The Huntington's Scrapbook Collection is a particularly rich source for early-twentieth-century southern Californiana, housing numerous volumes on local personalities and institutions. The National Labor Relations Board collection at the National Archives, Pacific Region, Laguna Niguel Office, includes records from the state's National Recovery Association office and many letters from white-collar men discussing their career plight.

Early-twentieth-century popular periodicals from Los Angeles and elsewhere in the west illuminate the middle-class culture of the region; they include *Out West*, *Los Angeles Life*, *The American Globe*, *The Graphic*, *Saturday Night*, and *Sunset*. *The Atlantic Monthly* and *Century Magazine* provide a national vantage point. The *Los Angeles Times*, the *Los Angeles Examiner*, the *Los Angeles Evening Herald and Express*, and the *Los Angeles Record* are among the significant local newspapers. Robert S. Lynd's and Helen Lynd's *Middletown: A Study in Contemporary American Culture* (New York: Harcourt, Brace, 1929) and Frederick Lewis Allen's *Only Yesterday: An Informal History of the 1920s* (New York: Harper and Row, 1931) provide classic social portraits of middle-class experience. Numerous popular novels from the era explore business and white-collar life, including those of Theodore Dreiser and William Dean Howells. A lesser-known but important example of this genre is Kester Vaughn, *The Manager of the B&A: A Story of Modern American Life* (New York: Harper and Brothers, 1901). Among the many key cinematic portrayals of white-collar experience are King Vidor's *The Crowd* (MGM, 1928); *Safety Last* (Hal Roach, 1923); *Alice Adams* (RKO Radio Pictures, 1935); and *If I Had a Million* (Paramount Pictures, 1932).

The federal census samples used in this book come from Steven Ruggles and Matthew Sobek's *Integrated Public Use Microdata Series: Version 1.0* (Minneapolis: Social History Research Laboratory, University of Minnesota, 1995). The sample of 1917 draft registrants derives from data obtained at the Atlanta Branch of the National Archives by Douglas Flamming.

Secondary Sources

Just as innumerable forces and factors shaped the rise of corporate capitalism in the United States, big business growth transformed virtually every segment of American life. Not surprisingly, there exists a vast scholarly literature analyzing these processes. Rich historiographies on American business and labor, as well as excellent scholarship on middle-class formation and culture, "whiteness," masculinity, and southern California provide a broad basis for studying white-collar male experience and the building of corporate cultures in Los Angeles.

For a general introduction to the rise of big business, see Glenn Porter, *The Rise of Big Business, 1868–1910* (New York: Thomas Y. Crowell Company, 1973); Naomi Lamoreaux, *The Great Merger Movement in American History, 1895–1904* (New York: Cambridge University Press, 1984); James Oliver Robinson, *America's Business* (New York: Hill and Wang, 1985); Alfred D. Chandler, Jr., *Scale and Scope: The Dynamics of Industrial Capitalism* (Cambridge: Harvard University Press, 1990); idem, *Strategy and Structure: Chapters in the History of the American Enterprise* (Cambridge: Massachusetts Institute of Technology Press, 1963); and Alfred D. Chandler, Jr., and Louis Galambos, "The Development of Large-Scale Economic Organizations in Modern America," *Journal of Economic History* 30 (1970): 201–217. Louis Galambos charts public interaction with corporate emergence in *The Public Image of Big Business in America, 1880–1940: A Quantitative Study in Social Change* (Baltimore: Johns Hopkins University Press, 1975).

Alfred D. Chandler, Jr.'s *The Visible Hand: The Managerial Revolution in American Business* (Cambridge: Harvard University Press, 1977) has become the starting point for studies of American management. Richard R. John discusses its significance in shaping subsequent scholarship in "Elaborations, Revisions, Dissents: Alfred D. Chandler, Jr.'s *The Visible Hand* After Twenty Years," *Business History Review* 71 (summer 1997): 151–206. While Chandler presents an approach to corporate formation that is driven by technology and modernization, William G. Roy's *Socializing Capital: The Rise of the Large Industrial Corporation in America* (Princeton, N.J.: Princeton University Press, 1997) seeks to "de-naturalize" big business formation by emphasizing the social and political pressures that led to American corporate structures and strategies. Sanford M. Jacoby's *Employing Bureaucracy; Managers, Unions, and the Transformation of Work in American Industry, 1900–1945* (New York: Columbia University Press, 1985); Walter Licht's *Working for the Railroad: The Organization of Work in the Nineteenth Century* (Princeton, N.J.: Princeton University Press, 1983); and Daniel Nelson's *Workers and Managers: Origins of the New Factory System in the United States, 1880–1920* (Madison: University of Wisconsin Press, 1975) explore and underscore the significance of personnel and labor management to business growth. Sharon Hartman Strom's *Beyond the Typewriter: Gender, Class, and the Origins of Modern Office Work, 1900–1930* (Urbana: University of Illinois Press, 1992) presents a rich exploration of the rise of scientific and personnel management in the white-collar workplace. Dan Clawson's *Bureaucracy and the Labor Process: The Transformation of U.S. Industry, 1860–1920* (New York: Monthly Review Press, 1980) and Richard Edwards's *Contested Terrain: The Transformation of the Workplace in the Twentieth Century* (New York: Basic Books, 1979) present illustrative workplace perspectives on economic bureaucratization. John T. Landry's "Corporate Incentives for Managers in American Industry, 1900–1940" (Ph.D. diss., Brown University, 1995) focuses on business efforts to cultivate effective and loyal personnel in the upper ranks, while Daniel Wren's *The Evolution of Management Thought* (New York: John Wiley and Sons, 1987, 3rd ed., 1987) offers a broad survey of management history. For a valuable anthology on the subject, see Sanford Jacoby, editor, *Masters to Managers: Historical and Comparative Perspectives on American Employers* (New York: Columbia University Press, 1991). On the growing importance of internal communication networks to corporate growth, consult Joanne Yates, *Control through Communication: The Rise of System in American Management* (Baltimore: Johns Hopkins University Press, 1989).

Recent histories of corporate America have increasingly focused on the ways in which social and cultural contexts shape business growth. Thomas C. Cochran's *Business in American Life: A History* (New York: McGraw-Hill, 1972) and *Challenges to American Values: Society, Business, and Religion* (New York: Oxford University Press, 1985) foreshadowed the emerging synthesis of social and business history. Walter Licht's excellent *Industrializing America: The Nineteenth Century* (Baltimore: Johns Hopkins University Press, 1995) offers a rich survey of the social, cultural, political, and economic dimensions of nineteenth-century industrial development. Olivier Zunz's *Making America Corporate, 1870–1920* (Chicago: University of Chicago Press, 1990) presents a compelling exploration of the interplay between structural and technological pressures towards corporate formation, prevailing cultural attitudes, and the personal expressions of individuals involved in the process. Zunz argues that middle-level managers played key roles in designing the structures and cultures of corporate capitalism. His work on the social and cultural contexts of business growth highlights a wave of research on the concept of "corporate culture." Key works on individual firms or industries include Charles Delheim's "The Creation of a Company Culture: Cadbury's, 1861–1931," *American Historical Review* (February 1987): 13–44; Alan R. Raucher, "Dime Store Chains: The Making of Organization Men, 1880–1940," *Busi-*

ness History Review 65 (spring 1991): 130–63; Roland Marchand, "The Corporation Nobody Knew: Bruce Barton, Alfred Sloan, and the Founding of the General Motors 'Family,'" *Business History Review* 65 (winter 1991): 825–75; David E. Nye, *Image Worlds: Corporate Identities at General Electric, 1890–1930* (Cambridge: Massachusetts Institute of Technology Press, 1985); and Terrence E. Deal and Allan A. Kennedy, *Corporate Cultures: The Rites and Rituals of Corporate Capitalism* (Reading, Mass.: Addison-Wesley, 1982). For an excellent analysis of the implication of cultural studies for business history, see Kenneth Lipartito, "Culture and the Practice of Business History," *Business History Review* 24 (summer 1995): 1–41.

Many scholars have positioned gender as one of the primary dynamics shaping personnel relations and corporate cultures. No study makes this point more persuasively than Angel Kwolek-Folland's *Engendering Business: Men and Women in the Corporate Office, 1870–1930* (Baltimore: Johns Hopkins University Press, 1994), which explores how gender shaped the structure and experience of office work in the financial industry, specifically in several major eastern and southern insurance companies. Kwolek-Folland's extensive research shows how gender fundamentally influenced job descriptions, managerial strategies, office interactions and relationships, and corporate architecture in this sector. Susan Porter Benson, *Counter Cultures: Saleswomen, Managers, and Customers in American Department Stores, 1890–1940* (Urbana: University of Illinois Press, 1986); Wayne A. Lewchuk, "Men and Monotony: Fraternalism as a Managerial Strategy at the Ford Motor Company," *Journal of Economic History* 53 (December 1993): 824–856; and Lisa M. Fine, "One Big Factory Family: Masculinity and Paternalism at the Reo Motor Car Company of Lansing, Michigan," *Labor History* 34 (spring/summer 1993): 274–91, similarly reveal how gender relations shaped managerial designs. A valuable guide to gender's centrality in labor relations is Ava Barron, editor, *Work Engendered: Toward a New History of American Labor* (Ithaca, N.Y.: Cornell University Press, 1991).

An interest in women's history and gender relations has sparked much scholarship on clerical workers, including not only Kwolek-Folland's *Engendering Business*, but also Margery Davies, *Woman's Place is at the Typewriter: Office Work and Office Workers, 1870–1930* (Philadelphia: Temple University Press, 1982); Lisa Fine, *The Souls of the Skyscraper: Female Clerical Workers in Chicago, 1870–1930* (Philadelphia: Temple University Press, 1990); Carole Srole, "'A Position that God has not Particularly Assigned To Men': The Feminization of Clerical Work, Boston, 1860–1915" (Ph.D. diss., University of California at Los Angeles, 1984); and Mary Christine Anderson, "Gender, Class, and Culture: Women Secretarial and Clerical Workers in the United States, 1925–1955" (Ph.D. diss., Ohio State University, 1986); and Strom, *Beyond the Typewriter.*

Jürgen Kocka's *White Collar Workers in America, 1890–1940: A Social Political History in International Perspective* (Beverly Hills, Calif.: Sage Publications, 1980) provides the broadest history of white-collar employees, and one of the few with significant attention to male workers. Ileen A. DeVault's excellent *Sons and Daughters of Labor: Class and Clerical Work in Turn-of-the Century Pittsburgh* (Ithaca, N.Y.: Cornell

University Press, 1990) looks at both male and female workers in the clerical ranks and evidences a keen sensitivity to the importance of place in economic relations. Cindy Sondik Aron's *Ladies and Gentleman of the Civil Service; Middle-Class Workers in Victorian America* (New York: Oxford University Press, 1987) offers a valuable portrait of white-collar life in a very early time period and in the public sector. C. Wright Mills, *White Collar: The American Middle Classes* (New York: Oxford University Press, 1956) provides an important complement to the available historical literature on white-collar workers.

In comparison to the relatively small body of studies of white-collar employees that they have produced, labor historians have probed the experience of blue-collar workers in considerable detail. Some of the most notable studies with rich implications for any historian interested in American business or labor relations include Douglas Flamming, *Creating the Modern South: Millhands and Managers in Dalton, Georgia, 1884–1984* (Chapel Hill: University of North Carolina Press, 1992); Lizbeth Cohen, *Making a New Deal: Industrial Workers in Chicago, 1919–1939* (New York: Cambridge University Press, 1990); and David Montgomery, *The Fall of the House of Labor: The Workplace, the State, and American Labor Activism, 1865–1925* (New York: Cambridge University Press, 1987).

The issue of "welfare capitalism" or "corporate paternalism" has been a major focus of labor and industrial history, and the literature on these topics offers valuable insights for understanding white-collar employment as well. Stuart Brandes, in *American Welfare Capitalism, 1880–1940* (Chicago: University of Chicago Press, 1970), provides a solid, descriptive history of business programs, while Andrea Tone presents a newer perspective in *The Business of Benevolence: Industrial Paternalism in the Progressive Era* (Ithaca, N.Y.: Cornell University Press, 1997), which emphasizes the role of gender and political pressures in stimulating welfare capitalism. Sanford Jacoby's *Modern Manors: Welfare Capitalism since the New Deal* (Princeton: Princeton University Press, 1997) carries the study of welfare capitalism through the twentieth century. Helpful studies of welfare capitalism in specific firms include Stephen Meyer III, *The Five Dollar Day: Labor Management and Social Control in the Ford Motor Company, 1908–1921* (Albany: State University of New York Press, 1981) and Gerald Zahavi, *Workers, Managers, and Welfare Capitalism; The Shoeworkers and Tanners of Endicott Johnson, 1890–1950* (Urbana: University of Illinois Press, 1988). David Vrooman emphasizes the power that individual leaders exercised over labor relations in *Daniel Willard and the Progressive Management on the Baltimore and Ohio Railroad* (Columbus: Ohio State University Press, 1991). For other sources useful in creating a background and critique of the welfare capitalism paradigm, see Bruce E. Kaufman, *The Origins and Evolution of the Field of Industrial Relations in the United States: Cornell Studies in Industrial and Labor Relations Number 25* (Ithaca, N.Y.: ILR Press, 1993) and H. M. Gitelman, "Welfare Capitalism Reconsidered," *Labor History* 33 (winter 1992): 5–31.

According to many scholars, personnel relations and other aspects of business life became avenues through which firms legitimized corporate power. Studies of "corporate liberalism" include Jeffrey R. Lustig, *Corporate Liberalism: The Origins of Modern American Political Theory, 1890–1920* (Berkeley: University of California Press, 1982); Neil J. Mitchell, *The Generous Corporation: A Political Analysis of Economic Power* (New Haven, Conn.: Yale University Press, 1989); James Livingston, *Origins of the Federal Reserve System: Money, Class, and Corporate Capitalism: 1890–1913* (Ithaca, N.Y.: Cornell University Press, 1986); James Weinstein, *The Corporate Ideal in the Liberal State: 1900–1918* (Boston: Beacon Press, 1968); Ellis Hawley, "The Discovery and Study of Corporate Liberalism," *Business History Review* 52 (autumn 1978): 314; and Kim McQuaid, "Corporate Liberalism in the American Business Community, 1920–1940," *Business History Review* 52 (autumn 1978): 342–368.

Other historians have argued more broadly for the connection between political and business history, notably Martin J. Sklar, *The Corporate Reconstruction of American Capitalism, 1890–1916: The Market, The Law, and Politics* (New York: Cambridge University Press, 1988); Licht, *Industrializing America;* James Livingston, *Origins of the Federal Reserve System;* Neil Fligstein, *The Transformation of Corporate Control* (Cambridge: Harvard University Press, 1990); Gerald Berk, *Alternative Tracks: The Constitution of American Industrial Order, 1865–1917* (Baltimore: Johns Hopkins University Press, 1994); Gabriel Kolko, *The Triumph of Conservatism: A Reinterpretation of American History, 1900–1916* (New York: Free Press, 1963); as well as Louis Galambos and Joseph Pratt, *The Rise of the Corporate Commonwealth: U.S. Business and Public Policy in the Twentieth Century* (New York: Basic Books, 1988).

This study benefits from the writings of many historians who have researched particular business sectors and industries. Several studies, for instance, survey the insurance industry's history; they include Viviana A. Rotman Zeilizer, *Morals and Markets: The Development of Life Insurance in the United States* (New Brunswick, N.J.: Transaction Books, 1983) and Morton Keller, *The Life Insurance Enterprise, 1885–1910: A Study in the Limits of Corporate Power* (Cambridge: Harvard University Press, 1963). Two significant histories of the Pacific Mutual Life Insurance Company exist: C. I. D. Moore, *The Pacific Mutual Life Insurance Company of California: A History of the Company and the Development of its Organization, the Sixtieth Anniversary, 1928–1969* (Los Angeles: Pacific Mutual Life Insurance, 1928) and Doyce B. Nunis, Jr., *Past Is Prologue: A Centennial Profile of the Pacific Mutual Life Insurance Company* (Los Angeles: Pacific Mutual Life Insurance, 1969).

Benjamin J. Klebaner provides a general study of banking in *American Commercial Banking: A History* (Boston: Twayne Publishers, 1990). On banking in California, consult Lynne Pierson Doti and Larry Schweikart, *Banking in the American West: From the Gold Rush to Deregulation* (Norman: University of Oklahoma Press, 1991); Rockwell Hereford, *A Whole Man and a Half Century: Henry Mauris Robinson, 1890–1940* (Pacific Grove, Calif.: Boxwood Press, 1985); and Gerald D. Nash, *A. P. Giannini and the Bank of America* (Norman: University of Oklahoma Press, 1992).

For the electric utility industry see David E. Nye, *Electrifying America: Social Meanings of a New Technology, 1880–1940* (Cambridge: Massachusetts Institute of Technology Press, 1990); Harold L. Platt, *The Electric City: Energy and the Growth of the Chicago Area, 1880–1930* (Chicago: University of Chicago Press, 1991); and Richard F. Hirsch, *Technology and Transformation in the American Electric Utility Industry* (New York: Cambridge University Press, 1989). The best history of Southern California Edison is William A. Myers, *Iron Men and Copper Wires: A Centennial History of the Southern California Edison Company* (Glendale, Calif.: Trans-Anglo Books, 1983). William Charles Jones presents further data in "The Corporate Evolution of the Southern California Edison Company and Its Financial History from 1909–1928" (master's thesis, University of Southern California, 1929).

Robert O. Anderson, *Fundamentals of the Petroleum Industry* (Norman: University of Oklahoma Press, 1984) provides a general history of the oil industry. On the oil sector in California, see Walker A. Tompkins, *Little Giant of Signal Hill: An Adventure in American Enterprise* (Englewood Cliffs, N.J.: Prentice-Hall, 1964) and William Rintoul, *Spudding In: Recollections of Pioneer Days in the California Oil Fields* (San Francisco: California Historical Society, 1976). Union Oil histories include Fred L. Hartley, *The Spirit of 76: The Story of the Union Oil Company of California* (New York: Newcomen Society in North America, 1977); Earl M. Welty and Frank J. Taylor, *Black Bonanza: How an Oil Hunt Grew into the Union Oil Company of California* (New York: Whittlesey House, 1950); idem, *The 76 Bonanza: The Fabulous Life and Times of the Union Oil Company* (Menlo Park, Calif.: Lane Magazine and Book Company, 1966).

On electric railways, consult George H. Hilton and John F. Due, *The Electric Interurban Railways in America* (Stanford, Calif.: Stanford University Press, 1960) and Thomas H. Shanks, *From Horse Car to Red Car to Mass Rapid Transit: A Century of Progress* (Virginia Beach, Va.: Donning Company, 1991). Histories of Pacific Electric include Glen Dumke, "The Growth of the Pacific Electric and Its Influence upon the Development of Southern California to 1911" (master's thesis, Occidental College, 1911) and Spencer Crump, *Ride the Big Red Cars* (Corona del Mar, Calif.: Trans-Anglo Books, 1977).

Robert Fogelson's *The Fragmented Metropolis: Los Angeles, 1850–1930* (Cambridge: Harvard University Press, 1967) remains one of the most important historical and demographic portraits of Los Angeles in the early twentieth century. Kevin Starr's multivolume study of California contains rich descriptions of Los Angeles and valuable source material. See particularly the volumes entitled *Material Dreams: Southern California through the 1920s* (New York: Oxford University Press, 1990) and *Endangered Dreams: The Great Depression in California* (1996). Other essential studies of Los Angeles include Lynn Bowman, *Los Angeles: Epic of a City* (Berkeley, Calif.: Howell North Books, 1974); Mike Davis, *City of Quartz: Excavating the Future in Los Angeles* (New York: Verso, 1990); and Carey McWilliams, *Southern California: An Island on the Land* (1946; reprint, Salt Lake City, Utah: Peregrine Smith Books, 1990).

No one has yet published a comprehensive business and economic history of Los Angeles. An invaluable source on the topic for the 1920s is James Clifford Findley's, "The Economic Boom of the Twenties in Los Angeles" (Ph.D. diss., Claremont Graduate School, 1958). Important studies that include discussions of specific economic sectors, industries, or business issues include: William B. Friedricks, *Henry E. Huntington and the Creation of Southern California* (Columbus: Ohio State University Press, 1992); William F. Deverell, *Railroad Crossing: Californians and the Railroad, 1850–1910* (Berkeley: University of California Press, 1994); Norris Hundley, *The Great Thirst: Californians and Water, 1770s-1990s* (Berkeley: University of California Press, 1992); Greg Hise, *Magnetic Los Angeles: Planning the Twentieth-Century Metropolis* (Baltimore: Johns Hopkins University Press, 1997); Mansel G. Blackford, *The Politics of Business in California, 1890–1920* (Columbus: Ohio State University Press, 1977); and Jules Tygiel, *The Great Los Angeles Swindle: Oil, Stocks, and Scandal during the Roaring Twenties* (New York: Oxford University Press, 1994). For Los Angeles political contexts consult William Deverell and Tom Sitton, editors, *California Progressivism Revisited* (Berkeley: University of California Press, 1994) and Norman Klein and Martin Schiesl, editors, *Twentieth Century Los Angeles: Power, Promotion, and Social Conflict* (Claremont, Calif.: Regina Books, 1990).

On labor in Los Angeles, see Paul Greenstein, Nigey Lennon, and Lionel Rolfe, *Bread and Hyacinths: The Rise and Fall of Utopian Los Angeles* (Los Angeles: California Classic Books, 1992); Grace Heilman Stimson, *The Rise of the Labor Movement in Los Angeles* (Berkeley: University of California Press, 1955); Louis B. Perry and Richard Perry, *A History of the Los Angeles Labor Movement, 1911–1941* (Los Angeles: University of California Press, 1963); and Michael Kazin, "The Great Exception Revisited: Organized Labor in San Francisco and Los Angeles, 1870–1940." *Pacific Historical Review* 55 (August 1986): 371–402. For an excellent look at working-class culture in Los Angeles, see Becky Nicolaides, "In Search of the Good Life: Community and Politics in Working-Class Los Angeles, 1920–1955" (Ph.D. diss., Columbia University, 1993).

My research into white-collar men has benefited enormously from a flurry of recent scholarship on the middle class, "whiteness," and masculinity. On the formation of the middle class based upon specific family structures and nonmanual forms of labor, see Mary Ryan, *Cradle of the Middle Class: The Family in Oneida County, New York, 1790–1865* (New York: Cambridge University Press, 1981) and Stuart Blumin, *The Emergence of the Middle Class: Social Experience in the American City, 1760–1900* (New York: Cambridge University Press, 1989). John S. Gilkeson, Jr., in *Middle-Class Providence, 1820–1940* (Princeton, N.J.: Princeton University Press, 1986) and Jeff Charles in *Service Clubs in American Society: Rotary, Kiwanis, and Lions* (Urbana: University of Illinois Press, 1993) explore organizational associations' importance in middle-class culture. Margaret Marsh provides a rich analysis of the domestic dimensions of middle-class experience in *Suburban Lives* (New Brunswick, N.J.: Rutgers University Press, 1990). Frederic Cople Jaher's *The Urban Establishment: Upper Strata in Boston, New York, Charleston, Chicago, and Los Angeles* (Urbana: University of Illinois Press, 1982) presents a detailed study of Los Angeles's upper-middle class and elites. Margo Anderson's "The Language of Class in Twentieth-Century America," *Social Science History* 12 (winter 1988): 349–375, is important background for studies of social class.

Historical investigations of racial identity have increasingly focused on the construction of "whiteness" as a racial category. Ronald Takaki's *Iron Cages: Race and Culture in Nineteenth-Century America* (New York: Knopf, 1979) presents an introduction to the process of racial formation. Other critical studies include Grace Elizabeth Hale, *Making Whiteness: The Culture of Segregation in the South, 1890–1940* (New York: Pantheon Books, 1998); Alexander Saxton's *The Rise and Fall of the White Republic: Class, Politics, and Mass Culture in Nineteenth-Century America* (New York: Verso, 1990); and Stephen Steinberg's *The Ethnic Myth: Race, Ethnicity, and Class in America* (New York: Atheneum, 1981). John Higham's *Strangers in the Land: Patterns of American Nativism, 1860–1925* (New York: Atheneum, 1963) and Dale Knobel's *"America for the Americans": The Nativist Movement in the United States"* (New York: Twayne Publishers, 1996) explore the patterns of nativism that provided a basis for racial Anglo-Saxonism, which is itself the subject of Ronald Horsman's *Race and Manifest Destiny: The Origins of American Racial Anglo-Saxonism* (Cambridge: Harvard University Press, 1981). David Roediger's *The Wages of Whiteness: Race and the American Working Class* (New York: Verso, 1991) and George Lipsitz's *The Possessive Investment in Whiteness: How White People Benefit from Identity Politics* (Philadelphia: Temple University Press, 1998) analyze the significance of white identity in class and economic relations. For histories of the process of racial formation in California, see Lisbeth Haas, *Conquests and Historical Identities in California, 1769–1936* (Berkeley: University of California Press, 1995); Tomás Almaguer, *Racial Fault Lines: The Historical Origins of White Supremacy in California* (Berkeley: University of California Press, 1994); and Alexander Saxton, *The Indispensable Enemy: Labor and the Anti-Chinese Movement in California* (Berkeley: University of California Press, 1975). On whiteness in Los Angeles history specifically, see Eric Avila, "Reinventing Los Angeles: Popular Culture in the Age of White Flight, 1945–1963" (Ph.D. diss., University of California, Berkeley, 1997).

E. Anthony Rotundo's *American Manhood: Transformations in Masculinity from the Revolution to the Modern Era* (New York: Basic Books, 1993), provides a detailed survey of masculinity in American history. Gail Bederman's *Manliness and Civilization: A Cultural History of Gender and Race in the United States, 1880–1917* (Chicago: University of Chicago Press, 1995) focuses on the Progressive Era and offers a rich introduction to definitional and theoretical perspectives on masculinity. Elliott J. Gorn's *The Manly Art: Bare-Knuckle Prize Fighting in America* (Ithaca, N.Y.: Cornell University Press, 1986); Mark C. Carnes's *Secret Ritual and Manhood in Victorian America* (New Haven, Conn.: Yale University Press, 1989); and Michael C. Adams's *The Great Adventure: Male Desire and the Coming of World War I* (Bloomington: Indiana University Press, 1990) present illuminating case studies of masculine identity during the era of corporate formation. Other key general texts and anthologies include Mark C. Carnes and Clyde Griffen, editors, *Meanings for Manhood: Constructions of Masculinity in Victorian America* (Chicago: University of Chicago Press, 1990); Peter Filene, *Him/Her/Self: Sex Roles in Modern America* (Baltimore: Johns Hopkins University Press, 1998, 3rd ed.); Peter N. Stearns, *Be a Man! Males in Modern Society* (New

York: Holmes and Meier, 1990, 2nd ed.); and Harry Brod, editor, *The Making of Masculinities: The New Men's Studies* (Boston: Unwin Hyman, 1987).

Many historians have addressed the relationship among work, identity, and cultural constructions of success. For the best of this literature, consult Judy Hilkey, *Character is Capital: Success Manuals and Manhood in Gilded Age America* (Chapel Hill: University of North Carolina Press, 1997); Daniel T. Rogers, *The Work Ethic in Industrial America: 1850–1920* (Chicago: University of Chicago Press, 1984); Richard Weiss, *The American Myth of Success: From Horatio Alger to Norman Vincent Peale* (Urbana: University of Illinois Press, 1969); Rex Burns, *Success in America: The Yeoman Dream and the Industrial Revolution* (Amherst: University of Massachusetts Press, 1976); James Gilbert, *Work without Salvation: America's Intellectuals and Industrial Alienation, 1880–1920* (Baltimore: Johns Hopkins University Press, 1977); and John G. Cawelti, *Apostles of the Self-Made Man* (Chicago: University of Chicago Press, 1965). A fabulous study of the actual realities of securing employment is Walter Licht's *Getting Work: Philadelphia, 1840–1950* (Cambridge: Harvard University Press, 1992).

The literature on social mobility is an important companion to exploring white-collar identity. Key studies are Peter Decker, *Fortunes and Failures: White-Collar Mobility in Nineteenth-Century San Francisco* (Cambridge: Harvard University Press, 1978); Seymour Lipsett and Reinhard Bendix, *Social Mobility in Industrial Society* (Berkeley: University of California Press, 1967); and Stephan Thernstrom, *The Other Bostonians: Poverty and Progress in the American Metropolis, 1880–1970* (Cambridge: Harvard University Press, 1973).

Corporate efforts to create "community" occurred within rapidly shifting patterns of social organization. These are described in Thomas Bender's *Community and Social Change in America* (Baltimore: Johns Hopkins University Press, 1978). For a broad survey of community transformations, see Gerald W. McFarland, *A Scattered People: An American Family Moves West* (Amherst: University of Massachusetts Press, 1985). Excellent studies of the contestation between occupational, public, and personal realms of community for working-class Americans include John Bodnar, *Workers' World: Kinship, Community, and Protest in an Industrial Society, 1900–1940* (Baltimore: Johns Hopkins University Press, 1982); Thomas J. Jablonsky, *Pride in the Jungle: Community and Everyday Life in Back of the Yards Chicago* (Baltimore: Johns Hopkins University Press, 1993); and James R. Barrett, *Work and Community in the Jungle: Chicago's Packinghouse Workers, 1894–1922* (Urbana: University of Illinois Press, 1987).

On the rise of mass culture and American cinema and their intricate connection to middle-class corporate culture, see Lary May, *Screening out the Past: The Birth of Mass Culture and the Motion Picture Industry* (Chicago: University of Chicago Press, 1980). Steven J. Ross illuminates the class and political dimensions of silent film in *Working-Class Hollywood: Silent Film and the Shaping of Class in America* (Princeton: Princeton University Press, 1998). Corporate athletics emerged amidst rapid changes in recreation and leisure. Roy Rosenzweig traces this evolution in *Eight Hours for What We Will: Workers and Leisure in an Industrial City, 1870–1920* (New

York: Cambridge University Press, 1983), as does Steven A. Riess in *City Games: The Evolution of American Urban Society and the Rise of Sports* (Urbana: University of Illinois Press, 1989). On sport history in particular, see Alan Guttmann, *A Whole New Ball Game: An Interpretation of American Sports* (Chapel Hill: University of North Carolina Press, 1988). For a study sensitive to the ethnic and class dynamics of sporting cultures, consult Melvin Adelman, *A Sporting Time: New York City and the Rise of Modern Athletics, 1820–1870* (Urbana: University of Illinois Press, 1986).

Broad sketches of this study's time period which I found helpful include Alan Trachtenberg's *The Incorporation of America: Culture and Society in the Gilded Age* (New York: Hill and Wang, 1982); Robert Wiebe's *The Search for Order, 1877–1920* (New York: Hill and Wang, 1967); Mary Klein, *The Flowering of the Third America: The Making of an Organizational Society, 1850–1920* (Chicago: University of Chicago Press, 1993); John Milton Cooper, Jr., *Pivotal Decades: The United States, 1900–1920* (New York: Norton, 1990); and Lynn Dumenil's *The Modern Temper: American Culture and Society in the 1920s* (New York: Hill and Wang, 1995).

Valuable accounts of the Great Depression include Michael A. Bernstein, *The Great Depression: Delayed Recovery and Economic Change in America, 1929–1939* (New York: Cambridge University Press, 1987); T. H. Watkins, *The Great Depression: America in the 1930s* (New York: Little, Brown, 1993); and Robert S. McElvaine, editor, *Down and Out in the Great Depression: Letters from the "Forgotten Men"* (Chapel Hill: University of North Carolina Press, 1983). On the Depression in California, see William H. Mullins, *The Depression and the Urban West Coast, 1929–1933* (Bloomington: Indiana University Press, 1991); Richard Lowitt, *The New Deal and the West* (Bloomington: Indiana University Press, 1984); and James N. Gregory, *American Exodus: The Dust Bowl Migration and Okie Culture in California* (New York: Oxford University Press, 1989). On the Depression in Los Angeles, consult Leonard Leader, *Los Angeles and the Great Depression* (New York: Garland Publishing, 1991).

INDEX

The Library of Congress has cataloged the hardcover edition of this book as follows:

Davis, Clark, 1966–
Company men : white-collar life and corporate cultures in Los Angeles, 1892–1941 / Clark Davis.
p. cm. — (Studies in industry and society)
Includes bibliographical references and index.
ISBN 0-8018-6274-4
1. Executives—California—Los Angeles—History. 2. White-collar workers—California—Los Angeles—History. 3. Corporate culture—California—Los Angeles—History. I. Title. II. Series.
HD38.25.U6D38 2000
302.3′5′0979494—dc21 99-38677

ISBN 0-8018-6275-2 (pbk.)